THE GOOD NEWS

A Modern Christian Apology

by R. J. Wagener

Published by Robert Wagener

Copyright © Robert Wagener 2016

First published in the UK 2016

ISBN 978-1-5262-0587-2

This book is sold subject to the condition that it shall not, by way of trade or otherwise, be lent, re-sold, hired out or otherwise circulated without the publisher's prior consent, in any form or binding or cover other than that in which it is published and without a similar condition including this condition being imposed on the subsequent purchaser.

CONTENTS

CHAPTERS	PART	SUB-SECTIONS	PAGE
PREFACE			
INTRODUCTION			1
1. THE SOUL			
	1.1.	Background	3
	1.2.	Definitions	3
	1.3.	Arguments against the Soul	4
	1.4.	Counterarguments	5
	1.5.	Attributes of the Soul	9
	1.6.	Proof of the Soul's Existence	10
	1.7.	Animals	15
	1.7.1.	General	15
	1.7.2.	Biology	16
	1.7.3.	The Bible	17
	1.8.	Conclusions	23
2. EVOLUTION			
	2.1.	Introduction	24
	2.2.	The Biblical Account	24
	2.2.1.	Outline	24
	2.2.2.	Interpreting the Creation Account	25
	2.2.3.	Interpreting the Flood Account	27
	2.2.4.	Interpreting the Chronologies	117
	2.2.5.	Conclusions	128
	2.3.	The Scientific Evidence	128
	2.3.1.	Light	128
	2.3.2.	Radiometric Dating	146
	2.3.3.	Geology	175
	2.3.4.	Biology	188
	2.3.5.	Palaeontology	240
	2.4.	Conclusions	255

3. SUFFERING & SIN

3.1.	Introduction	257
3.2	The Traditional Explanation	258
3.2.1.	Outline	258
3.2.2.	Free Will	259
3.3.	Sin	260
3.4.	Suffering	264
3.4.1.	Introduction	264
3.4.2.	The Existence of Suffering	264
3.4.3.	Inequalities in Suffering	267
3.5.	Conclusions	268

4. SALVATION

4.1.	Introduction	269
4.2.	Logic	269
4.3.	Justice	272
4.4.	Scriptures about Hell	273
4.5.	Scriptures about Salvation	290
4.6.	Conclusions	303

5. MIRACLES & REVELATION

5.1.	Introduction	305
5.2.	Miracles and the Early Church	305
5.3.	The Gift of Prophecy	307
5.4.	The End of Prophecy	309
5.4.1.	Introduction	309
5.4.2.	Daniel 9:21-27	310
5.4.3.	Related Texts	312
5.4.4.	Interpretation	341
5.5.	The End of Miracles	345
5.6.	Conclusions	345

6. KNOWLEDGE & FAITH

6.1.	Introduction	347
6.2.	Certainty	348
6.2.1.	Scepticism	348
6.2.2.	The Basis for Certainty	350

6.2.3	Summary	353
6.3.	The Bible	353
6.3.1.	General	353
6.3.2.	Knowledge	354
6.3.3	Faith	355
6.4.	Conclusions	356

7. SUMMARY & CONCLUSIONS 358

Appendix 1. Mammal Species

Appendix 2. The Sumerian King List

Appendix 3. Ancient Egypt, C^{14} Dating: 1970 Results

Appendix 4. Ancient Egypt, C^{14} Dating: 1984 Results

Appendix 5. Ancient Egypt, Old and Middle Kingdom C^{14} Dates

Bibliographical Tables

General Index

PREFACE

I dedicate this book to my two lovely daughters, Kitty and Evie, and also to my wife Karen, without whose love and support I could not have seen the project through to its completion.

I would also like to thank my mother, Lyn Wagener, both for her moral support and for her unstinting help with the proof reading.

INTRODUCTION

Science has improved many aspects of modern life and given us a much clearer understanding of the world in which we live. Religion, on the other hand, does not offer any material benefits and appears to provide little tangible evidence for its beliefs. Not surprisingly, therefore, most people reject religious ideas, particularly when they come into conflict with scientific theories.

That conflict began as far back as the Renaissance and Galileo, but its defining moment came with the publication of Darwin's Theory of Evolution in 1859. This cast doubt, not only on the reliability of the Bible, but on the need to believe in a creator at all. And since then, scientists have developed a much better understanding of the brain and the mind, which has dealt a serious challenge to another cornerstone of religion: belief in the soul.

Although science has had a major impact on our thinking, for many people the most unacceptable facet of religion is the idea that a loving God would allow innocent people to suffer. Others reject religion, because they are unable to reconcile their everyday experiences with the world that is portrayed in the Bible. As they have no knowledge of miracles, they assume that all biblical accounts that describe them were simply invented to lend credence to religious beliefs.

In response to these arguments, some have defended their beliefs by questioning the assumptions made by science. Others have claimed to possess miraculous powers, arguing that any differences between modern and biblical times are due to our lack of faith.

Few have been convinced by these counter-arguments, however, as they have simply not addressed people's fundamental doubts and misgivings. They provide no justification for belief in the soul, and fail to reconcile the idea of a loving God with the existence of suffering and evil.

Furthermore, orthodoxy has repeatedly reaffirmed its belief in the idea of everlasting punishment. This teaching, perhaps more than any other, has reinforced people's reasons for rejecting Christianity, by presenting it as a religion which ultimately has no 'gospel' for the vast majority of mankind.

This book examines the main arguments against religion and aims to show that belief in God *can* be justified. It also seeks to prove that the idea of everlasting punishment is unbiblical, and that Christianity *is* a religion that brings 'good news' to *all* men.

CHAPTER 1. THE SOUL

1.1. BACKGROUND

Establishing the existence of the soul would not prove that there was a God or even an afterlife. We could argue that the formation of the brain gave rise to the soul's existence, which might then cease to exist when the brain was destroyed. Like gravity, these phenomena might simply be the result of fundamental laws of the universe.

If we *could* prove that the soul existed, however, it would demonstrate that there was a spiritual dimension to the universe. And this, in turn, would remove one of the most powerful objections to belief in God and the afterlife.

1.2. DEFINITIONS

One of the difficulties with many discussions about the soul is that they are often clouded by philosophical and scientific terms, which make the subject virtually inaccessible to the average person. Before we can begin to consider the issues in any detail, therefore, we need to clearly define what is meant by the words that are central to the argument. At the same time, it is equally important to bear in mind that other writers may well use some, or perhaps all, of these terms in quite different ways.

The first group of words we need to consider are 'matter', 'material' and 'physical'. Here, they refer to anything that has length, breadth or depth. 'Materialism', therefore, is the belief that everything that exists has one or more of these physical dimensions.

The words 'soul', 'mind' and 'spirit' are also used quite interchangeably in this chapter. By contrast to 'matter', however, they refer to something that does not have any physical dimensions whatsoever, but which is nevertheless capable of both influencing and experiencing matter.

Finally, there is the all-important word, 'consciousness'. The term is used in this chapter in its widest possible sense, to denote the awareness of anything, whether this takes the form of a thought, an emotion or a bodily sensation.

1.3. ARGUMENTS AGAINST THE SOUL

According to materialists, everything that exists has dimensions and must therefore occupy some 'space' in the universe. The idea of an entity that does not have a physical dimension is therefore dismissed as a logical impossibility.

Some materialists also contend that two entities must be in actual contact to affect one another. If the mind is not physical, however, there would be no contact between it and the body, and this, it is argued, would make it impossible for one to interact with the other.

If something immaterial were to affect matter, this would also require an introduction of energy into the physical universe, an event which would contradict the Law of the Conservation of Energy. Some consider this point to be so strong that they see it as decisive proof against the soul's existence. Dennett, for example, refers to the Conservation Law and concludes that anything that can move a physical thing must itself be a physical thing[1].

Many scientists also argue that there is no *need* to believe in the soul, as medical evidence shows that brain functions alone fully account for consciousness. They point out that nerves from our sensory organs carry stimuli to the brain, and that when a nerve is severed that particular faculty or sensation is lost. Thoughts and other mental processes can also be directly related to changes in the brain, damage to which can apparently prevent us from being conscious altogether. If all of our experiences can be explained in terms of brain functions, the idea of the soul would be completely superfluous, which would place it at variance with the principle of *Occam's Razor**.

These conclusions are said to be further supported by the evidence of brain surgery. Parfit argues, for instance, that epileptics whose brain hemispheres have been surgically disconnected have two separate streams of consciousness, each of which is unaware of the other[2]. This, he argues, completely refutes the notion that we are 'separately existing entities, distinct from our brains and bodies, whose existence must be all-or-nothing'[2].

Perhaps due to the influence of materialism, some religious people also appear to think of the soul as possessing some kind of shape or form. This, however, is simply materialism in another guise, as it does not require us to believe in anything that does not have physical dimensions. In such a belief system, there would be nothing to require us to believe that God Himself did not possess some kind of shape or form. Moreover, if the soul was 'somewhere', materialists would argue that it should be possible to locate it and to verify its existence scientifically.

1.4. COUNTERARGUMENTS

There are, however, several fundamental flaws in these arguments. To begin with, to be illogical an idea must contain a contradiction, and there is nothing contradictory in the idea that something could exist that did not occupy space. In fact, many physicists believe that a star collapsing under its own gravity may eventually shrink to something that occupies zero volume[3].

There is also nothing to prove that entities must be in contact to affect one another, and even in the physical world there are examples that would contradict such a notion. All objects, for instance, exert a gravitational force on one another. Gravity waves

---

* The principle that hypotheses should involve as few assumptions as possible.

and particles have been postulated, but there is no direct evidence of the former[4] and the latter are 'virtual particles', which mean they are impossible to detect by definition[5]. The key point is that there is no contact between objects affected by gravity, so one cannot argue that the soul must be in contact with the body to affect it.

The argument concerning the conservation of energy is invalid, as it assumes the very thing to be proven, namely, that there is nothing outside the physical universe. If souls exist, however, they are part of the total order of things, and any laws we describe must therefore take account of their existence. In such a universe, there would be nothing to prevent the amount of energy from increasing.

Furthermore, there is no experimental evidence to prove that the soul does not alter the amount of energy in the physical universe. As the brain specialist John Eccles points out, the brain already possesses the energy to create nervous impulses, and the additional energy required to direct those impulses in a particular way would be far too small to measure[6].

The arguments concerning the brain are equally inconclusive. This kind of evidence can only ever tell us what changes in the brain accompany mental activity. It cannot tell us what causes those changes or what kinds of entities possess consciousness. The materialist's account also singularly fails to explain what laws of physics require us to conclude that consciousness will arise whenever matter is arranged into certain configurations. It is completely unable to explain, therefore, why some parts of the brain are believed to be conscious whilst others are not.

As regards unconsciousness, believing in the soul does not alter the fact that the brain is still the channel through which we experience the world. Damage to it can therefore affect *what* we experience. It does not follow from this, however, that the brain determines everything we experience. When we are 'knocked out', we may simply be unable to recall what we experienced during that period of time.

Whilst this may appear unlikely to some, it is worth pointing out that most of us cannot remember being born and a large percentage of people cannot recall certain dreams except under hypnosis[7]. We do not assume, however, that we are unconscious as babies or when we are dreaming. We believe that we are simply unable to remember these experiences, just as amnesiacs are unable to recall many of theirs.

If God does exist, it is also possible that He might prevent us from being conscious when we are 'knocked out'. After all, if we experienced another plane of consciousness every time this happened, life would not be a test of faith at all!

As regards epileptics, these operations sever some of the nervous connections between the two halves of the brain. This prevents that person from being conscious of events in both hemispheres at the same time. A patient might, for example, be able to see one colour through one half of the brain and another colour through the other half, but not be able to see both colours simultaneously[9].

This does not prove, however, that there are two simultaneous 'streams of consciousness', each of which is unaware of the other[9]. It simply means that when the brain is damaged in this way, we have to switch our attention from one half of the brain to the other.

It is worth remembering that the brain takes in large amounts of information, and controls many functions that we are completely unaware of until we turn our conscious attention to them. And it is worth adding here that this information includes the fine details of many of our *voluntary* movements. So we are constantly unaware of details relating to things that we choose to do. Most cognitive psychologists also now believe that we are not conscious of many of the mental processes that influence our behaviour[9].

It clearly does not follow from any of this that the areas of the brain that are responsible for different functions, such as the two visual centres, constitute 'separate streams of consciousness'. It simply means that there is a limit to the number of things that we can be conscious of at the same time.

An interesting footnote to this discussion is the case of the Siamese twins that was presented by Dr. Winston in, 'The Secret Life of Twins' (BBC1, 14 July 1999). The women in the case study shared those parts of the frontal cortex that are widely believed to be responsible for consciousness. Despite this, the twins reported experiencing independent thoughts, dreams and sensations, and appeared to have quite different personalities.

As they shared the supposedly conscious parts of the brain, materialists should conclude that only one consciousness was involved. It seemed abundantly clear, however, that there were in fact two conscious individuals. This suggests that something other than the brain is responsible for consciousness.

If the brain is not conscious, it might be argued that it should be possible to obtain evidence of consciousness outside the brain. This might perhaps be provided by the large body of remarkably consistent 'out of body' and 'near death' experiences. However, most regard these accounts as inconclusive. And materialists dismiss the phenomena as culturally induced hallucinations caused by drugs or a lack of oxygen to the brain.

It is unclear why a chemical change of this kind would induce virtually identical hallucinations in quite different people. The problem with empirical evidence, however, is that it is never entirely conclusive. In this case, for instance, even if someone provided information from an out-of-body experience that they could apparently not have otherwise known, it would still be impossible to prove beyond all doubt that they had not obtained this information from elsewhere, perhaps subconsciously. If conclusive proof of the soul's existence is to be found, therefore, this must be provided by logical argument rather than empirical evidence.

To consider the possibility of a logical proof for or against the existence of the soul, we need to closely examine the qualities that are attributed to it, and decide if these reveal any clear contradictions on either side of the argument.

1.5. ATTRIBUTES OF THE SOUL

The principal qualities that are attributed to the soul are *will* and *consciousness*, by means of which the soul is believed to affect, and be affected by, the material world. In relation to *will*, we have already shown that there is nothing illogical in the idea of a force that enables something immaterial to affect something physical.

Obtaining scientific evidence that such a force exists, however, is not possible at present, as its effect on the brain is too small to measure[6]. What distinguishes *will* from other forces, however, is that it involves *conscious* effort. To take the argument a stage further, therefore, we clearly need to develop a fuller understanding of the nature of *consciousness*.

The natural first step here would be to define consciousness. Knowing what consciousness is should make it possible to determine how it arises. The problem with this, however, is that our understanding of consciousness is derived entirely from our own internal experience. We know about consciousness, because we are conscious. Analysis of what happens in the brain only tells us what chemical changes accompany consciousness, not what it is.

We might say, for example, that consciousness involves the relaying of information to a central point. However, computers relay large amounts of data to central processors, but few people believe this means that computers are conscious. We clearly cannot define consciousness more closely, therefore, without falling back on synonyms such as 'awareness'. Trying to explain consciousness to someone who is unconscious, would be like trying to explain 'red' to someone who had been born blind.

1.6. PROOF OF THE SOUL'S EXISTENCE

Although it is impossible to define consciousness more closely than this, we can take the argument a stage further by considering whether it is logical to attribute consciousness to material things.

The materialist's analysis is that the conscious 'you' consists of certain parts of the brain. And when any of these areas receives a stimulus, it gives rise to a conscious experience. If different stimuli affect the same brain, the same person would experience those stimuli. However, this account of consciousness fails to explain two fundamental realities: the unity of consciousness and personal identity.

Materialism does not account for the unity of consciousness, as it fails to explain how a group of chemical structures, many parts of which are not directly connected to one another, can act as one in terms of consciousness. As Popper and Eccles put it, there is no 'neurophysical theory that explains how a diversity of brain events comes to be synthesised so that there is a unified conscious experience…The brain events remain disparate, being essentially the individual actions of countless neurones'[10].

To give an every-day example, when I see a car and hear its engine running, two different parts of my brain undergo two quite separate chemical changes. One receives visual information and the other receives acoustic data. However, there is no central part of the brain to which both of these 'experiences' are relayed. The problem with this is that whilst no part of the brain 'experiences' both stimuli, 'I' experience them both and at the same time. This indicates that 'I' am something apart from the brain.

The materialist's usual response to this is to try to define the problem away by simply saying, 'I am the brain, the brain experiences both things, therefore I must experience them both'.

However, the brain does *not* 'experience' both things. One *part* of the brain is affected by sight and another is affected by sound. Neither the brain as a whole nor any part of it 'experiences' both of these things together.

It is also clear that this problem is a lot more deep-seated than might at first appear, as it cannot be resolved by simply altering our view about how the brain works. We might conclude, for example, that everything we experience *is* in fact brought together in a central part of the brain. The problem with this, however, is that any part of the brain could be sub-divided into further parts. And if two parts of the brain are conscious, why would they not be two separate 'persons'? After all, even if they experienced the same things at the same time, they would still be two conscious bits of matter.

The nature of this problem is perhaps made clearer by considering a well-known thought experiment. In this, due to advances in medical science, doctors are able to remove your brain whilst keeping it alive and maintaining consciousness. As they separate the nerve endings from your body, you lose physical sensation, but are still conscious and able to think.

The supposedly conscious parts of the brain are then divided in half. The only nerves that are damaged are those connecting the two hemispheres, and consciousness is unaffected, as no anaesthetics are used and a steady supply of blood and oxygen is maintained throughout. The two halves of the brain are then placed into two new bodies that do not contain brains. All of the nerves to which those brain halves would normally be attached are then re-connected. The question is: 'What would you experience after this experiment and through which body?'

The materialist could not say that you would be conscious through neither of the new bodies, because the matter that was assumed to be 'you' has been kept 'alive' throughout. It would also be illogical to say that one of the brain halves would be you and the other would not, because both came from the brain that was assumed to be 'you' in the first place. The materialist would therefore be left with only one logical alternative: you would be conscious through both of the new bodies.

This operation might of course mean that, like some epileptic patients, you would be unable to experience things through both brain hemispheres simultaneously. But the materialist would have to accept that events affecting both brain halves would be experienced by the same person, because he defined that person as being the conscious matter of the brain in question.

Here, then, we have a clear contradiction. On the one hand, there is a unity of consciousness, as the events in the two brain halves are experienced by *one* person. On the other hand, there is no physical unity, because the two brain hemispheres are now as separate as two different brains; they have absolutely no physical connection with one another whatsoever. We can summarise the argument as follows: *if there is a unity of consciousness, but no physical unity, consciousness cannot be the attribute of something physical.*

Parfit considers this conundrum and, perhaps realising the inevitable contradiction, concludes:

I may ask, 'But shall I be one of these two people, or the other, or neither?' But I should regard this as an empty question.[11]

Parfit regards all such questions as 'empty', because there is simply no logical place at which one could 'draw the line'. So we could not, for example, meaningfully ask, 'at what point would I cease to be me if, one by one, I swapped my brain cells with someone else?' It follows from this, Parfit argues, that all such questions are meaningless or 'empty'.

The first point to make here is that there is an alternative to dismissing such questions as 'meaningless': we could accept that consciousness was the attribute of something immaterial, which was incapable of being sub-divided like the brain. The second point is that the question raised by our thought experiment is not concerned with the problem of identity. It simply asks, 'through which of the two new bodies would you be conscious after the operation?' This cannot be a meaningless question, and even Parfit concedes that such an operation might be possible in the future. If the brain halves are fully functional throughout, as a materialist you must say that you would experience something. What that is, is a straightforward question of fact.

As already indicated, however, the issue of personal identity does represent a further serious difficulty for the materialist, as illustrated by the following thought experiment.

A

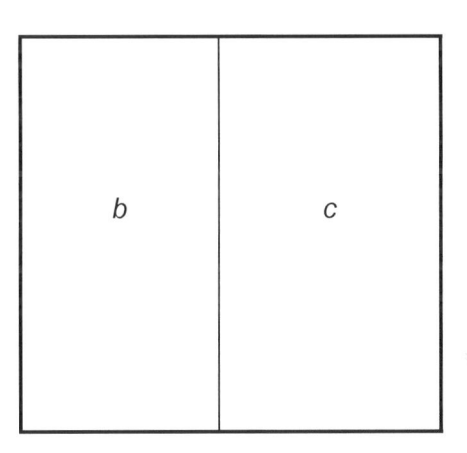

b	c

In the diagram, A represents all of the matter from a human brain that is assumed to be conscious. To the materialist, therefore, A represents an individual conscious being, like you or me. The areas b and c are simply the two halves of A.

Now, let us imagine that this individual has two strokes. After the first, c is unable to function at all. As soon as it is able to function again, however, b is similarly affected. In terms of consciousness, therefore, the materialist would have to conclude that there were three distinct periods of time, during which -

1. *b* and *c* were conscious;
2. only *b* was conscious; and,
3. only *c* was conscious.

If I were A, *b* and *c* would be parts of me. As a materialist, therefore, I would have to conclude that I would be conscious throughout. However, the matter that is assumed to be conscious in time period 2 is completely different from the matter that is assumed to be conscious in time period 3. In short, *if the same person is conscious, but different matter is involved, that person cannot be composed of matter.*

Despite this, some may question why a conscious being cannot be composed of two or more parts of matter. The answer is that *if* our conscious individuality stems from the fact that we are made of *different* brain matter, then *b* and *c* must be two conscious beings. They are made up of different matter, and if they were conscious they would be capable of experiencing different things at different times. Even if they had exactly the same experiences simultaneously, they would still be two conscious bits of matter, and to that extent they would be as separate as two different brains.

It should now be clear, therefore, that the problems with materialism are actually indissoluble, as all physical things can be divided up an infinite number of times. And even if an entity were too small to be physically dissected, it would still be possible to 'divide' it up by distinguishing between different parts of it. Whenever, therefore, we tried to pin-point something physical to put forward as being the conscious 'me', we would always be able to sub-divide this into further and further sub-parts. And so the contradictions referred to above would always arise.

In view of these insuperable problems, materialism is simply unable to provide a coherent account of consciousness, a fact which materialists occasionally acknowledge. David Chalmers, for example, concedes that consciousness cannot be explained by neuroscience or cognitive science[12], and several years before this Quine was forced to conclude:

Consciousness is to me a mystery, and not one to be dismissed. We know what it is like to be conscious, but not how to put it into satisfactory scientific terms[13].

The arguments of materialism are not only inconclusive, therefore; they inevitably lead to contradictions whenever the nature of consciousness is considered. The only way of resolving these contradictions is by accepting that consciousness must be the attribute of something that does not possess physical dimensions, namely, the soul.

1. 7. ANIMALS

1.7.1. General

If the soul is responsible for consciousness, then animals must either have souls or not be conscious. Many religious people appear to be uncomfortable with either of these conclusions, however, which perhaps explains why orthodoxy has never sought to establish a direct link between consciousness and the soul.

Denying that animals are conscious appears to ignore the evidence of our senses. And if they were not conscious, there could be no such thing as animal cruelty, and for most people this would be a completely untenable conclusion.

On the other hand, believing that animals have souls appears to undermine man's unique position in God's creation. It also gives rise to a number of difficult questions, such as, why does the Bible allow us to eat animals? And how could apparently unthinking and amoral creatures attain salvation?

To deal with those scriptures that appear to indicate that animals have souls, we could accept that animals have souls, but say that only humans are conscious in this life. That would remove concerns around issues such as eating animals. Alternatively, we could say that animals are conscious, but that their souls are not immortal.

The problem with the first suggestion is that we would have to deny that there was any empirical or intuitive evidence that animals were conscious. Many people would find it very hard, if not impossible to accept this. However, the second proposition raises even more serious concerns, as it would make God the cause of unnecessary suffering. If animals' suffering did not lead to an afterlife for them, why did God give them souls in the first place? Why did He not simply create them as unconscious biological machines instead?

1.7.2. Biology

Some people argue that whilst animals display the outward signs of consciousness, these could simply be inbuilt responses to protect other members of their species. Others point out that according to brain specialists even if an animal's cerebral hemispheres were removed altogether, it would still react to 'pain' and show signs that looked like rage and fear[14].

In considering whether animals are conscious, some draw attention to differences between the structure of animal and human brains. Others see significance in animals' lack of linguistic skills or a sense of humour. However, none of this evidence actually proves that animals are *not* conscious. Animals might experience pain; they certainly react to it in a very similar way to humans. Animals also communicate with one another, albeit at a more basic level, and they indulge in behaviour that could be regarded as amounting to practical humour.

The absence of a highly structured language does, of course, make it difficult to obtain further evidence that animals *are* conscious.

Having said that, some mentally handicapped people can only communicate at a very basic level, but most of us do not assume that *they* are unconscious.

1.7.3. The Bible

Many people base their religious beliefs almost entirely on the Bible. Some of them would no doubt point out that the Bible makes no reference to an afterlife for animals, and only tells us that *man* was made in God's image (Genesis 1:27). It also says that we are more important than animals (Matthew 10:31; 12:12), and that we may kill other creatures for food (Genesis 9:3; 1 Timothy 4:3,4). All of these facts, it is argued, are incompatible with the idea that animals have souls or an afterlife.

However, the scriptures do not actually say that animals do not have souls. In fact, the words 'soul' and 'spirit' are used in relation to animals on a number of occasions. In some instances, these words clearly have the meaning of 'life' (Deuteronomy 12:23, Philippians 2:30) and 'breath' respectively (Job 15:30, 2 Thessalonians 2:8). In other contexts, however, it is equally clear that these words are being used in a spiritual sense. For example, Ecclesiastes 3:21 refers to what happens to the 'spirits' of man and animals after they have died.

There are also numerous statements in the Bible which indicate that animals are conscious. We are told that they experience fear (Genesis 9:2; Psalm 104:29; Joel 2:22), desire (Psalm 145:16), confusion (Joel 1:18), pleasure (Job 39:21) and pain (Romans 8:22). They are also said to possess attributes that are closely associated with consciousness, such as subtlety, cunning (Genesis 3:1), knowledge (Isaiah 1:3, Jeremiah 8:7), and understanding (Jude 1:10).

A vivid example of animal consciousness is also provided by Numbers 22:21-34. Here, we are told that Balaam's donkey rebukes him for kicking her after an angel had blocked their path. The passage makes it clear that the donkey's ability to speak (verse 28) and see the angel (verse 31) were miraculous. However, the same cannot be said of the donkey's awareness of being kicked, which appears to be entirely natural.

Furthermore, Proverbs 12:10 says that 'the righteous man has regard for the life of his animal, but the compassions of the wicked are cruel.' This proverb contrasts the actions of a righteous and a wicked man. It only makes sense, therefore, if the good man's behaviour is an act of compassion. And it can only be an act of compassion if 'his animal' is conscious. It is clearly impossible to be compassionate towards something that is unconscious and therefore incapable of suffering.

As regards the reference to man being created in the 'image of God', this could refer to attributes other than consciousness, such as man's creativity or his ability to reason. These qualities, coupled perhaps with man's greater capacity for mental suffering, might also explain why man was given dominion over animals, and why Jesus said that a human being was 'worth more than many sparrows' (Matthew 10:31).

It should be noted here that man is said to be worth more than animals, not that animals are of no worth whatsoever. And elsewhere, Jesus said that flesh and blood are of no value (John 6:63), which suggests that animals are more than flesh and blood.

The Bible does of course say very little about an afterlife for animals. However, it also provides no information about the creation of angels. The reason for this perhaps is that the Bible was written for us, and its revelations are therefore limited to what human beings need to know. As Deuteronomy 29:29 reminds us -

The secret things belong to the Lord our God, but the revealed things belong to us and to our children for ever, that we might follow all the words of this law.

They also feature in certain key prophecies and visions relating to the renewal and redemption of mankind.

This leaves one final question: why have man and carnivores been permitted to eat animals if they have souls? To answer this question, it is important to note that the Bible effectively divides history into three periods:

1. from creation to the Fall* - man, birds and land animals eat plants (Genesis 1:29, 30);

2. after the Fall - man is allowed to kill and eat animals (Genesis 4:4; 9:3); and,

3. from the new creation - meat eating is prohibited for all (Isaiah 11:6-9; 65:17-25).

Eating animals, therefore, was not part of the original creation and it will also not be part of the 'new heaven and earth'. It should be obvious from this that the Bible does not regard eating animals as an ideal state of affairs; it is simply something that was permitted after sin had entered the world.

The Bible does not tell us why eating meat was permitted, but the reasons are not hard to see. Sin brought death into the world (Roman 5:12) and with this came a new set of moral problems. Death was now inevitable for all, so speeding up that process was no longer the worst thing that could happen to a sentient being. There was something potentially far worse: suffering.

Had we not been allowed to eat animals, many people would have died slowly of starvation. This would have occurred during periods when there was insufficient plant food, such as after the Flood or following serious crop failures. This would also have been a significant problem in very hot or cold areas of the globe where there was little or no vegetation.

---

* This refers to man's first disobedience and his fall from grace

Although the Bible is silent about the salvation of animals, however, there are some key references to animals in relation to God's dealings with mankind. We are told that God's grief about creation applied not just to man, but to the whole animal kingdom. As a result, both man and animals were punished by the Deluge (Genesis 6:7). And after the Flood, we are told that the covenant and the laws given to Noah also applied to animals (Genesis 9:5,10-16), as did certain Mosaic laws relating to the Sabbath (Deuteronomy 5:14) and to sexual conduct (Leviticus 20:15,16).

Later in the Old Testament, we are also told about animals repenting (Jonah 3:8) and honouring God (Isaiah 43:20), and in Isaiah's famous prophecy, animals are portrayed as an integral part of God's vision of a perfect world:

The wolf also will dwell with the lamb, and the leopard will lie down with the kid; and the calf and the young lion and the yearling together; and a little child will lead them. The cow will feed with the bear; their young ones will lie down together; and the lion will eat straw like the ox. And the sucking child will play on the hole of the asp, and the weaned child will put his hand on the viper's nest. They will neither hurt nor destroy in all of my holy mountain, for the earth will be full of the knowledge of the Lord, as the waters cover the sea. (Isaiah 11:6-9)

Paul identifies this prophecy with the reign of Christ (Romans 15:12), and Isaiah 65:17-25 contains a similar vision in relation to the 'new heaven' and the 'new earth'. Paul also refers to the 'the *whole of creation*' being liberated to the freedom of the glory of the children of God' (Romans 8:21, 22). And the book of Revelation contains this vision:

Then I heard every creature that is in heaven and on the earth and under the earth and on the sea and all therein, say, 'Blessing and honour and glory and power be unto him that sits upon the throne, and unto the Lamb for ever and ever'. (Revelation 5:13)

Whilst the scriptures do not explicitly refer to an afterlife for animals, therefore, animals are included in various covenants and laws.

In addition, if herbivores had been allowed to reproduce without restriction, they would soon have depleted the supplies of plant food until both they and humans died slowly of starvation. Without predators, there would also have been nothing to reduce the risk of sick animals spreading disease to other members of their species.

If people and animals had been allowed to die slowly as a result of old age, sickness, and starvation, this would have resulted in much more suffering than allowing some of those creatures to be killed for food. As animals have a lower level of consciousness than man, the least cruel option was to allow us to eat certain animals. Some carnivores were also allowed to survive the Flood to ensure the number of herbivores was kept under control in areas where human population levels were low.

This created a balance in nature that prevented excessive suffering. This balance, however, also provides us with a permanent daily reminder that the world in which we live is a stark contrast to the paradise that God originally created for us. Violence and death are now an indelible part of our existence, a painful reminder of our disobedient past.

Some disagree with this analysis. They point out that Genesis 1:29,30, does not actually say that land animals could not eat meat. It also says nothing about sea creatures not being allowed to eat meat, many of which are now carnivores. They also argue that the Hebrew names for some of the carnivores have meanings that allude to violence and predation. And as Adam named the animals before the Fall (Genesis 2:19,20), it is suggested that he must have also witnessed animals killing one another before then.

It is also pointed out that the Bible only refers to death entering the *human* world as a result of sin (Romans 5:12). Some contend, therefore, that there is no reason to believe there was no death of any description before the Fall. The wages of sin may be death (Romans 6:23), but that does not mean that all death is the result of sin. After all, plants were eaten from day one of creation, so some of them presumably died, together with other creatures such as fungi and bacteria. If some of God's creatures died from day one, it is argued, then there is no reason to assume that higher animals may not have also died before the Fall.

However, the fact that eating meat was not explicitly prohibited in Genesis 1:29,30 does not mean that it was permitted either. These verses set out the sole dietary conditions that applied to both man and animals. If they did not permit man to eat meat before the Fall, they could hardly have allowed animals to do the opposite.

As regards the names Adam gave to the animals, any trace of their linguistic roots could easily have been lost following the Tower of Babel (Genesis 11). Any carnivorous connotations in their Hebrew names might only therefore reflect the natures some animals developed *after* the Fall (Genesis 6:11).

It is also clear from Isaiah 11:6-9 that animal predation is not acceptable in an ideal world. And if no creatures killed one another before the Fall, the only way they could have died would have been as a consequence of accidents, disease or old age.

Widespread deaths from disease and accidents, however, are incompatible with a world that is 'very good' (Genesis 1:31). In addition, as well as being 'the wages of sin' (Romans 6:23), death is also described as an 'enemy' of God, which will therefore be destroyed in His new creation (Isaiah 25:8;1 Corinthians 15:26; Revelation 20:13, 21:4).

The idea that animals died from old age before the Fall is also incompatible with Romans 8:18-23. This passage refers to creation being subject to 'the bondage of decay', under which it will suffer until it is liberated into 'the freedom of the glory of the children of God'. It is clear from this that decay and death from old age have no place in an ideal world.

1.8. CONCLUSIONS

The arguments against the soul are not only inconclusive; the soul's existence can be proven beyond all reasonable doubt, because belief in the soul is the only way of providing a logically coherent account of consciousness.

As consciousness and the soul are inextricably linked, other conscious beings must also have souls. There is therefore good reason to believe that many animals have souls. And this means that we must treat all such creatures with kindness and respect.

It is true that the arguments against materialism do not prove that there is a God or an afterlife. However, placing the existence of the soul beyond all doubt removes one the most important and long-standing objections to those beliefs.

CHAPTER 2. EVOLUTION

2.1. INTRODUCTION

The publication in 1859 of, 'On the Origin of Species by Means of Natural Selection' marked a turning point for religion. Darwin not only presented evidence to contradict the biblical account of creation; he put forward a theory that removed the need to believe in a creator at all.

In response, many have defended their religious beliefs by arguing that the biblical accounts are symbolic and were never intended to be taken literally. Others have supported a literal interpretation of Genesis, and argued that the scientific evidence is flawed and that its theories are based upon unprovable assumptions.

The purpose of this chapter is to examine exactly what the Bible does say about creation, and the extent, if any, to which these accounts should be interpreted symbolically. It then goes on to identify and evaluate the assumptions that are made by the prevailing scientific theories. Each of these sections then considers the extent to which the generally accepted scientific facts actually conflict with the biblical account of creation.

2.2. THE BIBLICAL ACCOUNT

2.2.1. Outline

Exodus 20:11 tells us that 'in six days the Lord made the heavens and the earth, the sea and all that is in them'. A detailed account of those six days is provided by chapter 1 of Genesis, which tells us that the order of creation was as follows:

Day 1. the earth, the heavens and light;
Day 2. the sky, separating two expanses of water;
Day 3. the land, sea, plants and trees;

Day 4. the sun, moon and stars;
Day 5. creatures of the sea and air; and,
Day 6. land animals and man.

Genesis chapter 3 tells of the fall of man. Cast out from God's presence, mankind becomes increasingly corrupt and the earth is 'full of violence' (Genesis 6:11,12). To remove this corruption and violence, God brings a flood to destroy the vast majority of mankind and most of the creatures of the land and air (Genesis 6:7,17).

To preserve a remnant, however, God tells a righteous man, Noah, to build an ark. God commands Noah to take onto the ark pairs of all 'flesh', comprising seven pairs of each kind of bird and 'clean' land animal, and one pair of each kind of 'unclean' land animal (Genesis 6:19,20; 7:2,3,14).

The animals come to Noah (Genesis 6:20; 7:9,15) and when they have boarded the ark, 'all of the springs of the great deep burst forth and the floodgates of the heavens' are opened (Genesis 7:10,11,13). The land and air creatures outside the ark perish (Genesis 7:21-23), and the flood waters do not subside until 150 days later (Genesis 7:24; 8:3). However, a year and ten days after rainfall begins, Noah and the animals are able to leave the ark to re-populate the earth (Genesis 7:11; 8:14-18).

2.2.2. Interpreting the Creation Account

The 'days' in the creation narrative appear to be literal days, as each contains an 'evening' and a 'morning'. And the literalness of the account is confirmed by the way in which it is interpreted in the New Testament. Luke and Paul refer to Adam as an historical person (Luke 3:38; 1 Timothy 2:13,14), and Jesus says that God made man and woman 'at the beginning of creation' (Mark 10:6).

Many religious people reject this literal interpretation of Genesis, on the grounds that it is contradicted by the scientific evidence. They argue that the Hebrew word for 'day' is sometimes used for a longer period of time (e.g. Zechariah 14:8), and they point out that to God a day and a thousand years are alike (2 Peter 3:8; Psalm 90:4). It is also argued that the first three periods of creation could not have been literal days, as they occurred before the creation of the sun.

Adherents to this view contend that the words 'evening' and 'morning' in chapter 1 of Genesis represent the beginning and end of periods of creative activity[1]. And this interpretation is developed further by equating each 'day' with periods in the geological timescale. On this basis, it is suggested that the account in Genesis reflects the evolutionary progression from simple animals and plants to higher life forms and finally to man.

An alternative explanation was put forward by Dr. Thomas Chalmers in 1814, which has come to be known as 'the Gap Theory'. According to this, Genesis 1:2 onwards only tells us about the present creation. Before this, he argued, there must have been an earlier creation, the history of which is reflected in the fossil record. He concluded that this original creation was destroyed because of its wickedness, following which the earth became 'formless and void' (Genesis 1:2).

This theory was restated in 1876 in George H. Pember's book, 'Earth's Earliest Ages'. It has become known as 'the Gap Theory', as it postulates a vast gap in time between the original creation 'in the beginning' (Genesis 1:1), and the six days of creation described in Genesis chapter 1.

The principle difficulty with any interpretation of the Bible that relies upon modern science, however, is that, if is correct, then believers in previous generations must have been completely misled by those passages of scripture. And if the Bible is misleading, then it cannot also be the word of God.

The evolutionary interpretation of Genesis must also be rejected, as the order of events in Genesis contradicts the Theory of Evolution. According to Genesis, the earth, light, and plants were all created before the sun and stars; plants were created before marine life; and flying creatures were created before land animals.

A further problem is the interpretation of the seventh day, on which we are told that God rested from His work (Genesis 2:2). An evolutionary interpretation of chapter 1 would have to equate the seventh day with the period *after* the emergence of man, i.e. the *present* era. According to Exodus 20:11, however, the seventh day is in the *past*.

As regards the Hebrew word for 'day', although this can represent a longer period of time, 'morning' and 'evening' are never used in this way in the Bible. And the statement that 'a day is *like* a thousand years' simply reminds us that God is eternal and that both periods of time are equally insignificant when compared with eternity.

It also does not follow that the first three days of Creation are figurative, simply because they occurred before the creation of the sun. It should be remembered that light through which the earth could rotate was created on day one.

As regards the Gap Theory, this is contradicted by Mark 10.6, which says that '*at the beginning of creation* God made them male and female'. It cannot be argued that Jesus was merely speaking here of the beginning of human creation. He does not refer to the beginning of mankind, but to the 'beginning of creation' itself.

2.2.3. Interpreting the Flood Account

2.2.3.1. Historicity

Noah is referred to as an historical person in the New Testament (Matthew 24:37-39; 1 Peter 3:20; 2 Peter 3:3-6), and the Jewish historian, Josephus wrote this about the ark in the first century AD:

Now all the writers of barbarian histories make mention of this flood and of this ark; among whom is Berosus the Chaldean *(330-250 BC);* for when he is describing the circumstances of the flood, he goes on thus: - "It is said there is still some part of this ship in Armenia, at the mountain of the Cordyaeans *(Garduchi);* and that some people carry off pieces of the bitumen, which they take away, and use chiefly as amulets for the averting of mischiefs". Hieronymus the Egyptian, also, who wrote the Phoenician Antiquities, and Mnaseas *(3rd century BC)*, and a great many more, make mention of the same. Nay, Nicolaus of Damascus, in his ninety-sixth book, hath a particular relation about them, where he speaks thus:- "There is a great mountain in Armenia, over Minyas, called Baris, upon which it is reported that many who fled at the time of the Deluge were saved; and that one who was carried in an ark came on shore on top of it; and that the remains of the timber were a great while preserved. This might be the man about whom Moses, the legislator of the Jews, wrote'[2].

On the basis of these facts, some have accepted that the account of the Flood should be interpreted literally, but have concluded that the Deluge might have been limited to the region in which Noah lived. This idea is discussed in 'The New Bible Dictionary' (pages 427,428), which points out that the Hebrew words translated as 'heaven' and 'earth' could simply mean 'sky' and 'land' respectively. Similarly, the word for 'the world' in 2 Peter 3:5,6 could simply mean 'the inhabited world'[3].

In *The Genesis Flood* (pages 1 to 88), however, Whitcomb and Morris list several strong arguments against interpreting the Flood as a local inundation. For example, if the Flood had been confined to a geographical region, why did Noah not simply leave that area or build a much smaller ark?

One conclusive argument in support of a worldwide flood is that Noah was told to take all kinds of birds onto the ark, and all those that were not taken, perished (Genesis 7:21). There are numerous species of sea bird and many birds migrate thousands of miles across oceans of water every year. Furthermore, birds on the periphery of a local flood could have easily survived by flying to dry land. The Flood must, therefore, have covered more than just the 'land' in which Noah lived. In this context, therefore, the Hebrew word must refer to the whole 'earth'.

2.2.3.2. Logistical Problems

However, numerous practical objections have been raised against the idea of a worldwide flood, each of which is considered below. Some argue that these objections are so strong that the Flood narrative must be interpreted figuratively. If this is correct, then it has important implications for the interpretation of Genesis generally. If the Flood is symbolic, then the biblical account of creation might also be figurative.

The main objections to a literal interpretation of the Flood are that:

1. Noah could not have taken all of the species then living onto the ark, or even enough animals to account for the species living today;

2. all seawater fish would have been killed by the sudden changes in salinity levels;

3. if all of the animals were originally herbivorous, a literal interpretation would not explain the emergence of carnivores;

4. most animals would have starved to death when they left the ark, as plant life would have been decimated and other meat supplies would have been exhausted;

5. land animals could not have re-populated islands after the Flood;

6. seabirds and all animals in the Arctic would have been unaffected by the Flood;

7. a global flood 4,500 years ago is incompatible with present-day human population levels;

8. the uninterrupted sequence of various ancient dynasties contradicts the idea that there was a worldwide deluge during this period of time; and,

9. there is insufficient water in the oceans and the polar ice caps to account for the amount of water that would be required to flood the entire planet.

1. The Number of Animals

(a) General

Genesis 6:17 tells us that God brought the Flood to destroy 'from under the heavens all flesh in which was the breath of life, all which was in the earth'. These phrases are explained by Genesis chapter 7, where we also learn that the creatures that perished were all those that moved or flew 'upon the earth' (verses 21, 23) and all those 'in the dry ground in whose nostrils was the breath of life' (verse 22).

To preserve a remnant Noah was told to take 'of all living things of all flesh' that were 'beasts', 'creeping things', or 'fluttering things' (Genesis 6:19,20). Genesis 7:8,14 then tells us that these 'creeping things' were creatures that moved '*upon* the earth'. As regards, the 'fluttering things', these encompassed all kinds of '*birds*', but the Hebrew word used here also specifically included bats (Leviticus 11:13-19; Deuteronomy 14:11-18).

The first question that arises from this is, 'what does the phrase 'of all' mean?' Does it mean literally every single species that was then living on the planet or does it have a more general meaning? Before considering these questions further, we need to understand what biologists mean by 'species' and how the concept of 'species' relates to other biological classifications.

In terms of where species sit in the overall classification structure, biologists divide life forms into the following groups, starting with the largest: domains, kingdoms, phyla, classes, orders, families, genera and species. Below this, biologists also occasionally refer to sub-species to reflect important locally-adapted traits. Last of all are different 'varieties' that may exist within a particular species or sub-species. Obvious examples of 'varieties' would include strains of roses and the different breeds of domestic dogs.

The word 'species' is generally used to refer to groups of organisms that can produce offspring together. This definition, however, clearly cannot be used to categorise fossils or organisms that only reproduce asexually. Furthermore, whether or not living creatures are physically incapable of reproducing is not something that is usually known by biologists. Consequently, the number of animals Noah had to take on board the ark might have been significantly smaller than is assumed in the calculations below.

All that we can say is that each category of creatures that boarded the ark comprised all of the animals in that group, divided 'by *their* kind' or 'according to *their* kind' (Genesis 6:19,20; 7:14). For example, Genesis 7:14 says that they included 'all fowl according to its kind'. To gain a better idea of the number and type of animals that are likely to have boarded the ark, therefore, we need to have a clearer understanding of what is meant by the words 'according to their kind'.

The phrase literally means 'by' or 'to' its 'division'. The word translated as 'kind' is the Hebrew noun מִין, which denotes some kind of 'division' and has a cognate verb meaning 'to split'[4]. In the context of Genesis 6 and 7, therefore, this word simply refers to some form of 'division' in the animal or plant kingdom. The question is, 'what kind of division?'

It has been suggested that מִין refers to individual 'species'. However, although the word is sometimes used in relation to a species, its meaning is clearly not limited in this way. For example, in Leviticus 11, it is used in relation to a species, the ostrich (Leviticus 11:16; Deuteronomy 14:15), but in the very same sentence it is also used to describe much larger divisions of the animal kingdom, such as the stork (Leviticus 11:19), an order of birds that comprises one family, 6 genera and 19 species.

Some might feel that it is inconsistent to use the same word to refer to 'species' and 'families' in the same sentence. Others might argue that this classification simply betrays the writer's ignorance of taxonomy. As explained above, however, the Hebrew word merely denotes some form of 'division' in the animal or plant kingdom; it does not refer to any particular kind of division.

It is also clear that the Flood account is concerned with very broad groupings or divisions within the animal kingdom. In fact, all of the animals that boarded the ark are divided into just three categories and 'their kinds'. It clearly does not follow, therefore, that these 'kinds' refer to individual species. So we cannot assume, for instance, that Noah took every species of lizard onto the ark, including all of the dinosaurs.

We can, however, at least estimate the maximum number of animals Noah *might* have taken onto the ark, by considering the approximate number of species living today, viz.[5]:

1. Plants, fungi, moulds, microbes	405,300
2. Marine animals, worms, amphibians, gastropods	306,100
3. Insects and arachnids	975,000
4. Birds	9,100
5. Reptiles	6,000
6. Mammals	4,200
Total	1,705,700

Of the above, Noah had to take amphibians and marine reptiles, as they 'crept upon the earth' at least part of the time. He did not, however, have to take any of the other creatures in the first three categories, as they either did not move upon the earth and/or they were not creatures 'in whose *nostrils* was the breath of life'. This raises an immediate question: 'how did these organisms survive the

Flood, given that many of them spend a lot of time above ground?'

The first point to make here is that dry land began to appear seven and a half months after the start of the Flood (Genesis 7:11; 8:5). For one of these species to be preserved, therefore, it was only necessary for one pair of each species to survive for several months. Some organisms might have done this by living underground in pockets of air, beneath large rocks or in and around rotting trees and animals. Others might have entered a state of dormancy, known as diapause, which frequently occurs when these creatures or their eggs find themselves in hostile environments.

Diapause should have allowed these organisms and their eggs to remain dormant underground for at least three to four months during winter every year. For a particular species to survive, therefore, all that was necessary was for one adult female to stay alive for four months before laying her eggs underground. These could then remain dormant for a further three-and-a-half months.

We also know that many of these creatures could have remained dormant for much longer periods of time. The San Xavier Talussnail can remain dormant for up to three years and the brown garden snail for four years. In addition, the eggs of many insects stay in diapause for several months over winter each year[6], and locusts' eggs can survive for over 3 years[7].

These abilities are also quite widespread. In chapter 3 of 'Book of Insect Records' (1994), for example, Marcos de Faria observes:

Diapause lasting more than a year...is known in many species of insects (Danks 1987). Sunose (1903) summarised cases of prolonged diapause and tabulated 64 insect species that present this phenomenon. In fact, prolonged diapause seems to be more common than one could imagine. Powell (1987) referred to approximately 90 species of Lepidoptera, in 10 superfamilies, that diapause for over one year.

Barnes (1952), studying wheat-blossom midges (Diptera: Cecidomyiidae), reported the emergence of *Cantarinia tritici Kirby* after the larvae had been in soil up to three years, whereas larvae of *Sitodiplosis mosellana Géhin* spent as many as 12 winters in the soil before the emergence of the adults. However, Powell (1989) reported the emergence of adults of the yucca moth *Prodoxus y-inversus* Riley (Lepidoptera: Prodoxidae), after prepupae spent 19 years in diapause.

Prolonged diapause may have appreciable adaptive value in habitats where resources are available only briefly...and/or undergo erratic fluctuations in abundance (Sunose 1978)... The physiological mechanisms of prolonged diapause are poorly understood (Tauber et al. 1986).

Consequently, there is no reason to believe that these kinds of organisms could not have survived underground for several months. Noah only therefore needed to take the following animals:

Birds and bats[8] (10,050 x 7 x 2)	140,700
Reptiles (6,000 x 2)	12,000
Clean mammals[9] (170 x 7 x 2)	2,380
Unclean mammals[10] (2,885 x 2)	5,770
Amphibians[11] (4,000 x 2)	8,000
TOTAL	168,850

As stated above, this assumes that marine reptiles 'crept on the earth' some of the time and need to be included in the above list per Genesis 6:20. As regards mammals, the number of recognised species has not altered greatly since 1970, so the above is based on the analysis provided by R. van Gelder, instead of the figure of 4,200 (see Appendix 1). The number of 'clean' mammals is an estimate based on the 164 living species of ruminantia, as these are the mammals that meet the criteria set out in Leviticus 11:1.

As regards the 'birds', some have argued that the figure would have been much lower than suggested above. This contention is based on the fact that the Greek, Syriac and Latin versions of Genesis 7:2,3 say that Noah was only told to take 'seven, seven' of each kind of clean bird and animal, but 'two, two' of each kind of unclean bird and animal[12]. It is argued that if the phrase 'two, two' means 'in twos', then 'seven, seven' must mean in 'sevens'[13]. It is also pointed out that Genesis 8:20 refers to Noah sacrificing 'clean birds' and this, it is suggested, indicates that a distinction must have been made between the numbers of clean and unclean birds that Noah was required to take on board the ark.

However, the Old Testament was originally written in Hebrew, and the Hebrew text does not include the phrase 'two, two'. Nor does it say that fewer 'unclean' birds were taken on board the ark. It simply says that Noah was required to take a pair of all unclean animals ('two'), and seven pairs ('seven, seven') of all birds and clean animals. Genesis 7:9,15 confirms that the phrase 'seven, seven' must mean 'seven pairs', as its says that all of the birds and animals entered the ark in pairs of male and female. This clearly rules out the possibility of an odd bird or animal.

As regards the reference in Genesis 8:20 to 'clean' birds, this merely tells us that a distinction was made for the purpose of determining which birds were appropriate for sacrifice. It does not follow from this that a fewer number of unclean birds were taken onto the ark.

(b) Collecting the Animals

One common question is how Noah and his family gathered all of the creatures together, particularly if some of them lived in remote parts of the world at the time.

The answer to this is provided by Genesis 6:20 and 7:15. These verses tell us that the birds and animals came to Noah after he and his family had boarded the ark. They also arrived in the correct numbers for each of the categories concerned, and presumably then went to the appropriate places on board the ark. As this was clearly miraculous in nature, the logistical problems that are raised in relation to this issue simply do not arise.

(c) Boarding the Ark

Some have concluded that Genesis 7:11-14 indicates that Noah and his family only had one day in which to get on board the ark. This, it is argued, would have been physically impossible.

However, Genesis 6:18-7:16 indicates that there was at least a week for embarkation. This passage begins with God telling Noah which creatures would come to him and what food he had to collect for their sustenance. Later, God forewarns that the rain will begin in *seven d*ays time, and following this Noah, his family and the animals enter the ark. The floodwaters break on the day of embarkation and Genesis 7:13 emphasises the providential nature of this, by stressing that they were on the ark 'on the selfsame day' that the 'windows of the heavens were opened.'

If this last phrase were translated using the simple past tense, it would suggest that they inexplicably starting boarding the ark on the day on which the deluge began, despite having received seven days' forewarning! Genesis 7:13 should therefore be translated in the pluperfect tense to read, 'by the selfsame day' Noah and all the animals '*had* boarded the ark.' It is worth adding here that Noah and his family also only had to collect *food* for the animals; they did not need to organise their embarkation in any way. As we have seen already, Genesis 7:9,15 says that the animals 'came to Noah into the ark' *after* he and his family had boarded it.

A period of a week would have only allowed about 7 seconds for each pair of birds and animals to board the ark, i.e. 60 x 60 x 24 x 7 ÷ 84,425 = 7.16 seconds. Genesis 7:9,15, however, does not say that the animals boarded the ark two at a time; it simply says that they entered in pairs of male and female. They could therefore have boarded eight, ten, or twelve at a time, depending on the kind of animal and, of course, the size of the ark's entrance.

Moreover, based on the above figures over 83% of the animals would have been birds, which could have flown onto the ark very quickly. Taking this into account and the fact that the animals' arrival was an act of God, there is no reason to believe that the whole operation could not have been performed within seven days.

(d) Caring for the Animals

The following details are provided purely to illustrate how many animals eight people could have tended to during an average ten-day period. There was no need for Noah to have provided so many cages, however, particularly for the non-carnivorous birds.

SPECIES	CAGES	MINS	FREQUENCY	TOTAL MINS
Carnivorous land mammals	249	2	8	3,984
Carnivorous birds	710	2	8	11,360
Other birds and bats	4,670	1	1.4	6,538
Rodents	169	1	1.4	237
Clean mammals	340	3	8	8,160
Primates	42	2	8	672
Elephants	2	3	8	48
Other Mammals	194	2	5	1,940
Totals	6,376	16	48	32,939

This comes to 6.86 hours per day for each person (32,939 ÷ 60 ÷ 10 ÷ 8), and assumes the cages contained the following animals:

SPECIFS	CAGES	NUMBER	TOTAL	REF.
Carnivorous land mammals	249	2	498	10
Carnivorous birds	710	14	9,940	14
Other birds and bats	4,670	28	130,760	5
Rodents	169	18-20	3,374	10
Clean mammals	340	7	2,380	9
Primates	42	7-8	332	10
Elephants	2	2	4	10
Other mammals	194	8-9	1,562	10
Reptiles	See below	See below	12,000	5
Amphibians	See below	See below	8,000	11
Totals	6,376		168,850	

The rest of each person's time might have been spent on:

Fishing, meat preparation	5.00 hours
Eating, washing	1.50 hours
Sleeping	7.00 hours
Sundry	3.64 hours

This breakdown assumes that more time was devoted to the larger mammals, on the basis that they would still have been fairly young. By contrast, no time has been specifically allocated to reptiles and amphibians, as many may have hibernated for fairly long periods in these conditions. A large part of the 'sundry' time could have been used to take care of these animals in between periods of hibernation.

Clearly, these assumptions would have created some significant time pressures. However, they could have been alleviated in a number of ways. To begin with, the cleaning of the cages might have been speeded up by using a simple sewerage system, such as a series of rudimentary channels running beneath the floors of the cages. This process could have been aided by the use of sloped or slatted floors, so urine and excreta collected automatically. The animals that produced the most excreta could also have been placed on the upper level of the ark, so that the waste could be sluiced through portholes directly out to sea.

On the lower levels excreta could have been collected from the channels and taken or pumped up to these waste portholes. This could have been done less regularly for birds and smaller animals, as their droppings can be left to accumulate for quite long periods with no adverse effects.

As an alternative or supplementary system, Noah could have employed vermicomposting, i.e., using earthworms or beetles to biodegrade the excreta. An important benefit of this method is that any surplus earthworms and beetles could have been used as a further food source for some of the birds and animals.

As regards feeding, most of the food would have been in a dried or preserved form, so that it could be stored for up to a year. It would not have been necessary, therefore, to replace most of the food on a daily basis. Many birds and rodents, for example, could have been fed using controlled self-feeding containers.

The distribution of the food could have been speeded up by using a simple system of chutes or pipes to deliver the foodstuffs into or near the cages. Similarly, water could have been supplied via a system of pipes, perhaps using hollowed out bamboo like those employed by the ancient Chinese. Steep sided or semi-enclosed water troughs could have prevented any significant water loss due to the movements on the ark. The ark was, however, shaped like a chest, so it would not have rolled from side to side in the same way as a traditional ship.

The task of preparing and distributing food for this number of carnivores would clearly have required a considerable amount of time and planning. Here, it has been assumed that this could firstly have been reduced by only feeding the carnivores every four days out of five, as is common in many zoos.

Some meat could have been preserved before the journey, but other meat must have been obtained from fishing, or slaughtering some of the surplus birds and animals. One benefit of the latter is that it would have reduced the total time needed to tend to all of the animals. It would also have reduced the time allocated to the meat-eaters, if some of the carnivorous birds were fed to the other carnivores.

Another possibility is that the carnivores were still relatively omnivorous. All animals were, after all, originally created to be plant eaters (Genesis 1:30). If this was the case, then it would have considerably reduced the time pressures by completely removing the need for fishing, slaughtering and meat preparation.

Given the tight schedule, any significant increase in the number of animals would clearly have presented a major problem. This could have been prevented, however, either by separating males and females or by feeding some of the offspring to the carnivores.

Most birds and animals would have been able to get sufficient exercise in their enclosures. For larger animals, the floors of their cages might have been fitted with some kind of exercise drum, which could have been released periodically. Apart from keeping the animals fit and healthy, this would also have removed the need to have animals' hooves and claws trimmed. These drums might even have been used to drive some of the equipment on the ark, such as the water pumps mentioned above.

Even taking these factors into account, this would still have been an arduous timetable for eight people. It has been suggested, therefore, that many of the animals and birds might have been dormant for quite long periods of time. Whitcomb and Morris, for example, point out that all groups of animals are known to hibernate, and they go on to suggest that most animals might have simply lost this ability with the passage of time[15].

This may seem implausible today, as the ability to hibernate appears to be confined to a relatively small group of bats, rodents, marsupials, amphibians and reptiles. These so called 'true hibernators' can survive drops in body temperature to below 10°c, following which they enter a dormant state that can last for several months at a time.

In addition to these animals, however, there are many others that are able to enter a less extreme version of hibernation, which involves higher body temperatures and shorter periods of dormancy. These include 'winter sleepers', such as badgers, raccoons, skunks and some species of bear, which can remain in this semi-dormant state for months with very little food or drink.

There are also a number of creatures that experience what is known as 'torpor'. In this type of dormancy, the animal may become inactive at any time of the year, and for various periods lasting from less than a day ('daily torpor) to a few weeks[16]. Torpor is widespread among deer, badgers, skunks, shrews, mice, gerbils and lemurs. And daily torpor has been found in quite a range of different bird species, including nighthawks, nightjars, pigeons, hummingbirds, swifts, martins and swallows.

The theory advanced by Whitcomb and Morris does not seem to be an untenable one, therefore, particularly given the dark and cold conditions that may have existed inside the ark. It also appears to be supported by more recent scientific evidence. One survey of hibernation, for example, stated that 'torpor was widely used in mammals and birds even in thermally moderate environments', and concluded that it might be 'an ancestral trait rather than an evolutionary adaptation.'[17]

If torpor was widespread, this would have considerably alleviated the burden of taking care of the birds and animals, particularly if different groups 'hibernated' during different periods of time. In these circumstances, there are clearly no grounds for saying that it would have been physically impossible for Noah and his family to have coped with the number of creatures on board the ark.

It is also worth remembering that the numbers of animals taken onto the ark might have been considerably lower than we have assumed. If our understanding of animals' genetic incompatibilities is incorrect, then the number of bird and animal species Noah needed to preserve might have been much lower.

(e) Living Space

An obvious question is: would the ark have been big enough to carry this number of animals? Genesis 6:15,16 tells us that the ark had a volume of 450,000 cubic cubits (300 x 50 x 30), and excavations have shown that the Hebrew cubit was about 17.5 inches[18]. Consequently, the ark would have had a volume of about 1,395,670 cubic feet (437.5 x 72.91667 x 43.75).

If 30% of the ark was taken up by family living quarters, storage space, floors, corridors, walls and other internal structures, this would have left 976,969 cubic feet. This is an average of 11.57 cubic feet for each pair of creatures (976,969 ÷ 84,425), which is equivalent to a cube with sides of just over 2.25 feet in length. Although this may appear to be very low at first sight, it seems plausible when the following factors are taken into account:

1. 95% of the animals were amphibians, birds and reptiles;

2. 42% of all land mammals are rodents[10], 89% of which are made up of members of the mice and squirrel families[19];

3. 11.5 cubic feet is enough space, therefore, for the vast majority of amphibians, rodents, birds and reptiles;

4. many of these smaller creatures could also have been kept in larger groups to allow more space for larger animals;

5. the larger birds, mammals and reptiles could have been represented by young animals; and,

6. some birds and animals would presumably have been slaughtered to feed the carnivores, thereby steadily increasing the amount of space available.

Some have argued, however, that all of the animals were adults, and that there would have been insufficient space, due to the number of large mammals. In support of this, it is suggested that the reference in Genesis 7:2 to 'a male and his mate' indicates that the animals were sexually mature. It is also claimed that many young animals could not have survived without the care of adults, and those that do not need close parental care tend to mature quickly and would be close to adult size within a year anyway.

However, the Hebrew text at Genesis 7:2, simply says that each pair consisted of 'a male and *its female*'. All this tells us is that each male was paired with a female of the same species. It does not say they were capable of reproducing at that stage.

As regards the larger species, although weaning can take several years in the wild, this can be speeded up in captivity. Elephant calves, for example, can be weaned by 15 months, and by 6 months giraffes can be completely independent of their mothers. Some animals would have needed time to adjust when they were released to the wild, but their instincts, coupled with human help, should have been enough to enable them to survive.

As regards growth rates, this is of course an important factor in evaluating the adequacy of the space onboard the ark. This has, however, been taken into account in estimating the average weights at (f) below. In addition, if the animals hibernated for prolonged periods, they would have grown at much lower rates. This would also have reduced the areas that were required for food storage, which would in turn have increased the amount of living space available for the animals.

(f) Storage

Noah was not told to take any water on board the ark. However, rain water would have been available throughout the first 40 days, some of which could have been stored in tanks on the roof of the ark. There must also have been some rain after this, as it was not until 150 days after the rain started that 'the windows of the heavens were stopped' altogether (Genesis 7:24 – 8:2). After this, some of the flood waters may also have been drinkable, as the vast majority of this came from rain and underground springs.

As regards food, the amount of space required for storage would have depended on various factors, in particular:

(a) the extent to which the birds and animals hibernated; and
(b) whether surplus birds and animals were fed to the carnivores.

Both of these issues were considered on pages 39-41 above. Hibernation would clearly have reduced the need to store food to a significant extent. And if some of the surplus birds and clean animals were fed to the carnivores, the number of animals for which food had to be stored would also have steadily reduced over time.

At the end of the Flood, we are told that Noah sacrificed some of 'every clean animal and clean bird' immediately after they disembarked (Genesis 8:20). Assuming that all but the carnivorous birds were 'clean' (see Leviticus 11:13-19; Deuteronomy 14:11-18), and that Noah sacrificed one of each clean animal and bird, we can assume that he needed to retain at least one of each of these species for the purpose of the sacrifices. This would have left the following animals on board the ark:

Details	Start	Eaten	End	Ave.	Notes
Carnivorous land mammals[10]	498	0	498	498	
Carnivorous birds[14]	9,940	0	9,940	9,940	
Amphibians[20]	8,000	0	8,000	8,000	
Carnivorous reptiles[21]	5,200	0	5,200	5,200	
Sub-totals	**23,638**	**0**	**23,638**	**23,638**	
Clean mammals	2,380	1,870	510	1,445	11/14 slaughtered, 1 sacrificed, leaving 1 pair of each species
Other mammals	5,272	0	5,272	5,272	
Clean birds	117,460	92,290	25,170	71,315	11/14 slaughtered, 1 sacrificed, leaving 1 pair of each species
Bats	13,300	11,400	1,900	7,600	12/14 slaughtered, leaving 1 pair of each species
Non-carnivorous reptiles	6,800	0	6,800	6,800	
Sub-totals	**145,212**	**105,560**	**39,652**	**92,432**	
Grand Totals	**168,850**	**105,560**	**63,290**	**116,070**	

According to field studies wild mammals consume about 20% of their weight each day; birds about 25%[22]. As the animals would have needed much less energy on board the ark, however, an average of 12.5% would appear to be a reasonable estimate. If 20% of the ark's capacity was used for storage, this would have provided 279,134 cubic feet. This could have held something in the order of 13,119,298 lbs of bird seed (47 x 279,134). And this amount of food could have fed around 92,430 animals for about 227 days (about 7.5 months), assuming they had an average weight of 5 1bs, that is 13,119,298/(92,430 x 5 x 12.5%). If so, it would have been necessary for the animals to be dormant for between 4 and 5 months of the voyage. This period could have been a fair bit lower, however, as some of the food could have been obtained from other sources, as explained on pages 46 and 47 below.

As regards the average weight of 5lbs, the following gives a possible breakdown, although it should be stressed that this is purely for illustration purposes. The source of the figures is explained on 44 above and Appendix 1.

Species	No.	Weight (1bs)	Total	Examples
Clean birds and bats	78,915	0.375	29,593	Collared dove
Clean mammals	1,445	203.5	294,058	Fallow deer
Rodents	3,374	0.656	2,213	Brown rat
Primates	332	13.5	4,482	Lar Gibbon
Elephants	4	635	2,540	African, 6 months
Other unclean mammals	1,560	68	106,080	Peccary
Non-carnivorous reptiles	6,800	3	20,400	Jackson's chameleon
Totals	92,430	Ave = 4.96	459,366	

It should be born in mind that these figures do not include carnivores, which account for most of the largest birds and reptiles. It is also assumed that the larger herbivores would have been represented by young animals.

The calculations of the storage capacity of the ark are based on bird seed, because over 75% of the non-meat eaters would have been birds. It was chosen for illustration purposes only, however, as Noah clearly had to take other kinds of food on board the ark. In fact, Genesis 6:21 tells us that he had to take 'of all food that is eaten'.

This should not, however, be regarded as meaning Noah had to take every single kind of foodstuff onto the ark. The phrase 'of all' is used throughout these passages to denote 'from each kind of'. Noah only therefore had to take from each 'kind' of foodstuff. So, he had to take some fruit, vegetables, cereals, meat and insects. He did not have to take every single kind of edible fruit, for example!

Some have questioned whether even this task would have been logistically possible. To begin with, a variety of animals require specialised diets consisting of things such as insects, bamboo shoots or eucalyptus leaves. How could Noah have assembled a wide enough range of foodstuffs to cater for such a diversity of dietary needs for the better part of a year? The second problem relates wastage. How could large quantities of food have been kept from spoiling when temperature or humidity levels may have been high at least for some of the time? And how could the cubit-sized window referred to in Genesis 6:16 have been large enough to have even kept the animals alive?

In relation to the first question, we know that by the time of Noah people had developed ways of storing food for long periods of time. In fact scientists believe that people in the Stone Age knew how to store various types of grain for several years[23], and from 3,500 BC dried fruit and fish were common parts of the diet[24].

In terms of catering for herbivores, grass silage can be stored for 18 months. In addition, most dried fruit can be stored for up to a year and dried vegetables can be preserved for up to 6 months[25]. It might also have been possible to grow some shade-loving plants on the ark, and given the large number of birds, there would also have been an almost inexhaustible supply of eggs! As regards the carnivores, fresh meat was available in the form of the surplus birds and animals. It could also have been obtained by fishing.

To feed insectivores, Noah could have taken insects on board the ark and bred them during the voyage. In addition, thousands of terrestrial insects may well have sought refuge on the Ark and it should not have been difficult to collect them by using various foodstuffs as bait. Moreover, a large number of insects could have been caught when fishing simple aquatic insect nets. Apart from the millions of insects that must have died during the Flood, these nets could also have been used to catch live aquatic insects as well.

Noah could therefore have stored quite a wide variety of foodstuffs, covering all of the main food types. It is true that some animals now have very specific dietary habits. However, this does not mean that they could not have survived for twelve months on similar, but not identical, foodstuffs at the time of the Flood. It is also worth bearing in mind that the ancestors of these animals may have enjoyed a more varied and omnivorous diet than their modern counterparts.

As regards the conditions on the ark, the first problem is that we simply cannot determine what the temperature on the ark would have been. This would have depended to a large extent on the temperature outside, about which the Bible is silent. As far as ventilation is concerned, this would certainly have been a problem if the only opening in the ark was an 18 inch square window. This assumption is based on Genesis 6:16, according to which God said to Noah, 'You shall make a צֹהַר to the ark and unto a cubit you shall finish above.' The noun צֹהַר in its plural form simply means 'midday', the time when the sun is at its highest and usually therefore at its brightest. As a result, many translators have taken this word to mean 'window', in the same way that the words 'sky' and 'light' are combined in English to mean, 'skylight'.

This interpretation appears to be confirmed by most translations of Genesis 8:6, which tells us that 'Noah opened the window he had made in the ark'. The Hebrew word for 'window' that is used here (הַחַלּוֹן) is never used to mean anything else. Furthermore, the use of the definite article ('the') indicates that the passage is referring back to 'a' window that was mentioned earlier in the text. (As in English, where an indefinite noun is mentioned again in Hebrew, the definite article must be used in the later references, e.g. 'he built a castle…and the castle was destroyed'.)

There are, however, various problems with this interpretation. To begin with, what Genesis 8:6 actually says is that 'Noah opened a window of the ark he had made'. The word 'window' is not preceded by the definite article (הַ), but by the accusative particle (אֶת). This particle simply tells us that the noun is the object of the sentence, and it is used for both definite and indefinite objects. For example, in Exodus 21:28, it is used in relation to 'a man' and 'a woman'. As already explained, however, when a noun has been referred to previously, it is preceded by the definite article in any later references. The fact that Genesis 8:6 refers to this as 'a window', therefore indicates that it is the first reference to this 'window'.

The second difficulty with the traditional translation of צֹהַר as 'window' is that Genesis 6:16 clearly indicates that it cannot refer to a window at all. According to this verse, Noah was told to make a צֹהַר and 'to finish a cubit above'. If Noah had to construct a window, however, he would have needed to know both its height and its width. Here, Noah was only given the former. This could not have been a 'window', therefore, at least not in the traditional sense. It also could not have been the door, as this is referred to later in the verse, using the indefinite article and a completely different Hebrew word.

In view of these problems, some have suggested that צֹהַר might refer to something else altogether. Some have proposed a roof[26], but some other commentators[27] believe that what Genesis 6:16 is describing is 'an opening' around the ark, which was a cubit from the top of the vessel.

This explanation has several things to commend it. To begin with, it ties in with the etymology of the word צֹהַר, which suggests some kind of 'opening'. It also makes sense of the phrase 'to finish a cubit above', the meaning of which would otherwise be unclear.

In addition, the concept of a gap around the top of the ark also makes perfect sense from a practical point of view. Such an opening would have provided not only light, but the ventilation the ark would clearly have needed.

With the assistance of breezes and convection currents, such an opening should have made it possible for air to circulate around all parts of the ark, assuming there were adequate gaps between the three sets of decking. In view of this, there is no reason to believe that ventilation would have been a serious problem.

(g) Seaworthiness

If the average weight of the animals was as much as 10 lbs at any point, then the cargo of food and animals would have weighed about 6,600 tons ((13,119,298 lbs* + 1,688,500* lbs) ÷ 2,240). This could easily have been accommodated by a vessel the size of the ark, which would have had a carrying capacity of at least 12,369 tons (437.5 x 72.91 x 36.45 /94)[28]. This is also a conservative calculation, as Genesis indicates that the ark was box shaped.

Some have questioned whether such a vessel would have been seaworthy. In particular, they point out that the longest wooden boats in modern times have been no more than 300 feet in length, and these had to be held together with iron straps. In fact, according to the Guinness Book of Records, the longest wooden ship ever constructed was the 377 foot long USS Dunderberg,

* see pages 37 and 45

which was built between 1867-72. Although this was an ocean-going vessel, it had to be clad with iron to hold it together.

As already indicated, however, the ark was not a ship, but a box-shaped vessel. In fact, the Hebrew word for 'ark' literally means 'chest'. It would therefore have been much more stable than any ship with a curved bow. We are also told that the ark was 'covered in asphalt within and without' (Genesis 6:14). This would not only have made the ark very waterproof, it would also have given it a considerable amount of flexibility and tensile strength.

Furthermore, the seaworthiness of the ark has been supported by detailed scientific studies[29]. These considered various hull designs and determined that the ark and its cargo capacity would have been about 20,640 tons. The various designs were converted into 1:50 scale models, which were then subjected to ocean conditions in the simulation tank of the Korean Research Institute of Ships and Engineering. The study concluded that the ark could have survived ocean going conditions with waves higher than 30 metres.

2. Salinity

Although the oldest water in the oceans is believed to be a few thousand years old, it is estimated that it would take between 68 and 260 million years for sodium to build up to its present levels, based on the current rates of accumulation[30]. According to a literal interpretation of the Bible, however, the Flood took place around about 2,350 BC[31].

One possible explanation is that the oceans were originally made up of freshwater. There was then a sudden increase in the salinity levels after the Flood, due to the torrential rains and the bursting of 'all the fountains of the great deep' (Genesis 7:11). This caused a huge amount of geological disturbance, which dramatically increased the rates of erosion and subsidence, resulting in huge amounts of rock salts being released into the oceans over a very short period of geological time.

Another possibility is that the sea was created with salt levels similar to those at present. The Flood did not significantly change the salinity levels, however, as the huge amount of rainwater coincided with a substantial release of rock salts for the reasons given above. Further salt was also released at that time by 'the fountains of the great deep', as these were mainly composed of salty or brackish water.

A third possibility is that the sea was created with similar salt levels to those at present, and the Flood altered this temporarily to a largely freshwater environment. This was caused by the massive amount of rainwater coupled with the eruption of huge numbers of underground freshwater streams. The salinity of the seawater then returned to its current levels, as a result of evaporation, increased rates of erosion, and the miraculous removal of the surplus floodwaters (Genesis 8:1).

The difficulty with the first explanation is that it may be hard to show that up to 260 million years worth of erosion could have been caused by this amount of geological activity. The second explanation is problematic, as it would require Noah's stores of water to have lasted for about seven months after the deluge had ceased (Genesis 8:2).

Large water tanks could have been situated on the roof of the ark, but these would probably have only been adequate if the animals that consumed most of the water hibernated for a large percentage of the time. John Woodmorappe calculates that almost 10% of the ark's volume would have been needed to provide a year's supply of water for about 16,000 birds and animals[32].

This suggests that the third explanation might be the most viable one. The problem with this, however, and to a lesser extent the first model, is that it is not immediately clear how fish and other sea animals could have survived such a dramatic and sudden change in salinity levels.

There is evidence, however, that the ability to adapt to changes in salinity may have been much more widespread than it is at present. But even today, although most fish are either marine or freshwater, many are much more adaptable than this. In the Kattegat, for example, where the salt content is about half that of seawater, Marshall reports 75 species of marine fish. And off the coast of Finland, where the salinity ranges from freshwater to about 20% that of seawater, freshwater fish can be almost as diverse as their marine counterparts[33].

Many further examples for both fish and other marine animals are cited by Woodmorappe, who also points out that marine fish are generally much more tolerant of reduced salinity than freshwater species are of salinity increases[34]. He also provides evidence that this tolerance can be significantly improved by higher temperature levels and the presence of other salts in the water, particularly those containing calcium.

More significantly perhaps, some fish, such as certain species of salmon and eels, are able to move between freshwater and marine environments quite freely. And there is evidence that this ability is linked to changes in the activity of the thyroid gland[35]. It is possible, therefore, that many fish and marine animals were originally able to adapt to changes in salinity levels much more readily than they are at present, an ability that has perhaps been lost by all but a few species. It also is interesting to note here that Darwin himself thought that this was a viable explanation for the presence of related freshwater species in remoter parts of the world[36].

3. Carnivores

The argument regarding the emergence of carnivores is inconclusive, as Genesis 1:30 only tells us that God gave plants as food to all 'birds' and land animals. It does not say that all of these creatures were physically incapable of eating meat. Apart from dentition, there are only few differences in the digestive systems of herbivores and carnivores[37]. Consequently, fish, birds, mammals and reptiles all include a mixture of carnivores and plant eaters, as did the dinosaurs before them[38]. The present-day carnivorous animals and birds may therefore have simply lost the ability to digest plant food with the passage of time.

Having said this, the Bible does clearly indicate that the emergence of carnivores was more the result of supernatural events than the laws of nature. Before the Fall, we are told that both man and animals had enjoyed a peaceful co-existence as plant eaters (Genesis 1:30). After man's disobedience, however, the Bible says that 'all flesh' became corrupt and the world was 'full of violence' (Genesis 6:11-13). This violence clearly affected animals and humans alike, as 'both man and beast' had to be destroyed by the Flood (Genesis 6:7).

However, as explained in Chapter 1, some carnivores had to be preserved to maintain a balance in nature. This prevented the depletion of human food resources. It also alleviated the suffering that would have occurred if herbivores had been allowed to reproduce unchecked, with the result that many of them died slowly of disease and starvation.

4. After the Flood

Although most plants would have been destroyed by the Flood, seeds[39] and spores[40] can survive in a dormant condition for at least a year. In more primitive plants, such as certain mosses[41] and algae[42], many of the plant parts can reproduce on their own, and this may occur even after many years of dormancy[43]. Some trees have also survived under floodwaters for periods of up to three years[44]. This last fact might account for the 'freshly plucked olive leaf' mentioned in Genesis 8:11, although this may also have come from a sapling that developed from a tree 'cutting'[45].

As regards the method of survival, many seeds can float for long periods, and this ability may have been even more widespread at the time of the Flood. Seeds and plant parts might have floated on flotsam, such as mats of vegetation or pieces of pumice. Other seeds and plants may have been buried by the Flood, with some of them then being exposed for germination or propagation by the erosive forces of the receding flood waters.

As dry land began to appear five months before the animals left the ark (Genesis 8:5,14), there would have been ample time for plant life to develop before the animals disembarked. In addition, the seed stores on the ark may not have been entirely depleted, particularly if some of the herbivores had hibernated for long periods of time.

The huge amount of geological activity (see 5(d) below) should also have made the soil extremely fertile. The annual flooding of the Nile was a major reason for the fertility of the surrounding land, and any volcanic activity would have increased the fecundity of the surrounding areas. Thus, plant life may have been able to develop much more quickly than usual after the Flood waters had subsided.

Carnivores emerging from the ark may have initially been able to feed on the carrion of animals that had died during the Flood. Given the huge numbers involved, some of their bodies must have been at least partially preserved by burial and then been re-exhumed when the Flood waters retreated. Some carnivores could have caught fish and other aquatic animals, whilst others may have been fed by Noah and his family from these sources for a period of time. Alternatively, many meat eaters may have been much more omnivorous than they are at present.

5. Re-population of Islands

(a) Background

Scientists believe that all life originated from a single land mass, from which it dispersed to colonise the rest of the world[46]. The process by which individual islands are believed to have been populated, however, depends on a number of factors.

To begin with, scientists divide islands into two categories, continental and oceanic. The former are believed to have been part of the original land mass, whilst geologists think the latter developed independently of it[47].

(b) Continental Islands

Scientists believe that terrestrial life forms could have populated continental islands in basically four ways: continental drift, glaciation, flotsam and human transport.

According to the theory of continental drift, the earth's surface is made up of plates, which have slowly moved apart over a period of about 200 million years[48], resulting in the separate continents we know today. This process also resulted in smaller areas of land becoming detached from the continents and forming islands, leaving their terrestrial animals isolated from the mainland. The concept of continental drift, which was developed in the 1960s, is considered to be one of the most important factors in explaining the present animal population of continental islands[49].

As regards glaciation, the last ice age is generally believed to have ended about 10,000 years ago and to have affected about 30% of the globe[50]. It has been calculated that this would have reduced the sea level by about 200 metres[51], thereby allowing some islands to become interconnected and for others to temporarily re-join the mainland[52]. The ice sheets would also have created a number of land bridges, enabling terrestrial animals to populate islands. And some of the animals on those islands could have become isolated when the glaciers eventually retreated[53]. Land animals from South America, for example, are believed to have migrated to Australia via Antarctica[54].

Transport by humans or by flotsam are important factors when considering the movement of small rodents, lizards and non-flying insects. Neill suggests that 'seldom can we be sure that a small, remote island received its meagre fauna without the help of man'[55]. The Pacific islands, for instance, contain hardly any land mammals apart from rats, which Pielou suggests have 'almost certainly been introduced by ships'[56].

(c) Oceanic islands

Human transport is also the only known means for small flightless mammals such as rats to populate oceanic islands. However, smaller creatures, such as insects and some reptiles, may also have been transported by flotsam. This would commonly include logs, trees, leaves and seeds[55,56], but it could also have included things such as pumice.

Although there is clearly a limit to the distances that insects and reptiles can be transported by flotsam, it also seems clear that in some cases their eggs must have travelled considerable distances in this way[57].

(d) The Scriptures

A literal interpretation of the biblical account does not require us to dispense with any of these scientific explanations. It simply means that we have to modify the timescale over which we believe they took place.

In the case of glaciation, we would have to assume that this occurred about 4,500 years ago instead of 10,000 years ago. As will be shown later in this chapter, however, scientific dating techniques are open to considerable doubt, so a more recent date is entirely possible.

As regards continental drift, Genesis 1:9, 10 says that there was one original mass of water, so there must also have been one land mass. Genesis 7:11 then tells us that God intended to destroy the earth in the form in which it then existed. This was brought about by global flooding, huge tidal waves and 'all the fountains of the great deep' bursting forth.

The latter could have released magma as well as water. And as continental drift is thought to be caused by currents within the earth's mantle[58], geological activity on this massive scale could have accelerated that process considerably.

Some may question whether the biblical account allows enough time for the earth to be repopulated. It should be borne in mind, however, that scientists believe that there has only been 10,000 years since the last ice age wiped out life from a large part of the globe[50], which has now been completely re-populated.

6. Seabirds and the Arctic

This objection assumes that the polar ice caps existed before the Flood and that these regions were inhabited by animals at the time. However, neither of these assumptions can be proven. The world may have been a much warmer place before the Flood. If so, the Arctic, a huge floating ice-sheet, may not have existed or may have been much smaller then and not therefore accessible to animals.

Some have seen a possible explanation for a warmer climate in the words of Genesis 1:7. This tells us that God separated the sea from the waters above the heavens. Whilst some assume that the latter refers to clouds, the word for 'clouds' is not used here as it is in Genesis 9:14. In addition, one would also expect clouds to be described as being 'in' the sky rather than 'above' it.

Some commentators therefore believe that Genesis 1:7 indicates that the earth was originally protected by a layer of water vapour, which created the stable, tropical environment which is traditionally associated with the Garden of Eden[59]. This protective water canopy, it is suggested, was released when the Flood occurred. This resulted in a dramatic fall in temperature and violent changes in the climate, which ultimately caused an ice age and the formation of the polar ice caps. This is only a theory, of course, but it would explain how land animals were able to populate certain islands after the Flood, and why the polar ice caps did not exist before then.

As regards seabirds, there are various reasons why they might not have survived outside the ark. Some may have been unable to find enough food due to the huge amount of disturbance in the sea. Others may have died from exhaustion, either because they could not settle on the water, or because they were continually seeking cliffs or dry land for nesting purposes.

7. Human Population Levels

According to the Bible, the Flood occurred around 2,350[31] BC, and historians estimate that by 50 BC the population of the world had grown to about 200 million[60]. The surviving group of 8 people, therefore, must have doubled between 24 and 25 times during this period of time, which is about once every 94 years.

At present, the world's population is probably increasing at a rate of around 1% per annum[61], which means that it is doubling about once every 65 years. And during the twentieth century, the world's population doubled at an average rate of once every 53 years[62]. Put in this context, the biblical account is certainly not impossible.

8. Ancient Dynasties

(a) General

It is often claimed that the records of the most ancient civilisations provide decisive proof against the historicity of the biblical Flood narrative. These records take the form of lengthy king lists, which suggest that there was an unbroken sequence of dynasties throughout the third millennium BC, when Noah's Flood is supposed to have taken place.

However, there are a number of problems with these accounts, which make it untenable to argue that they provide us with reliable chronologies. To begin with, we know that they were compiled hundreds, and in some cases thousands, of years after the events they describe. In the absence of supporting, contemporaneous evidence, it is fair to conclude that they probably contain a significant number of estimates and inaccuracies.

The second problem is that the king lists contain passages which are generally acknowledged to be mythological in nature. For example, all of the accounts begin with sections that describe periods of rulership by the gods, which are then followed by human kings with reign lengths that last for hundreds and even thousands of years. It is also not clear where legend ends and history begins. And if a writer was prepared to describe mythological events as if they were historical facts, this must cast doubt on the credibility of the others parts of the king lists as well.

Furthermore, even where these accounts seem to be largely historical in nature, they still appear to contain elements of exaggeration. Some of the over-statements may have been for political reasons, perhaps to emphasise the longevity of a particular ruler. In other cases, they may have been motivated by the more general desire to exaggerate the antiquity of the writers' ancestors. As Robert Morkot puts it, the Egyptian and Babylonian historians deliberately '*set* out to prove that his country was the oldest'[63].

Despite these weaknesses in the ancient king lists, historians have nevertheless continued to use them to construct extensive chronologies. This has been done by ignoring the mythological passages and replacing obvious exaggerations with more realistic estimates. In some cases, the proposed dates have received some support from archaeological evidence and carbon dating. However, this evidence has often been far from conclusive, as a result of which material differences of opinion still exist.

One reason for these disagreements is the significant number of differences between various texts and versions, which often make it impossible to determine which provide the most reliable data. There is also a further and more deep-seated problem. It was originally assumed that the total length of an historical account could be worked out by simply adding up the periods of the individual reign lengths, a process known as 'dead reckoning'. Over the years, however, it has become increasingly apparent that the accounts contain a significant number of overlaps, both in the form of parallel dynasties and as periods of co-regency within those dynasties. This realisation has resulted in some drastic reductions in the original calculations, and it is hard to exclude the possibility that further significant reductions may be necessary.

To disprove the account of the biblical Flood it is also not enough to simply show that there were rulers before and after 2,350 BC. One must also prove that there was either an unbroken series of reigns during this period of time or that the human population levels shortly after 2,350 BC were incompatible with a worldwide deluge in that year. The problem is that there is often no evidence to show that kings were related to their assumed predecessors. Consequently, it is frequently impossible to completely discount the existence of overlapping reigns or dynasties. It may also be impossible to rule out a significant gap between dynasties during which the Flood could perhaps have taken place.

One thing that the literature of these ancient civilisations does have in common with the Bible, however, is the concept of a global flood. This raises an important question: 'what gave rise to this idea in the first place?' Whatever the answer to this question might be, one thing is clear: the idea of a universal deluge has its roots in the very dawn of civilisation.

(b) Sumeria

The Sumerian King List (SKL) is represented by about 25 texts[64]. These exist in various forms, ranging from small fragments to extensive documents. None of the latter is complete, however, and several kings mentioned in other sources have been omitted from the SKL altogether.

The oldest version of the SKL is thought to be a clay tablet known as the Weld-Blundell Prism (WB)[65]. This contains the vast majority of the SKL, and most of the WB is dated to about 2,170 BC. This date is based upon the consistency in the style and language up to the reign of Utu-hegal, who is believed to have ruled around 2,170 BC. As the character of the writing in later sections is noticeably different, these are assumed to be the work of a later scribe.

This method of dating assumes that a scribe would not conclude an account if he knew that there were other rulers after this date. However, an historian writing at a later time may have simply wished to compile a record of these particular dynasties, just as someone writing today might, for example, wish to trace the history of English monarchs from Norman times to the beginning of the Tudor period.

To calculate the date of 2,170 BC, we also have to accept that the SKL is accurate back to this point in time and that the dynasties in question were sequential and do not contain any unknown periods of co-regency. As we will see, however, the SKL does contain several omissions and inaccuracies. It also does not mention parallel dynasties and co-regencies, which may have existed during various periods of Sumerian history.

As regards the style of writing in the WB, some scholars think that this could be as recent as the middle of the first dynasty of Babylon[66]. From a purely linguistic point of view, therefore, it might have been written as late as 1,650 BC, depending on the year in which Hammurabi's 42 year reign actually began. The latter is generally taken to be 1,792 BC, but some believe it could have been as late as 1,728 BC[67].

As regards the authorship of the WB, the contrasts in style could be attributable to stylistic differences in the source material, rather than the involvement of more than one scribe. The fact is that the inscription says that the whole of the WB is the work of one scribe, Nurninsubur. As the full text extends to Sinmagir, whose reign is believed to have ended in 1,819 BC, it is not unreasonable to conclude that the WB was completed at least 531 years after Noah's Flood.

Those who dispute the biblical account would presumably wish to support the earlier date of 2,170 BC, as this suggests that there could not have been a worldwide flood in 2,350 BC, assuming, of course, that the WB is historically accurate. After all, if a catastrophe of this magnitude had occurred only 180 years earlier, this should have been reflected in the SKL. Having said this, the SKL does tell us that there was a massive flood that 'swept over the land' and completely destroyed the previous dynasty. It is also clear from Sumerian literature that this was not merely a local inundation.

The Sumerian version of the flood is recounted in a tablet from Nippur. Unfortunately, only a third of this tablet now survives. However, the details in the text that remains bear remarkable similarities to the biblical account[68]. In the Sumerian version we are told that the gods resolved to bring a flood to destroy mankind. However, one of the gods decided to help a god-fearing king called Ziusudra, by telling him how to build a giant boat. Like Noah, Ziusudra followed these instructions and survived the flood, following which he made animal sacrifices to the gods as an act of thanksgiving.

Although the SKL attributes this event to a much earlier time, this may have been done to exaggerate the antiquity of the Sumerian people. Furthermore, as explained on page 67, there appears to be a gap in the SKL of about 400 years around the time of Noah's Flood. Although the date of this 400-year gap is uncertain, one cannot discount the possibility that the area was entirely flooded and was then re-populated during this period of time.

As regards the content of the SKL, there is a summary at Appendix 2, which is based mainly on Jacobsen's analysis[69] of the WB and 15 other texts. The dynasties are divided into reigns falling before and after a great flood. Those before the flood rule from heaven and have reigns of tens of thousands of years. These are accepted to be mythological, although some believe that the names may refer to actual kings who were later deified to reflect their legendary status.

The second part of the king list covers human rulers. The length of their reigns is believed to be apocryphal for at least the first 30,000 years, as many of the individual reigns span hundreds or even thousands of years. In addition, most of the reign lengths end in '0' or '5', which strongly suggests that they are not actual figures.

In the later periods there are also several instances of extremely long reigns, which are therefore also believed to be fictional. In the fourth dynasty of Kish, for example, we are told that Urzababa reigned for 400 years, and in a later dynasty a reign of 427 years is attributed to Utu-hegal.

Another notable feature of the SKL is the significant variation between different texts. Some of the anomalies could be due to scribal errors, but in other cases they are strongly suggestive of highly variant recensions. The absence of further information, however, often makes it impossible to be sure which version was the original one.

A further concern is the complete omission of rulers who are referred to in local inscriptions. In some periods, relatively few rulers appear in both the SKL and these other sources. None of the kings of Lagash or Umma are mentioned in the SKL; also absent are Zuzu of Ashak, Meskalamdug and Akalamdug of Ur, and Mesilim, Lugal, Urzaged and Utuk of Kish[70].

There are also a number of inconsistencies in the SKL. At the end of each dynasty, for example, the number of the kings is given together with the period covered by their reigns. As the notes in Appendix 2 indicate, however, on several occasions the summary totals contradict the details given in the main body of the text.

Despite these shortcomings, scholars have tried to use the SKL to produce a detailed chronology of Sumerian history. One of the most recent attempts to do this was *The Sumerian King List,* Thorkild Jacobsen's formative work of 1939. Jacobsen concluded that the SKL was derived from separate local sources, which gave details of the rulers of each city. Although he considered these sources to be largely reliable, he argued that later scribes had incorrectly organised the material to suggest that the dynasties occurred in a single sequence.

In addition, Jacobsen thought that internal and external evidence indicated that many of the dynasties overlapped with one another. He used these apparent synchronisms to align the accounts of each city and from this he produced a king list with a much shorter duration. Jacobsen then shortened this further by removing elements which he considered to be mythological or exaggerated. As a result, he excluded the first 20 kings and replaced about 30% of the remaining reigns with estimates of 20 to 30 years.

To complete his chronology, Jacobsen worked back from the reign of Hammurabi, the Babylonian ruler whose invasion brought the last dynasty of Sumeria to an end. Jacobsen used a date of 2,068 BC for Hammurabi, and from this he calculated that the first Sumerian king on the SKL would have reigned from about 3,110 BC.

It is now accepted that there are many parallel dynasties in the

SKL, as Jacobsen had argued. However, it is also thought that the dates of the Sumerian kings must have been somewhat later than Jacobsen originally suggested. The following summarises the general consensus[71]:

> The latter date [the beginning of the reign of Hammurabi], it is now generally agreed, is approximately 1,750 BC plus or minus fifty years. For the time span between this date and the end of the Third Dynasty of Ur, there is enough inscriptional material available to show by dead reckoning that it was approximately 195 years in length; the end of the Third Dynasty of Ur may therefore be placed at 1,945 BC, plus or minus fifty years. From this date backwards, there are enough historical inscriptions, date-formulas, and synchronisms of various sorts to carry us back to approximately 2,500 BC and a ruler by the name of Mesilim. Beyond this, all dating depends entirely on archaeological, stratigraphic, and epigraphic inferences and surmises of one sort or another and the results of carbon-14 tests, which, as already said, have not proved to be as decisive and conclusive as had been anticipated.

Based on the above the date of the first king in Jacobsen's list would have to be adjusted to 2,792 BC, as Hammurabi's reign would have begun in 1,750 BC, not 2,068 BC. More recently, though, some have argued that Hammurabi's reign began as early as 1,565 BC[72], in which case Jacobsen's king list would start at 2,607 BC.

In addition, there is evidence that the overlaps between the different dynasties were greater than Jacobsen had originally calculated. For example, in Jacobsen's reconstruction it is assumed that Gilgamesh preceded Mesannepadda by 38 years. According to the Tummal Inscription, however, Mesannepadda was an older contemporary of Gilgamesh and it was he, and not Gilgamesh, who brought the First Dynasty of Kish to an end[73].

As we have seen, the SKL does not take account of parallel dynasties. On the basis of the evidence of Gilgamesh, however, it also does not appear to recognise periods of co-regency. As co-regency does not appear to have been uncommon in the ancient world[74], it could have occurred on a large number of occasions in the SKL, for example when the next king was a near relative of his predecessor.

All of these conclusions cast serious doubt on the historical value of the SKL. If the author of the SKL was prepared to simply make up the reign lengths of 30% of the kings, how can we be sure that other figures are any more reliable? Furthermore, many of the kings' reigns occurred hundreds of years before the SKL was apparently written, and very few of those kings are referred to in other literature. Given this, it seems entirely possible that many of the rulers could be as fictional as their reign lengths.

Jacobsen's reconstruction also assumes that many of the dynasties of the SKL overlapped with one another. Throughout the SKL, however, we are told that each dynasty occurred in sequence, because it was only when one dynasty was defeated that the kingship passed on to the next city. For example, at the end of the Second Dynasty of Ur we read –

Ur was defeated and its kingship was carried off to Adab. In Adab, Lugalannemundu reigned 90 years as king. One king reigned 90 years. Adab was defeated, and its kingship was carried off to Mari.

Jacobsen's thesis, therefore, requires us to assume that the SKL is not only incorrect about this, but that many of the dynasties overlapped despite the clear statements in the SKL to the contrary. If the authors of the SKL were 4,000 years nearer to these events than we are, however, then they would presumably have had access to much better information regarding these events than we do. If, despite this, they created numerous fictitious reign lengths and then presented them as a long sequence of rulers, knowing full well that many of their reigns overlapped with one another, we must seriously doubt the reliability of any of the SKL.

As has already been stated, to challenge the biblical Flood account, it would be necessary to demonstrate one of two things. We would have to show that either (a) the population figures at the time were incompatible with a worldwide deluge in 2,350 BC, or (b) that there was an unbroken series of reigns during the period covered by Noah's Flood.

In relation to (a), detailed population information of this kind is simply not available in relation to Sumeria. In addition, the vast majority of the 'kings' in the SKL are rulers of individual cities, which suggests that the population would have been relatively small at that time. Given this, it would be hard to argue that a worldwide flood could not have occurred between two of the dynasties, following which the area was re-populated.

As regards (b), although the totals at the end of each dynasty imply a continuous sequence of rulers, the SKL frequently does not say if those rulers were closely related to their predecessors. We are also not told if there was any family connection between the rulers of different dynasties.

In theory, therefore, there could have been significant gaps in the SKL. One example of particular interest is Urzababa. He is believed to have reigned around 2,350 BC, as the SKL tells us that Sargon, who is dated to around this time, was originally his cupbearer[75]. The SKL also tells us that Urzababa reigned for 400 years, a figure which Jacobsen confirms is not a scribal error[76]:

...the dynasty total given in S, 586 years, presupposes that S originally had the same figure as WB, 400 years, for the reign of Urzababa...Why such an extremely high figure was assigned to Urzababa is uncertain.

It is generally accepted, of course, that Urzababa did not reign for 400 years. If the other dates from the fourth dynasty of Kish are correct, however, then there must have been a gap of about 400 years around the time of his reign. As 2,350 BC was also the year of Noah's Flood, this raises an intriguing question. Could the Flood have wiped out the Sumerian people in 2,350 BC, following which the area was entirely repopulated over the following 400 years?

It is interesting to note here that, unlike most Sumerian kings, Sargon and Urzababa were the subject of various legends[77]. This suggests that they were seen as rulers of a bygone age, as opposed to more recent kings whose reigns had ended little more than a 100 years before the SKL was supposedly written.

In conclusion, therefore, it is clear that the SKL is not a reliable document. Not only does it contain inaccuracies and omissions, but many of the reign lengths and sequences appear to have been deliberately fabricated. In view of this, it cannot be used to present a serious challenge to the veracity of the biblical account.

Having said this, like the Bible, the SKL tells us of a devastating flood at an early stage in human history. It also tells us that before and after the flood some people enjoyed incredibly long lifespans. Although the timescales for these events are somewhat different from the Bible, a gap of 400 years in the SKL suggests that there is a way in which the two accounts might at least be partially reconciled with one another.

(c) Egypt

(i) General

By contrast with Sumeria, the evidence to support the history of ancient Egypt appears to be much stronger. The main sources are:

- the Palermo Stone;
- the Royal Annals of Karnak, Abydos and Saqqara;
- the Turin Canon;
- the writings of Manetho;
- astronomical data;
- archaeological evidence; and,
- carbon dating.

We will look at these in turn to evaluate the content and reliability of each of them. Before doing so, however, it is worth outlining the conventional chronology of ancient Egypt, so that each of these sources can be viewed in its proper context.

The standard chronology of ancient Egypt is summarised in the table below, which is based on pages 480 to 482 of *The Oxford History of Ancient Egypt*. The first point to note here is that there is no evidence that the concept of dynasties existed during the time of the pharaohs. These dynastic divisions appear to have been entirely the creation of Manetho, a writer of the 3rd century BC. The periods or eras, however, are entirely modern divisions, although some of the demarcation lines vary from writer to writer. For example, some historians include the 7th and 8th dynasties in the First Intermediate Period, on the grounds that the downfall of the Old Kingdom was already evidently in progress at that stage.

Period	Dynasty	Start BC	End BC
Early Dynastic	1	3,000	2,890
	2	2,890	2,686
Old Kingdom	3	2,686	2,613
	4	2,613	2,494
	5	2,494	2,345
	6	2,345	2,181
	7	2,181	2,160
	8	2,181	2,160
First Intermediate Period	9	2,160	2,025
	10	2,160	2,025
	11*	2,125	2,055
Middle Kingdom	11*	2,055	1,985
	12	1,985	1,773
	13	1,773	1,650
	14	1,773	1,650
Second Intermediate Period	15	1,650	1,550
	16	1,650	1,580
	17	1,580	1,550

* The first involved rulership of Thebes only; the second covered the whole of Egypt

Period	Dynasty	Start BC	End BC
New Kingdom	18	1,550	1,295
	19	1,295	1,186
	20	1,186	1,069
Third Intermediate Period	21	1,069	945
	22	945	715
	23	**818**	**715**
	24	**727**	**715**
	25	747	656
Late Period	26	664	525
	27	525	359
	28	**404**	**399**
	29	399	380
	30	380	343
	31	343	332

The first noteworthy feature is the incidence of overlapping dynasties, here shown in bold. These are a common feature of the chronology, and before the Persian Period (27th Dynasty) they occur in 53% of the dynasties. And the history of ancient Egypt could be compressed into a significantly shorter period of time, if evidence of further overlaps came to light. This might take the form of parallel dynasties, co-regencies between pharaohs of the same dynasty, or perhaps a mixture of both.

Joint rulership also appears to have been much more likely during the 'intermediate' periods. These periods are so named, because they fall between eras of relative stability. The intermediate periods were apparently characterised by social upheaval and confusion, with various dynasties ruling from different parts of the country at the same time. The pharaohs therefore appear to have enjoyed relatively short reign lengths, particularly during the Second Intermediate Period.

(ii) Literary Sources

The first and apparently oldest piece of evidence is the Palermo Stone. This is inscribed on both sides and records details of the pharaohs from the last pre-dynastic kings up to Neferirkare in the mid 5th dynasty. This stone consists of a black basalt slab, which is currently located in the Palermo Museum in Sicily. Similar fragments are held in the Egyptian Museum in Cairo and the Flinders Petrie Museum in London. All of these are believed to have originally formed part of the same stela.

The Palermo Stone is generally believed to have been written during the 5th dynasty on the basis of the style of writing, the spellings of kings' names and the fact that it contains no rulers from later dynasties. Despite this, some scholars have argued in favour of a much later date, with one Egyptologist placing it as late as the 25th dynasty[78].

In terms of its historical reliability, the Palermo Stone records the names of several divine rulers, who are believed to be entirely mythological. Thereafter, the names of many kings are indecipherable, with some of the obscurer entries possibly being due to misunderstandings or copying errors by later scribes[78].

Moreover, in its damaged condition the Palermo Stone does not provide enough information to establish reign lengths. In view of this and its limitation to the first five dynasties, the Palermo Stone provides very little assistance in constructing a reliable chronology of ancient Egypt.

The same problem arises in relation to the Royal Annals. These only list the *names* of the pharaohs; no details of their reign lengths are provided. The content of the lists is also limited, as there are quite a large number of gaps and there is no information for periods beyond the 19th dynasty.

The Royal Annals of Karnak were found in the Karnak Temple of

Amun. They are dated to the reign of Tuthmosis III of the 18th dynasty, who is believed to have built the temple and whose name is the last to appear on the king list. The list records the names of many of the obscurer rulers of the Second Intermediate Period. However, of the 61 kings' names, only 48 are now legible. In addition, the list is in no obvious order and is clearly selective, as it excludes dynasties 1, 2, 8 to 10, 15 and 16[79].

The Royal Annals of Abydos are in fact two lists. These are both dated to Ramesses II, the 19th dynasty pharaoh who is believed to have been responsible for their completion. The first list was found on the walls of the Temple of Seti I, and comprises 76 kings from dynasties 1 to 8, 11, 12, 18 and 19. It is the sole source of the names of many of the rulers of the 7th and 8th dynasties, so it is highly valued for that reason alone. However, the Old Kingdom rulers are believed to be in the wrong order and several dynasties and many other pharaohs have been omitted altogether. The latter include the so-called 'heretic king', Akhenaten, and his assumed son-in-law, Tutankhamun.

The second Abydos king list was found in the Temple of Ramesses II. This is much more fragmentary than the first Abydos list and contains the names of only 52 kings from dynasties 7, 8, 12, 18 and 19. It is generally regarded as an updated copy of the first Abydos king list, with the name of Ramesses II added at the very end.

The Royal Annals at Saqqara are also attributed to the reign of Ramesses II. This list was discovered in the tomb of Thunery, a court official who held the titles of 'Royal Scribe' and 'Overseer of Works on all Royal Monuments'. It mentions the names of 58 kings from Merbiapen in the middle of the 1st dynasty to Ramesses II. However, only 47 names are now readable and numerous kings are missing, including the whole of dynasties 7 to 10 and 13 to 17.

None of the sources so far considered, therefore, provides any information that could be used to construct a chronology of ancient

Egypt. The Palermo Stone and the Royal Annals only provide evidence that the kings existed; they do not tell us when or for how long they reigned. Nor do they exclude the possibility of co-regency or parallel dynasties. In fact, the only ancient document that provides any details of the lengths of the reigns and dynasties of ancient Egypt is a papyrus called the Turin Canon.

Like the Royal Annals, the Turin Canon is usually dated to the time of Ramesses II. Unlike them, however, it provides the reigns lengths of each king in years, months and days. Unfortunately, it is now in an extremely fragmentary condition, which makes reconstruction of the list speculative at best and in some cases simply impossible.

The Turin Canon lists the Egyptian rulers from the divine kings until the end of the 17th dynasty, with the omission of the 7th and 8th dynasties. Of the 220 or so human rulers that are listed, however, only about 85 names are complete and a clear reign length is only given for 35 of those kings. In addition, period totals are only provided for dynasties 11 and 12 and for the period covered by the first six dynasties.

In terms of its reliability, there are significant differences between the generally accepted chronology and the Turin Canon. In particular, the Turin Canon assigns 955 years to dynasties 1 to 6, compared with 819 according to current chronologies. Thus, 6 of the 17 dynasties appear to have been overstated by 16.6%.

The reason for these differences is unclear, as the sources on which the Turin Canon is based are unknown. However, on occasions it appears to simply replicate the errors found in the Royal Annals, suggesting that its sources may have been more modern than ancient. For example, the name of Nebka is placed between Khasekhemwy (end of second dynasty) and Netjerikhet, although the archaeological evidence indicates that this would have been impossible[80].

A number of other anomalous differences between the Turin Canon and the archaeological evidence have also been discovered. For example, the Turin Canon allots 24 years to king Sneferu of the fourth dynasty. According to Egyptologists, however, this has been conclusively disproven by archaeological evidence[80]. Wilkinson says that this finding alone 'totally undermines the reliability of the Turin Canon as a source for the Old Kingdom and Early Dynastic period'[80]. The Turin Canon also attributes 19 and 39 years to the reigns of Senusret II and III respectively. However, the highest regnal years for these two kings recorded in contemporaneous documents are 6 and 19 years respectively[81].

As with the Palermo Stone, the Turin Canon also contains accounts that are regarded as obviously mythological in nature. These include the reigns of 6 gods, 9 demi-gods, 70 blessed spirits, 19 powers and 7 'speakers' for the blessed spirits. It is also worth noting that precise reign lengths are given for some of these rulers. For example, the demi-god Djehuti is said to have reigned for 3,126 years, and the 19 powers for 11 years, 4 months, and 22 days[82]. On the face of it, therefore, at least some the 'precise' dates in the Turin Canon are entirely fictional.

The final piece of literary evidence comes from the writings of Manetho. He is believed to have been an Egyptian priest of the 3rd century BC, who wrote a history of ancient Egypt called *Aegyptiaca*. This covers the period from the gods to the last pharaoh, and provides us with the dynastic divisions that are still in use today.

The first difficulty with Manetho is that *Aegyptiaca* only now survives through the works of other writers. These writers include Josephus of the 1st century AD, and Sextus Julius Africanus and Eusebius who wrote in the 3rd and 4th centuries AD respectively. A further issue is the fact that the writings of Africanus are only preserved via a work by an 8th century monk, George Syncellus. Consequently, not only was Manetho writing a long time after the events he describes, but none of *his* work has survived to the present day.

Furthermore, the two main sources of *Aegyptiaca*, Eusebius and Africanus, contain a large number of differences, the most significant of which are listed below[83].

Dynasty	Eusebius		Africanus	
	Kings	Years	Kings	Years
Gods	8	13,900	6	11,985
Demi-gods etc	44	11,025	9	2,646
4	17	448	8	284
5	31	100	9	218
7	5	75	70	0.19
8	5	100	27	146
9	4	100	19	409
14	76	484	76	184
16	5	190	32	518
Totals	195	26,422	256	16,390

Like the Turin Canon, Manetho contains details of rulership by the gods, which historians clearly regard as mythological in nature. Furthermore, the apocryphal material is not confined to the pre-dynastic era. For example, Manetho tells us that the 18th dynasty king Amenophis was believed to have been 'a talking stone'. He later records that a lamb spoke during the reign of the 24th dynasty ruler, Bocchoris. The presence of these elements clearly casts further doubt on the reliability of Manetho generally. It also supports Josephus's claim that Manetho's sources included 'nameless oral traditions' that amounted to no more than 'myths and legends'[84].

However, an even more serious problem exists in relation to the length of time that Manetho attributes to various reigns and dynasties. In fact, historians have found it quite impossible to reconcile many of his dates with other sources. As a result, the modern chronology of ancient Egypt occupies less than half the length of time allocated to it by Manetho, as shown by the following table. (This is based on the version of the *Aegyptiaca* provided by Julius Sextus Africanus, as this is generally considered to be more reliable than that of Eusebius.)

Dynasty	Manetho	Modern
1 to 6	1,478	819
7	0	8
8	146	13
9 & 10	594	135
11	43	40
12	176	212
13 & 14	637	123
15 to 17	953	100
18	262	255
19	204	109
20	135	117
21	114	124
22 to 24	211	230
25	40	59
26	151	131
27	124	121
28	6	5
29	20	19
30	38	37
Totals	5,332	2,657

In some cases these differences are due to Manetho's failure to acknowledge parallel dynasties and periods of co-regency. In many cases, however, they appear to be the result of errors, overestimates and perhaps even deliberate exaggerations.

Similar problems exist in relation to the names of the pharaohs. The *Aegyptiaca* lists 486 kings in the above dynasties, but only 129 (26%) are named, and of these only 84 can be identified from other sources[85]. As a result, 34% of the rulers' names provided by Manetho cannot be verified in any way.

In summary, although Manetho's system of dynasties is referred to quite frequently by modern historians, the names of the pharaohs and their reign lengths have generally been obtained from other sources. In view of this, Manetho cannot be regarded as a reliable source of evidence for the purpose of determining the chronology of ancient Egypt.

(iii) Sothic Dating

In view of the numerous problems that exist with the literary evidence, Egyptologists have tried to verify certain dates independently, in an attempt to establish some firm 'anchors' in Egypt's ancient history. One way in which it was believed this could be achieved was by using astronomical data, in particular, so-called 'Sothic dating'.

This dating method was invented in 1904 by Eduard Meyer, and depends on two key factors:

- the reliability of various documents that refer to the star Sothis (Sirius); and,
- the belief that the ancient Egyptian year always consisted of 365 days.

The documents in question are discussed in detail below. The key point to note at this stage is that these documents are believed to refer to the first day on which Sothis becomes visible just before sunrise, an event known as the 'heliacal rising of Sothis'.

This 'heliacal rising' was associated with the start of the Egyptian year, which began with the flooding of the Nile in July. If the year was exactly 365 days long, however, it would have been about a quarter of a day shorter than the solar year. The Egyptian year would therefore be ahead of the solar year at a rate of one day in every four years. As a result, a heliacal rising would not occur on the same day until 1,461 years later (365.25 x 4) or 1,460 Julian years later (365 x 4). This period is known as a Sothic Cycle, and it allows any heliacal rising to be dated from its position in the cycle. This is simply done by multiplying by four the number of days between two heliacal risings, where the precise date of one of them is known. So if we knew, for example, that the last known heliacal rising took place on 20 July 1,000 B.C, and the next one was observed on 3 October, then we could date the latter to 700 BC, that is, 1,000 less 300 (75 days x 4).

For these calculations to be reliable, however, it is vital that no adjustments were made to the Egyptian calendar at any stage in its ancient history. Some scholars believe this is indeed the case, a belief that is largely based on a document of 239 BC, known as the Decree of Canopus.

This document tells us that in 239 BC Ptolemy III ordered that a leap year should be introduced to align the Egyptian year with the Sothic Cycle. There appears to have been some resistance to this reform, as leap years were not introduced in Egypt until this was decreed by Augustus in 25/26 BC. Even then, the old calendar still appears to have been used in daily life. And the statements of Censorinus and Theon discussed below indicate that the old calendar continued to be used for astronomical purposes as well.

The Decree of Canopus tells us, then, that during the 3rd century BC the Egyptians followed a year of exactly 365 days. It is also tells us that the Egyptians were very much aware of the discrepancy between their calendar and the solar year, but chose not to rectify this. What it does not tell us, however, is that the Egyptians used a 365-day year throughout their history. Nor does it rule out the possibility that *ad hoc* adjustments were made from time to time to bring the calendar back in line with the Sothic Cycle.

The possibility of calendrical adjustments appears to have been particularly likely during and after the Intermediate Periods. These eras were characterised by social unrest and the absence of any kind of central government. As a result, many of the names and dates of the pharaohs for these periods are unclear or are missing altogether. It seems quite possible, therefore, that other recording systems might have become less reliable during these periods as well, perhaps requiring the Egyptians to 'reset the clock' at various intervals.

Although there is evidence that a 365-day year was used as far back as the fifth dynasty[86], Manetho also says that 5 extra days were not officially added to the previous 360-day year until the 17th dynasty[87]. In addition, the Ebers manuscript discussed below is based upon a 360-day year, and this document is generally dated to the 18th dynasty. There is clear evidence, therefore, that a 365-day year was not used throughout Egypt's ancient history, which means that some calendrical adjustments must have been made.

This evidence is not necessarily at variance with the sources that indicate that a 365-day year was used earlier in Egypt's history. The 365-day year might have fallen into disuse during the Intermediate Periods. This seems particularly likely during the Second Intermediate Period, as Egypt was then ruled by foreign invaders known as the 'Hyksos'. Their influence possibly lasted until the end of the 16th dynasty, which would tie in with Manetho's statement that a 365-day year was introduced in the 17th dynasty.

As regards the Decree of Canopus, it is worth remembering that the 360-day year was made up of 12 lunar months of about 30 days, to which five 'epagomenal' days were added to avoid the Egyptian year falling behind the solar year. There was therefore a clear desire to keep the Egyptian year in line with the solar year. In view of this, it is hard to accept that the Egyptians regarded these five added days as sacrosanct, as some appear to suggest. They were, after all, simply calendrical adjustments by any other name.

The second factor to bear in mind is that at the time of the Decree of Canopus, Egypt was an occupied power, under the control of

Greece. The Egyptians' failure to adopt a leap year may therefore have owed more to their dislike of having changes imposed on them by their Greek rulers, than any firm belief in the sacredness of their 365-day year.

Not knowing what calendrical adjustments were made, or even when the 365-day year was introduced in ancient Egypt, presents serious problems for Sothic dating. Without this information, it would be simply impossible to date Sothic risings with any degree of certainty. Furthermore, during any periods of time in which a 360-day year was used, the calendar would have fallen behind the solar year a lot more quickly, making *ad hoc* calendrical adjustments much more likely.

So why did the ancient Egyptians wait until the Decree of Canopus before introducing calendar reforms to align the year with the Sothic Cycle? One possibility is that the Sothic Cycle was not that important to them. There is, after all, no explicit reference to the Sothic Cycle in the Decree of Canopus or in any other literature of ancient Egypt. Moreover, their most celebrated astronomer, Claudius Ptolemy, makes absolutely no mention of the beginning of a Sothic Cycle in AD 139, despite the fact that this is believed to have occurred during his most prolific period of writing. However, it is hard to believe they would not have been aware of the Sothic Cycle, given the importance they attached to Sothis and to astronomy in general. All of this suggests that calendar adjustments may have been made at some stages during Egypt's ancient history. Without precise details of when these took place, though, it is impossible to perform any reliable calculations.

The documents that are thought to refer to Sothic risings are listed in the table below. This also summarises the interpretation issues relating to the documents, each one of which is then discussed in detail below. The table is mainly based on the list provided by Lappin[88], but also includes details regarding the Ivory Tablet of Djer.

Text	Sothic Date	Assessment
Censorinus	139 AD	Written 100 years later; no evidence it is based on observation; contradicted by Theon; no reference to it by Ptolemy; coin evidence inconclusive; but agrees with the Decree of Canopus.
Theon	25/26 BC	Written 300 hundred years later; no evidence it is based on observation; contradicted by Censorinus; identity of 'Menophres' unclear.
Aswan Inscription	221 BC	Meaning obscure; adds little to the date provided by the Decree of Canopus.
Decree of Canopus	239 BC	Ties in with Censorinus, but the day of the quadriennium is unclear.
Medina Habu Inscription	1,279/1,184 BC	Only records the month of the feast day; unclear if this is based on an observed Sothic rising; or, when that took place.
Elephantine Stele	1,479 BC	The name of the pharaoh and their regnal year is missing; appears to contradict the Ramesside Star Clock.
Ebers Papyrus	1,517 BC	Pharaoh's name and year are unclear; the epagomenal days are missing; refers to 'going forth' of Sothis every month; believed by some to contain numerous scribal errors.
Graffiti at Gebel Tjauti	1,598 BC	Pharaoh's name is missing; the translation is unclear and disputed.
Illahun Papyrus	1,871 BC	Pharaoh's name is missing; the handwriting evidence is inconclusive; the meaning is unclear; it is contradicted by lunar dates; and, receives only limited support from the Book of Nut.
Ivory tablet	2,781 BC	Symbols unclear; Sothic date 200 years later than conventional chronology.

According to the third century Roman writer, Censorinus, in 139 AD the start of the Egyptian year coincided with the heliacal rising of Sirius on 19 July. If this is correct, then the previous Sothic Cycle should have begun on the same day about 1,460 years earlier in 1,321 BC and the one before that in 2,781 BC. However, more accurate calculations have shown that these dates should be 1,314 BC and 2,770 BC[88], after taking account of precession and the fact that the sidereal year is marginally longer than the Julian year.

Censorinus's key statements can be found in the following sections from chapters 18 and 21 respectively of '*De Die Natali Liber*'[89]:

> The moon has nothing to do with the Great Year of the Egyptians, which we call in Greek 'kuvikov' and in Latin 'canicularis', because its beginning is taken when on the first day of the month which they call [Egyptian month of Thoth] the Dog Star rises. Their civil year has 365 days only without being intercalated not even by a single day. Hence, with them, the quadriennium [a cycle of 4 civil years] is approximately one day less than the natural quadriennium. So it happens that in the 1,461st it has turned around to the same beginning. This year is called by some 'heliacos' ['related to the sun'] and by others ['the year of God'].

> ...100 years from the present this same day occurred on the 13th day before the calends of August at which time the Dog Star habitually rises in Egypt. Hence we may know that of this Great Year - which, as said above, is named 'year of the Sun' and 'year of the Dog Star' and 'year of God' - the present year is the hundredth.

Although this refers to the Dog Star 'rising', the precise meaning of this is not entirely clear. In addition, the date given by Censorinus appears to be contradicted by Theon, a scholar and mathematician of the 4th century AD who lived in Alexandria. Theon[90] also refers to the Dog Star and says:

> But said period of 1,460 years, begun since some instant, came to an end in the fifth year of the emperor Augustus and, from this last epoch, the Egyptians begin all over again to find themselves every year one quarter of a day in advance.

Despite this, Censorinus's date is generally regarded as the correct one, as Theon's account was written later, is considered to be less reliable, and makes a less explicit link with Sirius. In addition, Theon is said to support Censorinus' date elsewhere, as a Greek manuscript note attributed to Theon says[91] that 'since Menophres and until the end of the era of Augustus, or the beginning of the era of Diocletian, there were 1,605 years.' The end of the era of Augustus fell in 284 AD and by deducting Theon's figure of 1,605 years we arrive at 1,321 BC, exactly the same date calculated by Censorinus using Sothic dating.

This has been seen by many as confirmation of Censorinus's date. It is also generally agreed that 'Menophres' is a reference to Ramesses I, whose throne name was Menpehitre and whose one-year reign is believed to have occurred during c.1321/1320 BC. This agrees with the Sothic Cycle date, and is auspicious as it marks the beginning of the New Kingdom era.

However, no-one has ever proven to whom or to what 'Menophres' actually refers. Some have even questioned whether 'Menophres' was a pharaoh at all, or if this word refers instead to a place or even an era. There is also a fairly significant difference between 'Menophres' and 'Menpehitre'. A much closer fit is provided by 'Merneferre', the throne name of Ay. He has been rejected as a candidate, however, as his reign is dated to about 1,650 BC.

Apart from the lack of any clear agreement between Censorinus and Theon, the main problem with their evidence is that they were writing a hundred years and over three hundred years respectively after the events they were describing. Furthermore, there is no evidence that the dates that they used were based upon actual observations of Sothic risings. Having said this, Censorinus's account does appear to be supported by two further pieces of evidence, namely, a commemorative coin and the Decree of Canopus.

The coin in question is generally believed to mark the beginning of a new Sothic Cycle[92]. We know that it was minted in Alexandria in the second year of Antoninus Pius, and that this year ran from 10 July 139 to 9 July 140 AD. This period ties in with the date provided by Censorinus. And a further link with Sothic dating is provided by the details on the coin, which include a phoenix and the legend 'ΑΙΩΝ', the Greek for 'eternity' or an 'age'. The link between the phoenix and the Sothic Cycle is provided by Tacitus, who refers to the phoenix rising from its ashes every 1,461 years[93]. The legend 'ΑΙΩΝ' is therefore taken to signify the beginning of a new 'age' in the form of a new Sothic Cycle.

However, Tacitus does not explicitly link the phoenix with Sothis, and both he and Herodotus say that the phoenix was generally believed to have a life cycle of 500 years[94]. In addition, the phoenix features on a number of other coins associated with Antoninus that clearly do not have any connection with the Sothic Cycle. These include later coins in the names of his wife and daughter.

The phoenix was also a common symbol for immortality or regeneration in both Roman and Egyptian cultures, and it is found on many coins in the period from Trajan to Gratian, between 120 AD and 385 AD. Furthermore, from the time of Antoninus Pius the phoenix often appears standing on a globe as an attribute of the goddess Aeternitas or as a symbol of the goddess Perpetuitas[95], which would also explain the reference to 'eternity'.

One general problem with the coin evidence is that it is unclear why a Roman Emperor would celebrate an Egyptian date, particularly one that was only a quirk of a calendrical system that Augustus had tried to reform 165 years earlier. It might be argued that this was a conciliatory act by a moderate emperor, who is known to have been interested in other cultures. However, the Egyptians themselves did not appear to attach any significance to this year, as evidenced by the fact that there is not a single reference to it in the works of their foremost astronomer, Ptolemy.

A further issue is that an identical coin was produced in AD 143. Although a Sothic rising would generally have occurred on the same day for four consecutive years, if AD 139 was the first year of that Sothic rising, AD 143 would have been the fifth and not the fourth year.

Borchardt's explanation for this is that the dawn of the new Sothic era continued to be celebrated until the heliacal rising moved on to 2 Thoth on 19 July 143[96]. The question this raises is why the AD 139 coin was minted *after* the Sothic rising had fallen on 1 Thoth, whilst the AD 143 coin was minted *before* the Sothic rising had moved on to 2 Thoth? There is no obvious answer to this, as one would expect the Romans to mint coins at the same time each year.

Whilst some doubt may remain about the interpretation of the coins, a stronger piece of evidence appears to be provided by the Decree of Canopus. This dated to 239 BC, as it was issued in the 9th Year of Ptolemy III. It contains a number of decrees, including the following in relation to Sothis[97]:

Let there also be celebrated a great national feast...[on] the day of the rising of the goddess Sothis...called the Feast of the Opening of the Year...which corresponds in Year 9 to day 1 of the second month of Shemu.

When Sothic dating calculations are applied to this data, the result ties in very closely with Censorinus's date of AD 139. The second month of Shemu was the tenth month of the year and Censorinus says that a Sothic rising occurred on day one of Thoth, the first month of the year, i.e. three months later. Assuming three 30-day months plus 5 epagomenal days, a Sothic rising should have occurred on 1 Thoth in 142 AD ($95 \times 4 = 380 + 1^{*} - 239$).

The small difference between this and the date provided by Censorinus could be due to a number of factors. The Sothic risings might have been observed in different places, and the Decree of Canopus might not refer to the first year of the quadriennium. A variance of only one day in the latter would, of course, produce a difference in the result of four years.

However, although the Decree of Canopus largely agrees with Censorinus, the two do not necessarily support one another. As already mentioned, there is no evidence that Censorinus's date was based upon actual observation. It is entirely possible, therefore, that the agreement with the Decree of Canopus is due to the fact that Censorinus simply used this information to calculate his own date.

---

* As the 95 days takes us into the next year

The next document to be considered is known as the Aswan Inscription. This is a hieroglyphic text, which says[98] –

Hail to you Isis-Sothis...lady of 14 centuries and mistress of 16, who has followed her dwelling place for 730 years, 3 months, 3 days and 3 hours.

Clagett suggests that '14' is a rounding of the 14 centuries of the Sothic Cycle, but acknowledges that he does not understand the reference to '16'[98]. As regards the second part of the statement, Clagett suggests that these are 'mixed measures', comprising 730 years and the time it would take the Sothic Cycle to advance 3 months, 3 days, and 3 hours, i.e. 360 + 12 + ½ years. In all, this would mean that 1,102.5 years had elapsed since the previous Sothic Cycle began in 1,321-1,318 BC, using the dates derived from Censorinus. This means that the date must be between 219-216 BC, which ties in with the reign of Ptolemy IV Philopater, whose cartouches appear on the inscription.

This is an imaginative, but not an entirely convincing explanation. Moreover, it does not take us much further forwards from the Decree of Canopus, which already provides a clear reference to an actual Sothic rising.

We now turn to the Medina Habu inscription. This is a calendar on the southern wall of a temple in western Thebes, which details the ceremonial feasts during the year. There is no real doubt that this temple was built by Ramesses III, whose reign is now dated from 1,184 to 1,153 BC[99]. There are various inscriptions at the site that refer to Ramesses III, and Papyrus Harris I states that he built the temple complex.

However, the calendar only lists the times for celebrating various annual feasts. It does not record any astronomical events. Nor does it provide a specific date for the celebration of the rising of Sothis. The text simply says[100], 'First month of the season Akhet, day of the Feast of the Rising of Sothis'.

Clagett suggests that the reason for this was that the writer knew that the day of the Sothic rising was constantly changing. He argues, however, that this still limits this Sothic rising to a period of 120 years (30 days in the month x 4 days)[101] from 1,321-1,318 BC, the Sothic quadriennium for this month. This date, he contends, fits in with the fact that the chief source for this document appears to have been a similar calendar that is located in the mortuary temple of Ramesses II (1,290-1224 BC)[102].

The first problem with this is that at the time of Ramesses III's death, this part of the calendar would have already been out of date by at least 45 years, i.e. 1,318 less 120 less 1,153. If we assume that the scribe was aware of the fact that the day of the Sothic rising changed every four years, why would he not have at least changed the month of the Sothic rising to bring the calendar more up to date? In addition, although it is similar to the calendar of Ramesses II, they are not identical. If some details were changed, why was the information relating to Sothis not also altered, particularly if the Egyptians attached such importance to it?

A further problem is that, even if the calendar was based upon an actual Sothic rising, we do not know when this took place. If the Medina Habu calendar was copied from an earlier version without the Sothic rising being updated, by the same token the calendar of Ramesses II could also have been based on a yet earlier calendar.

The next document is the Elephantine Stele. This is a hieroglyphic calendar inscribed in stone, which was discovered on the island of Elephantine, near to the first cataract of the Nile. It contains the following statement regarding Sothis[103]:

Month III of the season of Shemu, Day 28, the day of the Feast of the going forth of Sothis.

The name of the pharaoh is not given. However, this is generally believed to be Thutmose III, as his name appears on another fragment, which is assumed to have come from the same inscription. This Sothic rising has then been attributed to his 7th regnal year by applying Sothic dating to the conventional chronology.

According to Courville, however, the evidence linking the document to Thutmose III is very weak, as the other fragment was not connected with the inscription and was found some distance from it[104]. On the other hand, the conventional date of the Elephantine Stele appears to be supported by the Ramesside Star Clock, which refers to the 'culmination' of Sirius at the beginning of the month II, Peret. Clagett argues this fact, combined with the terminology in the Book of Nut, means that there must have been a Sothic rising on III Shemu 26 in 1,472 BC[103], which is very close to the conventional date of the Elephantine Stele.

However, the four texts of the Ramesside Star Clock were found in the tombs of Ramesses VI, VII, and IX of the 20th dynasty[105], whose reigns are dated from 1,143 BC to 1,108 BC[106]. Clagett would therefore have to conclude that these documents are merely copies of a much older text, which he dates to around 1,470 BC based solely on the Sothic data that they contain.

This involves a somewhat circular argument, as it uses Sothic dating to deduce the age of a text, even when this is in conflict with the historical context in which it was found. It also raises the question why a pharaoh would want a star clock in his tomb that was hundreds of years out of date. Clagett also acknowledges that the Ramesside Star Clock documents are incomplete and contain numerous careless errors[105]. If that is the case, however, then it is hard to argue that they can also provide a reliable basis for determining key dates in Egypt's ancient history.

The next document listed above is the Ebers Papyrus. This is a lengthy medical treatise dated to around 1,550 BC, which was discovered in the 1870s by George Ebers. The reverse of the papyrus contains the following table[107]:

1	Year 9 under the person of the Dual King Djeserkare, living forever					
2	New Year's Festival	Month III	of Shemu	day 9	going forth of Sopdet
3	Tekhy	Month IV	.	day 9	.
4	Menkhet	Month I	of Akhet	day 9	.
5	Huther	Month II	.	day 9	.
6	Kuherka	Month III	.	day 9	.
7	Shefbedet	Month IV	.	day 9	.
8	Rekeh (first)	Month I	of Peret	day 9	.
9	Rekeh (second)	Month II	.	day 9	.
10	Renutet	Month III	.	day 9	.
11	Khonsu	Month IV	.	day 9	.
12	Khentykhet	Month I	of Shemu	day 9	.
13	Iptet	Month II	.	day 9	.

The line numbers do not appear in the text, but have been inserted for ease of reference. The columns then provide the names and numbers of the months, followed by the seasons. 'Sopdet' means 'Sothis' and Djeserkare was the throne name of Amenhotep. Assuming line two refers to a heliacal rising, it has been calculated that his 9th year must have fallen in 1,517 BC.

There are, however, several issues with this interpretation[108]. Firstly, there is the pharaoh's name, which some have read as 'Ba-en-ra' and therefore connected with Bicheres of the fourth dynasty. Others have questioned the reading of the regnal year, with alternative translations including the numbers 3, 6 and 30. Borchardt even argued that this is not a '9' at all, but a special term to denote 'day of the new moon'.

Although opinion on these matters is now relatively settled, a number of significant problems remain. To begin with, the yearly cycle to which the Ebers Papyrus refers consists of the twelve lunar months, each of which would presumably have lasted for 30 days. Consequently, the calendar year only contained 360 days (12 x 30). As has already been pointed out, however, Sothic dating rests on the assumption that a year of exactly 365 days was used consistently throughout Egypt's dynastic history.

Meyer argued that the five 'epagomenal days' were not considered to be part of the official year, although they were used in all of the Egyptians' calendrical calculations. In support of this contention, he cited the example of the astronomical ceiling of the Ramesseum[109]. One could equally argue, however, that both this and the Ebers Papyrus are evidence that a 365-year calendar was not always used throughout Egypt's dynastic history. It is clear that at least some scholars, such as Edgerton, were much more uneasy than Meyer about the apparent understatement of the length of the year in the Ebers Papyrus[108].

The second and more serious problem relates to the interpretation of the dots in columns three and five. In the third column these clearly must be read as ditto marks, as they have clearly been inserted to avoid repeating the name of the season in each line. Without some compelling evidence to the contrary, it would be unreasonable to interpret these marks any differently in column five. The problem with this, however, is that it means that there was a Sothic rising on the 9th day of every month, something which is of course an astronomical impossibility.

Meyer's response to this difficulty was to attribute the dots in column five to a scribal error[110]. This is hard to accept, however, particularly as it would mean that one would have to assume that the scribal errors were repeated in eleven successive lines! In view of these difficulties, Clagett concluded that there was no entirely satisfactory explanation for these marks[111].

Rohl argues, however, that the 'going forth' of Sothis does not refer to a heliacal rising at all, but to some form of ceremonial procession. It is not clear why such a ceremony would have been carried out in each month of that year, but this is perhaps not inconceivable if the year was especially noteworthy. And it may have been regarded as particularly auspicious, as it began on the ninth day of the third month of the third season in Amenhotep's 9th regnal year[108].

Whatever the explanation, if one concludes that the Ebers Papyrus contains numerous scribal errors, this alone must cast serious doubt on its reliability. It would seem reasonable in these circumstances to conclude with the Egyptologist Manfred Bietak that the Sothic date derived from the Ebers Papyrus is 'insecure and should not be used any more'[112].

The next document is the small section of graffiti on a rock at Gebel Tjauti, about 250 miles south of Cairo. The graffiti, numbered 'Inscription 11', simply says[113]:

Regnal year 11, second month of the Shemu season, day 20: observing the rising of Sothis

The main problem here is the absence of a pharaoh's name. Based on the style of writing and the character formation, however, Darnell concluded that the inscription was written after the Illahun Papyrus. He then used Sothic dating and Beckerath's reconstruction of this period to calculate that the heliacal rising occurred between 1,593 and 1,590 BC, during the reign of Seweserenre[113].

The first difficulty with this interpretation is that it relies heavily on the analysis of the style of writing. It is clear, however, that the writing has been considerably distorted by the physical problems the author apparently faced when making the inscription. As Darnell himself acknowledges:

A number of awkwardly drawn signs owe their unpleasant appearance to the position of the inscription, high within a sunken window of stone.

Darnell also notes that the inscription mixes full writing with highly abbreviated signs, something he acknowledges 'is the case in the Thirteenth Dynasty' (1,773 and 1,650) If the inscription related to this period, however, it would appear to place the Sothic 'rising' between 60 and 180 years before 1,590 BC.

The other main difficulty relates to the word translated as 'rising'. Darnell assumes that this means 'heliacal rising', but this is far from beyond doubt. To begin with, the concept of the 'heliacal rising' is not discussed in any Egyptian literature. Darnell also acknowledges that there is some doubt about his translation of this word, and other scholars have argued that the translation is at least 'suspect'[114].

A more significant piece of evidence appears to be provided by the el-Lahun or the Illahun Papyrus, also known as Papyrus Berlin 10012. This predicts that in the seventh regnal year '...the going forth of Sopdet (Sothis) will happen in the fourth month of Peret, day 16'[115].

Unfortunately, this does not tell us the name of the pharaoh to whom this relates. However, comparisons with the handwriting of other documents from this town have led most scholars to conclude that this was Senusret III of the 12th dynasty, whose seventh year would have fallen in 1,863 BC[116], or, to be more precise, 1,871 BC after the adjustments mentioned on page 81.

Clagett argues that this date is further supported by the Book of Nut[117], also known as the Cosmology of Seti I and Ramesses IV. This text describes the motion of the sun and stars through the year, and the earliest versions of the text are dated to the reign of Seti I, a reign that is believed to have started between 1,306 and 1,290 BC. The significance of the Book of Nut is that it mentions a rising of Sothis in IV Peret 16, the same date that is given by the Illahun Papyrus.

As with the graffiti at Gebel Tjauti, the interpretation of the Illahun Papyrus relies heavily on the handwriting evidence. It is perfectly possible, therefore, that this papyrus and the other documents found at this location, were not written at the same time at all. They might simply reflect a similar style, which was passed down through generations of scribes. Another possibility is that the documents are roughly contemporaneous, but were written some time after the reign of Senusret III.

A further question relates to the interpretation of the word translated as the 'going forth' of Sothis. This is in fact a ceremonial term, which is usually used to describe the 'procession' of divine statues. By contrast, the Canopus Decree of 239 BC refers to the 'appearance' of Sothis (*kha Sepdet*), a term which is believed to describe an astronomical event. This and the fact that the Illahun Papyrus refers to an event in the future, has led Rohl and others to suggest that the 'going forth' of Sothis in the Illahun Papyrus was in fact an instruction to the priests, rather than an astronomical prediction[118].

A further difficulty concerns the attempts to reconcile the date of 1,871 BC with the lunar records of other Illahun documents relating to this period. Rose calculated that the two sets of data provided a match with an accuracy of not much better than 50%[119]. More recently, Lappin calculated Senusret III's first year to be 1,698 BC on the basis of the lunar data[119], about 180 years later than the date that appears to be provided by Sothic dating.

As regards the Book of Nut, this is represented by nine sources, comprising three monuments and six papyri. The former are the Cenotaph of Seti I (1,294 - 1,279 BC), and the tombs of king Ramses IV (1,153 -1,147 BC) and lady Mutirdis (630 BC). The papyri are dated from the 7th century BC to the 2nd century AD.

Some believe that the astronomical data in the Book of Nut indicates that the original text was written around 1,850 BC, which ties in with the above interpretation of the Illahun Papyrus. However, the texts of the Book of Nut vary considerably, and this includes two sets of astronomical data which cannot be reconciled with one another[120]. Consequently, the Book of Nut provides limited support for the above interpretation of the Illahun Papyrus.

This brings us to the Ivory Tablet, which is usually attributed to the pharaoh Djer, in whose tomb it was found. On the tablet there is believed to be a representation of the goddess Sothis, who is depicted as a seated cow. Between the cow's horns is a young plant, which is believed to symbolise the year. Based on this evidence, it was thought that by the beginning of Djer's reign the Egyptians had established a firm link between the heliacal rising of Sothis and the start of the calendar year[121].

As a result, it was originally thought that this first Sothic rising must have occurred in 4,241 BC, i.e. 1,460 years before the 2,781 BC date given above. However, it is now widely accepted that the first dynasty of Egypt could not have begun before 3,100 BC. If the ivory tablet refers to a Sothic rising, therefore, this event would presumably have taken place in 2,781 BC. However, this would put Djer's reign 200 years later than its conventional date. As a result, it is now generally accepted that the ivory tablet does not provide any reliable evidence regarding Sothic dating.

Sothic dating does not, therefore, provide any firm anchors for the history of ancient Egypt. Furthermore, even if it did, the history before and after those dates could still not be calculated with certainty, as the possibilities of calendar variations and adjustments, co-regencies and parallel dynasties would still remain.

(iv) Archaeology

There is a wealth of archaeological evidence about Egypt's ancient history. As a result, there are very few rulers in the conventional chronology for whom no archaeological evidence is held. Having said this, the nature and quantity of that evidence varies considerably. In some cases, it is limited to one or two artefacts; in others, it comprises a long list of statues and buildings.

In terms of reconstructing the chronology of Egypt's ancient history, however, the archaeological evidence is of very limited value. In the vast majority of cases, the items in question simply indicate that a ruler existed; there is little or no detail about the length of a particular pharaoh's reign. Nor is there much, if any, information about which kings or dynasties might have ruled at the same time as one another.

In addition, the further one goes back in time, the scarcer the archaeological evidence generally becomes. Rohl points out, for example, that very few inscriptions are held to verify any of the Old Kingdom data[122]. Allied to this are the difficulties in dating any of the artefacts. In the vast majority of cases, carbon dating is not possible or is problematic. As a result, artefacts and monuments have usually been dated on the basis of the writing style, the design or the location at which the item was found. As we have seen, however, none of these methods is without its difficulties, and each relies upon other dated items, the assumptions about which may also be incorrect.

It is also worth sounding a cautionary note about the nature of archaeological evidence generally. The fact that a pharaoh's name appears on a stone inscription as opposed to a manuscript does not make it any more reliable. Just like handwritten material, the inscription could simply be following an erroneous literary tradition. It might also refer to someone who was legendary rather than historical, as with the bust of Odysseus on the Island of Ithaca.

Closer consideration of archaeological sites has also produced some unexpected findings. For example, David Rohl's examination of various tombs and monuments of the Third Intermediate Period led him to believe that there were significant errors in the conventional chronology of this period. He went on to conclude that the start of the 18th dynasty had been overstated by 377 years, and that there were no safe fixed points in the history of ancient Egypt before 664 BC[123].

According to Rohl, these miscalculations arose as a result of overestimates and the repeated failure to take account of parallel dynasties and periods of co-regency. And his views have been supported by a number of other scholars. Lappin, for example, agrees that Rohl's 'New Chronology' ties in very closely with a whole range of astronomical data from 900 BC to 1,700 BC[124], which are at variance with the conventional chronology.

It is fair to point out that Rohl's theories are rejected by the majority of Egyptologists. However, the very fact that a serious scholar could propose a tenable theory that reduces Egypt's history by several hundred years, clearly indicates that the conventional chronology is far less certain than many might believe. Furthermore, if significant errors have occurred in the calculation of later dynasties where we hold a relatively large amount of data, then it is hard to rule out the possibility that significant adjustments might also be required to earlier periods for which far less evidence is held.

These considerations are also very significant in the context of the present discussion. After all, if there were overstatements totalling 800 years, then the first king of Egypt would not have ruled until 2,200 BC and the pyramids of Giza would presumably have not been completed until 1,700 BC, 150 years and 650 years respectively after Noah's Flood. Another possibility is that these adjustments might mainly bring forward the more recent dynasties, leaving the dates of older dynasties largely intact. This would leave a large and unexplained gap in the chronology of ancient Egypt, during which the Flood could in theory have taken place.

(v) Carbon Dating

The shortage of reliable literary and astronomical evidence has made it very hard to disprove radical theories such as those put forward by Rohl. However, some believe that an answer to these challenges might be provided by carbon dating. Shaw, for instance, after referring to other sources of evidence, says that major adjustments to the Third Intermediate Period can be ruled out –

because the scientific dating systems (that is radiocarbon and dendrochronology) almost always provide solid independent support for the conventional chronology[125].

As we will see, however, the carbon dating evidence appears to fall some way short of providing 'solid support' for *any* chronology. Before considering the evidence in detail, however, it is worth going over the basic principles of carbon dating. A more detailed critique can also be found on page 167 *et seq*.

Carbon-14 or radiocarbon is formed when neutrons in the upper atmosphere collide with nitrogen. This carbon-14 then has a half-life of about 5,730 years, which means that in 5,730 years 50% of the carbon-14 will, in all probability, have changed back into 'ordinary' carbon-12. After another 5,730 years, 50% of the remaining carbon-14 should have decayed back to carbon, and so on.

As carbon-14 is formed in the atmosphere, it is readily incorporated into carbon dioxide. From there, it is absorbed into the tissues of plants and animals, whose bodies are believed to maintain a fairly constant level of carbon-14 until they die, when they stop absorbing carbon dioxide. If the level of carbon-14 at the time of a plant or animal's death is known, it should be possible to determine how long has elapsed since that plant or animal died.

One immediate problem, however, is that the amount of carbon-14 in the atmosphere is known to have varied quite significantly in the past. As a result, another method is used to try to correct for these variations. This method is known as dendrochronology, which involves checking the ages of trees from their growth rings and then comparing these dates with the radiocarbon 'age'. Although the oldest living tree is only about 5,000 years old, by matching growth rings with samples from dead trees, scientists believe that they can now extend the carbon-14 record back much further than this.

However, there are a number of problems with dendrochronology. The most serious of these is the fact that comparisons between dendrochronology and radiocarbon data produce a very convoluted curve with many 'wiggles' in it. This means that a single radiocarbon reading often corresponds to more than one place on the curve, with the result that dating is frequently ambiguous. Dates therefore have to be determined by finding the best 'wiggle match', a calculation so difficult that it often has to be carried out by computer analysis.

In addition, it has been suggested that major climate changes may have had a significant effect on radiocarbon dates, by releasing non-radiogenic carbon into the atmosphere. This would increase the ratio of ordinary carbon to radio-carbon (carbon-14), thereby making the sample appear much older than it is. There is also evidence that this could have occurred during major climatic events, such as the end of an ice age or perhaps a major flood, such as the one described in Genesis.

As regards carbon-14 dating, when Libby first invented the method in 1949, he tried to validate his results by showing that they closely correlated with the dates of various artefacts of a known age. Importantly, his first report included the following Egyptian objects[126]:

Dynasty	Item	Conventional	C14	Difference
3	Wood, tomb of Djoser	2,648	2,625	23
4	Wood, tomb of Sneferu	2,589	2,650	-61
12	Wood, funeral boat of Senusret III	1,831	1,843	-12

Despite this promising start, more extensive carbon dating results did not provide anything near to such a close agreement with the conventional chronology. In fact, the differences were so significant that more than two decades later Edwards reported[127]:

I cannot pretend that ^{14}C has yet made any actual impact on our reconstruction of Egyptian chronology.

In his article, Edwards also reported a large number of carbon-14 dates, and these, together with the details relating to the pharaohs of the first 26 dynasties are summarised in Appendix 3. This Appendix compares the carbon-14 dates with the last year of each pharaoh's reign, based on the dates provided by *The Oxford History of Ancient Egypt*. As the latter does not provide regnal years for Dynasty 1, however, these have been estimated in this and the other carbon-14 appendices by simply dividing the dynasty length by the number of pharaohs.

As will be seen, Edwards' results comprise two sets of carbon-14 dates. The first are the unadjusted results, which yield dates between 130 and 569 years younger than those assigned by the conventional chronology. The second set of results has therefore been adjusted to take account of the fluctuating levels of carbon-14 in the atmosphere.

However, the authors of the adjustment factors, Stuiver and Suess, acknowledged that this was little more than 'a crude approximation'. Furthermore, although it produces average carbon-14 dates that are nearer to the conventional chronology, it also increases the span of dates, which range from 347 years older to 225 years younger than the conventional chronology.

The carbon-14 technology used up to this point involved counting the carbon molecules at the beginning and end of the process. In the early 1980s, however, another method emerged called Accelerator Mass Spectroscopy or AMS for short. With this technique, carbon-14 atoms were detected and counted directly. This improved the accuracy of the results and also allowed very small items to be dated for the very first time. AMS is particularly useful, therefore, when dealing with valuable artefacts from which only very small samples can be taken.

Both traditional and AMS methods were therefore used in a further study of the carbon-14 dates of ancient Egyptian materials, which was carried out between 1984 and 1987[128]. The report begins by acknowledging that[129] –

Soon after initial applications of the radiocarbon method to Egyptian materials, significant disparities between the radiocarbon dates and well-established historical dates became apparent.

It also refers to the 'very wide error ranges' of previous 'calibration curves', which were designed to correct the carbon-14 data[130].

These 'new' test results, which are summarised in Appendix 4, also produced a very wide range of carbon-14 ages. In fact, these dates covered an even wider period than the previous ones, extending from 1,333 years younger to 1,243 years older than the conventional chronology. In addition, even after excluding what were considered to be spurious dates, the average carbon-14 results were still 374 years older than those provided by the conventional chronology.

The authors of the report attributed some of these variances to factors such as measurement errors, charcoal made from old wood and the existence of repair work that took place a long time after a building's original construction. They also pointed out that the length of time it took to build some of the larger monuments could have produced differences of several decades.

It is clear, however, that these factors alone could not explain the 374 year age difference. For example, if the burning of old wood was a significant factor, then there should have been a marked difference between results based on charcoal compared with those involving other materials. However, although the charcoal results showed average age differences of 414 years, those for straw/grass and wood still yielded averages of 325 years and 294 years respectively[131].

In addition, although some apparently spurious dates could be removed, such as those that appeared to relate to later repairs, other differences could not be so easily eradicated. For example, the report mentions that[132] -

One of these samples (ARCE 54C), however, was scraped out of the mortar *in situ* in the monument and submitted to the lab as an assortment of small pieces. Both laboratories dated this sample and obtained quite different results (Table 2).

The dates in Table 2 in fact differed by 770 years, and a 600-year discrepancy was also found in another sample that was obtained in similar circumstances[133].

As a result of these findings, even after all of the spurious dates were removed, the report was forced to conclude that the first six dynasties appeared to have occurred at least three hundred years earlier than was suggested by the conventional chronology[134]. The report was also left with very wide age differences overall. This perhaps casts doubt not only on the validity of the conclusions, but also on the reliability of the carbon-14 method itself.

In view of the significant differences between carbon-14 dates and the conventional chronology, a further project was begun in 1995[135]. This involved members of the 1984 team, who examined similar materials, again using a mixture of traditional carbon-14 and AMS dating techniques.

The results of this exercise are summarised in Appendix 5. Here, the conventional date is the death of the pharaoh to which the monuments relate, and the carbon-14 date is the mean of the range with the highest probability percentage. The data reveals a much closer fit with the conventional chronology, as the carbon-14 results are only 86 years older on average than the conventional dates. However, the range of differences is still very wide at 740 years (524 years older to 216 years younger).

In addition, the published results only represent a minor part of the 353 samples that were taken. To begin with, 183 samples were not used at all, but were simply held in a 'reserve pool'. Of the other 170, any results that deviated from the average by a certain amount were screened out, on the assumption that they must have come 'from another context'.

Despite this, on a number of occasions several samples showed distinctly different ages from the main body of results. In these circumstances, the data was reported, but a separate average date was calculated for this sub-group[136]. Given all of these adjustments, it is perhaps not that surprising that the results produced a much closer data set than those in previous exercises.

None of the carbon-14 projects, therefore, takes us much further forward. Many of the dates in the projects differed significantly from the conventional chronology. Moreover, each dataset produced a wide range of dates, raising doubts about the reliability of the carbon-14 method itself, at least in relation to the dating of ancient Egyptian materials.

It is of course possible that some of the anomalies were due to later repairs or the re-use of old materials. The former may have been indistinguishable from the original building. And it is even harder to rule out anachronisms of this kind with moveable artefacts. These can easily be introduced into much older or younger contexts, just as one might place antique furniture in a modern house or furnish a period property with modern artefacts. In ancient Egypt, this phenomenon has even been found to occur with objects as personal as coffins and mummy wrappings.

One way of eliminating these difficulties might be to directly date the body tissues of the pharaohs' mummies. Providing the carbon-14 dating method is sound and we can be sure of the identity of the pharaoh, we should be able to secure a reliable carbon-14 date for each of the pharaohs tested.

A list of pharaohs' mummies is given in the appendices of *The Mummy in Ancient Egypt*[137]. This, together with the discovery of Queen Hatshepsut's remains in 2007, provides us with mummies for 38 of the 173 pharaohs of the first 31 dynasties[138]. There is also at least one mummy for most of the first 22 dynasties, so it should in theory be possible to accurately carbon-date large parts of Egypt's ancient history.

However, several of these 'mummies' amount to little more than a few bones, as many were seriously damaged by tomb raiders. Consequently, four of the mummies cannot be identified with any certainty. Furthermore, the list only provides details of two carbon-14 results, and both of these diverged significantly from the conventional dates.

The carbon-14 date for Menkaure, for example, was only 1,650 years BP, although he died 4,500 years ago according to the conventional chronology. And as regards Djoser, an article at www.ancient-egypt.org states that the carbon-14 date for what was assumed to be his mummy was 'several centuries younger'* than it should have been. The article explains that -

> ...some mummy parts, among which was a foot, were found in the burial vault. The mummification technique used on these remains are characteristic of the oldest mummies of the Old Kingdom, so it was long assumed that these were the remains of Netjerikhet (Djoser) himself.

This last point highlights some of the difficulties with trying to identify pharaonic mummies. However, these are not the only reasons for the discrepancies in the carbon-14 dates. According to the following extract of an E-mail from Jenefer Cockill, a researcher into carbon dating[139], there are several problems with the carbon dating of Egyptian mummies. She reported that:

> Bone samples have been submitted, but the results are often poor. Collagen is frequently poorly preserved and contamination is often present from resins applied to the body. We submitted tissue samples for AMS dating from several mummies. Some of these were successful, but many were not.

*2,000 years per *The Encyclopedia of the Egyptian Pharaohs (2008)*, D.D. Baker, page 99

The tissue is fragile and cannot withstand a rigorous pre-treatment process. The same issues with resin contamination were also found. It appears to be a bit 'hit and miss', making this sort of dating less likely to become universally applied to mummified tissue.

As a result, her 2006 article on carbon dating only gives one set of carbon-14 dates that can be directly linked to a pharaoh. This relates to the mummy of Wah[140], who is known to have been a dignitary in the house of Mentuhotep III. His well-preserved body was found wrapped in linen sheets bearing the marks for years 1 to 5 of Mentuhotep III. Parts of the brain and skin tissue were dated using AMS, and these yielded carbon-14 results ranging from 1,960 to 2,150 BC, in close agreement with the conventional dates for Mentuhotep III, who reigned from 2,004 to 1,992 BC.

(vi) Summary

There are only two literary sources that provide any dates for the chronology of ancient Egypt, namely Manetho and the Turin Canon. There are, however, many disagreements between these two texts, and between them and the archaeological evidence. The sources of Manetho and the Turin Canon are not known, but both were written hundreds, and for some periods, thousands of years after the Egyptian rulers to whom they refer.

Attempts to fix the chronology of ancient Egypt using astronomical data, in particular Sothic dating, are fraught with difficulties. There are serious problems in interpreting astronomical texts, and it is difficult to justify the assumption that calendrical adjustments were never made throughout the whole of Egypt's ancient history.

The final attempts to provide independent support for the conventional chronology have come from carbon dating. However, dating mummies and moveable artefacts is beset with difficulties, and the carbon-14 results for ancient monuments produce such a wide span of dates that they fail to provide any meaningful support for the conventional chronology.

As a result, the current chronology of ancient Egypt is a patchwork constructed from various sources, none of which has been shown to be particularly reliable. During the process of its construction, therefore, the ancient Egyptian history has already been reduced by over 2,500 years[141], and more recent discoveries threaten to reduce the chronology by further significant amounts. In particular, some scholars believe that the Third Intermediate Period may have been overstated by as much as 500 years.

We do not know if this radical reappraisal is correct, and many do reject it. However, the very fact that such a theory can be put forward by serious scholars shows that the conventional chronology is far less solid than it might at first appear. If changes of this order were required, however, it would raise the possibility that further significant reductions might be needed to other parts of chronology, particularly around the other Intermediate Periods.

(vii) Possible Solutions

There are only two ways in which the chronology of ancient Egypt can be reconciled with a worldwide biblical flood: either the Deluge preceded the first dynasty, or it must have taken place at some stage during Egypt's dynastic history, following which the area was repopulated.

If the first dynasty began after the Deluge, it presumably began quite some time after 2,350 BC, as the evidence suggests that there was a sizeable population at the start of the first dynasty. The very existence of a pharaoh, of course, implies that a well-developed society already existed at that stage. In addition, two statue inscriptions record a battle about 300 years later, in which Khasekhemwy's forces killed 47,209 men from the northern territory[142]. Furthermore, only 100 to 200 years after this, work on the Great Pyramids had apparently started, something which would clearly have required a very large workforce.

Despite this evidence, it is worth pointing out that we do not have any concrete information about population levels during any part of the Old Kingdom period. The inscription referred to above is not universally accepted, and there is no consensus about how the Great Pyramids were built exactly, with estimates of the workforce ranging from 30,000 to 200,000 men.

Furthermore, if the population doubled every 25 years, the survivors of the Flood would have increased to 131,072 after only 350 years and to over 2 million within 450 years. Whilst this might appear surprising, in 2005 many developing countries had growth rates of 2% to 3% per annum, which is equivalent to the population doubling every 24 to 35 years[143]. Even in Africa, with its many diseases, wars and famines, the growth rate has still been as high as 2.2% per annum.

If there was quite a large pre-dynastic population, however, it might be necessary to assume that the first dynasty began between say 2,100 and 2,000 BC. This would no doubt be rejected by most Egyptologists. However, it is worth remembering that the original chronology has already been reduced by over 2,500 years. In addition, a number of scholars now argue that the Third Intermediate Period alone needs to be reduced by 400 to 500 years. As this era is much nearer to us in time, it seems hard to rule out the possibility that reductions may also be required to other parts of the chronology, particularly earlier periods where far less information is held.

As regards the second possibility, a large gap in Egypt's history would of course arise if (a) various dynasties were brought forward by 450 years to accommodate a reduction in the Third Intermediate Period, and (b) earlier dynasties were pushed back by 300 years, as required by carbon dating results. A gap of several hundreds of years would clearly be long enough for Egypt to have been flooded and then repopulated.

In theory, such a gap could have occurred at any time between the end of the Old Kingdom and the start of the Third Intermediate Period. If the gap was earlier rather than later, however, there would be fewer ancient monuments to explain. For example, if the first 10 dynasties moved backwards by 300 years and the following dynasties were moved forwards by 450 years, then the Flood would have occurred during the First Intermediate Period. It would only then be necessary to explain how the monuments of the Old Kingdom had survived a worldwide flood in their present condition.

It is possible, of course, that many monuments could have been repaired or largely re-built by post-Flood generations. This possibility is supported by various references to Old Kingdom monuments being repaired, and by the carbon dating results discussed above. No matter how unreliable the latter might be, they do nevertheless clearly indicate that the older monuments contain much younger material, and researchers have attributed this to later repairs and reconstructions.

One question arising from this 'gap theory' relates to the extinction of the dinosaurs, which are generally assumed by believers to have perished with the Flood. If dinosaurs existed during some of the earlier Egyptian dynasties, why are they not depicted in artwork, literature or monuments? After all, numerous fossils have been found in Egypt, including the bones of a sauropod estimated to have been up to 100 feet in length.

The first point to make here is that we do not know what dinosaurs were living in the areas that might have been occupied by pre-diluvian Egyptians. In addition, if animals died in a worldwide Deluge, where some of their bones came to rest may have been different from where they originally lived. Consequently, the sauropod found in 2000 might have been washed into the area by the Flood, and may have never set foot in Egypt during its lifetime.

The next point is that only a handful of larger dinosaur remains have been found in Egypt[144], and most of the fossils are similar to modern hippopotamuses, rhinoceroses, primates and elephants. Given this, it is perhaps not surprising if the ancient Egyptians did not consider these kinds of animals to be deserving of any special mention in their art and literature.

Furthermore, even if a large dinosaur were mentioned in ancient Egyptian art or literature, that reference would probably not have survived the Flood, unless it was preserved in some durable form, such as metal or stone. It is also perfectly possible that such an artefact could have been buried by the Flood, either inland or at sea, and therefore still remains undiscovered, just as the sauropod bones remained undiscovered until very recently.

If the Flood did interrupt Egyptian history, one would expect Egyptian monuments to reveal at least some evidence of this. And a number of writers claim that this evidence does indeed exist. They draw attention, in particular, to various clues provided by the site of the Great Pyramids in Giza.

One of the first points that is often made is that none of the later pyramids come anywhere near to the Great Pyramids in terms of their size or the accuracy of their construction[145]. The site at Giza appears to mark the end of a golden age of pyramid building, the expertise of which was perhaps lost to later generations by some kind of sudden change or event.

Evidence that this sudden event might have taken the form of the biblical Flood was suggested in the writings of Albiruni (973 -1048 AD). He referred to watermarks on two of the pyramids and reported that[146] –

People are of the opinion that the traces of the water of the Deluge and the effects of the waves are still visible on these two pyramids half-way up, above which the water did not rise.

A number of later writers also linked these marks with the large areas of salt incrustation on the interior walls of the Great Pyramid, which was up to half an inch-thick in places[147]. Others, such as Strabo in the first century BC, referred to a substantial layer of silt that lay around the base of the Great Pyramid, which contained a large number of seashells[148]. Many have also commented on what appears to be a significant level of water weathering to the Sphinx, something which might also be explained by a flood.

If the water only rose halfway up the Pyramids, though, this would not provide evidence of a flood that covered the highest mountains, unless the world was much flatter then. Most therefore believe that the only geological upheavals that have affected the Great Pyramids were earthquakes, in particular one of 1301, which is believed to have dislodged many of the outer casing stones.

As regards the watermarks, some deny that these ever existed. One geologist, for example, said that he could find absolutely no evidence of watermarks[149]. This is perhaps not surprising after around 1000 years, particularly as the above passage from Albiruni suggests the marks were already very faint by the 11th century.

The existence of seashells may be explained by research in 2008, which indicated that the Great Pyramids were made from limestone that was formed in the sea. This limestone contains a huge number of seashells, which would presumably have been found in the silt around the Pyramids, particularly if that silt came from the original casing stones that were crushed during various earthquakes.

The salt encrustations inside parts of the Great Pyramid are perhaps less easy to explain. Most researchers attribute this phenomenon to the natural exudations of salt from the limestone. However, others such as Dunn, still describe this as 'one of the great mysteries' of the Queen's chamber[150]. It is not clear why the salt would have been limited to certain areas if it were the result of a worldwide flood. However, this is also a problem for the salt-exudation theory.

Opinion regarding the Sphinx is also divided. Although some have argued that the weathering of the Sphinx is consistent with long-term rain damage[151], the majority appear to believe that it is the result of other factors, such as sand erosion or perhaps even acid rain. The problem is that none of these theories on their own appears to explain why the Sphinx has aged so much when compared with the Great Pyramids.

Some have argued that the level of erosion indicates that the Sphinx must be thousands of years older than the Great Pyramids. This theory is, of course, firmly rejected by the vast majority of Egyptologists. If they are correct, however, it would give rise to another interesting possibility, namely that the Sphinx was built before the Flood, but that it only predates the Pyramids by hundreds of years. This would explain the substantial rain damage, the effects of which might have been magnified by the powerful floodwaters that followed.

One thing that is clear, however, is that the Egyptians, like the Sumerians, believed that in the distant past there was a major flood on the earth. And in their version of the flood story, the god Ra threatened to destroy mankind with the following words[152]:

For lo! I wish in my heart to destroy utterly that which I did create. All the world will become a waste of water through a great flood, as it was in the beginning...

As in the biblical account, though, the creator decides not to destroy literally all life on the earth. Instead, he resolves to preserve a remnant, and the floodwaters are eventually abated.

Manetho also refers to the flood of Deucalion[153], Noah's counterpart in the Greek version of the Flood. Manetho places this flood in the 18th dynasty, something he may have done to emphasise the antiquity of Egyptian history. Alternatively, he may have done this to play down the significance of the *Greek* deluge.

(viii) Conclusions

The conventional chronology of ancient Egypt is far more uncertain than is often suggested by the literature on this subject. Furthermore, that uncertainty increases quite significantly during the three intermediate periods, which currently account for almost a quarter of the entire dynastic history.

Apart from exaggerations in reign lengths, one of the major areas of uncertainty relates to the incidence of co-regency and parallel dynasties. As a result, several scholars have suggested that the Third Intermediate Period has been overstated by between 400 and 500 years.

The resulting view of Egyptian chronology is summarised by Jenefer Anne Cockltt and Ann Rosalie David, two scientists who specialise in radiocarbon dating[154]:

> Although the reconstructed chronology of ancient Egypt is an exceptional achievement, the calendar dates assigned to some periods are not as absolute as frequently implied. A large number of epigraphic, literary and archaeological sources have been used to produce a list of pharaohs who ruled over Egypt, their reign lengths and the dynastic 'family' to which they belonged. The two main textual sources are the surviving copies of the history of Manetho (Waddell 1940) and the Turin Canon (Gardiner 1949; Malek 1982). There are many contradictions between the two, both in terms of the identification of some pharaohs' throne names and the length of reign each one served. This is further compounded by problems such as suspected co-regencies, not documented in primary sources, and the three Intermediate Periods or 'Dark Ages' of Egypt. During these periods the political scene in Egypt was characterised by fragmentation of centralised authority, and increased evidence of regionalisation. As such, much of the chronological information sought by Egyptologists is missing, patchy or contradictory.

Given all of these doubts, it is clearly impossible to conclude with any certainty that the Flood could not have occurred at any stage before or during Egypt's dynastic history.

(d) China

The history of ancient China does not pose a serious challenge to the biblical Flood account. To begin with, the first dynastic period, the Xia dynasty, is not believed to have begun until about 2,000 BC[155]. This does not contradict the idea of a worldwide flood in 2,350 BC, however, as there are no records of the population at the start of the Xia dynasty. Furthermore, the date of 2,000 BC is not at all certain, being largely based on archaeological remains dated to between 1,900 and 1,350 BC[156].

Much more is known about the second period, the Shang dynasty (1,570 to 1,045 BC), as this saw the appearance of the first written records[157]. Despite this, the earliest undisputed date in China's history is no later than 842 BC. Scholars have used this date to reconstruct the chronology back to the 12th century BC, but this has only been achieved by using an uncertain mixture of literary and astronomical evidence[158].

The date of 842 BC is based on the writings of Sima Qian, whose work, *Records of the Grand Historian of China,* was written between the 2nd and 1st centuries BC. Despite the sources of information he presumably had at his disposal, Sima Qian was unable to provide any fixed dates before 842 BC. In fact, he wrote that 'the Shang dynasty and the ages before it are too far away to say much about…'[159]

It is also interesting to note that a little later in his work Sima Qian also says that –

The nobles who were descendants of Emperors Yao and Shun mentioned in The Book of Documents held their positions throughout the three dynasties of Xia, Shang, and Zhou, a period of over a thousand years.

As the Zhou dynasty ended in 256 BC, this implies that the Xia dynasty began not much earlier than the 13th century BC, instead of 2,000 BC as is often believed.

One possible explanation for this might be the existence of significant overlaps in the first three dynasties, a possibility that is now increasingly accepted by scholars, according to *The Cambridge History of Ancient China*[156]:

> The sequential view of the interrelationship among the Three Dynasties – Xia, Shang, and Zhou – is increasingly viewed by contemporary historians as inappropriate. Instead, a horizontal view has taken its place.

Before the Xia dynasty, folklore tells us that China was ruled by legendary heroes. These heroes were systematized during the Han period (206 BC to 220 AD) into the period of the three 'august ones', who were then followed by the 'five emperors'. The 'august ones' were Fu Xi, Sui Ren and Shen Nong, who invented hunting, fire, and agriculture/medicine respectively. These heroes are described as having the attributes of demigods and are therefore believed to be entirely mythical[161].

The five emperors that followed were, in order, Huang Di, Zhuan Xu, Yao, Sun and Yu. The first four rulers are believed to be entirely legendary, because of the various stories that are attributed to them. For example, one account tells of how, during the reign of Zhuan Xu, the gods Chong and Li prevented people from ascending and descending to and from heaven[161].

By contrast, some believe that the last of these 'emperors' was an historical figure, because of the way in which he is treated in traditional historiography. For example, Sima Qian places Yu at the start of the 'basic annals' of the Xia dynasty, thereby apparently affording him the same status as later historical rulers[161].

Although the accounts relating to rulers before the Xia dynasty are believed to be mythical in nature, one of these is of particular interest in this context. This account concerns a villain called Gong Gong, who, we are told, competed with Zhuan Xu and knocked his head against the Buzhou Mountain, one of the pillars supporting the heavens. As a result, the mountain fell, causing a hole to appear in the heavens and the waters from the heavens to then flood the earth. Fortunately, disaster was averted by a hero called Nü Wa, who melted the rocks of five colours to mend the break in the heavens. As a result, Nü Wa was able to stop the flood and restore the dome of the heavens to its previous condition[162].

It is interesting to note that Chinese literature not only contains an account of a devastating flood: it also links this with a character whose name sounds very similar to 'Noah'. The restoration of order following the flood is also associated with the rocks of 'five colours', a reference which appears to echo the seven colours of the first rainbow in Genesis chapter 9.

(e) Conclusions

For a literary source to disprove the biblical account of the Flood, it would have to (a) be completely reliable; and, (b) describe a sequence of events during the time of the Deluge that could not conceivably have been interrupted by a worldwide flood.

The Sumerian King List does not meet either of these criteria. It not only contains inconsistencies and mythological elements, it also contains an unexplained gap of 400 years around the time that the Bible says the Flood took place.

The chronology of Egypt is generally considered to be far more reliable. However, the literary records that contain actual chronological information are very limited and those that do exist contain inaccuracies and overestimates, and take no account of periods of co-regency and parallel dynasties. As a result, the original chronology of ancient Egypt has been virtually cut in half, reducing its length by about 2,600 years.

Although this still leaves an Egyptian chronology that goes back to 3,000 BC, serious doubts remain, and more recent evidence indicates that the orthodox chronology may have been overstated by a further 400 to 500 years at the very least. This and the scope for further periods of co-regency means that one cannot discount the possibility that the Flood occurred either before or during Egypt's dynastic history.

As regards the history of ancient China, this presents no real challenges to the biblical account, as the whole of it postdates the Deluge. It therefore provides no evidence to show that a worldwide flood could not have occurred in 2,350 BC.

Even if these chronologies did contradict the biblical account, however, it is not tenable to simply reject or give less weight to the Bible, simply because it was written by people who believed in God. All of the histories of the ancient world were written by people who believed in gods. To be consistent, therefore, we would have to either consider the biblical account on the same footing as these histories or reject all of them as being unreliable. The second approach would, of course, leave us with precious little history before the 19th century AD! It is entirely untenable, however, to believe that only atheists and agnostics are capable of writing trustworthy historical accounts.

It might be argued that, unlike the Bible, the history of Egypt is supported by a large amount of archaeological and monumental evidence. However, this is only partly true, as very little of this evidence actually provides any chronological data. Furthermore, statements inscribed on stone are no less prone to error, myth or exaggeration than those that are written on papyrus.

9. Amount of Water

This final contention is that, because there is insufficient water in the oceans and polar ice caps to flood the entire planet, a worldwide flood could never have taken place. In fact, if all of the ice in the world melted, sea levels would only rise by 200 to 250 feet. The resulting flood waters would not therefore come anywhere near to covering all of the mountains, as Mount Everest is over 29,000 feet above sea level.

The first weakness with this argument is that it ignores the providential nature of the Flood and the removal of the floodwaters from the earth. Both were clearly miraculous in nature, as both are described as being acts of God. It is not valid to assume, therefore, that every aspect of the account must be explainable in terms of the laws of nature.

As regards the removal of the floodwaters, Genesis 8:1 says that 'God made a wind to pass over the earth, and the waters subsided'. It is clear that this was no ordinary 'wind'. No natural wind would have caused the Flood to subside; it would simply have speeded up the currents and perhaps caused some of the water to evaporate, temporarily. This must therefore have been a supernatural wind, one that affected the whole 'earth', permanently removing substantial amounts of water from the planet for ever.

The fact that God used a natural phenomenon like the wind to achieve this, does not mean that it was an entirely natural phenomenon. Just like the great shout that brought down the walls of Jericho (Joshua 6:20) or the paste Jesus used to heal the man born blind (John 9:6), God used something natural to achieve something supernatural, thereby demonstrating His complete power over the whole of nature.

We also cannot assume that the planet's current topography was basically the same as it was at the time of the Flood. As already noted, the Flood could have been accompanied by a huge amount of geological disturbance, caused in part by the 'bursting forth' of 'all the fountains of the great deep'. This could have led to accelerated mountain building and plate tectonic activity. Consequently, the mountains at the time of Noah may have been significantly lower than they are at present.

2.2.3.3. Conclusions

The Bible describes the Flood as a real and worldwide event. Various logistical arguments have been advanced against this belief, but none has been proven that a single aspect of the account could not have taken place. And if we doubt that men could have built something like the ark 4,350 years ago, we only need to consider the baffling ingenuity that was involved in the construction of the great pyramids.

In addition, scientists' assumptions about what are and what are not 'species' and which animals could reproduce with one another may be significantly over-estimated (see page 194). If so, the solutions to many of the logistical problems referred to above could be reached a lot more easily.

2.2.4. Interpreting the Chronologies

2.2.4.1. General

If the accounts in Genesis chapter 1 are literal, chapters 5 and 11 provide a continuous chronology from the Creation up to Abraham. On the basis of this and other scriptures, it has been calculated that the earth is only about 6,000 years old[163].

However, some commentators have argued that the lists in Genesis chapters 5 and 11 do not represent an unbroken chronology. Instead, they simply provide details of our most prominent ancestors, who were interspersed with an indeterminate number of other generations[164]. If this interpretation is correct, they argue, the earth could be tens of thousands of years old[165]. And this, of course, would enable the Bible to be reconciled much more easily with some of the scientific and historical evidence.

It is clear, therefore, that the genealogies in Genesis chapters 5 and 11 are extremely important. In view of this, all of the main arguments relating to their interpretation are examined in detail in the following paragraphs.

Ages

If the lists in Genesis 5 and 11 are literally true, many of the ancestors must have lived for hundreds of years. This, it is argued, cannot possibly be the case, and so the language must be figurative and refer to the lengths of the family lines rather than the ages of individual descendants.

There is, however, nothing in the accounts to suggest that any of these statements are figurative. The lists follow a simple formula, which states the age of each ancestor when they had their first child, how long they lived thereafter and therefore what their age was when they died. The account relating to Methuselah, for example, says:

And Methuselah lived 187 years and begot Lamech. And after he begot Lamech, Methuselah lived 782 years and he begot other sons and daughters. And all the days of Methuselah were 969 years, and he died. (Genesis 5:25-27).

In addition to this, we are told elsewhere in Genesis that other patriarchs had very long life spans. Genesis 7:6, for example, states that Noah was 600 years old at the time of the Flood. It should be noted that there is no reference here to Noah's descendants, so there is no scope for arguing that '600 years' refers to the length of Noah's family line.

So how could people have lived this long? Perhaps the first thing to note is that most of the descendants' lifespans become progressively shorter, particularly after the Flood. Some commentators have linked this to the destruction of a protective water canopy apparently indicated by Genesis 1:7, the removal of which allowed harmful cosmic rays to penetrate the atmosphere and so speed up the ageing process (see pages 57 and 58).

Whilst the Bible is silent on this point, what is clear is that before man's disobedience there was no death, decay or even infirmity. After man's fall from grace, however, any protection from these things ceased to exist altogether.

However, Genesis 5 and 11 also indicate that this process did not happen immediately. Instead, the adverse effects of old age and infirmity increased gradually over a number of generations. This may have been the result of natural or supernatural forces or perhaps a combination of both.

Totals

As the total number of years is not given at the end of the genealogies, some suggest that they were not intended to be used to construct a complete chronology. One could equally ask, however, why figures were provided for every individual, if part of the purpose was not to enable a chronology to be constructed. It should also be noted that the figures for each individual are added up, as indicated above.

Furthermore, in every single case we are told how old each person was when they fathered the next person in the genealogy. This creates an unbroken chain of ancestors, which leaves no scope for arguing that there are gaps in the chronology.

Cainan

Whitcomb and Morris argue that the Hebrew text is incomplete, as it does not include Cainan, who is mentioned in Luke 3:36 and the Septuagint version of Genesis 10:24, 11:12,13 and 1 Chronicles 1:18. This omission, they argue, means that the Flood cannot be dated, as the ages in the Septuagint are 'obviously false'. Consequently, it is impossible to determine how old Cainan was at the birth of his son[166].

They do acknowledge, however, that Cainan's name is also missing from Luke 3:36 in some Greek texts, including a major fifth century manuscript, the Codex Bezae. As regards the Septuagint, Cainan's name is also absent from most texts at 1 Chronicles 1:24, which means that most of these manuscripts contain an internal contradiction.

In view of this, there is insufficient evidence to prefer the Septuagint over the original Hebrew text. Not only does the Septuagint contain ages that Whitcomb and Morris describe as 'obviously false', most Septuagint texts are contradictory, as they include Cainan at 1 Chronicles 1:18, but then exclude him only a few verses later. Whitcomb and Morris also recognise that the years and names in the Septuagint version may have simply been added to make the account symmetrical[166].

Symmetry

Following on from this point, the next objection is that the inclusion of Cainan's name produces a perfect symmetry between the genealogies of Genesis 5 and 11, which suggests that they are not strict chronologies, viz.:

Adam			Shem	
	Seth			Arphaxad
	Enosh			Cainan
	Kenan			Shelah
	Mahalalel			Eber
	Jared			Peleg
	Enoch			Reu
	Methuselah			Serug
	Lamech			Nahor
	Noah			Terah
	(Shem, Ham, Japheth)			(Abram, Nahor, Haran)

Whitcomb and Morris point out that in each case there are ten patriarchs, the last of which has three sons. From this, they suggest that the genealogies might have been drawn up in this way as an aide-memoire, with the number ten having obvious significance for any Jew[166].

Whitcomb and Morris go on to suggest that even if Cainan was not in the original text, the genealogies would still be symmetrical, as both Adam to Noah and Shem to Abram would involve ten generations. This would involve a repetition of Shem's name, but an analogy is drawn here with the genealogy in Matthew's Gospel, which, they argue, requires the name of David to be counted twice (Matthew 1:17).

Whilst this may appear persuasive, a closer examination reveals that it involves a number of inconsistencies. To begin with, as we have already seen, Whitcomb and Morris reject the years included in the Septuagint text, on the grounds that they have, in their view, been made artificially symmetrical. To be consistent, therefore, they should reject the inclusion of Cainan on the grounds that it was similarly motivated.

If Cainan's name is excluded, however, the symmetry is removed, leaving only some rather weak arguments based on the remaining parallels in the account. The generations from Abram to Noah, for example, cannot be compared with those of Shem to Abram, because the former only counts as far as the father of the three sons, whilst the latter extends to a member of the next generation.

It is also worth recalling here that in the Hebrew text there is no symmetry in the lengths of the various generations. Unlike the Septuagint, therefore, there is no evidence that the Hebrew genealogies were compiled for any purpose other than to provide an accurate historical account. The long, irregular ages of the patriarchs in the Hebrew text can hardly be said to represent a simple, handy mnemonic!

As regards the genealogy in Matthew's Gospel, this cannot be compared with Genesis chapters 5 and 11. No dates or years are given in Matthew 1, so it could not have been compiled to provide a chronology. Instead, as Matthew 1:1 explains, its purpose was to trace Jesus's lineage through Abraham and David.

As regards the genealogy in Matthew's gospel, it is also worth noting that David's name does not need to be counted twice. If Jehoiakim's name is included in Matthew 1:11, as it is in some Greek Manuscripts and at 1 Chronicles 3:16, then there are three quite separate groups of 14 names, as stated in Matthew 1:17.

Additional Information

Whitcomb and Morris argue that, as the genealogies contain details that have nothing to do with the length of the overall period, it is 'unnecessary to press them into a rigid chronological system.'[167]

There is also no reason, however, why the accounts could not have been compiled for more than one purpose. And the chronological data that is derived from these chapters is not the result of imposing a rigid 'system' on the passages. The genealogies tell us how old each patriarch was when he became the father of the next descendant. This and this alone produces a continuous chronological chain from Adam to Abraham.

Postdiluvian Patriarchs

Whitcomb and Morris argue that if the chronologies in Genesis 5 and 11 were to be interpreted literally, we would have to conclude that all of the patriarchs who lived after the Flood, including Noah, must have been alive when Abram was 50 years old. This, it is argued, creates a problem in interpreting Joshua 24:2, which indicates that the patriarchs who were alive when Abram received his calling were still worshipping other gods at the time. If this were true, they argue, it would mean that Noah must have fallen into idolatry after the Flood, a conclusion which Whitcomb and Morris reject, as Noah is elsewhere described as being a righteous man (Genesis 6:9)[167].

These conclusions, however, are incorrect on two counts. Firstly, Whitcomb and Morris assume that Abram was born when his father was 70 years old (Genesis 11:26). As Mauro points out, however, this verse does not in fact mean that Terah became the father of triplets at the age of seventy[168]. This becomes clear when we compare Genesis 11:32, 12:4 and Acts 7:4, which tell us that Abram left Haran when he was 75 'with the death of' his father at the age of 205. Terah must therefore have been 130 when Abram was born and not 70.

It is interesting to make comparisons here with Noah. We are told that he was 500 years old and he became the father of 'Shem, Ham, and Japheth' (Genesis 5:32). But even though Shem is mentioned first, Genesis 10:21 tells us that he was not in fact the eldest. Furthermore, a comparison of Genesis 7:6 and 11:10 reveals that Noah was in fact 502 years old when Shem was born, so they clearly could not have been triplets.

It is clear from this that Genesis 5:32 and 11:26 refer to the time when the wives of Noah and Terah gave birth to their firstborn sons, not to the time when they gave birth to triplets. This date was given prominence, as the birth of the first son was a very significant event for the Jews[169]. Despite this, Shem and Abraham are mentioned first in the lists, presumably because it is through them that the line of descent is to be traced.

What this all indicates is that Noah would have died two years before Abram was even born, so the apparent problem based on Joshua 24:2 does not arise[168]. Furthermore, Joshua 24:2 does not say that *all* of the patriarchs living at that time were worshipping other gods. It only refers in name to Terah, Abram, and Nahor and says that '*they* served other gods'. It is going beyond what is written to assume that this statement refers to every ancestor living at the time. So even if Noah was still alive then, this verse would not present a problem.

The Tower of Babel

Whitcomb and Morris point out that a literal interpretation of the Genesis genealogies would mean that the tower of Babel must have been built no more than 340 years after the Flood. Even taking into account the above adjustments, this would mean that Abraham must have left for Canaan only 427 years[168] after the Flood. This sort of timescale, it is suggested, is out of keeping with the various descriptions in Genesis, which indicate that the population of the region was too large to be accounted for by only a few hundred years of history[170].

We are told, for example, that 26 Canaanite cities and several different peoples existed during Abraham's lifetime. In addition, one of these tribes, the Philistines, came from Caphtor (Crete?) and took over an area that had previously been occupied by another ethnic group, the Avvim (Deuteronomy 2:23; Jeremiah 47:4; Amos 9:7). These facts, it is argued, imply that the events relating to the tower of Babel must have occurred many centuries before the time of Abraham.

These arguments, however, are far from conclusive, as Genesis provides no information about population levels or even the size of the towns to which it refers. We also cannot be certain that Caphtor is Crete or even an island[171]. Nor do we know how long the Avvim had occupied the area that was later conquered by the Philistines.

What we *are* told, however, is that the people of the time enjoyed a lifespan several times that of our own, and that polygamy had been practised since the time of Lamech (Genesis 4:19). This indicates that the population after the Flood would have doubled more frequently than once every 53 years, as it did in the twentieth century[62]. And if the population had doubled once every 20 years, for example, then there would have been over 16.7 million people (8×2^{21}) in the region before Abraham had even set out for Canaan!

Firstborn Sons

In view of their comments about Joshua 24:2, it is perhaps surprising that Whitcomb and Morris go on to acknowledge that Abraham was in fact born when his father was 130 years old. They also accept that the sons of Noah and Terah are not listed in chronological order. Despite this, they then suggest that this is further evidence that there could be gaps in the genealogies. They argue that, just as Abraham was born 60 years after the date that is apparently provided by Genesis 11:26, so other descendants might have been born much later than appears to be suggested by a literal interpretation of the text[1/2].

A closer examination of the actual wording, however, shows that there is no evidence to support this conclusion. Genesis 5:32 and 11:26 simply tell us how old Noah and Terah were before they had children. By contrast, in the main body of the genealogies we are told exactly how old each patriarch was when they 'begot' the next descendant on the list, and then it tells us how long they lived after that point in time.

In the case of the Genesis 5 genealogy, we are also told how long each patriarch lived in total, and this figure is invariably the sum of the years before and after they fathered the next descendant. There is therefore no evidence of any possible gaps, and, as only one descendant is mentioned in each of the other generations, there is no possibility of any ambiguity either.

Moses

Whitcomb and Morris point out that the words 'begat' and 'son' are sometimes used in a figurative sense, when they clearly denote a more distant ancestral connection, as opposed to a literal father-son relationship (e.g. 1 Chronicles 26:24; Matthew 1:8). They refer in particular to Exodus 6:20, because of the similarity between this verse and the formula used in Genesis 5 and 11.

Although Exodus 6:20 and 1 Chronicles 23:13 indicate that Amram and Jochebed were Moses' immediate parents, Whitcomb and Morris argue that this is impossible, because shortly after the Exodus the families of Amram and his three brothers included 8,600 male offspring (Numbers 3:28). This, they argue, proves that Amram was a more distant relative, a conclusion which they say is supported by the fact that the narrative of Moses' birth in Exodus 2:1-10 omits the names of his parents[173].

It has been suggested, however, that the names of Moses' parents were omitted from Exodus chapter 2, because the account portrays the 'dark environmental background' to his birth[174]. It is also worth noting that we are not given the name of Moses' sister or pharaoh's daughter, and Moses' own name is not mentioned until the very end of the account. Whatever the reason for these narrative features might be, however, the passage provides no evidence whatsoever that Amram and Jochebed were not Moses' actual parents.

As regards Numbers 3:28, we know that Amram lived 137 years (Exodus 6:20) and that Moses was 82 years old when the census was taken (Exodus 7:7; Numbers 1:1). We do not know, however, how old Amram was when Moses was born. We also do not know how old Amram was compared with his brothers, and the genealogies show that there were sometimes very large gaps between the births of different children. Furthermore, we are not told how many wives each of Amram's brothers and their descendants had, something which would obviously have had a significant effect on the total number of offspring.

It is perfectly possible, therefore, that Moses was born quite a long time after his uncles, who, consequently, could have had a large number of descendants by that time. If we assumed, for example, that each of the brothers had four wives and that the population doubled once every 20 years, then, after 200 years, the population would have been 16,384. If just over one half of these were male, this would account for the figure of 8,600 in Numbers 3:28.

As regards the meaning of the words 'begot' and 'son' in Genesis 5 and 11, what is clear is that where further information is ever provided the words never refer to distant ancestors. Adam and Lamech, for example, are said to have named their descendants (Genesis 5:3,28), which indicates that they were living at the same time as those descendants. We are also told that Shem, Ham and Japheth boarded the ark together with their father Noah (Genesis 7:13), and Genesis 11:28 tells us that Haran died before his father Terah. Whitcomb and Morris' interpretation, therefore, requires us to believe that in one sentence the word 'begot' is used literally, but In the very next verse it is used to denote a distant ancestor, who lived hundreds or perhaps even thousands of years earlier!

Peleg

Whitcomb and Morris refer to the reference in Genesis 10:25 to 'Peleg', who was so named because 'in his days the earth was divided'. This 'division' is taken to refer to the Tower of Babel (Genesis 11:1-9), as God then 'divided' people into different linguistic groups.

Whitcomb and Morris contend that it would be senseless to say that the earth was divided 'in the days of Peleg', if all the previous patriarchs were also still living at that time. They argue that this must mean that the genealogies cannot be interpreted literally, something which they say is further supported by the fact that the lifespans of Peleg and his descendants are significantly shorter than their predecessors. This, they argue, is a further indication that there must be a significant gap in the genealogy at this point.

However, Genesis 10:25 simply tells us why Peleg was given this name. It does not justify this, or say no-one else could have been legitimately given that name. He may have been so named, for example, because he was born in the year of the 'division'. As regards the argument about lifespans, this is speculative. It also ignores the fact that we are told how old Eber was when he 'begot' Peleg and how many years he lived after then.

Enoch

Jude 14 states that Enoch was the 'seventh *from* Adam'. It might be argued that this means the genealogy in Genesis chapter 5 is incomplete, as this indicates that Enoch was only the sixth after Adam. It is clear, however, that Jude 14 simply means that Enoch was of the seventh generation, with Adam's being the first.

2.2.5. Conclusions

We have shown that the creation and flood accounts in Genesis must be interpreted literally, as must the genealogies in chapters 5 and 11. We have also established that the Flood was a worldwide deluge, and that this and the bursting forth of 'all the fountains of the great deep' could have had very profound effects on the earth's geology. We will now consider if the Bible does in fact contradict the scientific evidence. If it does, then we must either reject the Bible or the interpretation or reliability of this scientific evidence.

2.3. THE SCIENTIFIC EVIDENCE

2.3.1. Light

Introduction

According to astronomers, the most distant stars are billions of light years away, and the light we receive from them therefore reflects how they appeared billions of years ago. This, of course, clearly contradicts the biblical account of creation, which, as we have seen, indicates that God created the stars 6,000 years ago.

To consider this issue further, the following sections firstly review the various star distance measurement techniques that are used by astronomers. There is then a brief review of the account in Genesis, together with some further analysis to show how the biblical account could be reconciled with the scientific evidence.

The Speed of Light

The first assumption that astronomical calculations make is that the speed of light is constant through time and space. This is a fundamental tenet of Einstein's Special Theory of Relativity, which states that nothing can travel faster than light, the speed of which is identical for all observers irrespective of their own speeds[175].

Since Einstein, however, scientific evidence has emerged which indicates that the 'normal' speed of light is not an absolute barrier. This evidence comes from a variety of different sources. For example, in one experiment light was sent through optical filters, which were so fine that they caused the light to undergo something called 'tunnelling'. The resulting measurements showed that the light beams had travelled at around 1.7 times the normal speed of light. In addition, electromagnetic waves, which usually travel at the same speed as light, apparently attained speeds of up to 4.7 times that value[176].

Star Distances

The second assumption is that some stars are billions of light years away. This belief rests on a number of other assumptions, which are discussed in detail below.

(a) Parallax

Parallax is the most direct method of star distance determination, which has been used to measure stars that are up to 10,000 light years away[177]. In this method, a star's position is measured from either side of the earth's orbit around the sun. These two angles are then used to construct a triangle, the base of which is the distance between the earth's position on either side of its orbit. As the latter is known, the triangle can be solved and the distance to the star can then be calculated using simple trigonometry.

One complicating factor is the movement of the star itself, known as its 'proper motion'. This can be measured by comparing a star's position from identical places in the earth's orbit over several years. This data can then be combined with the star's red or blue shift to calculate its movement away from or towards the earth. One problem with this, however, is that red shift is not always due to radial velocity, as explained in sub-sections (c) and (n) below.

(b) Open Clusters

This is another geometric technique. It has been used for distances of up to 3,000 light years[178], but the Hubble telescope means that it can now be used for distances several times greater than this.

This method relies on the fact that objects moving away from us in parallel lines appear to travel towards a convergent point, like lines on a railway track. The rate at which stars appear to converge depends on two factors: their radial velocities and their distances. The radial velocity is deduced from a star's red shift. This is then combined with the angle produced by the convergent point to calculate the distance implied by the stars' motions.

One problem with this method is that it is only 92% accurate at 150 light years[179]. Moreover, it assumes that the stars are travelling in parallel lines[180], because, if they were not, they would have moved apart billions of years ago. If the stars are no more than 6,000 years old, however, we clearly cannot make this assumption.

(c) Indirect Methods: General

Parallax and open clusters provide the only direct methods of star distance determination; for greater distances astronomers have to rely on a number of indirect methods. Most of these techniques are based on the fact that objects appear smaller and dimmer the further away they are. Consequently, if we know the actual size and brightness of a star, we should be able to estimate its distance.

There are, of course, several problems with these kinds of estimates. To begin with, we cannot be sure how large or bright more distant stars or galaxies actually are. It is therefore necessary to assume that certain types of stars or galaxies have roughly the same size or brightness throughout the universe. We also have to assume that these objects have not changed significantly over time, as the most distant objects are thought to be billions of times older than their nearer counterparts.

A further issue is that the spectrum of light from a star only tells us about its chemical composition and temperature. However, a star's brightness may also be affected by other more variable factors, such as its size, mass and density[181]. For example, brightness is usually proportional to a star's mass raised to the 3.5 power. It is known, however, that this ratio can vary quite considerably[182].

A further factor that interferes with distance calculations is interstellar dust, which causes stars to appear much dimmer than they actually are. Astronomers have taken account of this by comparing stars of known distance with the same spectral type. Analysis has shown that the dimming caused by interstellar dust is accompanied by a reddening in the star's appearance, as light of shorter wavelengths is absorbed by the interstellar material. By studying the correlation between these two effects, astronomers have formulated a reddening versus dimness ratio, which is then taken into account when performing brightness comparisons[183].

One problem with these calculations, however, is that they require us to assume that interstellar dust has exactly the same properties throughout the universe. Whilst this may appear reasonable, we cannot be sure that it is in fact the case, and the properties of even relatively near objects have occasionally taken astronomers by surprise. For example, a ring around Saturn more than 8 million miles thick was not discovered until 2009!

One of the most difficult factors to compensate for is 'dark matter'. Like interstellar dust, dark matter can absorb light. However, as it does not re-radiate any form of energy, it cannot be seen. Consequently, it can be very difficult, if not impossible, to quantify the effect dark matter may have on a star's brightness.

It is now generally accepted that dark matter and dark energy account for 90% to 99% of the universe[184]. It is also thought that there are no more than 300 primordial black holes per cubic light year of space[185]. If this is correct, then dark matter should apparently exist in dense enough forms for it to be detected.

One way of doing this would be by deducing its existence from the gravitational effect it has on objects, or from the changes in brightness or multi-imaging that it may cause[186]. Dark matter may also be detected via the energy that is believed to be emitted by mass as it falls into a black hole[187].

This is still a relatively new area of research, however, and it is possible that dark matter and dark energy may be distributed far more evenly than astronomers have assumed hitherto. It may even exist in a form that is undetectable at present. If that is the case, however, then many stars may appear considerably dimmer and therefore more distant than they actually are.

(d) Main Sequence Fitting

This method has been used for distances of up to 65,000 light years[178]. It is mainly based on studies of the Hyades and Pleiades, two star clusters about 150 and 490 light years away respectively.

These clusters are used, as they contain a large variety of different stars, yielding data about the spectra and brightness of 100 different types of star[188]. These outputs have been represented diagrammatically, by plotting the brightness of these stars against their spectral types. Diagrams for other clusters are then matched against these, and differences in the brightness of each star type are then used to estimate their distances.

As indicated above, however, there are various problems with these comparisons. To begin with, there are the possible effects of variations in size and mass of the stars being compared. These difficulties may then be augmented by the presence of interstellar dust, which has a reddening versus dimness ratio that differs from the 'standard'. Finally, there is the possibility of undetected and therefore unquantified amounts of dark matter.

(e) RR Lyrae Variables

These stars are commonly found at the centre of the Galaxy in concentrated groups, known as globular clusters. The prototype for the RR Lyraes is about 200 light years away[189], and around 4,500 have been found in our Galaxy[190]. RR Lyraes differ in their periods of variation and are divided into several classes[190]. Despite this, RR Lyraes are believed to have the same intrinsic brightness, an assumption which has enabled astronomers to estimate their distances for up to about 2.8 million light years away[191].

If this assumption is incorrect, however, then all of the resulting distance calculations will be wrong. In addition, the accuracy of those calculations could be adversely affected by other factors, such as the presence of dark matter or 'atypical' interstellar dust.

(f) Cepheid Variables

Cepheid variables were first studied in detail in the Large and Small Magellanic Clouds, believed to be about 169,000 and 190,000 light years away respectively[192]. These studies indicated there was a relationship between their median brightness and periods of variation. So once the intrinsic brightness of a nearby Cepheid was established, the distances of other Cepheids could be calculated, based on their periods of variation and apparent luminosities.

The prototype Cepheid variable is a star known as Delta Cephei, which is about 1,300 light years away[193]. Some Cepheid variables are believed to be a lot brighter than RR Lyrae stars. As a result, they have been used to measure distances of up to 125 million light years away[194].

In addition to these classic Population I Cepheid variables, a second type has been discovered, which is believed to be about four times fainter[190]. Many of these Population II Cepheids have been found in globular clusters, but they have also been discovered in other locations.

Astronomers assume that there are no other types of Cepheid variable in the universe, and that the Cepheids within each category exhibit exactly the same period versus luminosity ratios. However, it is impossible to completely rule out the existence of other types of Cepheid variable, and the fact is that some clearly have exhibited 'atypical' period versus luminosity ratios.

For example, the North Star, Polaris is about 430 light years away, and is categorised as a classic Cepheid variable. However, it has perplexed astronomers, because over the years its pulsations have rapidly decreased, so much so that by the year 2000 the star had almost ceased to vary at all[195]. Whilst Polaris may be atypical, it does at least show that it may not be safe to assume that all Cepheids behave in exactly the same way.

(g) Novae

Although their name suggests that these are new stars, novae are in fact believed to be two closely linked stars called binaries, which undergo a temporary eruption that results in mass being transferred from one star to the other[196].

Novae are used in star distance determinations, as they are believed to have roughly the same maximum brightness, the magnitude of which is believed to be related to the subsequent rate of decline[197]. On the basis of these assumptions, novae have been used to estimate distances of up to 33 million light years[178].

It is accepted, however, that the behaviour of novae is not fully understood[196] and that they only offer a fairly crude way of estimating distances[197]. Those calculations also rely heavily on assumptions regarding their behaviour, size, mass and composition.

(h) Bright Stars

This technique uses very luminous stars with known distances and then compares their brightness with more distant stars of the same category. The apparent brightness of the latter is then used to estimate their distances, a technique that is believed to be reliable for up to 65 million light years[178].

The Pleiades contains a number of very bright stars[198], which can be used as distance markers. Another candidate is Alnitak. This is about 1,100 light years away and represents one of the brightest known categories of stars[198].

The technique of using very bright stars assumes that similar stars have the same intrinsic brightness throughout the universe. This might not be the case, however, and the distance calculations may be further invalidated by variations in the size and mass of the stars, coupled with the effects of interstellar dust and dark matter. Their brightness might also vary with age, a point that needs to be considered if they are as far away as astronomers maintain, and we can only see how they looked many millions of years ago.

(i) Globular Clusters

These are concentrated groups of stars found at the centre of our Galaxy, which have also been located in other galaxies. Because of their brightness, it is believed that they can be observed at considerable distances.

The distances of some globular clusters have been estimated from the presence of RR Lyrae stars. For example, they were used to calculate the distance of M4, which is believed to be about 6,800 light years away[199]. In the case of other globular clusters, the distance calculations assume that all of these clusters have roughly the same average size[199]. As their properties are believed to be observable for up to 330 million light years[200], globular clusters potentially serve as very powerful distance markers.

According to astronomers, however, the most luminous globular clusters are 100 times brighter than the faintest, and the number of stars they contain varies by a similar factor[201]. There are also striking variances in the chemical composition of the stars within different globular clusters[201]. Consequently, the use of average sizes in distance determination contains a potentially large margin for error. In addition, in common with other indirect methods, the results may be distorted by other factors, such as the presence of interstellar dust or dark matter.

(j) H II Regions

These are large clouds composed mainly of ionised hydrogen and dust particles, which are heated by the bright stars within them[202]. The distances of the nearest clouds are measured by reference to the Cepheid variables they contain. And the distances of others have then been estimated up to 260 million light years away, by assuming that all H II Regions have roughly the same diameter[202].

As with globular clusters, however, there is believed to be quite a considerable variation in the sizes of H II Regions. The Orion

Nebula, for example, is believed to be about 1,500 light years away and 15 light years in diameter. Some H II Regions, however, are believed to be 650 light years across[203]. Furthermore, there is no direct evidence that H II Regions stay within these parameters elsewhere in the universe.

(k) SC I Galaxies

These are bright spiral galaxies, which have open arms and small nuclei. The distances of the nearest Sc I galaxies have been estimated on the basis of the Cepheid variables and the H II Regions they contain[178]. The distances of other Sc I galaxies have been estimated up to 300 million light years away, on the assumption that all of these galaxies have the same intrinsic brightness[178].

Astronomers accept, however, that the sizes of most galaxies differ quite significantly. The diameters of galaxies within our local group, for example, are believed to vary by a factor of more than 80[204]. Although this figure includes different types of galaxies, there appears to be no compelling reason to assume that all galaxies of a certain shape should also have the same size. The brightness of a galaxy is also affected by how active it is, which could give a misleading impression of its distance[205].

In addition, it is questionable to assume that a galaxy would have the same brightness as one that was thought to be much younger, an issue that has been acknowledged in recent decades[206]. This would not be an issue for creationists, of course, as they believe that all of the stars and galaxies were created at the same time.

(l) Supernovas

A supernova is an exploding star, which is believed to increase in brightness by a factor of hundreds of millions[207]. Astronomers also believe that whilst there are several types of supernova, they all attain the same maximum brightness, an assumption which enables them to be used as markers for distances of up to 11 billion light years [208].

It is estimated that there is one supernova per galaxy every 30 to 50 years[209]. However, the last one to be seen in our own galaxy was observed by Kepler as far back as 1604. As a result, there is no firm evidence of their absolute brightness. Moreover, it is impossible to prove that all supernovae must have the same maximum luminosity. In view of this, it now appears to be generally accepted that supernovae are not particularly reliable distance markers[210].

(m) Bright Cluster Galaxies

Some astronomers have concluded that the third brightest galaxies in small clusters have the same luminosity[211]. Assuming that this is true of all such galaxies, astronomers believe this method will enable them to estimate the distances of other galaxies up to 26 billion light years away[212].

In addition to the problems referred to above, however, the difficulty with his method is that it does not explain what physical law would cause the third brightest galaxies in small clusters to have the same intrinsic brightness. As a result, there is no clear scientific basis for verifying the accuracy of this assumption.

(n) Redshift

When an object moves away from us the wavelength of the light it emits appears to be shifted towards the red end of the spectrum. In the case of stellar objects, the extent of this so-called 'redshift' is also believed to be directly related to its distance.

The idea of using redshift to determine distances was first proposed in 1929 by Edwin Hubble. He undertook measurements of various galaxies, and found that redshift and distance appeared to be related to one another. Hubble concluded that the universe must have begun with a huge explosion, following which it expanded very rapidly. As the speed of expansion is proportional to the distance between two points, Hubble concluded that this explained the correlation between distance and redshift.

One way of understanding this is to compare the expanding universe with a balloon that is covered with dots of ink. As the balloon inflates, the dots that are furthest apart move away from one another at the greatest speed[213]. Likewise, in a uniformly expanding universe, the most distant galaxies would recede at the fastest rate.

The speed at which a galaxy moves away from us can therefore be used to gauge its distance, once the relationship between distance and recessional speed has been calibrated. This relationship is known as Hubble's constant (H_0), and is generally believed to be between 40 and 50 km per second per megaparsec, or 25 to 31.25 miles per second for every 3.26 million light years.

The most distant objects measured using this method are quasi-stellar sources or quasars. These are believed to be extremely bright galaxies that are up to 15 billion light years away[214]. According to the redshift method, some quasars are moving away from us at more than 90% of the speed of light and are millions of times brighter than normal galaxies[215]. Despite this, the visible areas of some of these quasars are believed by some to be a millionth of the size our own galaxy.[216]

Hubble's constant is calibrated using the indirect methods of distance determination referred to above. It therefore contains a number of unproven assumptions. In addition, a significant amount of evidence indicates that redshift is not necessarily always caused by recessional speed, and conflicting redshifts have been recorded for a number of quasars and other galaxies[217].

(o) Summary

The speed of light does not appear to be an absolute barrier, and most star distance determinations involve several unproven assumptions. Astronomers may argue it is reasonable to assume that we inhabit a representative part of the universe. However, there is evidence that the universe is far from uniform. In 1985, for example, studies of galaxies revealed that the universe contained a number of huge cosmic voids, and that the galaxies bordering these voids were configured in the form of gigantic filaments. In commenting on this, Nathan Cohen concluded:

> Do voids and filaments make sense with a Big Bang model? In the strictest sense they do not....We speak of galaxies as moving with the *Hubble flow*, the expansion velocity of the universe. This flow should prevent galaxies and clusters from connecting over very great distances.[218]

If the universe does not have a uniform structure, however, it seems unreasonable to assume that similar stars and galaxies will necessarily be of the same size and brightness throughout the whole universe, particularly as the ages of what we are able to see on earth are believed to differ by millions and even billions of years.

It is also worth remembering that astronomers are only able to calculate the distance of stars up to 10,000 light years away using 'direct' methods. This means that assumptions about the rest of the universe are based on direct knowledge of what astronomers believe is about three ten billion billionths (quintillionths) of the visible universe ($4/3\pi 10{,}000^{3*} \div 4/3\pi 15{,}000{,}000{,}000^{3*}$). Arguments based on this amount of extrapolation must surely be open to serious doubt on statistical grounds alone.

Creationists' Explanations

General

According to Genesis 1:14-18 (with emphasis added), God said:

---

* $4/3\pi r^3$ is the formula for the volume of a globe.

<u>14:</u> ...Let there be lights in the firmament of the heaven to divide the day from the night; and let them be for signs, and for seasons, and for days, and years:

<u>15:</u> And let them be for lights in the firmament of the heaven to give light upon the earth: <u>and it was so.</u>

<u>16:</u> And God made two great lights; the greater light to rule the day, and the lesser light to rule the night *and the stars*.

<u>17:</u> And God set them in the firmament of the heaven to give light upon the earth,

<u>18:</u> And to rule over the day and over the night, and to divide the light from the darkness: and God saw that it was good. (Authorised Version)

The first point to note here is that the words in italics are a literal translation of the Hebrew, Instead of the text of the Authorised Version (AV), which at this point reads, ':he made the stars also'. The omission of the word 'and' from the AV, coupled with the addition of a colon and the words 'he made', clearly alter the meaning quite significantly. From the literal translation, however, it is clear that this verse is simply telling us that God made both the 'lesser light' (the moon) to rule over the night together with ('and') the stars, something which is confirmed elsewhere in the Old Testament (Psalms 136:9; Jeremiah 31:35).

For our purposes, however, the most important section of this passage is to be found in verses 14 and 15. These tell us that God ordained four things:

1. the creation of 'lights', to
2. separate day and night
3. serve as signs, seasons, days and years, and
4. shed light upon the earth.

Immediately after this we are told, 'And it was so'. As the words of verses 14 and 15 form a single sentence, the phrase, 'And it was so' that follows them must relate to everything in that sentence.

This is important, because it means that all of these things came to pass on day four of Creation. The 'luminaries' were not only created; they also immediately separated day from night and began to serve as signs to differentiate the seasons, days and years. And, most importantly in this context, the stars also immediately began to 'shed' light upon the earth.

The phrase, 'to shed light upon the earth' means literally to 'cause light on the earth', the word here being the causative form of אוֹר, which means, 'to be or become light'[219]. This cannot, therefore, be interpreted to simply mean that light was shed in the direction of the earth; the luminaries actually *caused* light to reach the earth.

Light Speeds

This is significant, as it implies that starlight must have travelled at incredibly high speeds to reach the earth on day four of Creation. Ignoring the sun, the nearest star is over four light years away. So for light from this star to arrive in just one day implies a light speed of at least 1,461 times (365.25 x 4) faster than the usual speed of light. Moreover, if the most distant stars really are over 15 billion light years away, this implies light speeds trillions of times faster than the normal speed of light.

The important point to note here is that the light reached the earth on day four of Creation as a result of a direct command from God. If the constancy of the speed of light is a fundamental law of the universe, these phenomenal light speeds must have been miraculous, unless some other valid explanation can be found.

To disprove this we would have to be able to show that starlight did not travel at different speeds in the past. We do, of course, have a good idea of the current speed of light based on something known as 'the aberration of starlight'. This works on the principle that the angle of light from a star, and hence its apparent position, is distorted by the earth's transverse speed compared with the speed of the incoming light. However, this only tells us the speed of the incoming starlight at the time of the measurement; it does not prove what its speed was over the rest of its journey.

We also do not have to calculate how and when the speed of starlight might have declined. All we need to say is that the light we receive from stars that are 15 billion light years away, must have travelled at an average of 2.5 millions times the 'normal' speed of light (15 billion/6,000 years). We do not need to make any other calculations or assumptions. We do not even have to assume that all light travelled at these speeds throughout this period of time.

Physicists would argue that fantastic light speeds contradict a fundamental law of the universe. They might also say that light travelling at such speeds would create huge blueshifts, which are conspicuous by their absence. However, the Bible clearly tells us that starlight reached the earth on day four as the result of an act of God. Miracles, by definition, operate outside the laws of nature, so it is circular to construct arguments based solely on those laws.

Blueshifts are just one of those laws of nature. They occur when an object emitting light moves towards us at very high speeds, which results in the crests of light waves reaching us more quickly, with the result that its colour is shifted towards the blue end of the spectrum. Here, however, we are proposing that the speed of light was affected, not the speed of the object emitting the light. Moreover, if this was miraculous, God might have overridden this blueshift law. According to the Bible, God created stars to shed light on the earth and to help divide seasons, days and years. None of these purposes would have been fulfilled, if the phenomenal light speeds created blueshifts that made the stars virtually invisible against the night sky.

Relativity

An alternative explanation to miraculous light speeds has been advanced by Professor John Hartnett. In his book, *Starlight, Time and the New Physics,* Hartnett points out that according to the Big Bang Theory space expanded rapidly after the beginning of the universe. This fact, he argues, is also clearly reflected in the various biblical passages that refer to God 'stretching out the heavens' (Psalms 104:2; Isaiah 40:22, 42:5, 44:24, 45:12; 51:13; Jeremiah 10:12, 51:15; Zechariah 12:1.)

The key to Hartnett's theory is his proposition that virtually all of this expansion took place on day four of Creation. This phenomenally fast expansion of space, he contends, meant that time would have run much more slowly on earth compared with cosmic clocks[220]. As a result, starlight could have travelled billions of light years in one day whilst still moving at the normal speed of light.

The universe must have expanded rapidly for us to be able to see objects 15 billion light years away after only 13.7 billion years – the generally accepted age of the universe. Nevertheless, Hartnett's theory is rejected by the vast majority of cosmologists, presumably because it requires a *miraculous* acceleration in the expansion of the universe.

Hartnett's explanation is also not something that can be deduced from scripture. The Bible simply says that God created the heavens and stretched them out. It does not tell us how big the heavens were before they were stretched, the extent to which they were stretched, or the period over which this stretching took place. It is also worth noting here that some of these verses also talk about God 'spreading out the earth' as well.

However, Hartnett maintains that his model uses 'an economy of miracles'[221]. This, he argues, makes it preferable to other creationist explanations, as these require a belief in various miracles, some of which are not mentioned explicitly in the Bible. However, Hartnett's explanation does still appear to rely upon a miracle, as it requires God to accelerate the expansion of the universe. Whilst this theory may be attractive to creationists in some ways, therefore, in reality it only replaces the idea of miraculous light speeds with miraculous space-expansion speeds.

Distances

It is also worth remembering that starlight may not have travelled as far as astronomers estimate. As we have seen, astronomical calculations depend on numerous assumptions, so the resulting distance calculations should not be simply taken for granted.

Furthermore, these distances have been built up progressively by several different methods, each of which depends to some extent on the accuracy of previous ones. Consequently, if the results of six linked methods were overstated by a factor of 10, the resulting distances would be exaggerated by an order of one million.

It is also worth pointing out that astronomers have come to quite different conclusions about the distances of stars and galaxies, even in the relatively recent past. For example, in 1930 most astronomers still thought that our Galaxy constituted the entire universe[222]. And in the 1950s astronomers suddenly concluded that the universe was twice as large as they had previously thought[223]. More recently, data from the Hubble telescope in 1994 caused a stir when it indicated that some of the most distant stars were 8 billion, rather than 13 or 14 billion, light years away[224].

Conclusion

Scientific methods include numerous unprovable assumptions about the distances of stars and galaxies. Although there is nothing in the scriptures to contradict these assumptions, Genesis 1:14,15 tell us quite plainly that starlight reached the earth on the fourth day of Creation. This is, of course, emphatically rejected by most astronomers, who have calculated that it would take billions of years for light from the most distant stars to reach us.

However, one cannot dispute the accuracy of these biblical statements on the basis of the scientific evidence alone. The reason for this is that the Bible tells us that starlight reached the earth on day four of Creation, not in accordance with the laws of nature, but as a direct result of divine intervention. According to the Bible, therefore, our ability to see the stars is the result of a miracle. No further evidence may be available to support this belief. On the other hand, there is no scientific evidence to disprove it either.

2.3.2. Radiometric Dating

Introduction

This is the principal method used by geologists to date rocks and estimate the age of the earth. As this presents a serious challenge to Creationism, this section contains a thorough appraisal of this dating method and the key assumptions it makes. This is followed by a detailed review of the main dating processes and techniques.

General

Radiometric dating was developed in the first part of the twentieth century, following the discovery of radioactivity. It is based on the observation that a radioactive 'parent' element decays at an apparently constant rate into a 'daughter' element. If we know the ratio of parent to daughter elements at the beginning of this process, therefore, we should be able to calculate how much time has elapsed by measuring their present-day ratios.

This method therefore requires us to accept that -

(a) the rate of decay is constant;

(b) apart from this, the parent and daughter elements have not changed; and,

(c) the initial ratios of the parent:daughter elements can be established accurately.

(a) The Rate of Decay

The possibility that the rate of decay could be affected by outside factors, such as temperature and pressure, has been carefully considered. Tests revealed that elements that decay by the capture of an electron, such as potassium, can be affected by changes in pressure. However, when elements were subjected to 270,000 bars of pressure, the rate of decay only increased by 0.59%[225]. This amount of pressure would only exist in rocks at considerable depths, however, which are generally not used for dating purposes.

Moreover, other elements used in radiometric dating are unaffected by changes in pressure, and according to some of these the earth is about 4.5 billion years old. To reconcile this with a biblical timescale on the basis of the rate of decay alone, would require us to assume that the elements previously decayed at an average rate that was about 750,000 (4.5bn/6,000) times faster than at present.

Not only is there no evidence for this, there are other serious objections to such a proposal. One of the decay products in the uranium series, for example, is radon, a highly toxic gas. In the UK today, this gas is still produced by uranium decay at levels which mean some homes have to be fitted with radon pumps, because of the serious health and safety risks[226]. If the levels of radon were 750,000 times higher in the past, it is very hard to see how any life on earth could have survived.

(b) Loss and Gain of Parent or Daughter Elements

Scientists accept that very few rocks have remained undisturbed since their formation[227]. In fact, they have been continuously destroyed and reformed by geological processes[228], and changes in temperature have materially altered their chemical composition. In fact, increases of only 100 to 200°c may have had drastic effects on the parent-daughter relationship[229].

In addition, the rocks used for dating are often collected from surface outcrops, where they would have been exposed to the effects of weathering[230], and this can have further dramatic effects on the parent-daughter ratios. For example, it is believed that some uranium-bearing minerals have lost 85% of their radiogenic lead solely as a result of weathering[230].

The way in which these problems are tackled varies, and the strategies employed by different methods are discussed below. The main point to make here is that the seriousness of some of the problems was not fully appreciated until quite recently. The Rubidium-Strontium 'whole-rock method', for example, was widely used until the 1980s, when further evidence regarding the mobility of these two elements discredited the process[231].

(c) Initial Parent to Daughter Ratios

The evidence for the initial parent-daughter ratios that are used in radiometric dating comes from two sources. To begin with, geologists use what they call regression calculations, known as 'isochrons', to estimate how much of the daughter element existed before any radioactive decay had taken place. These calculations are then supplemented by data gleaned from meteorites and lunar samples, as these are believed to provide reliable clues regarding the chemistry of the earth at the time of its formation.

The word 'isochron' means 'same age'. So the isochron method assumes that the minerals in a rock are of the same age and have experienced the same geological conditions[232]. The procedure involves measuring the ratios of the 'parent' and 'daughter' elements in each of the minerals, and then using this data to work out the relationship between these minerals in the rock as a whole.

These calculations produce dates for the apparent age of the rock, as they provide evidence of the proportion of the 'parent' element that appears to have decayed. The resulting calculations also indicate how much of the 'daughter' element appears to have been present before any radioactive decay had taken place.

For this method to work, it is important that the amount of the 'parent' element varies from the mineral to mineral. This allows the concentrations of the 'parent' to be related to the varying levels of the 'daughter' element in the different minerals. This in turn allows the proportion that has undergone radioactive decay to be quantified, so that the age of the minerals, and hence the age of the rock as a whole, can be calculated.

We have placed the terms 'parent' and 'daughter' here in inverted commas, as some of the 'daughter' element may not have actually been produced by the assumed 'parent'. Instead, it may have come from other rock systems or, in the case of gases, from the atmosphere. For example, the magma from which a rock formed may have come from other rocks, which already contained quantities of the 'daughter' element as a result of previous radioactive decay.

To establish the amount of the 'daughter' element at the time the rock sample formed, it is necessary to deduct the quantity produced by radioactive decay from the total amount of the 'daughter' element. This, combined with the original amount of the 'parent' element, enables the initial 'parent'-'daughter' ratio to be calculated.

The easiest way to understand how this method works is probably by examining a typical isochron graph. An example is therefore provided on the following page. This does, of course, involve a fair amount of over-simplification, as the data points would be much more scattered than this in practice. However, the diagram does at least illustrate the essential principles that are involved in the construction of isochrons.

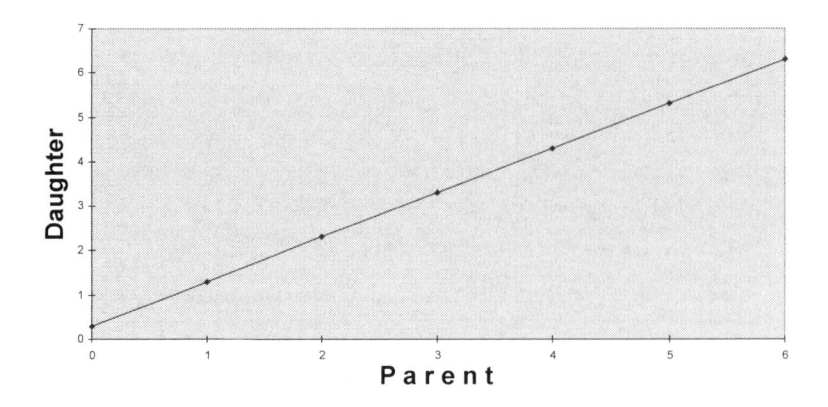

The points on the graph are the results of examining different minerals in the rock. As the graph describes a straight line, this suggests that the minerals share the same age, initial ratios and geological history. If this is the case, the slope of the graph combined with the decay constant can be used to calculate the age of the rock. In addition, the intercept with the y axis indicates how much of the 'daughter' existed when no 'parent' element was present. This therefore tells us how much of the 'daughter' element existed before any radioactive decay had taken place.

There are, however, a number of problems with this method. To begin with, few isochrons produce an exactly straight line, which casts doubt on the assumption that all of the minerals in the rock sample are of the same age. In fact, Brooks et al have argued that a line fitted around a set of data that displays a scatter in excess of experimental error should not be regarded as an isochron at all[233].

It is also accepted that fairly straight-line graphs can be produced by other factors as well. These false isochrons are known as errorchrons, and various sophisticated statistical methods have been developed to try to identify them[234]. Inevitably, however, any results that do not produce a perfectly straight line must be open to some doubt.

Furthermore, even straight-line graphs do not necessarily mean that the minerals in those rocks are of the same age. According to geologists, perfect isochrons can also result from the:

(a) mixing of rocks with different initial ratios[235, 236];
(b) mixing of minerals with different closure temperatures[237];
(c) progressive contamination by crustal rocks[238]; and,
(d) variable depletion of mantle rocks[239].

The graphs that are produced in these circumstances are referred to as pseudo-isochrons, and as rocks are constantly forming and reforming, there is plenty of scope for these phenomena. In 1976, for example, Brooks listed 30 volcanic and plutonic rocks that yielded pseudo-isochrons[240]. And one rock believed to be 1 million years old produced an isochron age of about 773 million years[240]!

Geologists identify results as pseudo-isochrons, if the dates disagree with the ages of adjacent rocks or other minerals in the rock. If processes such as mixing are involved, however, it may be impossible to correct the dates by reference to other minerals, as these kinds of processes may well have generated pseudo-isochrons. Adjacent rocks may not be of assistance either, as these may have experienced quite different geological histories.

Frequently, therefore, isochrons are classed as pseudo-isochrons, when their ages do not accord with geologists' assumptions, which are often based upon the strata in which the rock was found. As a result, geologists do not always agree upon what is and what is not a true isochron. For example, various diagrams based on the decay of uranium to lead have been interpreted as isochrons by some geologists and as mixing lines by others[241].

Theoretically, it is possible that all supposed isochrons are the product of mixing lines and other geological processes that have no age significance, and which therefore provide no evidence of initial 'parent'-'daughter' ratios. However, meteorites appear to offer some evidence to support the initial ratios produced by terrestrial isochrons.

Meteorites are used, as they are believed to capture the isotopic composition of the minerals at the time their parent bodies became inactive following rapid heat loss[242]. Unlike terrestrial rocks, geologists believe meteorites have not been affected by metamorphism or other geological processes[228]. And the isochrons of some meteorites are thought to reflect ages that are close to that of the solar system[243]. By contrast, terrestrial rocks of this age are assumed to be buried too deep in the earth for them to ever be accessible[228].

The meteorites used by geologists fall into two main categories: chondrites and achondrites. Chondrites contain rounded granules called chondrules and yield ages of up to 4.6 billion years[243]. By contrast, achondrites do not contain chondrules and many produce ages well below this, some as low as 165 million years[244]. It is thought that the latter either formed much later than chondrites[245], or that they only appear to be much younger due to subsequent changes in their composition[246].

The exceptions to this are achondrites that contain basalt. These are thought to closely resemble terrestrial rocks, because they appear to have crystallised from silicate liquids[247]. As they yield similar ages to chondrites, they are also used to provide evidence of the parent-daughter ratios at the time of the earth's formation.

The most frequently quoted example of the use of meteorites is in relation to the initial ratio for strontium. This element is produced as ^{87}Sr by the decay of rubidium, but strontium also occurs in a non-radiogenic form, ^{86}Sr. Meteorites have been used to locate minerals that contain no rubidium, but which also contain both ^{87}Sr and ^{86}Sr. This has enabled geologists to calculate the initial $^{87}Sr/^{86}Sr$ ratio, which has then been compared with the initial ratios calculated using terrestrial isochrons.

The latter contain higher $^{87}Sr/^{86}Sr$ ratios, which is seen as evidence that they inherited radiogenic ^{87}Sr from older rocks. This is regarded as confirmation of geologists' assumptions about the growth of terrestrial ^{87}Sr. However, further measurements revealed significant differences among the initial $^{87}Sr/^{86}Sr$ ratios of several meteorites[242]. They do not therefore provide an unambiguous answer regarding the $^{87}Sr/^{86}Sr$ ratio at the time of the earth's formation[247].

In addition, the belief that certain meteorites had the same chemical composition as minerals on the earth is an assumption. And if the universe *was* created supernaturally, then there would be no basis for making such an assumption. Furthermore, there is good evidence that the chemical composition of meteorites is quite different from that of the earth.

For example, unexplained isotopic anomalies have been found in chondrites involving common elements, such as oxygen, sulphur, calcium and the noble gases[248]. According to Faure, this is 'unequivocal evidence that the solar nebula was not isotopically homogenous with respect to certain elements'[248], and that the earth's chemical composition may have originally been quite heterogeneous[249]. There is no reason to assume, therefore, that the solar system must have been isotopically homogenous in terms of strontium or any of the other elements used in radiometric dating.

Similar arguments can be made against the use of lunar samples. Whilst the rocks that have been examined have similar strontium ratios to basaltic achondrites[249], significant variations were found in the isotopes used in the lutetium-hafnium[250] and samarium-neodymium[251] dating methods. And, as explained above, it is only an assumption that the moon and earth evolved from a chemically homogenous solar nebula.

Patterns and Cosmic Abundances

Before examining specific dating methods, we need to consider the general arguments that are advanced in support of radiometric dating. To begin with, it is often argued that the virtual absence of isotopes with a half-life of less than 100 million years (except those that are produced by radioactive decay), indicates that the earth is billions of years old. In short, it is argued that isotopes with much shorter half-lives cannot be found, as they have all decayed by now.

There is then the fact that there is 1000 times more argon in the atmosphere than other noble gases. This is understandably attributed to the decay of potassium over billions of years[252]. Similarly, the fact that there is far less ^{235}U than ^{238}U is ascribed to the differences in their half lives, which are 0.7 and 4.47 billion years respectively[253]. The half-life of ^{235}U is much shorter than the age of the earth, so it is argued that most of it has now decayed[253].

There is also a general assumption that the presence of 'daughter' and 'parent' elements in the same mineral means that one must have decayed from the other. This is said to be supported by the fact that the resulting dates generally agree with those produced by different radiometric methods. Furthermore, these dates also agree with those derived from astronomy, geology and palaeontology. And in connection with the latter, rocks nearer the surface generally yield younger dates than those deeper within the earth's crust. This, it is argued, vindicates the belief that rock strata must have been laid down progressively over long periods of time.

Before answering these points, it is worth summarising a few facts. There are 94 naturally occurring elements found on earth, 80 of which are stable. Most elements exist in more than one form, known as 'isotopes', and there are 339 naturally occurring isotopes, of which 269 are stable and 70 are radioactive[254]. However, only radioactive isotopes with half lives of 82 million years or more are found in nature, except those that are continually being produced by radioactive decay[255].

As radioactive isotopes generally decay into a stable isotope of another element, over 74% of those stable isotopes (199/269) are not the product of radioactive decay. So isotopes are commonplace and they are much more likely to exist as a result of processes other than radioactive decay. In addition, isotopes that *are* produced by radioactive decay may also occur naturally. ^{87}Sr, for example, is believed to have existed before any radioactive decay of rubidium had ever taken place.

As regards the abundance of various isotopes, as we have already noted, significant anomalies have been found in meteorites involving various common elements, including oxygen, sulphur, calcium and the noble gases[248]. Anomalies in the oxygen isotope ^{16}O have also been found in terrestrial rocks[256], and the amounts of lithium, beryllium and boron that are found in the solar system also require further research and explanation[257].

Scientists believe that these elements were created by nuclear reactions in supernovas, which ejected their matter into the solar nebula[258]. There are, however, quite a large number of elements whose abundance in the solar system needs to be explained. Some scientists now believe, therefore, that there must have been different types of supernovas, which must have occurred more frequently than once every 100 million years[259].

The fact that scientists have to invoke a theory of continuous supernovas to explain the chemistry of the solar system clearly indicates that the universe does not follow neat and predictable patterns. The relatively high concentration of a particular isotope, therefore, frequently cannot be attributed solely to the process of radioactive decay.

As regards short-lived isotopes, we cannot be sure that these do not exist on earth, as only a tiny percentage of the world has been subjected to detailed chemical analysis. However, God may not have created measurable quantities of these elements, because of the harmful effects of their higher levels of radioactivity. They could clearly have raised toxicity to dangerous levels, as most of these elements can form soluble compounds that could have found their way into water supplies.

As regards argon, minerals in mantle rocks have been found with $^{40}Ar/^{36}Ar$ ratios as high as 100,000[260], which compares with the atmospheric ratio of 295.5[261]. Detailed studies of these argon excesses have led geologists to conclude that there must have been a primordial argon reservoir, which was substantially degassed early on in the earth's history[262]. If there was a reservoir of argon in the earth, however, there is no reason to believe that the amount of argon that exists today is the result of radioactive decay over long periods of time. The earth might simply have been created with an initial surplus of argon.

A similar point arises in relation to helium. The earth's atmosphere is two orders richer in the isotope ^3He than can be attributed to the radioactive production of this element in rock minerals[263]. As with argon, geologists have concluded that the evidence clearly points to some kind of primordial reservoir of helium[264].

As regards uranium, geologists have calculated that there was 3.45 times more ^{238}U than ^{235}U at the time of the earth's formation[265]. To explain this, geologists have again resorted to models involving supernovas. Dickin admits that this involves a large amount of uncertainty[266], and accepts that there are an infinite number of possible models to explain these kinds of phenomena[267]. Once again, therefore, it is clear that radioactive decay alone cannot explain the relative abundance of different isotopes in the earth.

We also know that the presence of 'parent' and 'daughter' elements in the same mineral does not necessarily mean that one decayed from the other. As we have seen, both 'daughter' and 'parent' elements are quite mobile, so the amounts found in particular minerals may be partly due to movement between different rocks and minerals rather than radioactive decay.

In addition, some of the 'daughter' elements may have existed at the time the earth was formed. Rubidium, for example, decays into ^{87}Sr. However, the latter is believed to have been present at the time of the earth's formation, and this initial amount, therefore, has to be excluded when working out the ages of minerals. Consequently, some ^{87}Sr that is found in the same minerals as rubidium, is *not* believed to be the result of radioactive decay.

It is also inaccurate to suggest that radiometric dates usually agree with one another. In fact, most dates are discordant[268]. Similarly, ages based upon geology and fossil data rarely coincide with radiometric dates, a fact that has resulted in 'frequent revisions to the geological time scale'[269]. Furthermore, most radiometric dates come from igneous rocks, which are difficult to define stratigraphically and very rarely contain fossils[270].

We have already examined the astronomical evidence. At best, this only provides us with a lower limit for the age of the universe. In theory, there could be older objects in the universe that we have so far not encountered. In addition, as we have already seen, dates based upon astronomy make a number of key assumptions, including the constancy of the speed of light.

The observation that rocks that are found deeper in the earth generally yield greater ages than those nearer the surface, is also open to doubt. After all, we know that most radiometric dates are discordant[268]. What we do not know is how many of the dates are so discordant that they invert the assumed ages of the rock strata.

To draw meaningful conclusions regarding the extent to which results from different dating methods agree, statisticians would have to be satisfied that the data set was large enough and was both random and representative. They would also need to determine if what geologists define as 'concordant' was justifiable from a statistical point of view. Obviously, no two methods will produce exactly the same result, so we would have to establish just how near they would have to be to justify geologists describing them as 'concordant'.

The fact is that many test results are not published, so the details of many discordant results are simply not known. Unless every single radiometric date is known, it will be impossible for us to determine whether or not the amount of concordance that exists between different dating methods is statistically significant or could simply be a coincidence.

Certainly, whenever 'concordant' results point to unexpected conclusions, geologists are not averse to dismissing them as coincidences. In Alan Dickin's book, *Radiogenic Isotope Geology*, for example, 9 such results are described as pure 'coincidences'[271]. And, as we have already seen, there are also plenty of other examples of coincidences in the form of pseudo-isochrons.

Without further in-depth research, therefore, it is difficult to determine whether or not geologists' conclusions are reasonable. What we can say is that 'concordant' radiometric dates seldom coincide with geological ages, a fact that has led to frequent revisions in the geological time scale[269]. In some cases, this has caused scientists to conclude that older rocks were lying on top of younger strata, even when the geological evidence pointed unambiguously in the opposite direction[272].

Even if it were generally true that rocks nearer to the surface produced younger dates, this would be entirely inconclusive evidence. As we have seen, 'daughter' elements are very mobile and large percentages of these elements are readily lost due to weathering processes. During a universal flood of the kind described in Genesis, these processes would have been extreme and would have affected the rocks nearer to the surface to a far greater extent than those beneath them. This could easily have resulted in a loss of daughter elements from minerals in a way that decreased with depth, creating the impression that those deeper in the earth were significantly older than those nearer to the surface.

One final point is that the rocks and minerals used in radiometric dating are usually obtained from surface outcrops, as most of the mantle is inaccessible[230]. As we have seen, the data is then further refined to exclude supposedly 'discordant' dates. As a result, the data that is used represents an extremely small percentage of the earth. Any generalisations about the isotopic composition of the earth, therefore, must be open to a significant amount of doubt.

Uranium-Lead Methods

General

These methods are based mainly on the decay of two uranium isotopes into two isotopes of lead, namely:

$^{238}U \rightarrow \,^{206}Pb$ (half-life, 4.47 billion years),
$^{235}U \rightarrow \,^{207}Pb$ (half-life, 0.704 billion years).

As we have seen, the major problems with all radiometric dating methods relate to the potential loss or gain of 'parent' and 'daughter' elements, and the accurate determination of their initial ratios. The following outlines how these problems have been addressed in relation to the main uranium-lead dating methods.

Loss and Gain of Parent/Daughter Elements

According to Faure, most minerals lose or gain uranium or lead after crystallisation[273]. Some are believed to have lost 85% of their lead[230], and uranium is so mobile that conventional whole-rock isochrons have now been totally discredited[274]. As a result of these problems, many minerals produce discordant dates[275].

Lead and uranium can become mobile as a result of even superficial weathering or relatively small temperature rises[276]. In addition, ^{235}U can be lost due to fission, i.e. by the atom splitting into two. Although such events are believed to be rare, examples of otherwise unexplained ^{235}U deficiencies do exist, and some of these have been attributed to fission reactions[273].

Two principal methods are used to combat these problems. The first involves modelling and correcting for lead losses using zircon crystals, as these are believed to retain uranium well. The second involves making age calculations based on the ratio of the different lead isotopes. This method is unaffected by lead losses, and losses in uranium cannot distort the results, provided the system remained closed for most of the mineral's 'life'[277]. Attempts have also been made to establish another method using galena (lead sulphide), but this has now been largely discredited as a dating tool[278].

In the case of zircon, lead losses were found to be higher in the outer layers of the crystal, because they suffered more directly from the effects of weathering, temperature increases and radiation damage[279]. Although most zircon dates are discordant, therefore, the removal of these damaged areas substantially reduces the discordancy[280]. Faure, cites a reduction in discordant results from 18.6% to 3.8%[281].

The first point to make here is that this is only a decrease in the number of discordant results. Discrepancies do still exist, and this casts doubt on the age significance of the 'concordant' results. It is also clear that some of the discrepancies are quite wide. Analysis of individual zircon grains, for example, produced ages varying by over 1 billion years[282]!

The other problem with this method is that it assumes there has been no loss of uranium and no gain of radiogenic lead from external sources. The former is clearly possible[283], however, and if lead can be lost from one crystal it should be possible for it to be admitted into the lattice of another[284]. Whilst this method reduces the problems of element mobility, therefore, it clearly cannot rule them out altogether.

As a result of these difficulties, geologists are sometimes unable to obtain what they would regard as reliable ages for zircons[285]. Furthermore, in some cases, the data from zircons are regarded as being 'of high statistical quality', but the apparent dates are then dismissed as inaccurate, because they do not accord with geologists' assumptions about the ages of the rocks[286].

Turning to dating method based on ratio of ^{206}Pb to ^{207}Pb, this assumes that the two isotopes were not separated, as they share very similar chemical properties. Consequently, the loss of lead from a mineral should not alter the ratio of these isotopes, only the *amount* of lead within the mineral.

This method assumes that neither isotope existed at the time of the earth's formation, and that the present ratio is solely the result of the radioactive decay of uranium. Consequently, if the ratio of uranium isotopes is uniform, the ^{207}Pb/^{206}Pb ratio should reflect the amount of time during which uranium decay has taken place. This would also indicate the age of the mineral, unless it had suffered a complete loss of uranium at some stage.

As we have already seen, however, there are exceptions to the 'normal' ratio of ^{235}U/^{238}U, for which a variety of explanations including nuclear fission have been advanced[273]. There is also evidence of unexpected fractionation of uranium isotopes, which can undermine the accuracy of these age calculations. For example, the ratio of ^{234}U to ^{238}U has been shown to vary quite considerably[287].

One issue that might undermine the ^{206}Pb/^{207}Pb dating method are regional variations in these ratios. These might have existed at the time of earth's formation, following which those differences were largely homogenised. A further issue is that ^{235}U and ^{238}U pass through a range of different elements before becoming ^{207}Pb and ^{206}Pb respectively[288]. This branching series of elements provides yet further opportunities for the end products of radioactive decay to be separated from the parent elements.

It is interesting to note here that samples have been found with pure ^{206}Pb[289], and minerals have also been discovered which are enriched in ^{206}Pb but deficient in ^{207}Pb[290]. And in one case the ^{206}Pb/^{207}Pb dating method produced a discrepancy of over 1 billion years[291]. The Pb-Pb data in this example yielded what appeared to be a reliable isochron, but it was assumed that uranium had been lost at some point in the minerals' history, because the age did not agree with the results of another dating method. It is possible, however, that the results of neither of these methods had any age significance.

This leads us on to the other main objection to the ^{206}Pb/^{207}Pb method, which is that it assumes there was no 'radiogenic' lead in the earth at the time of its formation. This is a vital assumption, which, as we will see in the next section, is once again dependent on the interpretation of isochron diagrams.

Initial Parent/Daughter Ratios

As we have seen, the uranium-lead methods try to deal with the problem of lead losses. However, they do not eliminate errorchrons or pseudo-isochrons. They also do not resolve the problems related to meteorites mentioned on pages 152 and 153.

Consequently, uranium-lead methods suffer from the same difficulties as other techniques when it comes to trying to establish the initial parent-daughter ratios. Regarding attempts to establish reliable isochrons using the Pb-Pb method, Faure says:

Before we move on, we must add one word of caution: *not all linear arrays on the Pb-Pb diagram are isochrons.* Linear correlations of isotope ratios of Pb can also result from mixing of leads of different isotope compositions in varying proportions...the linear pattern of Pb ratios imposed by mixing is preserved to haunt us[292].

Faure does not explain how we can distinguish between true and pseudo-isochrons. It seems to be theoretically possible, therefore, that all apparent 'isochrons' might be the result of mixing processes.

Faced with this problem, geologists can only resort to making assumptions based on other scientific beliefs. Knowledge of the initial parent-daughter ratio, however, is absolutely central to radiometric dating. Assuming the initial ratio is tantamount to assuming the ages of the rocks that are supposedly being 'dated'.

Potassium-Argon Method

General

When potassium in the form ^{40}K decays, 11% of it forms an argon isotope as follows:

^{40}K → ^{40}A   (half-life, 11.93 billion years)[293].

The other main isotope of argon is the non-radiogenic ^{36}A. The 'normal' ratio of ^{40}A to ^{36}A in the atmosphere is 295.5[261], and this is used to calculate the amount of ^{40}A that has resulted from atmospheric contamination. The remaining ^{40}A is generally assumed to relate to the decay of the ^{40}K[294], from which the age of the mineral is then calculated.

Loss and Gain of Parent/Daughter Elements

As argon is a gas, it is obviously highly mobile. Consequently, it can be easily lost from or gained by minerals, which creates serious problems for age determinations. The method used to quantify argon losses is similar to the one described above for zircon crystals. Both involve modelling losses of the daughter element, to enable the original isotope ratios to be calculated. In the case of argon, the potassium in the sample must firstly be irradiated with neutrons to convert ^{39}K to ^{39}A. This avoids the need for difficult measurements of the absolute concentrations of potassium and argon, which may not be distributed evenly in the rock sample[295].

As only the ratios of ^{40}A and ^{39}A need to be measured, evidence of argon losses can be determined by heating the sample to successively higher temperatures, thereby releasing argon from the sample in stages. This is known as the 'step heating' technique, and it allows the losses of argon in the outer layers of the mineral to be modelled and quantified[296]. It may also help to understand samples which have inherited argon from other sources[297].

It is assumed that the first gas to be released at the lowest temperatures will come from sites that readily lose argon, and which therefore have relatively low $^{40}A/^{39}A$ ratios. By contrast, gas released at higher temperatures will be from more retentive sites, which will therefore have higher $^{40}A/^{39}A$ ratios. Ultimately, the ratios should reach a plateau, which is believed to indicate the amount of argon that existed before any losses took place. This in turn is considered to provide a reliable indication of the age of the mineral[298].

The problem with this method is that it is of limited value in quantifying argon that has been inherited from other minerals[299], and it provides no information about the loss or gain of potassium. Furthermore, it has produced many meaningless plateaus, some of which point to a decrease in age over most of the gas release[300]. Some samples, including meteorites, have produced no plateaus at all[301], whilst others form perfect but highly discordant plateaus. Faure cites one plateau age, for example, which was 2.5 billion years older than the age produced by the uranium-lead method and 0.7 billion years older than the assumed age of the earth[302].

The reason for these unexpected results is unclear, but they do cast doubt on the method as a reliable dating tool. In addition to these concerns, one known problem is that ^{39}Ar may be relocated by recoil of the nucleus during irradiation. If this happens to a significant extent, the sample will yield a plateau age which exceeds its true age[303]. In addition, it has been suggested by some geologists that plateaus may also result from mixing processes within the mineral itself[304].

Initial Parent/Daughter Ratios

The amount of argon inherited by a mineral is generally calculated from isochron diagrams. The problem with this method is that minerals in a rock sample may have had different initial $^{40}A/^{36}A$ ratios because of variable atmospheric contamination[305]. In addition, spurious isochrons may result from the mixing of minerals that come from different sources or which have different closing temperatures[306]. In some cases, the step-heating method has been used to try to determine the amount of inherited or excess argon. This, however, is not a reliable method for the reasons mentioned above, and in the example cited by Faure it was simply impossible to produce any kind of 'geologically meaningful result'[307].

Rubidium-Strontium Method

General

When rubidium in the form of ^{87}Rb decays, it produces an isotope of strontium as follows:

$^{87}Rb \rightarrow ^{87}Sr$

The standard half-life is 48.8 billion years, but there is still a fair amount of uncertainty about this. According to Dickin, for example, it is only possible to reconcile isochron calculations involving meteorites by assuming a half-life of 49.4 billion years[308]. The standard half-life may therefore have to be revised in the future.

Loss and Gain of Parent/Daughter Elements

Even modest temperature increases of between 100°c and 200°c can have a drastic effect on the parent-daughter relationship, without there being any evidence that the sample has been affected by metamorphism[309]. In addition, strontium is susceptible to mobilisation by fluids[310], and changes in the isotope ratios can also result from weathering, transport and the deposition of sediment[311].

In practice, where there is evidence that changes have taken place, it is usually assumed that these only involved the loss of radiogenic ^{87}Sr. This is an oversimplification, however, as the concentration of rubidium and other isotopes of strontium may well have been affected also. Faure therefore concludes that where rocks 'were chemically altered so that rubidium and/or strontium were either added or lost at any time after formation, they cannot be dated using the Rb-Sr method'[312].

Another important observation is the fact that the Rb-Sr ratios vary considerably throughout the earth's mantle[313]. In view of the long half-life of rubidium, it has been concluded that these heterogeneities must have existed for long periods of time[314]. This raises a serious question: how can the mantle be heterogeneous when it has been in continuous convective motion for billions of years, as required by the theory of plate tectonics and sea-floor spreading? According to Faure, 'the explanation to this paradox has not yet been given'[315]. One possible explanation, however, is that the earth has only been in continuous convective motion for a relatively short period of time and is not therefore as old as scientists assume.

Initial Parent/Daughter Ratios

As we have already seen, neither terrestrial isochrons nor studies of meteorites provide an unambiguous answer regarding the earth's initial ratio of ^{87}Sr/^{86}Sr[247]. The two general problems that arise from this fact are that: (a) the ratios of these isotopes may have varied from rock to rock; and, (b) subsequent disturbances may mean that it is now completely impossible to construct reliable isochrons.

Unexplained variations in meteorites have been found, which cast doubt on the reliability of their ages and the initial ^{87}Sr/^{86}Sr ratios derived from them[316]. Significant differences in ^{87}Sr/^{86}Sr ratios have also been found in terrestrial rocks. This includes volcanic rocks[317], together with rocks in the mantle[318], among ocean islands and along mid-ocean ridges[319].

Fluctuations in the $^{87}Sr/^{86}Sr$ ratio of the ocean also remain largely unexplained[320], and frequently there is no pattern to suggest that variations in the ratios are age related. One study of rocks in the Andes revealed that the $^{87}Sr/^{86}Sr$ ratio increased with decreasing age instead of vice versa[317], and measurements to gauge the ratios in seawater in the past have produced a similarly inverted picture[321]. In addition, research by Kistler and Peterman in California concluded that 'the initial ratios are independent of the age of the rocks and are controlled primarily by geography'[322].

As mentioned above, isochrons can produce straight-line graphs, which suggest that they are reliable indicators of age. These graphs may have no age significance, however, and might instead be simply the result of quite common geological mixing processes. The Rb-Sr method is no exception to this general observation[323].

The main problem with isochrons involving Rb and Sr is the evidence of disturbance in numerous environments, or what geologists call 'open-system behaviour'. According to Dickin, the problem is so widespread that it has 'discredited the Rb-Sr isochron method as a dating tool for igneous crystallisation'[324]. He also concludes that it is not a reliable method for dating shale and glauconite in sedimentary rocks[325], where, of course, most fossils are to be found.

Carbon Dating

When neutrons in the upper atmosphere collide with nitrogen in the form ^{14}N they produce carbon-14, also known as radiocarbon. This has a half-life of about 5,730 years and can be used to date objects up to 100,000 years old, although it may in practice be limited to about 30,000 years[326].

The significance of ^{14}C is that it is incorporated into carbon dioxide, which rapidly mixes throughout the atmosphere where it then stays at a fairly constant level. From there, it is absorbed by plants and animals, whose tissues maintain a constant level of ^{14}C whilst they are still alive. When the plant or animal dies, it stops absorbing ^{14}C from the atmosphere. And if the level of ^{14}C in living tissue is known, the ^{14}C in the dead tissue can be used to calculate the time that has elapsed since the plant or animal's death[326].

The main assumptions[327] required by the carbon dating method are:

(a) that the initial level of ^{14}C activity is a constant, which is independent of time, geography and species; and,

(b) that the samples used have not been contaminated by any radioactive impurities or other sources of ^{14}C.

There are also two main factors that affect the production of ^{14}C: the intensity of the sun's cosmic rays and the effects of the earth's magnetic field. The latter is, of course, much stronger at the poles, but this does not lead to geographical variations in ^{14}C, because of the rapid mixing of gasses that occurs in the earth's atmosphere[328]. However, the intensity of cosmic rays and the earth's magnetic field, are believed to have varied significantly in the past[328], and this can 'introduce serious errors into radiocarbon dates'[329].

The other factors that can affect radiocarbon dates are[330]:

- changes in the earth's carbon reservoirs due to climactic variations;
- increased production of non-radioactive carbon during the industrial revolution;
- the production of ^{14}C by nuclear tests and explosions; and,
- the fractionation of carbon isotopes in nature.

Taking these factors into account, it is estimated that the radiocarbon content of the atmosphere has varied by more than 20% since the nineteenth century[331]. Other methods have therefore been developed to enable scientists to model these variations and make suitable adjustments when performing age calculations.

The principal method that has been used in conjunction with carbon dating is known as dendrochronology. This technique involves independently checking the ages of trees from their growth rings, and then comparing these dates with the radiocarbon 'ages'. Although the growth rings of the oldest living tree only indicate an age of around 5,000 years, by matching growth rings with samples from dead and fossilised trees, it has been possible to extend the dendrochronological record as far back as 6,700 BC[332].

There are, however, a number of problems with this method. To begin with, matches have to be made between trees from areas with the same weather pattern so that they have similar growth variations[333]. Secondly, some trees miss growth rings altogether. For example, the widespread alder can have up to 45% of its annual rings missing[333].

The most serious problem, however, is the fact that a comparison with the radiocarbon dates produces a convoluted curve with many wiggles in it. As a result, a single radiocarbon date may well correspond to more than one dendrochronological age[334]. Consequently, if some of the older 'wiggles' have been matched incorrectly, it might be possible to reconcile the results with the biblical time scale of approximately 4,000 BC.

One of the methods that is used to extend the calibration of carbon dating involves couplets of strata known as varves. These are common in glacial lakes and are believed to be produced by seasonal climatic changes. The first layer is formed when summer melt-waters bring an influx of silt into the lake. This is followed later by winter freezing, which only allows finer clay particles and organic material to settle out. This results in the formation of the second layer[335]. Dickin concludes, however, that calibrations involving varves and ice cores are not very accurate, as they involve long interpolations between dated points, which are based upon estimated rates of sedimentation or precipitation[333].

Another method used to correct errors in radiocarbon dates was developed in 1990 and involves comparisons with ages calculated from the decay of uranium. According to Dickin, experiments involving corals produced results with 'good agreement' for samples believed to be less than 10,000 years old. For samples believed to be older than this, however, the results were 'more scattered', although this discordance was reduced after the experimental procedures were improved[333].

As regards the first set of results, the relative concordance did nevertheless require 400-year age corrections to be made[333]. The reason for this is that the ^{14}C content of carbonates in corals etc. is generally higher than that of carbon dioxide in the atmosphere by a factor of around 1.05. This varies in different localities, though, particularly between marine and freshwater environments[336]. As a result, many discordant radiocarbon dates have been produced, some of which report differences of several thousand years compared with their assumed ages[337].

It has also been suggested that climatic effects could have had a significant impact on radiocarbon dates, as this would have involved the release of non-radiogenic carbon into the atmosphere. This would have increased the ratio of ^{12}C to ^{14}C, giving the impression that a sample was much older than it was. There is evidence that this could have occurred during major climatic re-adjustments, such as at the end of an ice age[333,337]. So a worldwide flood, like the one described in Genesis, would certainly have had a dramatic effect on the % of radiocarbon. And this would certainly have made organic material appear much older than it was for a long period of time.

Whitcomb and Morris advanced another explanation for the fact that some ^{14}C dates exceed the biblical timescale by thousands of years. They point out that Genesis 1:6-8 tells us that on the second day God created the sky to separate the waters on the earth from those above it. They argue that this indicates there was a water canopy in the form of a vapour blanket in the lower atmosphere, which could have reduced the effect of cosmic rays and hence the amount of ^{14}C being formed in the atmosphere. In support of this argument, they point out that water vapour weighs only 0.622 times as much as dry air for the same conditions[338].

Whitcomb and Morris contend that this water canopy would explain the tropical conditions of the Garden of Eden and the huge amount of water released during the Flood. They argue that this would also explain why the tissues of animals and plants living before the Flood had a much lower ^{14}C content, making their radiocarbon ages appear much older than they were. In addition, they suggest that coal and oil were formed by the Flood, and point out that fossil fuels contain no trace of ^{14}C[339].

It might be argued that there is no description of a 'water canopy' in the Bible. The 'water above' could simply be an allusion to clouds, as in Proverbs 8:22-29, which refers to the beginning of creation, when God 'established the clouds' (verse 28). The word for clouds in Proverbs can also mean 'dust' or 'mist'[340], but there is no evidence of it being used in the Bible to mean a water canopy.

Although Genesis provides no description of the 'water canopy', it also does not say that these 'waters' were 'clouds'. Clouds are not mentioned until Genesis 9:13. Moreover, Genesis 1:7 says that these 'waters' were '*above* the sky'. If they were clouds, one would expect it to say that they were '*in* the sky'.

The idea of a canopy of water vapour, therefore, follows the literal meaning of Genesis. It also explains various aspects of the biblical account of creation and the Flood. And together with the Flood, it explains the ^{14}C evidence at the same time.

Fission Tracks

Uranium in the form ^{238}U spontaneously divides into two product nuclides. When this occurs, a large amount of energy is released and the nuclides travel in opposite directions, leaving a trail of damage known as a fission track[341]. As the rate of fission is believed to be a constant, the age of the mineral can be estimated from the density of the fission tracks[342].

There is, however, some uncertainty about the decay constant of ^{238}U[343]. To overcome this, dates produced by the fission track method are calibrated against other radiometric dating techniques[344]. As has been shown, however, there are doubts about the accuracy of these methods as well.

Another problem is that fission tracks fade when they are exposed to elevated temperatures[345]. Methods have therefore been devised to calculate a mineral's thermal history, so that adjustments can be made. Even with these methods, however, results can vary by as much as 20%[346], and various further assumptions have to be made to reconcile the discordant results[345].

The main problem with the method is that the density of the fission tracks is also related to the concentration of uranium[342]. As we have seen, however, uranium is a very mobile element[274]. A mineral might therefore have previously contained a high concentration of uranium, during which time a large number of fission tracks were formed. It is impossible to say with certainty, therefore, whether a high density of fission tracks is attributable to a low concentration of uranium over a long period of time, or a high concentration of uranium over a relatively short period of time.

As we have seen, to reconcile geological dates with the biblical timescale, we might have to assume that the uranium in some of the minerals had fallen by as much as 750,000 times (4.5 billion/ 6,000 years) or by 99.99%. In the case of fission tracks, however, it is not necessary to assume this, as the effects of temperature rises mean that the method is mainly used to date 'relatively young samples'[347]. There is, however, nothing to prove that those minerals could not have lost such a substantial amount of their uranium content. As indicated earlier, some uranium-bearing minerals are believed to have lost 85% of their lead as a result of weathering[230], and uranium is such a mobile element that conventional isochrons have been totally discredited[274].

Pleochroic Haloes

This method is based on the fact that when certain radioactive elements decay, they emit alpha particles. These particles create visible damage to some minerals by creating an area of discolouration in the form of a halo; hence the name.

Experiments have therefore been conducted to establish if there is a measurable link between the size of the alpha dose and the degree of discolouration. This has been done by irradiating minerals with a known dose of alpha particles and then observing the intensity of the resulting haloes[348].

As with fission tracks, however, pleochroic haloes are partially erased by heating during metamorphism. It is also difficult to measure the alpha dose and correlate this with the discolouration in the mineral[348]. The main problem, however, is that it is necessary to assume that the concentration of radionuclides emitting the alpha particles has not altered since the mineral formed, except by radioactive decay. As we have already seen, however, there are good reasons for believing that this last assumption is not a valid one. The method has in any event now been abandoned in favour of other isotopic dating techniques[348].

Thermoluminescence

When radiation interacts with certain solids, some of the excited electrons become trapped in the crystal lattice. The energy the electrons have absorbed is not then released until the sample is heated, when it is liberated in the form of light or thermoluminescence.

In this dating technique the sample is heated at increasing temperatures and the light output is recorded to produce a 'glow curve'. The area under this curve reflects the amount of radiation the sample has absorbed since it was last heated to about 450°C.

The annual radiation dose is calculated by measuring the concentrations of radioactive materials, or by irradiating the sample and measuring the resulting thermoluminescence[349]. Once the annual radiation dose is known, the number of years over which the sample was exposed to these radiation levels can be calculated.

As with dating techniques based on fission tracks and pleochroic haloes, however, this method cannot provide any evidence of the absolute age of a rock; it only tells us the time that has apparently elapsed since the sample cooled below a certain temperature. Thermoluminescence has not, therefore, been able to seriously compete with the various isotopic methods mentioned above, and it is also mainly used to date geologically young rock samples[349].

Some of the practical problems with this method have been addressed by measuring what is known as the electron spin resonance (ESR). This process detects the amount of microwave radiation that electrons have absorbed by the use of strong magnetic fields, thereby avoiding some of the sample preparation problems that are associated with thermoluminescence[349].

In both methods, however, it is assumed that the concentrations of radioactive elements have only been altered by radioactive decay. As we have seen, however, there is plenty of evidence that this is not a reliable assumption, as radioactive elements and their daughters can be very mobile.

Conclusion

As we have seen, radiometric dating techniques require us to make some very basic assumptions. The two main assumptions concern the initial ratios of parent and daughter elements in the minerals being dated, and secondly the mobility of those elements after the minerals have formed.

We have also seen that most of the ages produced by different dating methods are discordant[268]. Geologists' arguments therefore rest on whether the degree of concordance is statistically significant enough or if it is simply a coincidence. To date, no attempt appears to have been made to justify radiometric dates statistically.

What is also clear, however, is that the movements of the earth's layers and the formation of a large number of different types of rock, is a very complicated subject. If scientists cannot model the atmosphere to reliably predict the weather a few days in advance, it is hard to accept that they can accurately model and calibrate what the structure of the earth's minerals would have been billions or even millions of years ago.

2.3.3. Geology

General

The three principal methods for dating rocks are based upon radioisotopes and the evidence provided by palaeontology and palaeomagnetism[350]. The first of these was considered at 2.3.2., and this remains the most important method for dating rocks. However, it relies upon some basic assumptions and it generates a significant number of anomalous results. In addition, its application is generally limited to igneous and metamorphic rocks, which means that it cannot generally be used to directly date sedimentary rocks, which contain the vast majority of fossils.

The second dating method is considered in section 2.3.5. For the present, the most important point to note is that this method requires us to assume that life on earth evolved over very long periods of time. Dating rocks by this method is something of a circular process, therefore, as we have to *assume* the existence of the very long periods of geological time, solely because the Theory of Evolution requires us to do so.

As the first two dating methods are considered elsewhere, a large part of this section focuses on the third method, namely palaeomagnetism. In addition, there is also some discussion of another dating method called astrochronology, which has grown in significance since the 1990s. The latter is based upon rock formation patterns, which are believed to be linked to regular changes in the earth's position in relation to the sun.

This section also looks at some specific rock formations, the very structure of which is said to be incompatible with the biblical account of creation and the Flood. This is then followed by a more detailed consideration of particular rock formations, varves, which were briefly discussed on page 169 in relation to carbon dating.

The discussion concludes by considering the philosophical issues raised by the opposing arguments of geologists and creationists. In particular, we take a closer look at the problems that arise from the view that objects can be reliably dated on the basis of current rates of change, a philosophy known as 'uniformitarianism'.

Palaeomagnetism

Palaeomagnetism is the study of the earth's magnetic field, as it is preserved in various minerals. These studies indicate that geomagnetism has varied substantially through time, both in its intensity and direction.

These changes appear to be fairly random in nature[351], however, and many are believed to have been short-lived[352]. Consequently, there is no natural cycle to geomagnetic fluctuations to enable us to date individual changes directly. A further problem is that it is often unclear if these geomagnetic changes were local in nature or if they affected the whole globe[353]. This makes it very difficult, if not impossible, to correlate geomagnetic changes across different geographical areas.

Because of these problems, changes in the earth's magnetic field are calibrated by reference to other methods, such as radiometric dating and palaeontology[354]. Only when this is done, can geologists date other sedimentary rocks that have the same geomagnetic 'signature'.

In addition, the geomagnetic time scale can only be used to date rocks up to 180 million years old. In addition, it has only been possible to extend it this far back by assuming a constant rate of seafloor expansion over the last 80 million years[355]. Extending the timescale further would require a painstaking analysis of overlapping sections of rock[356], which could lead to the kinds of identification problems encountered by dendrochronology (see pages 98 and 169). It is also worth noting here that some of the earlier palaeomagnetic extrapolations have already been dismissed as spurious[357].

The most important problem with palaeomagnetism, however, is that it is only as good as the supporting methods that are used to date the magnetic minerals in the first place. Radiometric dating requires us to make some basic assumptions and, even then, it still results in some significant anomalies (see section 2.3.2. above). As we will see, the other traditional methods for dating rocks suffer from these same difficulties.

Astrochronology

This method is based upon geological features, which are thought to have been caused by changes in the relative positions of the sun and earth. Some believe this method may be capable of dating rocks up to tens of millions of years old[358]. At present, however, it is limited to formations that are thought to be no more than several million years old[358]. Consequently, astrochronology can only be used to check a very small part of the 4.5 billion geological timescale.

The most well-known astrochronological method is based upon the theories of Milutin Milankovitch (1879 to 1958). Milankovitch was a Serbian mathematician, who undertook numerous calculations of the amount of insolation (solar radiation energy) that the earth should have received at various latitudes. He then compared these predictions with the ice advances and retreats that were believed to have taken place over the last 600,000 years.

Milankovitch's calculations were based upon the three main cycles involving changes in the position of the sun and the earth, namely:

(a) eccentricity – the shape of the earth's orbit around the sun;

(b) obliquity – the extent of the earth's tilt on its axis; and

(c) precession – the gyroscopic motion of the earth on its axis.

Of these, (a) has been calculated to have a cycle of roughly 100,000 years, whilst the cycles of (b) and (c) are about 41,000 and 26,000 years respectively.

Milankovitch's theories were largely ignored for 50 years. Then, in 1976, a study appeared to confirm that his calculations were correct. Since then, however, a number of unresolved problems have arisen with Milankovitch's theories. In particular, geologists are still unclear why, based on their calculations[359] -

- 800,000 years ago the glacial cycle changed from 41,000 to 100,000 years, even though the latter is the weakest component of the Milankovitch cycle in terms of its impact on the climate; and,

- the northern and southern hemispheres enter ice ages at basically the same time, when Milankovitch's calculations predict that ice ages should always begin in the northern hemisphere.

There have also been problems in trying to reconcile calculations based upon astrochronology and those provided by traditional dating methods. For example, an update of the palaeomagnetic time scales was published in 2004, which was calibrated using astrochronological data. However, the results implied very sharp changes in the rates of seafloor spreading, which contradicted dates based on other methodologies. It is likely, therefore, that future calibrations using astrochronology will only be undertaken in partnership with other methods, such as radiometric dating[360].

Particular Structures

Some geologists argue that floods always result in two distinctive features[361]. The first arises from the fast-water stage, which is said to produce coarse-grained and poorly sorted deposits of sand, gravel and boulders. The second is a single layer of mud, which should be left once the flood waters have receded. As we do not find these features in the same position throughout the world, some argue that a worldwide flood could not have taken place at any point in the earth's history.

For rock strata to occur in exactly the same relative positions in different areas of the globe, we would have to assume that those areas did not have different rock strata when the world was formed. For the reasons mentioned in the section on uniformitarianism below, however, this is not an assumption that is required by the biblical account of creation.

Furthermore, this argument does not take account of possible geographical differences in the layers of rock that were laid down during the 1,655 years between the creation of the world and the Flood. During this period of time, some of those rock strata may have been eroded in some parts of the world but not in others, creating further differences in the geological landscape.

It is also worth remembering that the Flood was accompanied by the bursting forth of 'all the fountains of the great deep', something which alone could have triggered some significant and widespread geological changes as well as regional differences. These changes might have included a sharp increase in tectonic plate movements, and related changes such as mountain building. Given all of these factors, it would not be surprising if the geological evidence of a worldwide flood was not easy for us to discern 4,350 years later.

As regards the second distinctive feature mentioned above, it is not clear why a flood must always result in a layer of mud. Mud is a mixture of clay and silt. Clay is made up mainly of silica and alumina, and silt consists of particles with diameters of roughly between 0.002 and 0.05 millimetres. Why could the final layer of a flood not be composed of different material, reflecting the nature of the particles taken up by the flood waters? After all, as the section below on varves indicates, floods can produce several different layers of rock within a short space of time.

Even if a single layer of mud was formed at the time of the Flood, it does not follow that this layer must have been preserved entirely intact right up to the present day. In some regions, this layer may have been eroded; in others, it might have been partly destroyed or perhaps distorted beyond recognition by the various geological changes mentioned above.

Furthermore, one cannot necessarily apply the laws of nature to the Flood, as both the arrival and the removal of the floodwaters were clearly acts of God. In relation to the removal of the floodwaters, Genesis 8:1 says that God caused the waters to recede by sending 'a wind' to pass over the earth. As pointed out on page 116, this could not have been a natural 'wind', as this would only have speeded up the water currents, perhaps causing some of the water to evaporate. Whatever mechanism was involved, the supernatural manner in which the flood waters were removed makes it impossible to draw any firm conclusions about the kinds of deposits that would have remained after the flood waters had subsided.

A commonly cited source of evidence against what is termed 'Flood geology' is the Grand Canyon. Here, thousands of feet of rock strata are exposed, allowing geologists to study many different layers of rock without the need for any form of excavation.

Various features of the rock strata are said to be at variance with the biblical account. Firstly, there are hundreds of mud cracks, which are sometimes stacked in long sequences. These, it is argued, show that each layer of the rock must have dried and cracked before the next layer was deposited[361]. From this, it is inferred that they could not have been laid down by a single flood.

The first point to be made here is that at least some of these formations could have been laid down during the 1,655 years before the Flood. It is also possible that the mud cracks, or at least some of them, could have occurred as a result of the Flood. Underwater mud cracks, known as 'syneresis cracks', are often confused with subaeriel cracks, and are usually due to shrinkage following changes in factors such as salinity[362].

It has also been suggested that some mud cracks are caused by strong earthquakes. It is believed that the resulting increases in ground pressure can cause clay to lose water. This can then liquefy layers of sand and silt in between the layers of mud, causing the sand and silt to be injected into the resulting mud cracks[362].

If earthquakes could have affected layers of mud in this way, it seems possible that other environmental changes could have had a similar effect. For example, pressure is proportionate to temperature, so a significant increase in the temperature of a land mass could have caused clay formed at lower temperatures to crack at lower levels as well as at the surface. The resulting de-watering of the clay might then have liquefied the layers of silt and sand, resulting in similar formations to those mentioned above.

A further feature that is often mentioned in this context are the

Cardenas lava flows of the Grand Canyon. Here, it is argued that the molten rocks could not have erupted into flood waters, as this would have resulted in blobs of igneous rock known as 'pillow lavas'. Instead, the Cardenas lavas show signs of having erupted onto dry land, following which they appear to have cooled and then been eroded before the next sequence of rocks was deposited[361].

It is also pointed out that all of these rock strata are tilted on their sides and were apparently eroded before the other strata of the Grand Canyon were deposited on top of them. These features, it is argued, are inexplicable in terms of a worldwide flood, which would have produced a soft soupy layer of sediments, showing obvious slump folds where those strata were tilted on their sides[363].

However, some of these rock strata could have been formed when the earth was created; others might have been laid down before or during the Flood. In addition, a substantial amount of new rock formations could have been created after the Flood as a result of the huge geological changes referred to above.

There is no way, therefore, in which one can prove which rock layers existed when the world was formed. Without radiometric dating, geologists cannot even determine if particular rock strata were laid down over thousands, millions or billions of years[364].

Varves

One set of formations that *are* dated independently of radiometry, however, are varves. These structures consist of two layers of rock, which are believed to be the result of seasonal changes in the climate. Varves are therefore common in glacial lakes, where the summer melt-water brings an influx of silt, but winter freezing only allows the very finest particles to settle out from the suspension.

Where a formation consists entirely of annual varves, its age may be calculated by simply counting the 'annual' couplets. In larger structures the age may be estimated on the basis of the size of the formation and the average width of the couplets. Using these techniques, the 2000 foot high Castile Formation in Delaware, for example, has been calculated to be about 300,000 years old[365].

However, it is usually very difficult to prove that these couplets are *annual* deposits, particularly where episodic floods may have re-deposited old shoreline sediments[366]. It is also known that varves can be formed over much shorter periods of time than a year. In some cases, they may be the result of lunar rather than annual cycles[367]; in others, they may accumulate over a matter of days[368].

It is also accepted that varves can be formed in a whole range of different contexts, including proglacial, lacustrine and marine environments[369,370]. As a result, varves can assume a large variety of forms, with a wide range of differences in terms of structure, thickness, composition and colour[370].

The basic requirement for the formation of a varve is the existence of suspended matter (SM) within a column of water[370]. The SM may come from numerous sources, such as rivers, the air, chemical precipitation, bio-production, re-suspension or 'upwelling', e.g. subaqueous springs[371]. Differences in the density must then occur to stratify the water column. These differences in density can arise in a number of ways, including variations in temperature, salt levels and the concentration of the SM itself[371].

It seems likely that these conditions would have existed during the Flood. The water would probably have been stratified, as it came from various sources, namely the rain, the sea and the 'fountains of the great deep'. It is also likely that the water would have varied significantly in terms of its salinity and chemical composition.

In addition we know that turbidity currents can produce graded beds when inflowing rivers introduce an influx of sediment during flooding[372]. In Lake Walensee, for example, measurements have shown that more than two 'varves' a year can be produced by turbidity underflows alone, and in some cases the number of varves can be more than twice this amount[373]. Furthermore, in the Arkport Dam in New York, 2.5 to 17.8 cm of sediment were deposited during a two-week period of local flooding. And in many of these areas three layers were produced that were similar in appearance to glacial varves[374].

It has also been suggested that strong winds and storms can form varves in short periods of time, by suspending and winnowing sediment into different layers based on the different settling rates of the particles. It is thought that a single storm could produce numerous layers in this manner, providing the wind-driven turbulence abated slowly[375].

As varves can be produced in quite a wide variety of different ways, it is now accepted that numerous formations may have been incorrectly described as annual varves. These include, for example, sediment layers from Shilak Lake, Alaska, which are now believed to have been formed by depositional events. In addition, certain Precambrian laminites in Australia are now thought to be the result of tidal rather than annual cycles[367].

Despite the difficulties in determining how particular varves were formed, it is believed that some rock formation layers could not have been created by a single flood. For example, in Kentucky the Ordovician rocks of the Cincinnati Arch contain hundreds of finely laminated layers of shale and limestone, each of which is full of delicate fossils of marine organisms in their life positions. It is argued that these organisms have clearly not been disturbed by flood waters, and the rock formations could not therefore have been deposited by Noah's Flood[376].

However, this evidence is far from conclusive. Palaeontologists believe that fossilisation generally occurs when an organism is buried almost *immediately* after death[377]. They also acknowledge that marine environments offer the best potential for fossilisation[377]. In addition, the fact that these aquatic organisms are in their life positions clearly suggests that they died suddenly before being buried rapidly. They must therefore have been 'disturbed', and disturbed by something that occurred fairly suddenly.

We have also seen how floods can result in the creation of many finely laminated layers that closely resemble varves. So there seems to be no reason why these particular laminates could not have been caused by a flood or by the steady, but gradual abatement of flood waters.

A further possibility is that these layers were formed before the Flood. It is worth remembering that according to the Bible, there was about 1,655 years of geological history before the Flood occurred. Consequently, there appears to have been plenty of time in which hundreds of laminated layers could have been formed.

Uniformitarianism

It is generally assumed that the sedimentary environments of today also existed in the past[378]. Another widespread assumption is that sedimentary rocks have accumulated over a very long period of time at the current rates of deposition. If these assumptions are correct, then it would clearly be possible to estimate the age of sedimentary rocks with a reasonable degree of accuracy.

However, we know from the stratigraphic record that some conditions that existed in the past have no modern counterparts[378], such as the circumstances that led to the formation of massive coal seams and huge oil wells. We also know that sedimentary rock can be formed in a matter of minutes[379], and that water is by far the most significant mechanism for the transportation of those sedimentary materials[380]. A worldwide flood that lasted more than a year could therefore quite conceivably have resulted in large amounts of new rock strata being formed.

Even if the Flood does not account for most of the rock formations we see today, the evidence of geology alone would still be inconclusive. The reason for this is that if the world was created in a completed state, then both the earth and the life upon it would always appear to be much older than they actually were.

For example, if the first trees God created were normal mature trees, then they would have contained annual growth rings. These might 'tell' a scientist that the tree was hundreds of years old, despite the fact that it had only been created minutes earlier. Similarly, God might have created many different types and layers of rock strata.

This argument cannot of course be extended to strata that contain fossils, particularly where those life forms do not exist today. It would clearly be pointless and misleading for God to create fossils of animals that never existed. However, many rocks do not contain fossils, so this is usually not an issue.

If the world was created with many different layers of rock strata, therefore, age calculations based on the current rates of sedimentation would be completely erroneous. The problem of applying scientific methods in these circumstances is well illustrated by the following passage taken from an article by R.G. Korthals[381]:

And now let us imagine that Adam was a scientist interested in determining the age of the earth. He starts his research on the 8th day after creation, in and around the Garden of Eden. He looks at himself and Eve, and realizing that they are both mature individuals, states that they and the earth are at least 20 years old. He cuts down a tree in order to build a fire, and counts the growth rings. According to this, the earth is at least 139 years old. He and Eve stroll down to the river banks, where he notices the deep channel cut by the stream. By carefully measuring the erosion rate, he estimates and concludes that 5,000 years have gone by since the stream started as a tiny trickle. They pause and marvel at the magnificent mountains in the distance, watching the sun as it slowly sinks beneath the peaks. He knows the internal pressures within the earth are slowly pushing these mountains higher, and, using the present established rate, he calculates that the mountain range is at least 1.5 billion years old. The next day they explore a canyon started 750,000 years ago by a river and marvel at the layers of rock, some formed almost 3 billion years in the past, according to his geologic time scale, which is based upon the rock formation phenomena...And so Adam, the scientist, determines the age of the world on which he is living – a world which according to his reasoning, observations, calculations, and assumptions, is at least 3 billion years old – yet it is a world which was created just 8 days ago.

The central problem with using geology to challenge the biblical account of creation, therefore, is that it seeks to explain phenomena entirely in terms of the laws of nature. Consequently, it begins by assuming that miracles cannot occur or at least that there is no evidence that they have ever taken place. As a result, geology can only ever tell us how old the world would have looked if there had been no miracles to affect its apparent age. Geology cannot therefore prove that God did not create the world miraculously in the recent past; this is a premise that science simply assumes. And one cannot prove that something is true by merely assuming that this is the case.

Equally, of course, one cannot disprove scientists' conclusions by asserting that they are at variance with the Bible. We must also *know* that the scriptures are true, a subject that we will revisit in chapter 6. The purpose of *this* chapter is simply to show that, although the claims of science might be plausible, they nevertheless require us to make a number of key assumptions, which may or may not be true.

In the case of geology, the central assumption is that the present is always the key to the past. As we have seen, however, it is untenable to believe that the same conditions existed throughout earth's history. Scientists believe that on several occasions a huge amount of life on earth was wiped from the face of the planet over short periods of time. Both scientists and creationists, therefore, believe that major catastrophes and extinctions occurred in the past, they only differ in terms of when they believe they took place.

2.3.4. Biology

Overview

Before we can consider the specific arguments in any detail, we need to set out the salient beliefs and contentions of both the biblical account of creation and the Theory of Evolution. This will provide the necessary background to the detailed arguments; it will also clarify several popular misconceptions.

The Biblical Account

During days three to six of creation God made all kinds of creatures of the land, sea and air, telling them to 'be fruitful and multiply' (Genesis 1:22, 28). Originally, there was no death in the world (Romans 5:12) and man and creatures of land and air had an entirely herbivorous diet (Genesis 1:30).

Man's disobedience, however, resulted in a number of immediate physical changes. Decay and death entered the world (Romans 5:12; 8:21-23), the serpent and its descendants were condemned to move along on their bellies, and women were told that they would endure a lot more pain in childbirth (Genesis 3:15,16).

By the time of Noah, the degeneration in man and the animal kingdom had clearly gone much further. All flesh was now so 'corrupt' that both man and beast had to be destroyed (Genesis 6:13). The nature of this corruption is not explained. However, the earth is said to have been 'full of violence' (Genesis 6:12), indicating that animals may have begun to prey on one another.

To preserve a remnant, God selected pairs of each 'kind' of bird and land animal to survive. These creatures came to Noah miraculously and his ark saved them from the Flood (Genesis 6:20, 7:15). Outside the ark, all birds and all land animals that breathed through their nostrils perished (Genesis 7:21, 22). After the Flood, therefore, the surviving animals had to repopulate the earth. The relationship between man and animals, however, had now altered dramatically. The 'fear and dread' of man fell upon all creatures, and man was given power over the whole animal kingdom and was also allowed to take animals for food (Genesis 9:1-3).

The first point to make here is that the Bible does not say that the number of species God created remained unchanged. Nor does it say that organisms would not be affected by natural selection. What these passages do tell us, though, is that sudden and dramatic changes occurred in man and animals alike. They went from being 'good' to corrupt, and from being immortal to mortal.

In addition, there were some very specific biological changes. Some of the animals appear to have changed from being herbivores to carnivores; women's bodies and/or those of their children changed in a way that significantly increased a woman's pain in childbirth; snakes apparently lost their limbs, and the earth began to produce thorns and thistles (Genesis 3:14-18).

It is interesting to note here that snake fossils have been found with limbs and fully functioning hip bones, and some living snakes, such as boids, still retain vestiges of hind limbs and a pelvis. Biologists are unsure why snakes lost their legs or how they evolved, as their skeleton is so specialised that it is hard to compare with that of any other reptiles[382]. The Bible, however, provides a very clear answer to these questions. It also explains the sudden disappearance of many species, including the dinosaurs, and why other species survived. This was not the accident of natural selection; it was a deliberate act of supernatural deselection.

As we will see in the next section, abrupt changes in the fossil record have led palaeontologists to believe that there must have been a large number of mass extinctions. In the case of the dinosaurs, the most popular explanation is that a huge meteorite hit the earth 65 million years ago. However, some scientists remain unconvinced by this hypothesis, as it fails to explain why many species that should have perished did not do so[383].

The Bible not only explains this mass extinction, but also how some animals survived what might otherwise appear to be a rather arbitrary basis of selection. It also explains the dramatic changes in the biology of animals after the Fall. These changes were not the natural result of genetic modification, but the supernatural consequences of man's disobedience.

Following the Flood, man was told to be fruitful and to multiply on the earth (Genesis 9:7). To prevent people from becoming too powerful, however, God confused man's speech by creating different languages and scattering them across the earth (Genesis 11:6-8). From these dispersals, the different cultures, languages and ethnic groups that we know today finally emerged. It is worth noting here that scientists also believe that all of the races of the world came from an original pair of *homo sapiens.* They differ from creationists only inasmuch as they believe that this process occurred *naturally* over 100,000 years[384].

The Theory of Evolution

According to Evolution, DNA formed about 3.5 billion years ago perhaps via the formation of RNA. The probability of the chemical reactions that led to the formation of DNA is so low, however, that scientists believe DNA was probably only formed once in this way[385]. The existence of just one molecule of DNA, therefore, allowed single-celled organisms to exist, and this meant that DNA could be re-created whenever these organisms reproduced.

Single-celled organisms are believed to have been the only form of life on earth for the next 1.75 billion years. After this period of time, multi-cellular organisms developed. Unfortunately, however, many of these creatures were then wiped out by a mass extinction about 650 million years ago[386].

Despite this, there was a large growth in different life forms about 540 to 505 million years ago, a phenomenon that is commonly referred to as the 'Cambrian Explosion'[387]. At this stage, however, the resulting life forms were relatively simple. They consisted entirely of organisms that lived in marine environments, such as shelled invertebrates, sponges, starfish and jellyfish. In addition, the only plant forms that existed during this period of time were algae.

Following this, however, more advanced fish began to develop. Some of these went on to evolve into amphibians; some amphibians then evolved into reptiles. Later, some reptiles developed into mammals, whilst others evolved into birds[388]. The timescale for these events is believed to have been broadly as follows in terms of millions of years ago (mya):

Animals	Mya
Fish	540-505
Amphibians & reptiles	360-286
Mammals	245-208
Birds	208-144

During the first 1.75 billion years, therefore, virtually no evolution took place. However, in a period of about 400 million years very complex and specialised life forms evolved including birds and mammals. One explanation for this extremely rapid acceleration might be that organisms began to reproduce sexually, as this would have created much greater opportunities for genetic mutation.

Although mutations are random, those that occur during sexual reproduction are believed to be the main drivers for evolutionary change. When mutations provide a competitive advantage, the organism is able to reproduce more effectively than its competitors. As a result, the mutation survives and is replicated many times in future generations. If a mutation creates a serious disadvantage, however, the organism, and hence the mutation, would only survive for a relatively short period of time. This weeding out process is known as 'natural selection', and it is at the heart of the Theory of Evolution.

Natural selection is often described as 'the survival of the fittest'. However, that is a very inaccurate description of the process. Although the fittest do survive, so do many other organisms. Those that have competitive advantages may have a better chance of survival, but that does not mean that they will eliminate all other life forms around them. If that were the case, then all apes, for example, would have developed into human beings.

Instead, natural selection generates a huge range of different life forms, as a result of which ancestors and descendants are able to live with one another side-by-side in a harmonious, but nevertheless competitive, balance. Evolution is therefore often described as producing a pattern of development that is akin to a huge bush with many branches and offshoots, as opposed to a simple ladder of linear development, in which only the most recent mutations survive to the next generation.

One problem for natural selection is that large mutations seldom survive[389]. It is therefore generally believed that the huge number of physical changes required for the evolution of all life forms to take place would have involved many billions of mutations. Without this, it would have been impossible for animals to move into completely different habitats. And this would have prevented them from exploiting the many opportunities provided by those new environments, including the acquisition of new skills, such as the ability to fly.

Although the initial evolutionary steps saw a move from the sea to land, it is thought that there were also later emigrations back to the sea, as different development opportunities presented themselves. Crocodiles, turtles, sea snakes, seals and whales, for example, are all believed to have descended from land animals that returned to the sea for food[390]. Whales, for example, are believed to have descended from an ancestor of the hippopotamus, whilst seals are thought to have evolved from an ancestor of the bear[391].

However, not every step of the evolutionary path involved progress. As already mentioned, evolutionists believe there was a serious mass extinction event around 650 million years ago. On the evidence of various abrupt changes in the fossil record, it is also believed that there were several mass extinction events after this as well. The most significant of these were[392]:

No.	Mya	Species Lost
1	445	70% to 85%
2	375	70% to 80%
3	250	70% to 95%
4	200	About 80%
5	65	40% to 76%

The most recent of these catastrophic events is perhaps the most well known, as it is believed to have caused the extinction of the dinosaurs. This is thought by most to have been caused by a meteorite. However, others believe that it may have been due mainly to changes in the climate, and this might provide a better explanation for the apparently selective nature of this extinction[393].

Of the other extinctions, 1 and 2 above were confined to marine plants and animals, which are believed to have been the only organisms that existed at that time[394]. Flooding is believed to have played a major role in the latter part of 3 above, as well as a further mass extinction between 4 and 5[395]. Quite a lot of the extinctions, therefore, involve marine environments in one way or another.

Following the extinction of the dinosaurs, the development of mammals continued apace, and between 60 to 55 mya the only flying mammals, bats, are believed to have evolved[396]. It was not until between 6 and 7 mya[397], however, that human-like apes are thought to have appeared. Modern man *(homo sapiens)* is believed to have developed some time after then, between 1.6 million and 200,000 years ago.

There are, however, still some misunderstandings about the evolution of *homo sapiens*[398]. For example, Neanderthals and *homo erectus* are often thought of as distant relatives of modern man, with Neanderthals being regarded as an entirely separate species[399]. However, scientists now believe that Neanderthals and *homo erectus* survived alongside *homo sapiens,* only disappearing about 36,000 and 27,000 years ago respectively[399]. Neanderthals are also no longer regarded as our ancestors[400]. In fact, in May 2010 genetic studies indicated Neanderthals and *homo sapiens* were not even separate species, as they must have interbred[401].

What makes something a separate species, however, is still a controversial question, and at least 22 competing definitions of 'species' have been developed[402]. One common definition says that organisms are different species if they are genetically incapable of reproducing with one another. This definition cannot be applied to organisms that only reproduce asexually. Nor can it be applied to the vast majority of fossils, as DNA is missing. It is also not feasible to test the genetic incompatibility of the millions of different varieties of organism that exist today[403]. And if it were possible, this definition might well result in a vast reduction in the number of species[404].

In practice, therefore, evolutionists use different definitions of species, depending on whether they are considering living animals or fossils. In the case of the vast majority of fossils, whether something is a different species is determined on the basis of the fossil's appearance and structure. This approach has serious limitations, however, as there are many similar looking organisms, especially amongst birds, that are thought to be genetically distinct. Conversely, some animals may manifest considerable variations in form, whilst remaining members of the same species, a classic example of which is the extremely diverse range of different breeds of domestic dogs[405].

There are also quite divergent views about how evolution took place. Some believe that evolution occurred very gradually and at broadly the same rate ('phyletic gradualism'). At the other end of the scale are those who believe that there were vast periods of stasis that were punctuated by short bursts of evolutionary change, with the changes mainly occurring in isolated communities This variant form of Evolution is known as 'punctuated equilibrium'.

One area of research that appears to support the idea of rapid evolutionary change relates to regulatory genes. These are genes that control the expression of other genes, and changes in them can make a big difference to an organism, even within the space of a single generation. The most important development here has been the discovery of master regulator genes, known as homeotic or 'Hox' genes. These genes are found in nearly all multicellular organisms, where they regulate the fundamental development of the body plan and the major organs. For example, simple changes in these genes have been known to cause unusual mutations in insects, such as legs growing out of their heads and a second pair of wings[406].

These discoveries raise the possibility that some evolution occurred over much shorter periods of time than previously believed. Whatever the timescale, however, and whatever definition of species is employed, the vast majority of evolutionists appear to be united by one central belief: all animal and plant life that has ever existed on earth developed from one single-celled organism[407].

Introduction to the Arguments

The sub-sections that follow consider the four main biological arguments that are advanced in support of the Theory of Evolution.

These are that:

(a) numerous remarkable similarities in organisms' physical structures, embryology and DNA, can only be explained if those organisms shared a common ancestor;

(b) there are many examples of makeshift, poor design, and unnecessary suffering, all of which are incompatible with the idea that life was created by a perfect God;

(c) many animals have vestigial structures, which means that the original use of those structures must have been modified as a result of previous evolutionary change; and,

(d) the unique fauna and flora of places such as Australia can only be understood if those life forms evolved along different lines from other organisms as a result of their geographical separation from other species.

Before considering each of these arguments in detail, we will firstly look at one general issue relating to these arguments, namely evolutionists' claim that Creationism is not a scientific theory.

The Scientific Method

The scientific method involves collating evidence from observations and creating an explanation (hypothesis) to account for that evidence. The hypothesis is then tested against new observations, including data drawn from experiments. This testing may corroborate the hypothesis or it may require it to be modified. Alternatively, it may completely falsify the hypothesis, in which case the hypothesis would have to be abandoned[408].

Men have put forward basically three explanations to account for their observations about the nature of life on earth, namely that it -

(1) originated from other planets;
(2) was created by a superior being or beings; or,
(3) evolved over a very long period of time by natural processes.

All of these ideas are based upon observations about the attributes of life on earth. At face value, therefore, each of them meets the requirements to fulfil the general definition of a scientific hypothesis. The first hypothesis, however, does not seek to explain the existence of life as such; it only attempts to explain the origins of life on this planet. We will not, therefore, consider this particular hypothesis any further.

The appeal of the second hypothesis for many people is that it explains the powerful impression we have that nature has been consciously designed, something which is even acknowledged by evolutionists. Dawkins, for example, refers to the 'breathtaking illusion of design'[409]. This hypothesis is usually modified to attribute creation to one superior being or 'God', something which would also be in line with the principle of Occam's Razor (see page 5).

It is further hypothesised that this God must be benevolent, given the beauty, fertility and harmony that is so evident in nature. And If God is benevolent, it is also proposed that He would have communicated with mankind. This in turn has led many to conclude that the creator of life on earth is the God of the Bible.

Evolutionists argue that this is not a scientific hypothesis on two counts. Firstly, it is not based upon detailed observations, but on the teachings of the Bible. Furthermore, it is contended that the 'God hypothesis' is not a scientific proposition, as it is not testable, so its main ideas are incapable of being falsified in any way[410].

In relation to this last point, evolutionists argue that scientific methods must exclude any proposition that involves the supernatural, as explanations of this kind cannot be reproduced, tested and therefore falsified. Everything that is supernatural, therefore, must be regarded as 'unscientific' by very definition[411].

Although some believers may not approach this issue in a scientific way, it does not follow that Creationism is itself an unscientific proposition. We find ourselves in a highly complex and beautiful world, and when we look at this closely it reinforces our impression that it has been deliberately designed in this way. The idea that life on earth was created, therefore, *is* based upon observation like any other hypothesis. We may argue that it is at variance with certain other observations, but that does not mean it was not a scientific hypothesis to begin with.

As regards the question of testability, evolutionists cannot reasonably argue that Creationism cannot be falsified, and then proceed to write lengthy books claiming to prove that Creationism is false. The fact is that biblical Creationism includes some very specific claims about how and when life originated, and many evolutionists argue that they can disprove these claims. If Creationism can be falsified, then the 'untestability' argument cannot be advanced as a reason for contending that it is an unscientific hypothesis.

It is also unreasonable to argue that all 'supernatural' explanations must be disregarded by science. 'Science' means 'knowledge' and the purpose of science is to expand the horizons of that knowledge. It cannot do this, if it insists that everything must conform to ideas that are based upon our present understanding of the world. In addition, something is only described as 'supernatural', because it presently lies outside the sphere of our knowledge. If God really does exist, however, then He is part of the total order of things and His existence is, in one sense, as 'natural' as any other aspect or part of the universe.

In addition, the ultimate goal of science is to arrive at 'facts'. If science must exclude the idea of God from the outset, however, then how could it ever arrive at the truth if God did in 'fact' create the world? To comply with a self-imposed rule that required everything supernatural to be excluded, scientists would be forced in those circumstances to proceed on the false assumption that God did not exist, and confine themselves to producing theories that were based solely upon this false premise.

It is also not entirely clear just how testable the Theory of Evolution actually is *itself*. When asked what might disprove the Theory of Evolution, the biologist J. B. S. Haldane is reported to have famously said, 'fossil rabbits in the pre-Cambrian.' The problem with this answer, however, is that rock strata are generally determined by reference to the fossils they contain. So if rocks contained rabbit fossils, it would be assumed that they did not date to the pre-Cambrian. And any unexpectedly 'old' fossils in those strata would be explained away on the basis that those organisms had simply survived longer than originally thought. Thus, the central tenets of the Theory of Evolution would remain intact, entirely unaffected by the discovery.

The coelacanth is an interesting example in this context. For many years evolutionists had taught that this large deep-water fish had perished with the dinosaurs 65 million years ago (mya). Then, when fishermen discovered a coelacanth in 1938, one astonished naturalist said, 'I would not have been more surprised if I had seen a dinosaur walking down the street.'[412]

So how would evolutionists have reacted if they had found the fossil of a modern man next to that of a coelacanth? Would they have assumed man's evolution went back to at least 65 mya or would they have concluded instead that the coelacanth did not in fact die out with the dinosaurs? It seems clear that they could easily have assumed the latter.

Similarly, if evolutionists found the fossil of a modern man next to that of a dinosaur, they could easily argue that, like the coelacanth, the dinosaur in question had simply survived for a lot longer than was previously assumed, at least in that particular area or region. As a result, evolutionists could once again avoid the conclusion that their ideas about the fact or timescale of human evolution were wrong, by simply making some modifications to their beliefs about the extinction of another species.

It is possible, of course, that evolutionists might accept that the theory had been falsified if a fossil of a modern man was found in very old rock strata that had been 'reliably dated' by radiometry. As we have seen, however, scientists accept that erroneously old radiometric dates can be caused by a variety of phenomenon. It could be argued, therefore, that this particular date was anomalous, on the grounds that it was only an isolated piece of discordant data, which was at variance with the large body of other evidence that supported the Theory of Evolution.

It should be clear from all of this that it is not reasonable for evolutionists to argue that biblical Creationism is untestable, given the various arguments which they claim so clearly disprove it. It is equally clear that falsifying the Theory of Evolution is far from straightforward, if not impossible, given the numerous explanations that evolutionists could advance to account for discordant data. If biblical Creationism is held to be an unscientific hypothesis on the grounds of testability, therefore, then the Theory of Evolution must be at serious risk of suffering the same fate.

Homologous Structures

Structures are said to be homologous when they are made of the same basic parts, but serve quite different functions. A frequently cited example is that of the five-digit structure at the end of the invertebrate forelimb, which is found in human hands, bats' wings, whales' flippers, and the front feet of lizards, frogs and various land mammals[413].

Evolutionists argue that homologous structures only make sense if the animals in question had a common ancestor. If they evolved independently, there would be no reason for these structural similarities to exist. Moreover, if animals were created by God, it is claimed, He would have produced optimum designs for each creature, rather than making apparently *ad hoc* adjustments to other structures. A perfect creator would have produced the best possible design for flight, for example, rather than making wings out of structures that served elsewhere as hands and flippers[413].

Some evolutionists clearly regard this as one of their strongest arguments, as they consider it to be even more compelling than the fossil evidence itself[414]. They also contend that the arguments relating to homologous structures are strongly supported by the similarities that exist between the *DNA* of different animals.

The similarities in DNA are said to directly correspond with the ancestral relationships that have been deduced independently by the Theory of Evolution. For example, the DNA of chimpanzees is 98% similar to that of human beings, which accords with the view that chimpanzees are our nearest living relatives[415]. Evolutionists contend that the similarities in DNA structure simply could not be explained without the Theory of Evolution. This, it is claimed, puts the argument 'beyond all conceivable doubt'[416].

One particular similarity in DNA structures has also been advanced to explain the evolution of the cells that make up all advanced life forms. These cells contain a number of functioning sub-units, called organelles (in animals) and plastids (in plants). Some of these sub-units, known as mitochondria (animals) and chloroplasts (plants) also have their own DNA structures. And closer analysis reveals that this is different from the DNA structure of the cell nucleus, but similar to that of the DNA of bacteria.

Evolutionists argue that this only makes sense if mitochondria and chloroplasts originally came from sources outside the cell, such as bacteria[417]. These bacteria, it is argued, must have been captured by single-celled organisms, with which they subsequently formed a symbiotic relationship. This explanation is said to be supported by the fact that examples of this kind of symbiosis can be found in nature today. For example, certain amoebas that lack mitochondria contain symbiotic bacteria, which perform the same respiratory functions that would have been carried out by mitochondria[417].

It could be argued, however, that homologies at both the structural and molecular level are attributable not to a common ancestor but to a common creator. The Bible tells us that God made each creature 'after its kind' (Genesis 1:21-25). As these 'kinds' clearly did not exist before creation, this must mean that all creatures were formed around various configurations or themes. Birds and animals that fell within the same 'kinds' could therefore be expected to share some common structures.

Another important facet of the creation account is the way in which God is described as taking pleasure in the creative process. We are told on several occasions that God beheld His creation and 'saw that it was good' (Genesis 1:4,12,18,21,25,31). And one of the attributes of the creation in which God took particular pleasure was the wide range and huge variety of life forms that He had created (Psalms 104:24, 25).

It pleased God, therefore, to create numerous variations on different themes, just as an artist might use common elements and similar techniques when composing quite different works of art. We should not be surprised, therefore, if we find common structures in creatures within the same groups of animals, even where those structures serve quite different purposes.

It is important therefore to see creation as a work of art, as opposed to a production line, designed to produce perfect biological efficiency. It is also worth noting that whilst the creation is described as being 'very good', no part of it is said to have been 'perfect', in the sense of being without any kind of biological weakness. The birds and animals God created were made of flesh, and without His protection any of them could easily have been damaged or killed.

Furthermore, if God had designed a perfect bird, for example, any bird that differed from this would, according to evolutionists, have been imperfect by comparison. If God did not wish to make imperfect creatures, therefore, He would only have been able to make just one perfect example of each 'kind' of creature. It is quite clear from the account in Genesis, however, that God did not wish to make plants and animals in this way. He took pleasure in creating diversity in a natural order, where living things complemented one another in a beautiful and harmonious co-existence. Whilst individual creations are described as being 'good', therefore, taken together they are 'very good' (Genesis 1:4, 10, 12, 18, 21, 25, 31).

As regards DNA, there is clearly a close correlation between an organism's outward form (phenotype) and its genetic make-up (genotype), as the latter largely controls the former. Initially, the Theory of Evolution was mainly based upon observed similarities in structure and appearance (phenotypes). Since then, however, data has also been collated about the DNA (genotypes) of these organisms. DNA evidence does not therefore provide an additional argument relating to homology. It simply looks at the same evidence from another perspective, by establishing the genetic similarities that lead to the structural relationships.

There is also no basis for arguing that similarities in the DNA of creatures with similar structures are incompatible with the idea that they were created by God. Why, after all, should God be obliged to give similar creatures markedly different DNA structures, when DNA is the means for passing on those similarities to future generations?

The similarities between the DNA of mitochondria, chloroplasts and bacteria are also inconclusive. Mitochondria supply the cell with energy and are involved in other key processes, such as cell growth. Chloroplasts also play a vital role in energy supply, as they are responsible for capturing and storing the light energy needed for photosynthesis. All of these functions are also vital to bacteria, so it is not surprising if there are similarities in their DNA structures.

Despite these similarities, there are also some important differences. Mitochondria and chloroplasts have small genomes compared with bacteria, as many of the functions of organelles and plastids are controlled by the cell nucleus. This fact also accounts for the structural differences between the DNA of the nucleus and that of organelles and plastids. They have different DNA structures, because they perform different functions.

As far as the general argument relating to homology is concerned, it should be clear that this is not a separate arguments against Creationism; it is simply a variant form of the 'bad design' argument. The basic contention is that it would not 'make sense' for God to create something by modifying other structures. To make creatures perfect, it is argued, God would have to create them from scratch using an ideal design. Anything less than this would be imperfect and hence an example of bad design, for which a perfect God could not therefore have been responsible.

Dawkins argues, for instance, that a bat's structure can be explained from the fact that it is descended from other mammals. As a result, most bats have fur, but none of them have feathers. Dawkins argues that if feathers were a good idea for birds, a perfect designer would have given them to bats as well[418]. As bats do not have feathers, he argues that they could not possibly have been created by God.

This argument is invalid, however, as it does not take any account of other differences between animals that may be relevant to their structure. There may, for instance, be significant differences in their eating and sleeping habits, reproduction, life cycles and habitats. And some or all of these factors may well have a bearing on why a particular structure makes perfect sense for some creatures, but not for others.

To take the example of bats, unlike most birds they hunt at night, which means that they avoid any competition from birds. Most bats also have poor sight, so they have to rely on the increased sensitivity of other organs. These specializations include their echolocation system, but they also have highly sensitive wings. And these contain some special developments that are vital to bats' ability to navigate and catch prey[419].

To begin with, bats' wings contain touch-sensitive receptors on small bumps called Merkel cells. Each of these bumps has a tiny hair in the centre, which makes those cells even more sensitive. This allows a bat to collect information about the air flowing over its wings, which in turn provides it with the necessary feedback so that it knows how and when to change its wing shape to fly more efficiently[419]. Furthermore, research has shown that without these hairs, bats are unable to make a number of important adjustments during flight[420].

Some bats also have receptor cells in their wing membranes, which allow them to catch prey. These cells are sensitive to any stretching of the membrane, and are concentrated in areas where insects are likely to collide with the wings. These cells therefore provide an early warning system, so that a bat is able to detect and capture insects during flight[419].

Bats would be unable to perform these functions if their wings were covered with feathers. In addition, bats' wings are much thinner than those of birds so they can manoeuvre more quickly and more accurately. This is important for bats when hunting at night, and feathers would seriously undermine this[419].

In addition, evolutionists no longer believe that feathers evolved for flight, but for insulation[421]. So there is no evolutionary basis for believing that bats should have developed feathers for flight at all. And if bats would have been more efficient with feathers, then why did evolution not cause them to develop them like reptiles?

The facts are that bats represent 22% of all mammal species, and they are one of the most widely distributed groups of mammals on the planet, occupying almost every type of habitat. In addition, many tropical plant species depend entirely on bats for the distribution of their seeds[422]. They also play a vital conservation role by keeping down the numbers of night-flying insects, which would otherwise threaten farmlands, gardens and house timbers[423]. In short, bats are highly successful and useful creatures, which are perfectly designed for their particular niche in the animal kingdom. Their lack of feathers is an integral part of that design.

Bad Design

General

This argument maintains that many aspects of nature are badly designed. If God is perfect, it is argued, then everything He does must be perfect. Hence, nature, or at least large parts of it, cannot be God's handiwork.

The examples of bad design that are advanced are said to provide evidence of both inefficiency and unnecessary suffering. This section concentrates on the former, as the question of suffering is covered in the next chapter. However, a number of general points can be made, which have a bearing on both kinds of 'bad design'.

To begin with, we cannot simply look at nature now and assume that it reflects how things were when they were created. As explained on page 189, following the Fall many significant physical changes took place. Sin resulted in the physical degeneration of all creatures, as death and decay spread to all living things. It also resulted in a breakdown in the harmony of nature, causing mutations and distortions of the original creation, which led, for example, to the emergence of carnivores and presumably also to the dinosaurs. At an individual level, other changes took place, some of which might now be regarded as examples of bad design, such as the pains of childbirth that arise from the relative size of a human baby's skull.

According to the Bible, these changes were the supernatural consequences of man's disobedience. However, since creation other natural changes have also taken place, some of which serve to further obscure how things were when they were originally created. The environment was changed dramatically by the Flood and the events that followed this. And animals had to adapt to these rapidly changing circumstances. As a result, there may now be some really significant differences between the animals we see today and their original ancestors.

Apart from adaptive changes, there have also been many generations of genetic mutations. These occur naturally, but increase significantly during the process of sexual reproduction. Once again, therefore, studying nature as it is today does not necessarily tell us how it was when it was created. Hence, any design faults we identify now may not have been present when God originally created life on earth.

It must also be remembered that the Bible does not actually say that any part of creation was physically perfect, in the sense of it being without any kind of biological weaknesses whatsoever. It only tells us that the creatures were 'good' and that the creation as a whole was 'very good'.

In addition, whilst imperfections might be identified at the level of an individual animal, these might be of value in maintaining the balance in nature that presently exists. The fact that not all gazelles can outstrip a cheetah might be considered an imperfection from the gazelle's point of view. However, it ensures that a balance is maintained and that all cheetahs do not starve to death.

Finally, evolutionists cannot push the 'bad design' argument too far, as this would undermine the Theory of Evolution itself. Evolutionary theory teaches that over time organisms undergo substantial physical changes in response to changes in their environment, making them well adapted, and in some cases tailor-made, to those environments. It is hard for animals to be both 'tailor-made' and 'badly designed' at the same time. Evolutionists have to accept, therefore, that any examples of bad design are too innocuous for natural selection to have weeded them out at any stage. Consequently, if there are any design faults, they cannot be serious enough to prevent creation, even now, from being regarded as at least 'good' from an evolutionary point of view.

The Recurrent Laryngeal Nerve (RLN)

The RLN is perhaps the most frequently cited example of bad design. The circuitous route this nerve takes in mammals, it is claimed, makes it impossible to believe that it could have been created by a perfect designer. It also claimed that the RLN provides firm evidence that mammals evolved from fish.

Dawkins points out that in fish various branches of the vagus nerve pass behind the gill arteries so that they can reach the gills by the most direct route. When mammals evolved, he argues, they developed necks that were supplied by the same blood vessels and nerves that had previously served the gills of fish. The result, Dawkins claims, was that in mammals one of these branches (the RLN) now takes a very long detour to the larynx ('voice box') via the heart[424]. These arguments are often accompanied by diagrams like the one below.

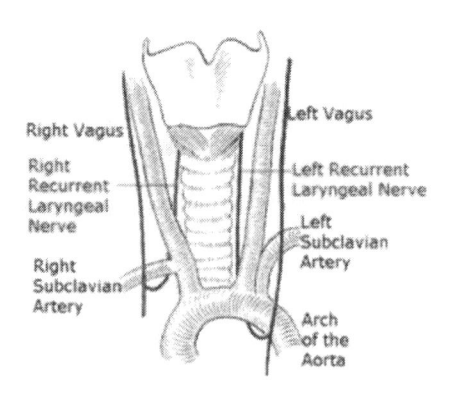

As can be seen, the diagram shows the circuitous route the RLN takes, looping around blood vessels on either side of the neck before finally making its way to the larynx. Dawkins argues that this 'design' makes absolutely no sense, particularly in animals such as giraffes, where the detour can be up to 15 feet in length[424].

This, however, is a very incomplete and misleading analysis of the structure and functions of the RLN. To begin with, the RLN takes the route it does, because it serves a number of other important organs along the way. This is illustrated by the following simplified diagram of the left RLN, which mirrors the functions performed by the right RLN.

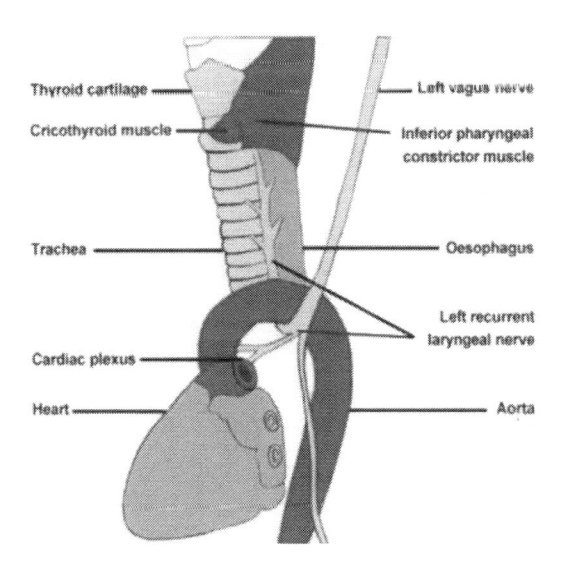

As the diagram indicates, the RLN firstly descends to the heart, where it provides several fibres to the deep cardiac plexus. Thereafter, it innervates the mucosal lining and the muscular coat and fibres of the trachea and oesophagus. It then supplies nerve fibres to the inferior constrictor pharyngis muscle and then to the larynx[425]. Within the larynx, the RLN communicates with the superior laryngeal nerve, which takes the direct route to the larynx from the vagus nerve[426].

The RLN delivers sensory and parasympathetic nerve (PSN) fibres to the heart via the cardiac plexus[426]. The PSN is part of the autonomic nervous system, which is responsible for the unconscious regulation of internal organs and glands. In particular, the PSN stimulates the so-called 'rest-and-digest' activities that occur when the body is at ease.

In the case of the heart, the PSN reduces the heart rate when the body is resting. It also reduces the strength of heart contractions, constricts the coronary arteries and reduces the intensity of the electrical impulses passing through the heart[427]. These are important functions, without which the heart would work far harder than it needed to during rest periods, which would place it under unnecessary strain.

After the heart, the RLN provides PSNs, together with sensory and motor nerves, to both the oesophagus and the trachea[428]. In the oesophagus, the PSN fibres increase oesophageal gland secretions to facilitate swallowing[429]. They also increase peristalsis[429], the contractions that are responsible for moving food down the digestive tract.

Motor fibres from the RLN control the upper oesophageal sphincter, a muscular section of the oesophagus that plays an important role in swallowing[430]. The RLN also provides all of the sensory nerves to the oesophagus, apart from those in the cervical section[431]. The RLN's sensory nerves communicate with the swallowing centre of the brain, which inhibits breathing during swallowing[432] and moves the food through the lower oesophageal sphincter and down towards the stomach[433].

In the trachea, the sympathetic nerves enhance the body's ability to breath during exercise by dilating the trachea. The PSN fibres from the RLN reverse these affects when the body is resting, by stimulating motor neurons to constrict the trachea and increase mucosal secretions[434].

As with the oesophagus, the sensory nerves from the RLN play an important role in the trachea. One major function is to trigger various defence mechanisms to protect the lower respiratory tract against foreign bodies that have been inhaled[435]. These defensive responses include coughing, bronchoconstriction and increased airway secretions[435].

After the trachea and oesophagus, the RLN innervates the inferior pharyngeal constrictor muscle. In most people, the RLN provides motor nerve fibres to this muscle, which is important in the swallowing process, as it contracts to force the bolus of food down into the oesophagus[436].

Finally, the RLN provides motor nerves to all of the muscles of the larynx, except the cricothyroid muscle[428]. The RLN activates the vocal cords by drawing them apart (abduction) to allow vocalisation. If one RLN is damaged, this results in hoarseness, and if both RLNs are cut, the voice is lost altogether[437]. Moreover, if both RLNs are cut, the adduction (bringing together) of the vocal cords is unopposed, and this leads to acute airway obstruction requiring an emergency tracheostomy[438].

The RLN is very fine when it reaches the larynx, having given off most of its nerve fibres by then. However, it is well protected over the upper third of its course, as it is located in a relatively safe position in the groove between the trachea and oesophagus[439].

The RLN follows the circuitous route it does, therefore, as it serves a number of functions along its pathway. Despite this, it might still be argued, as Dawkins does[424], that it makes no sense for the RLN to pass within such a short distance of the trachea on its way down to the heart. Several problems would arise, however, if the RLN travelled directly to the larynx.

To begin with, the connections between the RLN and the larynx would be a lot more vulnerable. Instead of being protected in the groove between the trachea and oesophagus, these connections would be in a fairly exposed position. Although the superior laryngeal nerve takes this direct route, damage to this section of the RLN would be a lot more serious, as it could be life threatening.

Secondly, if the most efficient route for the RLN were the shortest one, then it should also take the shortest route to the inferior pharyngeal constrictor muscle, the trachea and the oesophagus before it reaches the heart. Apart from exposing these nervous connections to greater danger, the RLN would then be at its finest and weakest in the section between the trachea and the heart, as it would have given off several fibres along the way. This would significantly enhance the risk of those connections being damaged.

Finally, Dawkins' re-design would eliminate the loops that the RLN takes around the aorta and the subclavian artery. Whilst these may seem unnecessary, like the cable hooks in ceiling light fittings, they reduce the strain on the nerve-end connections that could arise from accidents or sudden neck movements.

There is no evidence, therefore, that the route taken by the RLN is an example of bad design. There is also no evidence that the design of the RLN can only be understood by assuming that we evolved from fish.

The Vertebrate Eye (VE)

Evolutionists argue that the VE could not have been created by God, as it is wired 'back to front', with the nerve fibres in front of the retina's light sensitive cells, instead of behind them. As a result, light has to pass through a 'carpet' of nerves to reach the retina[440]. This also means that there is a 'blind spot' where the nerve fibres have to pass through the retina. Dawkins suggests that this should be more accurately described as a 'blind patch'[440]. And others argue that as the nerves do not pass through the choroid, the retina is at a much greater risk of becoming detached.

Evolutionists accept that the VE functions well, and acknowledge that these alleged shortcomings have little practical effect for most of us. They argue, however, that they are clear imperfections in the design of the eye, which contrasts with the much more efficient arrangement of invertebrate eyes, such as those of the octopus, where the nerve fibres are located behind, rather than in front of, the retina. The diagrams below illustrate this, by showing the structure of the human eye, followed by a comparison between the main features of human and octopus eyes.

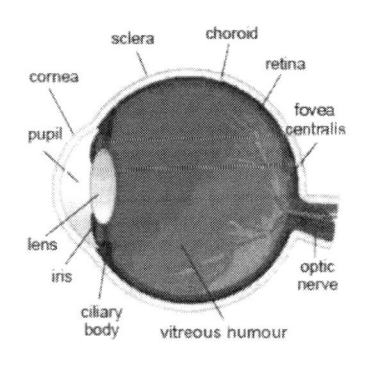

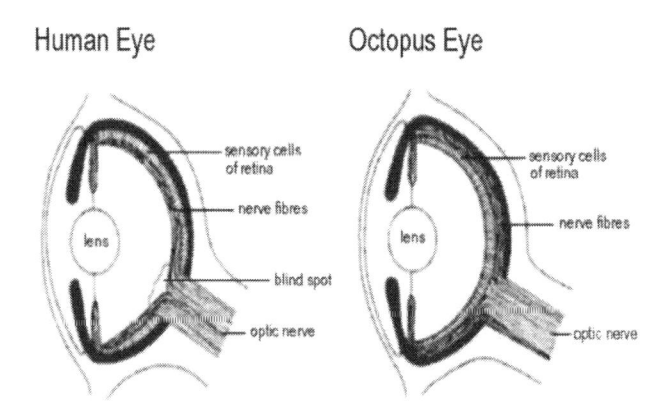

Apart from the blind spot, the other main difference in the diagrams above is the presence of the fovea centralis in the human eye. As with many VEs, the fovea is the focal point for light entering the eye[441]. It is densely populated with only colour-sensitive cells, so it plays an important role in daytime vision. And although it represents only about 1% of the area of the retina[442], it supplies information to about 50% of the visual cortex of the brain[443]. The fovea is also responsible for high-resolution vision, so it is the most critical part of the retina for many important visual tasks, such as object recognition, manipulation and reading[442].

In the area of the fovea centralis the inner layers of the retina are flattened laterally to maximise the light reaching it[444]. It is also worth noting that the retinal layers above the light sensitive cells are perfectly transparent[445], as are the nerve fibres above the retina[446]. There is no evidence, therefore, that these nerves obstruct the light reaching the eye any more than the large amount of clear gel (vitreous humour) in front of the retina does.

Furthermore, a research document in 2010 revealed that the VE does not rely on light passing though these media to reach the retina. Instead, glial (Müller) cells act like optical fibres, carrying the light down directly to the photosensitive cells[447]. This 'fibre optic' process both increases the resolution of the eye and reduces the chromatic aberration that would otherwise occur.

This research also considered the idea that the retina was poorly designed, because it was wired in the wrong order. The authors of the report came to the conclusion that, far from being badly constructed, the human retina was actually an 'optimal structure' for improving the sharpness of vision. This conclusion is certainly borne out by the highly effective vision that many vertebrates possess. We often talk, for example, about someone being 'eagle-eyed' or having 'eyes like a hawk'.

The arrangement of the VE does result in a blind spot. However, it is not accurate to describe this area as a 'blind patch'. To begin with, it only occupies about 0.2% of the visual field[448]. And as vertebrates have two eyes, what is a blind spot in one eye will not be 'blind' to the other eye. In addition, all high-resolution vision and 50% of all visual data is provided by the fovea centralis, which is completely unaffected by the existence of a blind spot in a peripheral area of the visual field.

As regards retinal detachment, this is relatively uncommon, affecting only one in 10,000 people per year or about one in 300 patients during the whole of their lifetimes. In addition, retinal detachment is often repaired with little or no residual loss of vision, making it a much less significant cause of irreversible blindness than other retinal diseases[449].

Despite these points, Dawkins and others still argue that the design of the VE is sub-optimal. Even if the drawbacks are relatively minor in their effect, they argue that they are nevertheless imperfections. Dawkins therefore insists that if the VE were designed in this way, it must have been created by 'a complete idiot'.

However, all designs must have potential advantages and disadvantages. One must therefore consider if any of the minor potential drawbacks in some areas exist to mitigate more serious risks elsewhere.

One obvious point here is that, unlike invertebrates, the VE eye socket is made of solid bone or cartilage[450], which means there is very little 'give' in them. If the nerve fibres were nearer to the surface of the eyeball, therefore, they would be in greater danger of damage from impacts. This would increase the risk of nerve damage in key parts of the retina, such as the fovea centralis, which might also be irreversible.

It is hard to compare the risks of retinal detachment and nerve damage with how those risks would be balanced if the VE was wired the other way round. It seems perfectly possible, however, that the current arrangement is the best possible design for the VE.

It is also sensible to exercise caution when considering things as complicated as the eye. Until we know much more about how it works, we are likely to make further discoveries like those relating to Müller cells, which may alter our assessment of how efficient the VE actually is.

In the meantime, it should be clear that it is not reasonable to argue that the VE could not have been designed by God. And Dawkins' assertion that anyone who designed it must be 'a complete idiot' stands in stark contrast to the assessment of eye specialists, who increasingly regard it as an 'optimal structure'.

The Vas Deferens (VD)

A diagram of the VD and its associated structures is below. Dawkins describes the VD as a pipe that carries sperm from the testis to the penis, taking a 'ridiculous detour' in the process around the bladder, where it is hooked over the ureter[451]. If the VD was designed, Dawkins argues, this huge detour would amount to a 'bad error'. He therefore concludes that it could not have been created by God; its path must be an accident of evolution, which occurred when mammalian testes descended to their current position. He says it is unclear why testes descended in this way, but speculates that it might have something to do with temperature control.

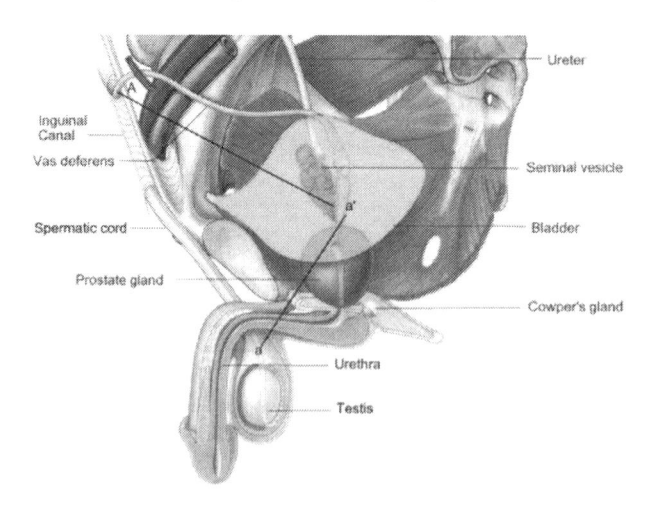

Before we consider the arguments outlined by Dawkins, it is worth commenting on some of these structures in the diagram above.

To begin with, we can see that the VD does not actually carry sperm to the penis; it is the urethra that performs this function. The VD transports sperm to the seminal vesicles, which explains why it needs to travel towards the bladder. There the seminal vesicles on either side secrete the fluids that make up a large part of the semen. To this are added secretions from the prostate and Cowper's glands, before the semen is ready to travel along the urethra to the penis.

Secondly, it is misleading to refer to the descent of the testes as something that is the result of evolution. The fact is the mammalian testes are formed inside the body, and in most cases, but not all, they descend to the scrotum at an early stage of development. In humans, this normally occurs before birth. So the path the VD takes is not an accident of nature arising from our distant evolutionary past, but a recent event that takes place during the normal course of mammalian development.

When each testis descends, it passes through the abdominal cavity via a passage called the inguinal canal. This passes through various linings of the abdomen (not shown above), including a layer of flat broad tendons (the aponeurosis of the external oblique muscle) and a thick, dense membrane (the transversalis fascia)[452]. Within the inguinal canal, the VD is further protected by a three-layered structure known as the spermatic cord.

Immediately before their descent to the scrotum, the VD follows a direct route from the testis to the seminal vesicle (A to a'). However, it has to take a more circuitous route when the testis descends to the scrotum, as part of the VD now passes through the abdominal wall via the inguinal canal. Dawkins argues that the VD should take the most direct route (a to a'), but it is not at all clear how he envisages this might take place.

Why then do the testes descend at all? Could we not be like birds or certain other mammals, such as elephants and rhinoceroses, which manage with internal testes? Research indicates that existence of external testes cannot always be related to the need for temperature control. More recent research suggests that they may instead be needed because of an animal's lifestyle[453]. In particular, mammals that have external testes are known to potentially need to undertake a lot of running or jumping, e.g. horses and humans. These activities can easily cause significant pressure changes within the abdominal cavity, which in turn could cause any part of the reproductive tract to expel its content[453]. This would clearly be a very significant challenge for internal testes, as it could seriously undermine the capacity of that species to reproduce and hence its ability to survive.

Another possibility that Dawkins might advance as an improved design would be for there to be no abdominal wall in this area. The VD would not then have to pass through any membranes when the testes descended, thereby avoiding the circuitous path it has to take as a result of that descent. Alternatively, the testes could develop in situ, so that they did not need to descend at all.

However, neither of these options appears to be viable. The muscles and membranes of the abdomen are important for the movement of the lower body and the protection of its internal organs. The testes benefit from this protection during the delicate stages of their early development, so it would clearly be much riskier for them to develop outside the abdomen. One particular risk in those early stages is 'torsion', something which occurs when the spermatic cord twists and cuts off the blood supply to the testis. This risk is higher before the testes descend, as the spermatic cord is attached quite loosely[454].

When it occurs, testicular torsion requires urgent medical attention to prevent the testis from being lost altogether. The seriousness of this risk perhaps explains why the VD takes the path it does. Not only do the inguinal canal and the spermatic cord afford considerable protection to the VD in its most exposed sections, they also suspend the testis and hold it in place, thereby reducing the risk of torsion and other injuries. The looping of the VD around the ureter helps to make this arrangement even securer, by reducing the stress that might otherwise exist at the connections between the VD, the testis and the seminal vesicle.

The argument that the VD is an obvious example of bad design, therefore, appears to be ill-founded. It assumes that the best biological arrangements always involve the shortest distance between two points. However, this line of argument takes no account of the possibility that there might be competing or even overriding biological requirements. These requirements might include, for example, the need to protect vital organs, even if this occasionally might require certain structures to take a more circuitous route in order to achieve this.

Maxillary Sinuses

This alleged example of bad design is not concerned with maxillary sinuses in general, but solely with their arrangement in human beings. It is argued that as the drainage holes are located at the top of the sinuses, their design is of little use to an animal on two feet, particularly if they suffer from sinus problems. This provides further evidence, it is argued, of our evolutionary descent from animals that clearly spent most of their lives on all fours[455].

The following diagram shows the position of the maxillary sinuses, together with their drainage holes, which are located at the top of the sinuses. This is the route that mucous has to take for it to pass into the back and middle of the nostrils. The middle 'meatus' is the central canal or opening through which the mucous drains. The 'turbinates' are narrow bone shelves, which force the air to flow in a steady, regular pattern. The 'nasal septum' is the structure that divides the nose into two nostrils.

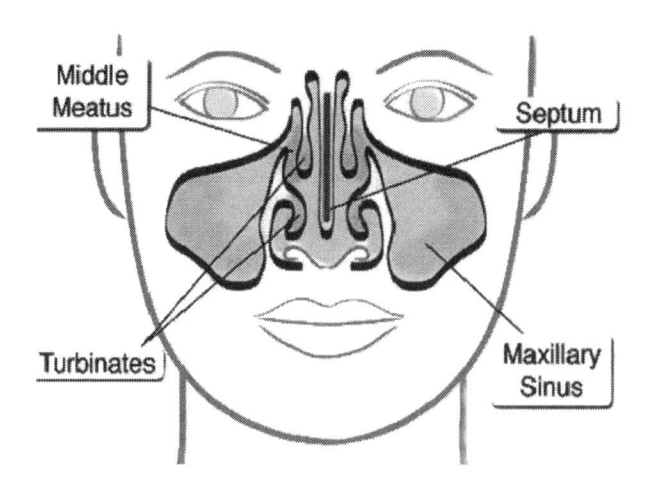

Diagram labels: Middle Meatus, Septum, Turbinates, Maxillary Sinus

There is no universal agreement regarding the purpose of the maxillary and other facial sinuses. Some refer to the fact that they lighten the weight of the skull. Others point out that they provide an insulating effect, warming the nasal cavity. One clear and undisputed benefit of the sinuses, however, is that they act as resonators for the voice, without which vocal quality would be significantly reduced[456].

As regards Dawkins' argument, the first point to make is that the movement of mucous out of the maxillary sinuses does not rely entirely on gravity. Instead, the sinuses are lined with ciliated columnar epithelium cells, which contain very small hair-like structures, called cilia. These beat back and forth and sweep the mucous out of the sinuses via the drainage channels[457]. It is also worth adding that we spend several hours a day in a horizontal position during sleep (and longer when we are ill), when any additional assistance needed by gravity can be provided.

Dawkins refers to people who suffer from sinus problems and advances this as evidence that they were poorly designed. However, suffering entered the world as a punishment for man's sin (pages 20, 21), so the existence of suffering cannot be attributed to faults in God's *original* design. The fact is that people who have perfectly healthy sinuses do not experience sinuses drainage problems. This clearly indicates that they were well designed when they were first created.

Flightless Birds

Of the 9,100 or so species of birds, about 60 are unable to fly[458]. The most well known of these are penguins, ostriches, cassowaries, emus, rheas and kiwis. In addition, certain types of duck, grebe, cormorant and parrot are also unable to fly. Evolutionists claim that it makes absolutely no sense whatsoever for God to have created birds that could not use their wings for flight. They argue, therefore, that these birds must have evolved from ancestors that *could* fly[459].

Evolutionists believe that many flightless birds lost the ability to fly due to the absence of predators or simply because they became too heavy to fly[460]. The lack of predators, together with a plentiful supply of food on the ground, made wings an expensive luxury. In addition, when it came to competing for food, natural selection favoured larger, stronger birds, particularly those that could also run quickly, like the ostrich or emu.

This explanation, however, does not contradict the Bible, which says nothing about the origins of flightless birds. The difference between evolutionists and the Bible, therefore, is simply a question of time. Evolutionists argue that the process took place over millions of years; creationists contend that it occurred over thousands or perhaps even hundreds of years.

When one considers the differences between flying and non-flying birds, it is hard to see why it would have taken millions of years for those differences to have developed. To begin with, birds have excellent mobility on land, which means that they can easily survive without their other main source of mobility, flight. Furthermore, evolutionists acknowledge that flight is 'readily lost' by birds that live on islands where there are no predators[461].

As regards the design of flightless birds, the common features are symmetrical wing feathers and a reduction in the sizes of their shoulder blades, coracoids, breast bones, arms and pectoral crests[462]. (The coracoids are small hook-like structures at the front of the shoulder blades, which help to stabilise the shoulder joints. The pectoral crest is a ridge on the upper arm bone, to which the chest muscle is attached.) There seems to be no reason why these changes could not have taken place within thousands or perhaps even hundreds of years. After all, huge differences in 400 to 500 breeds of dogs have developed over only a few hundred years[463].

It is also possible that some of the changes that occurred in flightless birds were not entirely the result of nature; they could also have been partly the consequence of the supernatural changes that resulted from man's disobedience. The Bible says that all of creation was affected by the Fall, and Job 39:13-18 says this about one particular kind of bird:

...she leaves her eggs to the earth and lets them warm in the dust; and forgets that a foot may crush them, or the beasts of the field may trample on them. She treats her young roughly, as if not hers. For her labour is vanity without fear, because God has made her forget wisdom, and He has not given her a share in understanding.

This reminds us of the following words from Romans 8:20, 21:

For the creation was subjected to vanity, not willingly, but by Him who subjected it in the hope that even the creation itself will be freed from the slavery to corruption to the freedom of the glory of the children of God.

So some birds might have lost the ability to fly as a result of changes in their biology or their environment. However, some of these changes could also have been partly the result of the degeneration in nature that accompanied the Fall.

One exception to this appears to be penguins. Penguins seem to be ideally suited to their environment. Instead of wings, they have perfectly designed flippers, which are ideal for swimming. There appears to be no good reason, therefore, to argue that penguins have been badly designed.

It is also interesting to note that according to evolutionists the oldest penguin fossils, found in New Zealand, are 62 million years old. Despite this, they look very much like modern penguins[464]. Evolutionists must accept, therefore, that penguins are well designed enough to inhabit a variety of environments, not just the post Ice Age habitat of the Antarctic.

It might be argued that by accepting that some birds have lost the ability to fly, creationists must also accept the Theory of Evolution. There is a significant difference, however, between degenerative changes, such as losing the ability to fly, and the genetic developments that are needed to transform simple life forms into human beings. The former involves the loss of one function; the latter would require a massive number of step-by-step increases in genetic complexity. Proving that some birds have lost the ability to fly provides absolutely no evidence that a massive number of macro-evolutionary changes have taken place.

It is also worth remembering that the Bible does not say that animals do not adapt to their environments. It is also silent about whether new varieties or even new species could develop. In short, the scriptures do not tell us that life *could not* have evolved from single cells; it simply teaches that this did not happen.

Sightless Animals

The same counter-arguments can be used in relation to animals that have eyes but cannot see. These include various salamanders, fish, shrimps, crayfish, millipedes, spiders and crickets. Evolutionists argue that all are further examples of bad design[465].

As with flightless birds, however, there is no need for creationists to assume that these animals were created with non-functioning eyes. They could simply have lost their sight due to changes in their biology or their environment, or as a result of the supernatural changes that resulted from man's Fall.

Trees

Evolutionists argue that trees provide yet another example of bad design. Dawkins begins by pointing out that their height is the result of competition to obtain better access to sunlight. This kind of competition, he argues, is entirely unnecessary from a creationist point of view, and concludes that it amounts to an extravagant waste of energy and resources[466].

Dawkins acknowledges that trees may have been created in part to supply human beings with timber, and that was certainly very important at the time of the Flood. He also says that it might be suggested that tall trees were created to inspire us with their beauty and majesty. Again, this repeats the point made on page 202, namely that God clearly takes pleasure in both the beauty and the variety of His creation, qualities which may well be even more important to Him than biological efficiency.

To these suggestions, however, we must also add another possibility, namely that trees may have been created differently in the beginning. Perhaps they did not originally compete with one another as they do now, but grew to an ideal height for each species. We certainly know that the plant kingdom was affected by the Fall of man, because God said to Adam: 'cursed is the ground because of you…it will produce thorns and thistles' (Genesis 3:17).

We cannot, therefore, simply consider how animals and plants are now, point out some potential shortcomings in their structures and then argue that they must have been designed badly. According to the Bible, we live in a sinful and broken world, which is a poor reflection of the original creation. Its shortcomings are the result of man's sin, not God's incompetence.

Predators

The existence of predators and unnecessary suffering are provided as further examples of 'bad design'. Dawkins compares physical improvements in the hunter and the hunted with a pointless arms race, which no perfect designer would have created[467].

As regards suffering, both Darwin and Dawkins cite the example of the ichneumon wasp, which paralyses caterpillars whilst keeping all of their sensory nerves active, and then slowly feeds on them. This is said to be an act of cruelty, which is incompatible with the existence of a beneficent God[468].

The Bible teaches, however, that predation and suffering only entered the world as a result of man's sin (see pages 20, 21). They cannot, therefore, be advanced as evidence of a biological design fault with the original creation. As regards the issue of suffering, the question of animal consciousness, even in higher animals, has been a fairly hotly-debated subject in scientific circles for a number of years[469]. So it seems strange to insist it is obvious that a creature as lowly and simple as a caterpillar must be conscious of pain.

Once again, it is clear that the observable attributes of our fallen world do not necessarily tell us anything about its original condition. Consequently, these kinds of observations cannot be advanced as evidence that the world was badly designed at the outset.

Vestigial Structures

General

To be vestigial, a structure must have lost its original function. It may still serve others purposes, but these will usually be of relatively little importance. Evolutionists frequently describe these secondary purposes as *ad hoc* adjustments that are contrived by nature to make 'the best of a bad job'.

There are clearly some potential overlaps between this and the 'bad design' argument (see page 206). The central thesis of the 'vestigial structures' argument, however, is that it provides additional evidence of evolution: the structures were not always vestigial, so they must have evolved. To be an effective argument against biblical Creationism, however, it also needs to show that these changes must have taken place over a much longer period of time than the Genesis accounts will allow.

However, the Bible does not say that organisms cannot change. So it does not rule out the possibility that some biological structures may have become less important or perhaps lost their original function altogether. In fact, it not only tells us that the Fall resulted in significant biological changes; it also seems to indicate that some of them led to vestigial structures, as the snake's pelvis clearly ceased to serve its original purpose after it was forced to crawl on its belly (Genesis 3:14).

There are, however, two key differences between Evolution and the Bible. In the scriptures, biological changes occurred relatively quickly, at the most over thousands of years. Secondly, all of the biological changes mentioned in the Bible are degenerative, not evolutionary, in nature. A woman's pain in childbirth worsened significantly, snakes lost their legs and all creatures became subject to death and decay. Given the degenerative nature of these changes, it is far from surprising if we now find biological structures that no longer serve their original purposes.

As regards the timescales over which evolutionists claim vestigial structures developed, many of these are relatively small or involve soft tissues that are not preserved in the fossil record. It is often very difficult, therefore, to advance any kind of argument about the lengths of time that might have been involved. Consequently, even if it could be shown that a vestigial structure was purely the result of biological change, it is very difficult to evidence the timescales over which these changes took place.

Evolutionists might argue that if some structures became vestigial, then the reverse should also have happened, with some organisms gaining more faculties or structures. The mere existence of vestigial structures, however, does not prove that this is the case or that any other parts of the Theory of Evolution are correct. The fact that structures in some organisms have lost their original function, provides us with absolutely no evidence that humans evolved from single-celled organisms.

As many of the structures in question are not fossilized, the main problem with arguments relating to vestigial structures is that there is little, if any, evidence regarding how something might have looked or functioned in the past. This makes it impossible to demonstrate what functions, if any, a particular structure may have lost. And this leaves open the possibility that it might have been created with only relatively minor functions in the first place.

The other significant problem with arguments relating to vestigial structures is that many of those structures do still have clear and valuable functions. This makes it harder to argue that these structures were not deliberately created in this way to begin with. And in these circumstances, it becomes increasingly difficult to argue that they are vestigial at all.

In view of this, the following discussions focus on the evidence that many of the alleged vestigial structures still serve important biological functions. Where a particular structure has apparently become vestigial, however, it is shown that these changes could have occurred over relatively short periods of time, either as a consequence of the Fall, or as a result of biological processes acting over thousands rather than millions of years.

Human Body Hair

Most human beings possess a very limited amount of body hair. Some evolutionists argue that these are vestigial hairs, which provide persuasive evidence that we evolved from hairy ancestors[470]. 'Goose bumps', they contend, are nature's way of raising hair follicles to keep us warm, and without body hair they serve no useful purpose at all.

However, goose bumps do clearly serve a purpose in modern man. Hair follicles are distributed over the entire surface of the human body apart from our soles and palms. And those parts of the body that are not covered by 'terminal' hair, do still have fine vellus hairs[471]. The latter become erect when we get goose bumps, and these hairs plus the muscular action that creates the goose bumps, help to keep us warm.

It is possible that man was less hairy at the outset, but became hairier for a period of time after being banished from the protective environment of the Garden of Eden. When Adam and Eve were expelled from paradise, God created garments of skin for them (Genesis 3:21). This was presumably done to keep them warm, which would suggest that they were relatively smooth skinned at the time. Subsequently, however, we learn of very wide variations in levels of hirsuteness. While Jacob was smooth-skinned (Genesis 27:11), his twin brother Esau is described as having a body 'like a hairy garment' (Genesis 25:25).

Even if we were a lot hairier in the past, however, it does not follow that we must have developed from apes. The existence of goose bumps and vellus hairs provides absolutely no evidence that evolution of this kind has ever taken place.

Male Nipples

All mammals have nipples, but in males they do not serve any obvious function. Evolutionists therefore argue that the male nipple is either a design fault or a vestigial structure that provides evidence of evolution[472].

However, both parents contribute genes to their offspring of both sexes. The only way in which all human males could avoid having nipples, therefore, would be if all of the genes that controlled nipple formation were sex-linked. In other words, all nipple forming genes would have to be located on the sex chromosomes, which in humans are known as the X and Y chromosomes.

For this to work, the female sex chromosome (X) would have to contain the genes needed to promote nipple formation. The male chromosome (Y), by contrast, would have to contain genes that actually inhibited these actions. The male genes would therefore have to be 'dominant', so that when the offspring was male (XY), the actions of the female nipple formation genes on the X chromosome would be overridden by inhibitory genes on the Y chromosome.

This would clearly result in a larger amount of genetic material and an increase in genetic complexity. This does not seem to be very efficient, particularly as it might not even produce the desired result for future generations. Gene dominance might change, for example, and this could give rise to examples of mixed or partial dominance, with the result that some males might have partially or fully developed nipples.

Furthermore, there is good evidence to suggest that there may be a much more basic reason why males have nipples. They might need them so that they can breast-feed offspring in certain extreme situations; a kind of lactic emergency plan to ensure the survival of offspring at times of serious hardship.

We know that male mammals have mammary ducts and can produce the hormone that stimulates milk production, prolactin. We also know of one male mammal that still produces milk to feed its young: the Dayak fruit bat. Other male mammals, such as billy goats, have also been known to spontaneously lactate[473]. It seems possible, therefore, that this ability existed more widely in the past, so that males could help with the rearing of their young. This may have been crucial during periods of hardship or when the female was injured, dead or had too many offspring to feed.

There is also plenty of fairly recent evidence of male lactation[474]. For example, the 1896 work, *Anomalies and Curiosities of Medicine* catalogued several instances. Among them was a South American man, who acted as a wet nurse after his wife fell ill. This work also mentions male missionaries in Brazil, who breast-fed their children because their wives had shrivelled breasts. More recently, Agence France-Presse reported in 2002 that a man from Sri Lanka had nursed his two daughters through their infancy following the death of his wife during the birth of their second child.

A significant number of boys develop breasts at puberty. In addition, certain drugs can increase prolactin, which may then cause some men to lactate. Thorazine, an antipsychotic drug used in the mid-20th century, often caused an overproduction of prolactin, and lactation is listed as one of the possible side effects of the heart drug, digoxin[474]. Pituitary tumours can also induce milk production in males. Moreover, in adult humans, starvation has been known to cause men to spontaneous lactate. For example, this was observed in survivors of the Nazi concentration camps and in the Japanese POW camps of World War II[474].

This last fact is the most interesting here, as it directly supports the view that male 'breasts' may originally have been a back-up source of milk during famines or times of serious hardship, when a mother's milk was less plentiful or may have dried up altogether. The fact that mammals seem to have largely lost this ability does not mean that it did not exist at the time of Creation. The Fall led to a general deterioration in nature, and genetic changes over thousands of years could also have significantly reduced this ability.

The Coccyx

The coccyx is often referred to as 'the tailbone'. It is the final segment of the spinal column in humans and tailless primates, and comprises three to five separate or fused vertebrae, a fact which allows for a certain amount of free movement. According to evolutionists, the coccyx serves no purpose whatsoever[475] and provides clear evidence that humans previously had tails.

The contention that human ancestors possessed tails, however, is not something that can be proven. The fossil evidence may contain examples of tailed primates, but one cannot show that these developed into *homo sapiens*. What is clear, however, is that the coccyx does serve a number of important biological functions.

To begin with, the coccyx protects an important part of the spinal cord membrane or pia mater[476]. In addition, various muscles and ligaments have important attachments to the coccyx. The muscles in question are the levator ani, coccygeus and the gluteus maximus muscles. And the ligaments that are attached to the coccyx are the anococcygeal, sacrococcygeal, sacrospinous and sacrotuberous ligaments. Finally, the spinal cord membrane or pia mater that is attached to the coccyx is known as the filum terminale.

The levator ani muscles consist of the iliococcygeus, pubococcygeus and pubo rectalis muscles[476]. These support the pelvic viscera and help to keep the vagina and the anus closed. They are needed to maintain the appropriate angle between the rectum and the anal canal. They also support the anal sphincter and effectively act as a vaginal sphincter[477]. As regard the coccygeus muscle, this supports the pelvic viscera and pulls the coccyx forward after defecation[477].

The gluteus maximus has several functions[478]. It extends the trunk of the lower limb and helps to stabilise the extended knee joint. Its main functions, however, are the rotation and extension of the thigh. Here, the gluteus maximus is mainly involved between the flexed and standing positions, for example when rising from a sitting position or when walking up a flight of stairs.

The anococcygeal ligament connects with the anal sphincter, which closes the anus[479]. The anterior and posterior sacrococcygeal ligaments improve stability[480], and support the sacrococcygeal joint[481], the cartilaginous connection between the coccyx and the sacrum. The lateral sacrococcygeal ligaments strengthen and stabilise the joints of the pelvis. They also complete the foramina for the fifth sacral nerve, which supplies the coccygeus muscle[482].

The sacrospinous and sacrotuberous ligaments close the greater and lesser sciatic notches of the ilium to form the greater and lesser sciatic foramina[482]. The main function of these ligaments is to prevent posterior rotation of the pelvis with respect to the sacrum[483].

As indicated above, an extension of the spinal cord membrane, the filum terminale, is attached to the back of the coccyx[484]. The filum terminale stabilises and anchors the spinal cord, attaching the dura within the lower part of the epidural space[485]. The dura is a membrane that surrounds the spinal cord and is responsible for retaining the cerebrospinal fluid.

Given the important functions it performs, surgeons consider removal of the coccyx to be potentially very harmful. Removing it altogether takes away a key anchoring point for a whole complex of muscles, which are critical to the proper functioning of the bowels and the stability of the pelvic floor[486]. In view of this, it is clearly untenable to argue that the coccyx is a vestigial structure.

Tonsils

Prothero says that the tonsils are vestigial organs[487], which now serve no function whatsoever[488]. Neither statement is supported by any evidence. Prothero also offers no evidence that the tonsils had functions that they have now lost. Consequently, there appears to be no evidence that they are vestigial either.

As regards the statement that they currently perform no function at all, this is contradicted by a large body of medical evidence. For example, one detailed treatise on ear, nose and throat diseases says that the tonsils serve both local and systemic immunological functions[489]. They achieve this by means of highly-developed structures in the crypts of their reticular epithelia, which ensure that the tonsils have intensive contact with the widest variety of antigens in the oral cavity. This enables the tonsils to form immunologically marked white blood cells and immunoglobulins, which are then released into the oral cavity.

These blood cells and immunoglobulins are also sent to various stations in the body's immune system. Some of the blood cells serve the cellular immune system, whilst others, together with the immunoglobulins themselves, target immune responses that involve body fluids, such as serum.

The Appendix

Evolutionists describe the appendix as a vestigial structure, which has become potentially dangerous because of the risks associated with appendicitis[490]. They argue that the appendix was originally needed as a functioning part of the digestive system called the caecum. This played an important role in the digestion of plant materials, such as leaves, as these contain cellulose[490]. As we became more omnivorous, however, the appendix shrank and eventually became too narrow to serve any digestive function.

Despite this, some scientists have argued that the appendix serves other important functions in humans. In particular, research in 2007 concluded that the human appendix acts as a safe repository for the retention of 'good bacteria', which might otherwise be flushed out of the digestive system during bouts of dysentery[491]. This function may not be of much significance to people in the developed world, where antibiotics are now readily available. However, it may have been vital in the past, and may still be very important in less developed societies today, where the risk of death from dysentery may be much more serious than the dangers of appendicitis.

Evolutionists do not deny that this function exists. They argue, however, that it is a derived function, the evolutionary by-product of the appendix becoming a vestigial part of the digestive system. They also maintain that the benefits of this supervening function are far outweighed by the drawbacks of having an appendix, in particular the potentially fatal risk of appendicitis[490].

Even if the evolutionists' functional analysis were correct, however, it is not clear why this would challenge the biblical account of creation. According to Genesis, man was created as an entirely herbivorous animal (Genesis 1:29; see also pages 20, 21). So it would be entirely in keeping with this, if man originally had a larger, wider appendix, which played an active role in digestion.

Following the Fall, however, mankind suffered many serious changes in its condition. Death and decay became an integral part of the natural order, which were accompanied by some specific biological changes, such as the serious increases in the pain and difficulty of childbirth.

After the Flood, there was also a change in man's diet, which now included meat (Genesis 9:3). We are not told exactly why these dietary changes were introduced, or if man's digestive biology was one of the things that changed as a consequence of the Fall. However, man clearly adopted a much more omnivorous diet, and it seems entirely possible that thousands of years of genetic changes favoured people with smaller appendixes. A large appendix would have become less and less important.

The evolutionists' argument, therefore, would have to show that the appendix could not have changed to this extent over thousands of years. They would also need to demonstrate that this functional change could not have been brought about by the Fall. There is, however, no evidence to support either contention.

In relation to the first point, the fact is that organs can and do shrink, and even today the human appendix can vary from an inch to over a foot in length[490]. Significant variances in the width of the appendix could have therefore developed over thousands of years, with nature gradually favouring a narrower appendix, as its digestive functions diminished with the passage of time.

As regards the possibility of supernatural changes to the appendix, for our bodies to have been transformed from a perfect and immortal structure to its present imperfect, decaying, and disease-prone condition, it must have been subjected to a lot of changes that are not specifically mentioned in the Bible. One cannot, therefore, rule out the possibility that some of those changes affected the structure of our digestive tract.

Furthermore, if evolutionists argue that the human appendix is a dangerous vestigial organ that has existed for over a million years, why has evolution not removed it? Professor Coyne posed this question, and admitted that scientists do not yet have an answer to it[490]. Unless and until these arguments are properly developed, however, the human appendix does not appear to provide any serious challenge to the biblical account of creation.

Non-Functional DNA

Evolutionists argue that a large amount of our DNA is useless. This non-functional or 'junk DNA' is said to include pseudogenes that were active in our ancestors, but which are now dormant. This includes, for example, the gene for making Vitamin C[487].

Scientists are clearly not certain how the chemistry of our ancestors functioned. According to the Bible, however, both mankind and nature changed significantly as a result of the Fall. All creatures became subject to death and decay, and their bodies changed in various ways. For these changes to have been passed down the generations, they must also have become part of our 'fallen' genetic blueprint; our DNA. It would not be surprising, therefore, if large parts of our DNA ceased to serve their original functions, or perhaps ceased to serve any function at all.

We must, however, sound a cautionary note here. The fact that man has not yet discovered a function for something does not mean that a function does not exist: 'absence of evidence is not evidence of absence'. Moreover, further work on DNA as part of the ENCODE project, which started in 2004, has produced some surprising results. These suggest that much, if not most, of our DNA still serves a range of important functions[492]. These functions may include regulating biological processes[493], maintaining gene function and chromosome order[494], organising the genome and determining which genes are expressed[495].

Biogeography

This argument is based upon differences between life forms in different parts of the world, particularly where these are geographically isolated. Why are animals so similar in North American and Europe, but so different in Africa and South America? Evolutionists argue that this is due to the effects of different dispersal patterns, which causes isolated communities to evolve along different lines. It is argued that this phenomenon cannot be easily explained by creationism[496].

The fact that similar animals occupy similar latitudes is perhaps not that surprising. When this is coupled with the differences between life forms where a land mass has been isolated for long periods, however, evolutionists argue that the only reasonable conclusion one can draw is that these patterns are the direct consequence of evolution. They argue that animals in isolated communities will evolve along similar but distinctive paths if they are isolated for long enough.

This phenomenon is known as 'adaptive radiation', of which Australia is a prime example. It has a very distinct population of marsupials and monotremes (egg-laying mammals), but almost no placental (live-bearing) mammals. Its fauna also include the marsupial versions of many placental mammals, including wolves, cats, flying squirrels, groundhogs, anteaters, moles and mice.

Prothero asks why only marsupial mammals would have migrated to Australia from Noah's Ark[497]. He also points out that the continents of the southern hemisphere possess at least one species of flightless bird from a group known as ratites. These include the rhea (South America), the ostrich (Africa), the cassowary and emu (Australia), and the kiwi (New Zealand). Prothero argues that this distribution would make absolutely no sense if the biblical account of the Flood were true. He argues that it makes perfect sense, however, if these birds had a close genetic relationship before the southern continents separated, following which they developed along different evolutionary paths[497].

The first point to make here is that creationists do not dispute that the geographical distribution of animals is the result of dispersal from a central point of origin[496]. They simply contend that the point of origin was the mountains of Ararat in Turkey, as opposed to somewhere in Africa.

Creationists also do not need to reject the idea of continental drift or argue that isolated life forms do not adapt to their environments. They only need to show that these changes could have taken place over much shorter periods of time than evolutionists contend.

In the case of plate tectonics, creationists could argue that this process might have been hugely accelerated by the cataclysmic events of the biblical flood. The Bible tells us that the Flood was accompanied by the bursting forth of 'all the fountains of the great deep' (Genesis 7:11). This huge amount of geological disturbance may have started a much more rapid separation of the continents. And this, coupled with the retreat of many land bridges by the end of an ice age, could easily have resulted in many land mammals becoming isolated very quickly.

As regards adaptation and natural selection, creationists do not need to argue that this does not take place. It is obvious from the inbreeding processes that have generated the hugely divergent varieties of domestic dogs, that isolation can produce significant physical differences. Creationists might argue, however, that this is one of the intended strengths of God's creation, as it makes the earth's fauna and flora capable of producing a broad spectrum of adaptations that can survive in a wide variety of environments.

The only point with which creationists need to take issue is the claim that these changes must have occurred over millions rather than thousands of years, because they allegedly involved the development of many new species. To consider this contention further, it is worth looking at the case of Australia more closely, to see if there is any evidence that the species living there today must have evolved from common ancestors from the mainland.

So how did Australian mammals get there in the first place; and, why do they differ so much from other mammals in the world? The first possibility is that ancient placental mammals moved to what became Australia before it separated from the mainland. Some of these mammals then evolved into marsupials and monotremes. And as they fared much better than the placental mammals, they became the dominant mammalian groups in Australia.

The second possibility is that all three mammal types dispersed to Australia before it was geographically isolated. As the marsupials and monotremes were better adapted to the environment, however, they survived but virtually all of the placental mammals died out.

The final possibility is that marsupials and monotremes moved to Australia before it was separated from the mainland, but only a small number of placental mammal species followed them. Marsupials and monotremes might have moved south, because they were not competing well with placental mammals. Few placental mammal species followed them, however, as they were the dominant mammalian force on the mainland and so did not need to seek out any 'pastures new'.

Only the first of these hypotheses creates potential issues for creationists, as it is the only one that involves the emergence of new species. Scenarios two and three assume that all three groups of mammal already existed before Australia was separated from the mainland. So what does the genetic and fossil evidence tell us?

The first point is that one cannot conclusively differentiate between the three groups of mammals from fossil evidence alone, as the reproductive differences are found in soft tissue parts, which are not preserved in the fossil record[498]. Consequently, marsupial fossils are generally identified on the basis of the formation of their feet and teeth[499]. It is impossible to prove, however, that these characteristics were not also shared by certain placental mammals.

Despite these difficulties, most scientists agree that the oldest marsupial and placental mammal fossils are about 125 million years old, both having been found in the same rock strata in Liaoning Province, north China[498]. Evolutionists now believe, therefore, that marsupials and placentals separated around this time, probably in Asia, from where they spread to other regions, including Australasia[498], reaching Australia and Antarctica about 55 million years ago[500]. So there is no fossil evidence that marsupials evolved from placental mammals or vice versa.

As regards monotremes, scientists date the oldest fossil in Australia to between 115 and 110 million years ago. As this is significantly older than the oldest Australian marsupial fossils, however, some scientists now believe it is also highly unlikely that monotremes evolved from marsupials or vice versa[501].

In addition to the fossil evidence, various tests have been carried out to compare the blood serum and DNA of various modern mammals. These tests revealed that although marsupials were not very much like placental mammals, there are also very large differences between different groups of marsupials[502].

In view of this, evolutionists have now concluded that all of the living orders of marsupials evolved before the southern super-continent broke apart, and that the present distribution of these orders is largely the result of migration and extinction[503].

In short, therefore, the most recent research provides no compelling evidence that the fauna of Australia is the result of adaptive radiation that led to the creation of new species. The existence of different mammals in different parts of the world is instead the result of migration and extinction. Australia has been held up as the strongest possible evidence of evolution by means of adaptive radiation. If so, that evidence is far from compelling.

2.3.5. Palaeontology

Introduction

Palaeontology is the study of ancient life forms, a study that is mainly undertaken by examining the evidence provided by the fossil record. In the public perception, it is this fossil record, more than anything else, which provides the definitive evidence that supports the Theory of Evolution.

For evolutionists, understanding that evidence is simple. Lower rock strata must have been laid down firstly and must be older than the layers above them. The succession of rock strata then shows a clear development from simple life forms to more complex ones.

Evolutionists argue this proves that life on earth must have evolved over long periods of time from the very simplest of beginnings.

However, creationists view the data in a completely different way. They argue that the fossil record does not tell us about *when* the creatures *lived*, but about *where* they *died*. Creationists also believe that the vast majority of those deaths were caused by the Flood, a huge cataclysmic event which laid down many of the rock strata that we see today.

In support of *their* position, evolutionists point to the evidence of radiometric dating. They also argue that, as many different animal groups share the same habitats, there should be a wide range of different species in each rock strata if Creationism were true. Creationists counter this by referring to the absence of intermediate forms and the large gaps in the fossil record. They also point out that the evolutionists' account has difficulties with the sharp demarcation lines in the fossil record, which they are forced to interpret as numerous mass extinction events (see page 193).

Both models, therefore, have to address some difficult questions. Before considering these further, however, we need to firstly outline the undisputed facts, so that we have a clear picture of the evidence upon which the arguments are based.

General

For a fossil to be formed, an organism's death must be accompanied by rapid burial[504]. The reason for this is that all organisms are part of the food chain, so their bodies would be consumed by predators or scavengers if they were not buried very swiftly[505]. And in the unlikely event that there were no predators or scavengers around at the time, a creature's body would probably be broken apart by natural forces such as wind and water, if burial did not occur within a short space of time after death.

As well as being a rapid burial, the layer in which the creature's body is buried would probably have to solidify quickly. If this did not happen, predators and scavengers could dig up the remains, which could also be disturbed more easily by natural forces. However, rapid burials of this kind are very rare[505], so fossils are believed to represent only 'a tiny fraction of 1%'[506] of the total species that have existed on earth. The fossil record may not therefore be particularly representative of the planet's biological past[507].

Fossils are found almost exclusively in sedimentary rock[508], which is formed when particles from other rocks are transported to a place of deposition. Transportation by water is by far the most significant of those transport mechanisms[509] and the potential for fossilisation is also at its highest in marine environments[510].

It is impossible to tell how long it has taken for a particular layer of sedimentary rock to be formed[511]. What we do know, however, is that individual strata can accumulate rapidly[512], and a thick bed of sedimentary rock can accumulate in the space of just one day[513].

It is true that there is a pattern in the fossil record from simpler to more complex life forms, but the picture is far from straightforward. Rock strata may have been eroded altogether, leaving no trace of their existence. In addition, in many places rock layers have been inverted[514], but it is not always clear that this has taken place.

Strata sequences may also differ significantly between locations, making it impossible to correlate rock sequences across different regions[515]. Even where there seems to be a continuous sequence of rock strata, we find many layers of rock containing fossils of simpler marine life on top of, and sometimes also below, more developed creatures, such as amphibians, reptiles and mammals[516].

The Evolutionists' Arguments

The vast majority of fossils are found in sedimentary rocks.

Evolutionists acknowledge these rock strata could have built up very quickly. They also accept that their ages cannot be calculated reliably without radiometric dating techniques. In fact, before the invention of radiometric dating, geologists were unable to say whether particular rock strata had taken thousands or billions of years to be deposited[517].

Palaeontologists argue, however, that these problems can be overcome, as sedimentary rocks can be assigned relative ages by using what are known as 'index fossils'. These fossils are the remains of creatures that are believed to have existed for only a short period of geological time, and which therefore act as markers to date strata immediately above and below the index fossils[518].

Before radiometry dating, evolutionists dated fossils by estimating the length of time it would have taken for various species to evolve. This assumes, of course, that evolution occurred in the first place, so this is clearly quite a circular argument. However, evolutionists argue that these conclusions are justified for two reasons.

To begin with, they contend that the rock strata containing fossils must have been laid down over long periods of time. If all of these species were living at the same time, as the biblical account suggests, there should have been some mixing of fossils within each rock stratum.

One might reasonably expect, for example, that at least one trilobite would have won a place in the upper strata, and the remains of at least one man would have been washed into the lower strata[519]. We have not, however, found any fossils out of their 'usual place' in this way. Evolutionists conclude, therefore, that the fossils in distinctive rock strata reflect the spectrum of creatures that existed during those distinctive periods of geological time.

The second argument is that there is a clear pattern of evolutionary development as one moves up through the successions of rock strata. One can clearly see, evolutionists argue, that life has evolved from very simple beginnings to the complex array of life forms that inhabit the world today. This overpowering impression, it is argued, is further supported by the wealth of evidence provided by various transitional forms, which clearly shows that later creatures must have developed from their immediate ancestors.

By way of evidence of transitional forms, evolutionists have drawn particular attention to the following:

(a) *acanthostega,* which had gills, fins and ears like a fish, but also had a spine and limbs like an amphibian[520];

(b) *archaeopteryx,* which had teeth and claws like a reptile, but the long 'arms' and feathers of a bird[521];

(c) *tiktaalik,* which had gills, scales and fins like a fish, but limb bones, wrist joints, rib bones and a mobile neck and chest like a tetrapod, together with spiracles, which point to the existence of lungs[522]; and,

(d) *pezosiren portelli,* which is described as basically a walking dugong, a sea mammal of the order sirenia[523].

The fact that these creatures not only existed, but that they appear in rock strata in between those containing their apparent ancestors and successors, is said to be the strongest possible evidence that one must have evolved from the other.

The example of *archaeopteryx* is well known. In the public perception, however, what is generally seen as the most compelling evidence for the Theory of Evolution are the fossils relating to human beings. Here, evolutionists draw attention to the reconstructions they have made, which in their view prove that apes not only became bipedal but were increasingly human-like in their appearance. The most significant developmental changes are said to be the large increases in apparent brain size, which are summarised below[524]:

Name	Fossils Found	Average Cranial Capacity (cm^3)
1. *Australopithecus*	6	440
2. *Homo habilis*	4	640
3. Javanese *Homo erectus*	6	930
4. Chinese *Homo erectus*	7	1,029
5. *Homo sapiens*	7	1,350

Skeleton reconstructions of these fossils are often presented in this order, to illustrate the progressive changes that are believed to have resulted in the emergence of modern man. And for many, this provides the most compelling evidence that we evolved from apes.

The Creationists' Analysis

The first point to recognise here is that it is not necessary for creationists to argue that all sedimentary rock and all fossils are the result of the Deluge; some may have been formed before or after the Flood. Having said this, creationists do believe that the vast majority of the fossils we see today *are* the result of the Flood.

As regards the progression of life forms through the rock strata, as already explained, creationists argue that what the fossil record actually tells us is *where* animals died, not *when* they lived. As sea level is below that of the land, marine creatures naturally occupy the lowest rock strata. Next are amphibians, as they lived in or near water. Reptiles follow, because, being cold-blooded, they would have been less mobile than mammals in inclement weather.

Of the mammals that follow, intelligent arboreal mammals such as primates might be expected to occupy the upper sections of these strata, because of their ability to escape all but the highest flood waters. Next, one might expect to find birds, as they could have flown over the flood waters for some time before finally succumbing to exhaustion. Man, as the most intelligent creature, might have survived the longest, as he would not only have had the wisdom to seek the highest ground, but could also have built watercraft to escape the deluge, at least for a period of time.

These might have been the initial factors that determined the relative positions of animals in the rock strata, starting from the lowest to the highest. Another factor might have been the size-related sorting that naturally occurs when objects settle down in water after a period of turbulence. Many children will have shaken a jar of different kinds of sediment and watched as the particles of different sizes, shapes and density settle out at different rates to create sharply defined bands of different types of sediment[525].

Floods can also create clearly defined banding in sedimentary rocks[526], giving the impression that they were laid down during separate periods of time. This process could also have affected organic material, causing animals' bodies to be roughly sorted according to their shapes, sizes and densities, so that they were grouped together to some extent. In the turbulence of a huge cataclysmic event, the extent to which this happened would no doubt have varied from place to place, which would explain why the patterns we see in the fossil record are not as neat and predictable as one might expect. Nevertheless, this kind of sorting could have been a factor in creating some of the segregation of fossil types that has been commented upon by palaeontologists.

Evolutionists argue that there would have been some mixing between the fossils in rock strata if the biblical account of the Flood were correct. The above explanation indicates why this may not have occurred. This model also accords with the fact that translation of material by water is by far the most significant transport mechanism[509], and that fossils are much more likely to form in water than in any other environment[510]. It also explains why we find rock strata containing fossils of simpler marine life on top of (and sometimes also below) more developed creatures, such as amphibians, reptiles and mammals[516].

It is also worth remembering that evolutionists believe that fossils represent only 'a tiny fraction of 1%' of the life forms that have inhabited the earth[506]. So it is hard to argue that the absence of a discernible mixing of fossils is statistically significant enough to draw any firm conclusions. The absence of mixing might simply be due to the fact that the fossil record is very incomplete.

A further point is that sedimentary rocks are generally dated by the fossils they contain. Consequently, if evolutionists found a skeleton of a man near to that of a dinosaur, they would simply conclude that that particular dinosaur species had survived longer than they had originally concluded, just as they once (incorrectly) believed that the coelacanth had died out at the time of the dinosaurs, although it has in fact survived to this very day (see page 199). If an argument cannot be falsified by the evidence, it is supposed to be unscientific, as it is completely untestable.

As regards intermediate species, the Bible teaches that God created a wide-range and a huge variety of life forms (Psalms 104:24, 25). It pleased God to create numerous variations on different themes. Given this, we should not be surprised if we find fossils from a wide spectrum of creatures with varying degrees of similarity. It is also not surprising that they are found in adjacent rock strata, as creatures with structural similarities may well have occupied similar habitats. Creationists also point out, though, that it does not follow from this proximity that creatures within higher strata must have developed from similar creatures in the rock layers below them. This is an assumption of Evolution, not a fact proven by it.

In addition, true intermediate forms are extremely rare[527]. Darwin himself acknowledged that this was a serious problem for the Theory of Evolution. He observed that the number of intermediate forms that ought to have existed must have been 'truly enormous'. As a result, he was forced to conclude that our failure to find these fossils would be 'the most obvious and gravest objection' that could be urged against his theory[528]. The only explanation he could offer was that their absence was due to the 'extreme imperfection of the geological record'[529].

If the fossil record is so incomplete, however, how can it provide strong evidence of anything, other than the fact that these creatures existed? Moreover, as Darwin says, if evolution is true, there must have been many millions of 'finely graduated' life forms. These must also have been more than just 'intermediate'. The vast majority must also have been 'transitional', in the sense of possessing things such as partially developed limbs or wings. However, transitional forms are entirely absent from the fossil record. Furthermore, if evolution is a continuous process, as scientists maintain, why are there no creatures today with partially developed limbs?

It is worth pointing out here that this is not just a creationist observation. Many evolutionists have also commented on the fact that transitional forms are extremely rare[527]. They have also acknowledged that many creatures appear suddenly in the fossil record without any obvious evidence of an immediate ancestor[530].

These observations led some evolutionists to develop a variant form of the Theory of Evolution, which became known as 'Punctuated Equilibrium'. This was first outlined by Ernst Mayr in 1954 and developed by Eldridge and Gould in 1972. In effect, the proponents of Punctuated Equilibrium argue that evolution involved long periods of stasis (periods without change), which were followed by sudden evolutionary changes in isolated communities. As these communities were relatively small, this allowed for the rapid emergence of new species. These factors also meant that the probability of finding fossils of transitional forms was very low.

The Punctuated Equilibrium Theory has not been universally accepted, but it did offer an explanation for the paucity of fossil evidence for transitional forms that clearly concerned Darwin. However, although it accounts for the sudden appearance of creatures in the fossil record, it leaves a further phenomenon still unexplained. If successive rock strata provide information about wide expanses of geologic time, why do many creatures seem to disappear so suddenly?

The evolutionists' explanation for these sudden disappearances is that they were the result of numerous mass extinctions, the most significant of which are summarised below in terms of millions of year ago (Mya)[392]:

No.	Mya	Species Lost
1	650	70%
2	445	70% to 85%
3	375	70% to 80%
4	250	70% to 95%
5	200	About 80%
6	65	40% to 76%

It is also interesting to note here that flooding is believed to have played a major role in a number of these mass extinctions[395].

So evolutionists' explanation is that the fossil record provides evidence of very slow developmental changes, which would require huge periods of geological time. However, animals appear suddenly and fully developed in the fossil record, which palaeontologists attribute to the extreme shortcomings of the fossil record. And when those fossils disappear with equal suddenness, evolutionists conclude this was the result of worldwide catastrophes, several of which involved massive floods. The first of these conclusions is self-defeating, as it undermines the value of the fossil evidence. The second runs counter to the concept of very slow, uniform changes over vast periods of geological time. It also supports the creationists' belief in at least one worldwide flood.

Turning to the specific examples of intermediate forms mentioned on page 244, evolutionists assume that the *acanthostega* was a wholly aquatic animal, as its limbs do not appear to have been strong enough to have borne its weight on dry land. It is described as being essentially a giant salamander[522]. However, giant salamanders still exist today, and they are also entirely aquatic. It is not surprising, therefore, to find the remains of such an animal lying between rock strata containing fish and other amphibians.

There is nothing like the *archaeopteryx* living today, although young hoatzins have claws at the end of their wings. However, evolutionists now believe that the *archaeopteryx* possessed only a few bird-like features[531]. It is not therefore thought to have been the direct ancestor of birds, and whether or not it was an ancestor of birds at all is no longer believed to be a testable hypothesis[532].

Evolutionists also believe that there were several species of non-flying reptiles that possessed well-developed feathers, which they now believe developed for insulation rather than flight[533].

If this analysis is correct, it is possible that whilst the *archaeopteryx* could presumably glide, it may not have been able to fly that well. From a creationist perspective, this would also explain why its remains are found in strata above other reptiles, but below the rocks in which bird fossils are generally found.

The tiktaalik fossil was discovered in 2004, and is estimated to be 375 million years old. *Tiktaalik* has been described as a crocodile without legs, and appears to have shared similarities with the 'walking' fish and lung fish that exist today. Doubts about its evolution into tetrapods, however, were not raised until 2010, when footprints attributed to a tetrapod were calculated to be 395 million years old[534]. Initially, some attributed these prints to environmental processes. Since then, however, other evolutionists have concluded that they may have been created by walking fish[535].

These concerns do not prove that *tiktaalik* did not evolve into a tetrapod. However, it is also impossible to prove that it did. In addition, the existence and location of *tiktaalik* fossils is entirely compatible with the biblical account. If most fossils were laid down by the Flood, then we would expect creatures such as *tiktaalik* to be fossilised between rock strata containing fish and amphibians, as they presumably would have inhabited areas with shallow or virtually no water.

Pezosiren portelli is advanced as evidence of the evolution of certain mammals, which led to them returning to the sea. *Pezosiren portelli* was a pig-sized animal with hands and feet[523], which had a skeleton that biologists believe would have allowed it to support its weight out of water so it could walk on dry land.

In addition, however, it also had the typical skull, teeth and ribs of sirenians, together with certain features that suggest it was aquatic. These include a retracted nasal opening, the lack of paranasal sinuses and numerous heavy ribs that could have been used as ballast. Evolutionists therefore believe that *pezosiren portelli* spent most of its time in the water [536].

These conclusions do not, however, mean that *pezosiren portelli* went on to evolve into modern sirenians. The latter differ quite significantly from *pezosiren portelli,* as they possess flipper-like forelimbs and have no hindlimbs at all. *Pezosiren portelli* may therefore have simply been a small hippo-like creature, which did not change significantly until it was made extinct by the Flood.

God may have created a huge spectrum of creatures, with numerous variations on a variety of anatomical themes, so they could exploit a wide range of different environments. The only thing that could challenge this belief would be huge numbers of partially developed creatures, such as animals with incomplete limbs. *Pezosiren portelli* clearly does not provide any evidence of this kind.

As regards human evolution, the basic facts are that *australopithecus* had a pelvis and legs similar to our own, but its height and cranial capacity were those of a chimpanzee[537]. *Homo habilis* was essentially the same as *australopithecus*, but with a larger brain capacity[538]. *Homo erectus*, however, was much more like modern man, with a cranial capacity of up to 1,200 cc[524] - well within the normal range for modern man. Evolutionists claim that this progression, particularly in cranial capacity, clearly demonstrates human evolution taking place. Creationists argue that these creatures were either apes or human beings. So how significant is cranial capacity in addressing this question?

The first point to make here is that a bigger skull does not necessarily mean a bigger brain[539]. The significance of the skull size also needs to take an accurate account of factors such as age and height. In addition, we know that the brain size of modern man varies considerably. For example, recent human skulls suggest brain sizes have varied from 1,000 and 2,000 cc[524]. These wide variations have also been reflected in more direct measurements using MRI technology. These revealed brain sizes from 1,052.9 cc to 1,498.5 cc in men, and 974.9 cc to 1,398.1 cc in women[540].

These ranges would be even greater if the subjects included extremely tall people and members of pygmy tribes. We also know that there is no simple correlation between brain size and IQ. So we cannot say how intelligent a *homo erectus* might have been, for example, compared with a modern man. All we can say is that *homo erectus* had a cranial capacity of up to 1,200 cc, which indicates a brain size that is not much smaller than modern man's.

More importantly, none of this proves that *homo erectus* was a separate species that evolved into modern man. In fact evolutionists now believe that *homo erectus* lived alongside *homo sapiens* until about 27,000 years ago[399], and in 2011 DNA evidence was unearthed, which indicated that modern man and *homo erectus* had even interbred at some stage[541].

This mirrors the findings relating to Neanderthals, which were originally considered to be an entirely separate species that evolved into modern man. It is now accepted, however, that Neanderthals were not in fact ancestors of modern man at all[400]. Moreover, in May 2010 genetic studies indicated that Neanderthals and *homo sapiens* had actually interbred[401]. It is perhaps also worth adding here that Neanderthals had a larger cranial capacity than modern man, at around 1,400 cc[542], so their popular cave-man image appears to be seriously wide of the mark.

Moreover, if *homo erectus*, Neanderthals and *homo sapiens* did interbreed, then they cannot provide any evidence of the evolution of different human species. They would simply be varieties of different types of human being, just as a Chihuahua and an Irish Wolfhound are different varieties of dogs.

Perhaps we should not be that surprised by any of this. Today, the different peoples of the world vary quite significantly in their appearance. They can also vary significantly in structure as well, if one compares pygmies, dwarfs and giants. One also has to bear in mind the possibility that some of the fossils we have found are not that representative of a particular group of hominids. They could be deformed in some way as a result of disease or mutation.

Creationists believe that the original man and woman contained within them the genetic make-up from which all of the peoples of the world have originated. And there have been some interesting phenomena in recent history which may lend support to this belief. This includes the case of Sandra Laing, the black girl born to Afrikaner parents in 1955, and a Nigerian couple with no mixed-race background who had a blue-eyed white, blond girl in 2010[543].

Adam and Eve may therefore have had within their genetic make-up the capacity to create a wide range of progeny with different appearances. And these differences could have become quite marked if they later interbred in isolated communities. In addition, creationists could also point out that the Fall led to many changes in nature, which could have augmented some of these differences.

Turning back to the fossil evidence, one key problem for palaeontologists is that they have to compare similarities in the skeleton and other hard parts of an organism in order to define a species, as the soft parts are only preserved in very unusual circumstances. However, these hard parts do not provide a reliable way of defining species. There are many examples of similar looking organisms that are considered to be genetically distinct; this is especially true of birds. Conversely, some species, such as dogs, show considerable variations in form. Furthermore, even if it could be shown that A and B were different species, how could one prove that B evolved from A?

These problems apply *a fortiori* in the case of human evolution, as palaeontologists only have a few good hominid fossils on which to base their conclusions[544]. Many of the fossils are very incomplete, which means that we have to piece together teeth and bone parts found at the same site. As a result of these problems, views about these skeleton parts are always controversial[544].

Given these difficulties, it is worth pausing to remember the salutary lesson of Piltdown Man. Palaeontologists believed that a collection of skull bones belonged to a missing link in human evolution, who they called 'Piltdown Man'. This error persisted for 40 years. However, it was eventually acknowledged in 1953 that the bones comprised parts of a medieval human skull, the 500-year-old lower jaw of an orang-utan and some teeth from a chimpanzee!

Conclusions

Fossils do not provide conclusive evidence against Creationism. Fossils have to be laid down quickly and the normal agent for doing this is water. This basic observation runs counter to the underlying premise of palaeontology, which assumes that sedimentary rock was laid down over hundreds of millions of years.

Palaeontologists have found it hard to explain the sudden

appearance and disappearance of creatures in the fossil record. This led to proposed changes to the Theory of Evolution, and caused palaeontologists to conclude that most of the life on earth was wiped out by a number of global catastrophes, several of which were caused by large-scale floods. These conclusions are at variance with the idea of gradual evolution, but accord well with the biblical account of the Flood.

Finally, it is impossible to prove that fossils of one creature evolved into another or that similar looking creatures were members of different species. In addition, evolutionists' are forced to conclude that the fossil record is extremely incomplete. They must therefore accept that it may be extremely unrepresentative, and hence extremely unreliable as a source of evidence about life on earth.

2.4. CONCLUSIONS

The purpose of this chapter was to examine the meaning of the biblical account of creation, and to consider if this was contradicted by the evidence of science or other extra-biblical sources.

It is clear from our review that the creation account is not symbolic; it clearly describes six literal days of creation. Whilst this obviously contradicts the beliefs of mainstream scientists and historians, it is equally clear that rational explanations do exist to reconcile the Bible with the *facts* of science and history.

Many will no doubt continue to dismiss the biblical account as entirely mythological, and accept the conventional views about evolution and human history. However, the purpose of this chapter was not to disprove science. It was merely to show that Christians do have answers to each and every one of the arguments that can be advanced against the biblical account of creation.

It is important to note here that there is no way in which one can compute the probability that either Creationism or Evolution is correct, as the former involves supernatural forces and the latter accepts that there will always be ignorance and uncertainties. The key point is that the facts of science do not disprove the Bible. They are not therefore an insuperable hurdle to believing in the God of the scriptures.

CHAPTER 3. SUFFERING AND SIN

3.1. INTRODUCTION

The existence of suffering and evil raises a serious challenge to belief in a loving God. If God is omnipotent, why does He not stop these things as soon as they occur? And if He also knows everything, including the future, why does He not prevent sin and suffering from ever happening in the first place?

To many people, these questions represent the most fundamental challenges to belief in God. The problems posed by the Theory of Evolution, for example, could be avoided by simply adopting a different view of the Bible. However, the questions raised in this chapter challenge the idea of believing in any kind of loving and omnipotent god, not just the God of the Bible.

It may appear paradoxical, therefore, that this is one of the shortest chapters in this book. However, this simply reflects the fact that we are solely concerned here with reasoning, as opposed to texts, empirical evidence or expert opinion. As a result, there is a lot less data to be examined and far fewer documents to consider.

Although suffering and sin raise similar problems, we will consider them separately, partly because most people do not see them as being connected in any way. We will, however, adopt a similar approach to examining the problems relating to each of these subjects. This approach will involve firstly considering whether any logical explanation can be found that might justify the existence of suffering or sin. We will then look at how these explanations accord with what the Bible teaches on these subjects.

Many believers might say this places things in the wrong order: we should derive our beliefs from scripture, and accept that human reasoning is often faulty, and can at best only take us part of the way towards trying to understand God's purposes.

One problem with this approach, however, is that the Bible actually says very little about the *ultimate* reasons for the existence of suffering and evil. In addition, we need to remember that reason is one of the few things that believers and non-believers can share. And the limitations of, and occasional failures in, human reasoning are clearly not good grounds for abandoning it altogether.

Before we turn to a more detailed examination of these arguments, however, it would be useful to firstly consider the 'orthodox' explanations of suffering and sin, so we can see why these 'explanations' do little to clarify the much more fundamental questions that are raised by these issues.

One of the first areas we need to consider is the concept of 'free will'. This idea is frequently introduced into these discussions, but it is seldom defined. The result of this is that no clear thought is given to the ramifications of this belief, either in terms of our behaviour and accountability, or in relation to wider issues, such as its implications for the principles of cause and effect.

3.2. THE TRADITIONAL EXPLANATION

3.2.1. Outline

The traditional explanation of sin is that it began with the disobedience of Satan, also known as the Devil and Lucifer, whose pride caused him to fall from heaven (Luke 10:18). Following this, Satan sought to undermine God's will by tempting and ultimately misleading humankind.

Man's sin was caused by the misuse of his free will, which caused him to disobey God. This resulted in man's separation from God and his expulsion from the Garden of Eden. Since man's Fall, all human beings have inherited these sinful characteristics from birth, a condition that is known as 'original sin'. Sin is not something that is caused by God, therefore, but something that ultimately stems from man's misuse of his free will.

Human suffering is the direct cause of man's sinful state, which has brought suffering on humans and animals alike. Although animal suffering serves no direct purpose, human suffering may have a positive effect on people, perhaps by leading them to repentance or by helping them to be stronger Christians. The suffering of Christians might also inspire fellow believers, strengthen their faith, or possibly convert some disbelievers to the Christian faith.

Although Christ came to save the world, sin and suffering will continue for ever in hell, where Satan, his angels and all non-Christians will remain for eternity. There, they will be tormented for ever and ever, because after death they will remain in a perpetual state of rebellion against God.

3.2.2. Free Will

'Free will' is defined by the dictionary as 'the power of acting without the constraint of necessity or fate'[1]. And 'fate' is defined as, 'the development of events outside a person's control, regarded as predetermined by a supernatural power'[2].

The traditional view is that as God is entirely without sin, He cannot be the cause of sin. As a result, it is impossible for there to be any cause-and-effect relationship between God and mankind's sins. Even though God created us and could foresee how we were going to misuse our free wills, He did not, and never has, *caused* us to sin: we remain entirely free agents.

In discussions of free will, it seems that most mainstream writers believe it is significant that man consists of a body and a soul.

Whilst they accept that the body is governed by the cause-and-effect rules of physics, they believe that the soul is not governed by such mechanistic principles.

The idea of free will has obvious attractions, as it broadly reflects how many people think, including non-believers. Few people appear to regard themselves as consisting of nothing more than a collection of atoms that react completely predictably in accordance with the laws of physics. Instead, they view the choices they make as things that are real and not apparent. They therefore believe that those choices are entirely within their own control.

3.3. SIN

The traditional view, therefore, offers an explanation for how sin could have occurred without it having been caused by God. It does this by proposing that our wills operate independently of the rules of cause and effect.

There are, however, two serious problems with this proposition. To begin with, it fails to explain why an omniscient God would have created us if He knew how we were going to misuse our wills. And, if He could not or did not know how we were going to use our free wills, why did He take the risk of creating us in the first place? This would mean that God was gambling with the eternal fate of mankind, all of whom could in theory have rebelled against Him and remained in hell for ever.

The second problem relates to the concept of free will. We can either believe that everything that happens has a cause, or we can believe that some, and possibly all, things happen without a cause. The latter is known as 'acausalism', and it leads to some very uncomfortable conclusions about human choices.

The reason for this is that if what we choose is not caused by anything, then our choices must 'just happen' to us. If that is true, however, there would be no continuity with the past whatsoever. We would just find ourselves in a state of having made a choice, which was entirely uncaused by anything that had gone on before.

Rather than implying control, therefore, acausalism is in fact the exact opposite. In an acausalistic world, choices simply arise in our minds without any cause and therefore without any possible explanation. We would simply find ourselves with desires and choices, which were entirely unconnected with anything that had preceded them. As a result, the characteristics with which we were created, or even those that we had two seconds ago would be quite irrelevant. How could this line of reasoning ever be reassuring to us? Our choices would not be under our control; they would not be under anyone's control - they would just happen.

A further issue with acausalism is that it would mean that how we behaved in the future would be completely unpredictable, as it would have no causal relationship with anything that had preceded it. How then could even God know the future? The future would not have been created yet; anything could happen.

The only solution to these problems is to believe that all things that happen have a cause. God knew we were going to sin, because He gave us good but imperfect natures when he created the souls of each one of us. God wants us to be tested and to fail, but then to find and love Him through repentance. And the reason for this might be that God knows that this is the only way in which we can achieve true salvation. We cannot fully appreciate good without a knowledge of evil, just as light cannot be fully appreciated without darkness.

Although this would make God the cause of sin, it would not mean that He was himself guilty of sin, as He would only be causing sin in others so that good would ultimately triumph over evil. When a *man* sins, he asserts his will without reference to God, concerned only with his narrow, self-centred aims. God is clearly not guilty of this, as He allows sin to exist solely because it is the only way in which He can bring us to salvation.

As regards free will, we could believe that whilst we clearly choose to be and act in certain ways, those behaviours are caused by a number of factors, principally the characteristics that we received when God created us. The interaction of these characteristics is extremely complicated, but to someone who is omniscient, who fully understands all of the causes, they are entirely predictable.

This does not mean that our wills are not free. We freely choose within the limitations of our circumstances. And one of those circumstances is that we have an imperfect nature, which in some situations will cause us to sin. We are like bridges. We can only bear a certain load before we crack and eventually collapse. We can choose how we like, but we cannot choose how we choose. And we choose as we do, because God created us in the way in which He did. We can change, but only if He created us so that a genuine and committed desire to change can arise within us.

Some will say that if this is true, then we are automatons. However, automatons are unconscious machines; we are conscious, living beings. Our predictability to God does not make us any less free than God Himself. God knows His mind perfectly and how therefore He will be and act in the future. He knows that He will never sin, as it is not within His nature to do so. None of this means that God is an automaton; our predictability to Him does not make us automatons either.

This explanation makes perfect, logical sense and it preserves the concept of cause and effect in all things. It also ties in with everything that is said in the Bible. The scriptures tell us that God cannot even be tempted by evil, and that in His nature there is 'no place for change or a shadow of turning' (James 1:13,17).

The Bible also tells us that God 'knows everything' (1 John 3:20) and that 'His understanding is infinite' (Psalm 147:5). That knowledge clearly includes the future, as Psalm 139:4 says of God, 'not a word is on my tongue, but you know it completely'. And Jeremiah 1:5 says that God knew him before he was even formed in the womb.

God therefore knew that we would sin and therefore made provision for our sins in advance, as Christ is described as the 'lamb slain before the foundation of the world' (Revelation 13:8). And as God's knowledge is infinite, He knows exactly how and when we will commit these sins. Jesus therefore *knew* that Judas would betray Him that night, and that Peter would deny Him three times before the cock had crowed twice (Mark 14:72).

God knew that we would sin, therefore, and yet He did not seek to prevent it from occurring. He also frequently does not stop sin from continuing when it does take place. The Bible says that God is all-powerful (Genesis 17:1; Jeremiah 32:27; Revelation 19:6) and that He 'accomplishes all things according to the counsel of His will' (Ephesians 1:11). It follows from this that sin must be part of God's plan and His will.

This purpose is made clear in several passages. Romans 5:20 says that God's laws were deliberately created 'so that sin might increase', because 'where sin increased, grace increased all the more'. And Romans 8:20, 21 tells us that:

For the creation was subjected to vanity, not willingly, but by Him who subjected it in the hope that even the creation itself will be freed from the slavery to corruption to the freedom of the glory of the children of God.

Similarly, Galatians 3:22 says:

But the scripture shut up all under sin, so that the promise by faith in Jesus Christ might be given to those that believe.

Mankind's initial fall from grace, therefore, together with our later sins are known by God in advance. And He neither prevents nor stops them, because they are part of His plan for our redemption.

3.4. SUFFERING

3.4.1 Introduction

The existence of suffering is the issue that probably concerns people more than any other when they consider the idea of a loving God. For many, the origins of sin can at least be explained as one of the consequences of our possessing free will. For the vast majority of people, however, significant amounts of suffering, particularly when it involves young children or animals, is completely unnecessary, and is not therefore something that would be permitted by an all-powerful and loving God.

The two biggest questions that the existence of suffering presents, are, 'why is suffering necessary at all?', and, 'why do there appear to be such large inequalities in the amount of suffering that different people endure?' We need to look at each of these questions separately.

3.4.2. The Existence of Suffering

To justify the existence of suffering, we would have to show that, despite its terrible immediate effects, it leads to a greater good that could not otherwise be achieved. Here, what we are considering is whether we have to suffer to attain salvation.

There does not appear to be anything untenable in the idea that experiencing suffering in others might be the only way in which we can learn true compassion and fellow-feeling. And our own suffering might be the only way in which we can ever be brought to fully understand and accept our ultimate dependence on God.

Perhaps we need to be 'brought to our knees' in suffering to be brought to our knees in a spirit of true repentance.

These potential explanations need to be explored further, however, because it is clear that many people die in suffering without ever having turned to God. And many do not even appear to be able to benefit from suffering in the ways we have just described, either because they are too young or because they do not appear to have the mental ability to make sense of their experiences in this way. How does their suffering ever help them?

There really can only be one answer to this question: there must be an after-life where previous suffering is a valuable part of our journey towards reconciliation with God. The fact that the value of that suffering is not recognised, understood or appreciated at the time or even in this life at all, does not mean that it is pointless or cruel, any more than a painful medical procedure would be cruel, simply because the patient did not understand its value at the time it was performed.

The idea that suffering is an essential part of God's redemptive purpose is also clearly taught by the Bible. Jesus said believers had to take up their crosses and follow Him (Luke 9:23, 14:27), and the early evangelists believed converts could only enter the kingdom of God by suffering 'many tribulations' (Acts 14:22). In the first epistle of the New Testament Paul explains this further (Romans 5:3-5):

> ...we rejoice in our sufferings, knowing that suffering produces endurance, and that endurance produces character, and character produces hope, and hope does not disappoint us, because God's love has been poured into our hearts through the Holy Spirit that has been given to us,

Later on in this letter, Paul emphasises the necessity of suffering as part of the redemptive process when he says that we are only heirs with Christ, 'provided we suffer with Him' (Romans 8:17). And in his second epistle to the Corinthians at chapter 4:17, Paul comments on suffering again and concludes that:

...this slight momentary affliction is preparing us for an eternal weight of glory beyond all comparison.

Later on in the New Testament, a lengthier commentary on suffering is provided by the following passage from Hebrews chapter 12, verses 4 to 11:

In your struggle against sin, you have not yet resisted to the point of bloodshed. And have you forgotten the exhortation, which addresses you as sons? -

'My son, do not regard lightly the discipline of the Lord, nor lose courage when you are reproached by Him. For the Lord disciplines those whom he loves, and scourges every son whom He receives.'

It is for discipline that you have to endure. God is treating you as sons; for what son is there whom a father does not discipline? If you are left without the discipline in which all have partaken, then you are illegitimate children, and not sons.

Furthermore, we have had earthly fathers who disciplined us and we respected them. Shall we not much more be subject to the Father of spirits and live? For they disciplined us for a short time as they deemed appropriate, but He disciplines us for our good that we might share in His holiness. For the moment, all discipline seems painful rather than pleasurable; later it yields the peaceful fruit of righteousness to those who have been trained by it.

Although the subject matter of the passage is 'discipline' rather than suffering, the kind of 'discipline' Paul has in mind is 'painful' (literally, 'of grief'). And the issue of Christian suffering is never far away. For example, the passage begins by alluding to believers possibly ('not <u>yet</u>') having to resist 'to the point of bloodshed'.

The key points of this passage are that not only does this suffering serve a divine purpose, but that this purpose cannot be fulfilled in any other way. Unless we share in this suffering, we will be 'illegitimate children' and not be sons of God at all.

3.4.3. Inequalities in Suffering

Whilst many people might acknowledge that suffering may occasionally have beneficial outcomes, most find it impossible to understand why some people suffer significantly more than others. If God is just, why does He allow these inequalities to exist?

Two points can be made in response to this challenge. The first is that some of the inequalities in suffering that we are aware of may be more apparent than real. Two people enduring the same physical pain might actually suffer to a different extent, either because one is stronger than the other or because one has endured the pain before and so is less distressed by the experience.

This last fact also reminds us that in assessing apparent equalities of suffering, we have to bear in mind mental suffering. This is often invisible to us, but it can be very considerable, as evidenced by the number of people who very sadly commit suicide every year.

The second point is that whilst there might be differences in the amount people suffer in this life, these inequalities might be rectified in the after-life. The Bible clearly recognises that there are significant inequalities in suffering in this life, but it also makes it clear that there will be equally significant role reversals in the after-life. This is vividly portrayed in Jesus's parable of the rich man and Lazarus (Luke 16:19-31). Jesus also refers on a number of occasions to major reversals in the after-life, reminding people that in the hereafter in many cases 'the first will be last' and 'the last will be first' (Matthew 19:30; Mark 10:31; Luke 13:29, 30).

It does not follow from this, of course, that everyone has to suffer in exactly the same way and for the same length of time for their suffering to be equal. People are different. They have different levels of strength and resilience and they have different spiritual and emotional needs for them to attain salvation. If God truly is just, however, then the amount each of us suffers must also be just.

3.5. CONCLUSIONS

Tradition teaches that God is not the cause of sin or suffering; man is. It accepts that sin and suffering may lead to good. However, it asserts that they usually do not, as most people go to hell for ever.

However, the Bible actually says that God works out *all things* according to His plan (Ephesians 1:11). Suffering and sin must therefore be part of that plan. This is why Christ is described as 'the Lamb slain before the foundation of the world' (Revelation 13:8). It also explains why an all-knowing and loving God would create us when He knew in advance exactly how we would choose.

Suffering and sin must therefore serve a good purpose that is linked to God's plan for our redemption. This good purpose is for suffering and sin to teach us true compassion, fellow-feeling and humility, and for us to recognise our ultimate dependence on God, so that we finally turn to Him in true repentance.

CHAPTER 4. SALVATION

4.1. INTRODUCTION

In the New Testament, the word 'salvation' usually refers to a person's liberation from sin to a state of grace and reconciliation with God, the ultimate realisation of which occurs when that person enters heaven after death. The view held by orthodoxy is that very few people achieve salvation; the fate of the vast majority of humanity is to be punished in hell for ever.

For many people the idea of eternal punishment is cruel, pointless and disproportionate. They also find it impossible to reconcile this doctrine with belief in a loving and all-knowing God. As well as being illogical and unjust, some believers raise a third objection to the doctrine of eternal punishment: it does not accord with the teachings of scripture.

4.2. LOGIC

The word 'logic' is used here to denote a process of reasoning that does nothing more than exclude contradictions. Whilst we must recognise that our powers of reasoning are limited and fallible, we also clearly cannot accept two statements that flatly contradict one another. Our understanding of language itself is founded in logic, without which we would have no common ground for debate or discussion, or for accepting one interpretation of the Bible over another. There would, in fact, be nothing to prevent us from believing that God both existed and did not exist at the same time, or that He was simultaneously completely evil and perfectly good. The doctrine of eternal punishment presents us with apparent contradictions that are equally impossible to resolve.

As we saw in the last chapter, the choices that lead us to sin must either be caused or uncaused. The proposition that things might just happen without any cause may seem illogical, but it might simply be a law of the universe that some things occur without being caused by anything.

If things did happen without a cause, this might also prevent God from foreseeing these events. On the other hand, God might possess limitless powers to see into the future, even where those events were not the result of cause and effect.

None of these conclusions, however, helps us to avoid a number of very tough questions. If God knew in advance who would never repent, why would He create those people in the first place? And if He could only know about people's futures *after* He has created them, why would He not destroy people whom He knew would never repent as soon as He was able to foresee their destinies?

Many further difficult questions follow on from this. If God takes no pleasure in suffering and sin, why did He not stop those things from continuing straight away? And if He hates sin, why would He not be equally against enhancing the risk that sin might occur? Why would God create us in the first place and take this risk? If sin is wrong, surely it would also be immoral to gamble with the eternal fates of billions of His creatures.

We considered some of these issues in the last chapter, and concluded that both sin and suffering could be reconciled with belief in a loving God *if* they were a necessary part of that person's path to redemption. However, if most people go to hell for ever, then their sins and suffering appear to serve no good purpose whatsoever.

It might be argued that the eternal punishments of those who go to hell may be an important part of the experiences of others, as these fearful realisations may lead some along the path of redemption, teaching them compassion and the fear of God. And if God simply destroyed the ungodly, as opposed to punishing them for ever, many might not see any point in turning to God. This might lead them into hedonistic lifestyles, safe in the knowledge that they would cease to suffer when they died.

These counter-arguments are clearly not sustainable. As soon as God knew the future, the only moral and reasonable action for Him to take in those circumstances would be to destroy those whom He knew would never turn to Him. This would prevent a huge amount of sin and suffering, which would far outweigh any good that might result from a small number of people becoming believers.

One might also question how genuine such believers would be, if their faith only existed because they were terrified of God and the possibility of eternal torment. Furthermore, by choosing to continue the existence of those who remained in a sinful state, God would be perpetuating sin for ever. If God hates sin and wants it to end, why would He keep sin 'alive' solely in order to punish it for ever?

Many believe that a man's soul is sinful from the very first millisecond of its existence. As God creates the souls of all men (Numbers 16:22; cf. Hebrews 12:9), He must have made them sinful. We can only make sense of this by saying that making us sinful is not a sin for God, because He does this for our ultimate good, just like a doctor who knows he has to make us sick before he can make us well again.

If God does not cure our sinful natures, however, then we must remain in sin. And if those in hell remain in sin because of their ongoing rejection of God, then they must have freewill. If they have freewill, though, what is there to prevent them from repenting? And if this is possible, how do we know they will remain in hell for ever? If, however, the souls in hell do not have freewill, how can they be capable of sin? And if they are no longer sinning, why would God mete out an infinite punishment for their finite crimes? This last question brings us onto the issues covered in the next section.

4.3. JUSTICE

In society, we recognise the need for punishment. It is not meant to be an act of revenge, however, but is intended to protect the public, deter others and restrain and reform the person being punished, so they can hopefully be safely released back into society.

In some cases, we may believe that the offender is so dangerous to society, that they can never be given their freedom again. In some societies, this is achieved by the death penalty; in others, the most serious of criminals are imprisoned for life. In all, however, there is a general recognition of the need for proportionality in punishment: the more heinous the crime, the more severe their punishment should be.

According to the gospels of Matthew (7:9) and Luke (11:11), Jesus said:

What man is there amongst you who, if his son should ask him for a loaf, would give him a stone? And if he asked for a fish, would he give him a snake? If you, then, being evil, know how to give good gifts to your children, how much more will your Father in heaven give good things to those who ask him!

This tells us very clearly that God is much kinder and more generous than we are. We must therefore ask ourselves, 'what human father would torture his children for ever for not trusting and loving him?' And, as far as proportionality is concerned, what father would mete out the same eternal sentence to all of his wayward children, even when some had only been alive for a few years, whilst others had spent decades in evil and criminal behaviour, ensnaring many others in the process? How can it be just to mete out the same punishment of eternal torment to Adolf Hitler as to a young, atheistic child who, perhaps reflecting on all of the evidence to hand, concludes that God does not exist?

Perhaps recognising some of these issues, orthodox believers draw attention to verses such as Luke 12:47,48. This relates to a parable Jesus told of a master returning to his household to bring his disloyal servants to account. Some he would beat with 'many stripes', but the less wicked would be punished with 'few stripes'. This, it is argued, is evidence that hell involves degrees of punishment, so that some people's suffering will be less intense than others. This, it is argued, preserves the principle of proportionality and shows that God *is* just.

If this reading were correct, however, do the degrees in the intensity of suffering make eternal torture a just and proportionate punishment to the crime of not loving God? After all, all non-believers would still be punished with an infinite number 'of stripes' and none of them would have any chance of escape from hell. If all received an infinite punishment for their finite crimes, how could this be said to be just and proportionate?

4.4. SCRIPTURES ABOUT HELL

4.4.1. Outline

The above arguments may convince some readers that the doctrine of everlasting punishment cannot be reconciled with belief in a loving God. However, many believers base their doctrines solely on the teachings of the Bible. This section, therefore, examines the key passages of scripture, and aims to show that eternal punishment is unbiblical.

There is one point that needs to be mentioned in advance. People often refer to 'the *Last* Judgement', language which strongly suggests that this is God's final verdict on the fate of each individual. However, this phrase does not appear in the Bible, which refers instead to 'the *Day of* Judgement'. The latter phrase is therefore used throughout the following discussions.

4.4.2 Psalm 103

This psalm opens with a personal testimony regarding the things for which David wishes to personally thank God (verses 1 to 5). This hymn of praise mentions Israel (verse 7), but it also clearly goes on to embrace the whole of mankind. Verse 6, for example, refers to 'all of the oppressed' and verses 14 to 17 refer to mankind in general and to any person who fears God. As the New Bible Commentary puts it[1]:

The psalm is an expression of praise evoked firstly by the psalmist's own experience (note the singular pronouns in vv. 1-5). But it is tremendously strengthened by the evidences of the Lord's amazing compassion and mercy toward men in general...'

Amidst these powerful general statements, there are two concerning God's nature that stand out prominently in the context of our discussion about eternal punishment:

He will not always strive, nor will He keep His *anger* for ever (verse 9).

The verb 'strive' has the meaning of 'to conduct a (legal) case against' someone[2]. Here, it refers to God taking mankind to task, and is therefore translated as, 'to chide', 'to chasten' or 'to accuse'.

In the second clause the word 'anger' has been placed in italics, as this does not appear as a separate word in the Hebrew text. Instead, this is implicit in the Hebrew verb, which is translated here as 'to keep', and which is used in exactly the same way in other biblical passages[3], e.g. Jeremiah 3:5, 12 and Nahum 1:2.

These two statements therefore present a problem for those who believe in eternal punishment, as they indicate that God's conflict with mankind will not last for ever. In relation to this, it is also worth referring to John 3:36, which says:

...he who does not obey the Son shall not see life, but God's wrath rests upon him.

If God is always angry with those who do not repent, but He will not be angry for ever, then the disobedient must either repent or they must cease to exist at some point in time.

It might be argued that God ceases to 'strive' with the disobedient when He metes out their final punishment on the Day of Judgement. However, if, as John 3:36 says, He remains angry with those who do not obey Christ, then that disobedience must cease to exist at some stage for Psalm 103:9 to be true.

It might be argued that anyone who is in hell cannot be said to be 'disobeying' the Son, as they are no longer capable of acting in any particular way. It might also be suggested that the above statements from Psalm 103:9 are directed solely at Israel, not the whole of mankind.

However, neither of these arguments is sustainable. 'Obeying' Christ must include obeying His commandment to love one another (John 15:12; 1 John 3:21). And the Bible teaches that people in hell do not posses true love, as 'everyone who loves has been born of God and knows God' (1 John 4:7). Anyone in hell must therefore remain in disobedience to Christ's commandment to love one another, as love and obedience are inseparable (2 John 6).

Unlike the similar statements in Isaiah 57:16 and Micah 7:18, it is untenable to argue that Psalm 103:9 only applies to Israel. To begin with, there is nothing in this context to require or even suggest that this is the case. Furthermore, according to orthodoxy, such a statement regarding Israel would be untrue anyway, as God does remain angry with at least parts of Israel for ever. All non-believers receive eternal punishment, including any Israelites who do not turn to Christ.

These two simple, but powerful statements from Psalm 103, therefore, make it quite impossible to believe in a God who punishes people for ever. God is always angry with non-believers, but He will not be angry for ever. Unless He destroys all non-believers, this can only mean one thing: everyone will eventually turn to Him and be saved.

4.4.3. Isaiah 24

This chapter and those that follow are acknowledged to refer to the Day of Judgement[4]. The New Bible commentary, for example, refers to Isaiah 24:23 as being 'essentially the same vision' as Revelation 21:22 et seq., which provides a post-apocalyptic vision of the New Jerusalem.

The eschatological nature of these chapters is also made clear by a number of the statements in these passages. Isaiah 25:8, for example, says that at this time God will 'swallow up death in victory' and 'wipe away tears from all faces'. According to 1 Corinthians 15:54, the first of these prophecies is fulfilled at the time of the 'last trumpet' and the resurrection of the dead. And Revelation 7:17 and 21:4 echo the second phrase when it says that God will 'wipe away all tears' at this time.

The passage we are directly concerned with here, however, is chapter 24 verses 21-22. This describes God's punishment of mankind after the earth has fallen 'never to rise again'. As the earth never rises again, this must be the Day of Judgement.

The important point to note here is that the passage goes on to say that the disobedient will be 'shut up in a prison, *and* after many days they will be *visited*'. The two words in italics here are vital. The first is a conjunction that can equally be translated as 'but'[5]. As regards 'visited', whilst this can mean to punish in the sense of a 'visitation', it can also mean to 'visit graciously'[6].

The latter is how this verb was used only 20 verses or so earlier in Isaiah 23:17. Moreover, the second reading ('visit graciously') is the only one that makes sense in this context. To begin with, 'prison' is clearly a punishment in its own right, so it does not make sense to talk about imprisoning someone and then punishing them later, particularly when the imprisonment in question lasts 'for many days'. In addition, the 'prison' here is clearly not a literal prison, but some kind of spiritual imprisonment following the Day of Judgement. 'Prison' in this context is always used in the Bible as a symbol of hell (Matthew 18:30; 1 Peter 3:19; Revelation 20:7).

Given this, the only tenable translation of verse 22 is the one provided by the New International Version, namely, 'they will be shut up in prison, but they will be released after many days.' Now, we know this is the end of the world, as the events occur when the earth has fallen 'never to rise again' (verse 20). This must therefore be the Day of Judgement described in the New Testament (e.g. Matthew 25:31-46). Consequently, this verse must be telling us that hell is not literally 'for ever', and that people will be released from it.

To argue against this reading, we would have to say that the 'prison' does not represent hell; hell is the 'visitation' that occurs 'after many days'. The problem with this reading, however, is that it would not explain what the 'prison' was. Nor would it reconcile with any of the New Testament passages about The Day of Judgement, which make no reference to a state of initial imprisonment that lasts 'for many days', which follows the destruction of the earth but which also occurs before people are actually sent to hell.

The only interpretation that can be reconciled with the rest of scripture is that the 'prison' here represents hell. Given this, the suffering of this 'prison' cannot last for ever, as God 'graciously visits' its inhabitants 'after many days'. This clearly points to God releasing people after a long period of spiritual incarceration.

4.4.4. Matthew 7

This chapter contains two statements, both of which suggest that most people will not go to heaven. The first of these (verse 14) states that few find the path and the narrow gate that leads to 'life'; most go through the wide gate that leads to 'destruction'.

This verse, however, merely describes the paths that people follow in this life. Many do indeed go through the wide gate that leads to hell. However, that does not mean, that hell lasts for ever.

It is also worth noting that the word 'destruction' in this context does not denote the end of existence. In Revelation 17:8, for example, the beast is condemned to 'destruction', but Revelation 20:10 says that his fate involves being 'tormented day and night' (see 4.4.7. regarding the phrase 'for ever' that is used here). 'Destruction' is also not necessarily an irreversible process. For example, Jesus said that if His body were 'destroyed', He would raise it again in three days (John 2:19).

The second statement in this chapter is found in Matthew 7:21-23. Here, verse 21 says that not all of those who say 'Lord, Lord' will enter the kingdom of heaven; only those doing God's will. However, it is clear that this statement is only describing what will happen on the Day of Judgement. This is made clear in verse 22, when Jesus explains the meaning of verse 21 by saying:

In that day, many will say to me, Lord, Lord…but I will say to them, 'I never knew you; depart from me, you evildoers'.

The phrase 'in that day' makes it clear that verse 21 is only telling us about what will happen on the Day of Judgement; it is not a prediction for all time. The fact that certain people will 'not' enter the kingdom of heaven 'on that day' does not mean that they will 'never' enter the kingdom of heaven.

All that we can conclude from Matthew 7:21, therefore, is that some people who say 'Lord, Lord' will not enter the kingdom on the Day of Judgement. This leaves open the possibility that these people could be saved *after* the Day of Judgement.

4.4.5. Matthew 12

Here, verses 31 and 32 tell us that a sin against the Holy Spirit will never be forgiven. It is argued that, as God always forgives the sins of believers who repent (1 John 1:9), those who sin against the Holy Spirit will never repent and therefore will never be saved.

However, the Greek word for 'forgive' that is used here has quite a wide range of meanings, which include, 'to send away; to allow to leave; to cry out; to omit; to expire; to leave alone; to not care for; to permit; to suffer; to give up; to yield; to resign; to relax; to forsake; to leave behind; and, to pass over'[7]. Earlier on in Matthew's gospel, Jesus said that God would 'forgive' us our sins if we forgave people when they sinned against us' (6:14). So in one sense of the word, God is always prepared to 'forgive' us, providing that we also 'forgive' others.

In Matthew 12:31, 32, therefore, what Jesus must be saying is that some sins God will 'pass over', i.e. He will not punish them. However, a direct and deliberate blasphemy against the Holy Spirit will never be 'passed over'; God will always punish it. That does not mean, however, that this punishment will last for ever.

4.4.6. Matthew 22

Verses 1 to 14 relate to one of Jesus's parables, in which He compared the kingdom of heaven with a wedding banquet. To this, selected guests were invited at first, but then the invitation was extended to anyone else. Despite this, an even greater number of guests was rejected along the way. Jesus concluded, therefore, by saying that, 'many are called, but few are chosen' (verse 14).

Similar comparisons to a wedding appear elsewhere in the New Testament (Ephesians 5:26, 27 and Revelation 21:9-13,). This parable could therefore be advanced as evidence that whilst God calls many to repentance, few do in fact repent, with the result that few go to heaven. The corollary of this must be that everyone else is either destroyed or goes to hell for ever, like the guest who attends without wedding clothes and is 'thrown into outer darkness', where there is 'weeping and gnashing of teeth' (verse 13).

As with several other passages, however, this parable only describes the kingdom of heaven on the Day of Judgement, as indicated by Matthew 25:1, which follows on from these parables. Nowhere in Matthew 22 does it say that those who do not enter the kingdom of heaven at this time cannot do so at any time thereafter.

4.4.7. Matthew 25

This chapter contains perhaps the most famous prophecy of the Judgement Day: the parable of the sheep and goats (verses 31 to 46). In this parable, Jesus foretells how the Son will come to judge every nation, dividing the righteous ('the sheep') from the unrighteous ('the goats'). The sheep are rewarded with 'eternal life', but the goats go away to 'eternal punishment'.

We know that the biblical terms that are frequently translated as 'eternal' do not always mean literally 'for ever'. Both the Hebrew and the corresponding Greek words can simply mean a long or indeterminate period of time[8]. For example, various Old Testament ordinances are described using this word (e.g., Exodus 27:21 and Leviticus 3:17). However, Christians clearly do not believe that these regulations will last for ever, as they were abolished with the creation of the New Covenant (Galatians 3:24,25; Colossians 2:14).

In Matthew 25, however, there is a clear problem with arguing that 'eternal punishment' only means punishment for a long or indeterminate period of time: if 'eternal punishment' does not necessarily last for ever, then presumably 'eternal life' might also come to an end. Many regard this as conclusive proof that 'eternal punishment' must also last for ever, as any other reading would undermine the clear parallels between the two phrases. This would also force one to read the word 'eternal' in two quite different ways in the very same sentence.

There are, however, several flaws with this line of argument. To begin with, if 'eternal life' simply meant 'living for ever', this would not, in itself, be any kind of reward, as it would tell us nothing about the quality of that life. Furthermore, if the goats were kept 'alive' for ever so they can be punished for eternity, they too would receive 'eternal life' in this narrow sense of the phrase. This would also destroy the clearly intended contrast between the fate of the sheep and that of the goats.

Moreover, reading 'eternal life' in a purely temporal way overlooks the fact that Jesus told us exactly what He meant by 'eternal life'. In John 17:3, He said:

And this is eternal life, that they may know you, the one true God, and He whom you have sent, Jesus Christ.

A similar definition of 'eternal life' is provided by 1 John 5:20, which equates God and communion with Him as 'eternal life'. In each of these passages, the word 'eternal' is clearly not being used in a temporal sense. It refers to the quality not the quantity of the 'life'. This life is 'eternal', not because it goes on for ever and ever, but because it involves a knowledge of the 'eternal' God. Unlike biological life, it exists in 'eternity', the realm that God inhabits (Isaiah 57:15), as opposed to the ephemeral, material world.

In both of these passages, it is important to note that the Bible is not telling us that 'eternal life' *involves knowledge* of God; it says that knowledge of God *is* eternal life. Furthermore, these are not isolated examples of a non-temporal use of the word 'eternal'. For instance, we are told that a believer 'has eternal life' (John 3:36; 5:24), but by contrast we are assured that 'no murderer has eternal life abiding in him' (1 John 3:15). 'Eternal life', therefore, is something that dwells within someone here and now; it is not something that will only exist at some stage in the future.

As already indicated, Matthew 25:46 requires there to be a symmetrical contrast between the fates of the sheep and the goats. If the phrase 'eternal life' uses the word 'eternal' in a non-temporal sense, therefore, 'eternal punishment' must also have a non-temporal meaning. The opposite of knowledge of God is separation from that knowledge. That, therefore, must be what 'eternal punishment' means. And this is exactly how 'eternal punishment' is portrayed in 2 Thessalonians 1. Here, the Day of Judgement is depicted in very similar language to Matthew 25. It then describes the punishment of the disobedient as being 'eternal destruction', and explains this by telling us that they suffer 'exclusion from the presence of the Lord and from the glory of His might' (verse 9).

Matthew 25 is not telling us, therefore, that the reward of the righteous is that they will carry on existing for ever, whilst the unrighteous will exist for ever as well, but also be punished for ever. It is telling us that the righteous will be rewarded with a knowledge of God ('eternal life'), whilst the unrighteous will endure the opposite fate, a complete separation from that knowledge ('eternal punishment'). The adjective 'eternal', therefore, describes the quality not the quantity of both the 'life' and the 'punishment'. They are both 'eternal' as they both relate to the eternal God and take place in 'eternity', the realm of God's habitation (Isaiah 57:15).

4.4.8. Mark 9

The key phrases in this passage are those Jesus used to describe hell. In verse 44, according to most translations, He refers to hell as having an 'unquenchable fire'. And in verse 48 Jesus says that in hell 'the worm does not die, and the fire is not quenched'. To many, these statements indicate that hell must last literally for ever.

However, the phrase in verse 44 can be translated as 'the unquenched fire'[9]. In addition, the fact that a fire is not quenchable now, does not mean that it could not be quenched at some stage in the future. Furthermore, even if the fire of hell could never be quenched, it would not mean that God could not cause hell to cease to exist, so that there was no longer any fire to be quenched.

As regards verse 48, once again, this only tells us that the fire of hell is not 'quenched' and that the worm 'does not die' now. It does not follow that they will not be quenched or die at any stage in the future. Nor does it tell us that hell will not itself cease to exist, so that there are no longer any worms to die or fires to be quenched.

The following verse also needs to be taken into account. Here, Jesus says: 'for everyone will be salted with fire'. The use of the word 'for' clearly shows that this is a direct thought development from the 'fire' in the previous verse. And the cathartic nature of this symbolic 'fire' is made very evident by the fact that Jesus then says, 'salt is good' and 'have salt in yourselves'. The fire is therefore ultimately to be linked with salvation, not with eternal suffering (c.f. 1 Corinthians 3:15).

The 'unquenched fire' and the 'undying worm' reflect the absolute constancy of God's anger against sin (John 3:36). That does not mean, however, that God will remain angry with or punish individuals who have sinned for ever. If everyone repented and ceased to sin, the fire of God's anger against sin would not be 'quenched'; it would simply no longer have any sinful behaviour against which it could be directed.

For all of these reasons, Jesus's statements in Mark 9 tell us nothing about the possibility of redemption from hell. They teach us that the fire of hell is not something that any man can extinguish. This does not mean, however, that hell will always exist or, even if it did, that people who went to hell would remain there for ever.

4.4.9. Luke 16

The chapter contains the well-known parable of the rich man and Lazarus. Both men die, but whilst the latter goes to a happy afterlife ('Abraham's bosom'), the rich man is tormented in the flames of Hades. The key verse is 26, where Abraham says that there is a huge chasm 'firmly fixed' between these two places, so that no-one may cross between them. This, it is said, proves that no-one can be redeemed in the after-life, as it is impossible to move between heaven and hell.

All that we can deduce from this passage, however, is that no-one can cross between heaven and hell whilst this 'great chasm' remains 'firmly fixed' between them. It does not follow that this will always be the case, and the Bible tells us of a number of exceptions. For example, it refers to Satan falling from heaven to hell (Luke 10:18; Jude 1:6; Revelation 20:7). It also says that Jesus descended into hell before ascending to heaven (1 Peter 3:19-22).

4.4.10. John 7 & 8

In each of these chapters Jesus made an identical statement to certain Jews, in which He told them that where He was going 'they *could* not come' (7:34; 8:21). It could be argued that this shows that some people cannot ever go to heaven.

However, Jesus did not say that these Jews would never go to heaven; He simply said they could not do so at that time. Jesus also made the same statement to His disciples (John 13:33), but then said that they would follow Him afterwards (John 13:36).

4.4.11. Hebrews 6

This chapter contains a well-known passage about followers of Christ who 'fall away' after they have been enlightened and have also been partakers of the Holy Spirit (verses 4 to 8). It tells us that it is impossible to restore such people to repentance, and compares them with land that only produces thorns and thistles, and whose 'end' is therefore to be burned.

This passage is part of a letter that was addressed to fellow Christians, and the first few verses of this chapter tell them what they must do to mature as believers. These verses are clearly linked to the passage in verses 4 to 8, as the latter starts with the words, 'for it is impossible to restore again to repentance...'

As the advice in verses 4 to 8 is addressed to Christians, it is concerned with what *they* could and should do. It is therefore saying that it will be 'impossible' *for them* 'to restore' people to repentance in these circumstances. This does not mean that God could not restore such people to repentance, because we know that 'with God all things are possible' (Matthew 19:26). It is worth remembering that even Jesus found it 'impossible' to perform miracles in certain circumstances (Mark 6:5).

Furthermore, even if Christians could lose their faith and go to hell, it does not follow that this would be their everlasting fate. The fate or 'end' of the land in verse 8 is to be burned, but that does not mean that it cannot be used for better things thereafter. On the contrary, the fire would only destroy the weeds, so that the land could be re-cultivated and used for better things thereafter. This might be a long process, but there is no reason to believe that it would be an 'impossible' one.

4.4.12. Hebrews 10

In this chapter verses 26 to 29 refer to someone sinning 'wilfully' after they have received knowledge of the truth. When this happens, we are told, there is no longer a 'sacrifice for sins'. Instead, all that remains is 'a fearful expectation of judgment' and a 'fire of fury that will consume the adversaries'.

We are not told what 'wilfully' means in this context, but it must mean much more than just 'deliberate'. Every sin is deliberate, as it involves a conscious misuse of our freewill. David deliberately arranged Uriah's death, so he could marry his wife (2 Samuel 12:9).

And Peter deliberately denied Jesus three times, despite being told by Jesus that he would do this (Matthew 26:74). Both men had clearly received a 'knowledge of the truth', yet neither of them will go to hell for ever.

Verse 29 provides some insight into what 'wilfully' means in this context, as it describes such sins as 'trampling on the blood of the covenant' and 'insulting the Spirit of grace'. This indicates that 'wilful' sins are deliberate acts of defiance, which are intended as direct affronts to God.

Whatever sins fall into this category, those who commit them are clearly beyond human intervention; they must be punished in the afterlife. The fact that a sin has to be punished, however, does not mean that this punishment must also last for ever.

4.4.13. 1 Peter 3

Verses 18-20 describe how Christ, being put to death in the flesh, went in the spirit and preached to 'the spirits in prison'. The spirits are said to be those who disobeyed at the time Noah's ark was being built, and 'prison' in this context is always used in the Bible as a symbol of hell (Isaiah 24:22; Matthew 18:30; Revelation 20:7). This interpretation appears to be confirmed by 1 Peter 4:6, which refers to the gospel being preached to the dead. All of this indicates that it is possible to escape from hell, which directly contradicts the notion that punishment in hell lasts for ever.

Some commentators have argued that this is not a reference to Christ's descent into hell, but to Him preaching via Noah to people at the time of the Flood. Others argue that the 'prison' is either their bodies or their present predicament[10]. According to the second reading, the passage refers to people who were alive when Christ preached to them, but who are now in hell.

Others conclude that Christ did descend to hell, as this is indicated elsewhere in scripture (Acts 2:31; Ephesians 4:9). They argue, however, that the preaching in question was not intended to save its hearers; it was purely 'vindicatory' in nature.

As regards 1 Peter 4:6, it is argued that this does not refer back to 1 Peter 3:19 at all. In line with their interpretation of 1 Peter 3:1, some conclude that this passage is talking about people who were dead when the epistle was written, but who were not dead at the time Christ preached to them. Others argue that the word 'dead' refers to people who are spiritually, rather than physically, dead[11].

None of these arguments, however, stands up to scrutiny, when the precise wording of the passage that runs from 1 Peter 3:18-20 and then to 1 Peter 4:5, 6 is examined:

For indeed Christ died once for sins, the righteous for the unrighteous, so that He might bring you to God, being put to death in the flesh on the one hand, but on the other being made alive in the spirit; in which he went and preached to the spirits in prison, to those who disobeyed when God's longsuffering waited during the days in which Noah's ark was being prepared, in which a few, that is eight souls, were saved through water.

...who will render an account to the One who is ready to judge the living and dead. For this is why the gospel was even preached to the dead, so that on the one hand they might be judged like men in the flesh, but on the other might live like God in the spirit.

Firstly, we are told that Christ was 'in the spirit' when he preached to 'spirits'. So neither He nor they were flesh and blood at the time of this preaching. Secondly, the spirits to whom He preached were clearly 'in prison' at the time this took place; the Greek literally says that he preached 'to the in-prison spirits'.

As regards the purpose of the preaching, 1 Peter 4 carries on the themes of the previous chapter, contrasting the 'flesh' and the 'spirit', which are central to an understanding of 1 Peter 3:18-20. There is, therefore, a clear thought development throughout the whole passage right up to 1 Peter 4:6.

We are also told in 1 Peter 4:6 that the gospel was preached to the dead so they might be saved and 'live in the spirit like God'. If they were beyond redemption why was this done? And why are people baptized 'on behalf of the dead' (1 Corinthians 15:29)? 1 Peter 3:19 could not therefore be 'vindicatory preaching', and preaching the gospel to people who have no chance of salvation is as pointless as it is cruel.

The idea that 1 Peter 4:6 is referring to those who are 'spiritually dead', is rendered untenable by the fact that the verse immediately before this refers to Christ judging the living and 'the dead'. The 'dead' here are clearly those who are physically dead, therefore, and verse 6 is linked logically to this previous verse by the word, 'for'. The word 'dead' must therefore have the same meaning in both verses.

The suggestions that 1 Peter 4:6 either refers to the spiritually dead or to those who are dead now, can also be discounted by the use of the word 'even' in this verse. This clearly indicates that preaching to the 'dead' would be seen as something surprising to the reader. However, preaching to people when they were still alive or preaching to those who are spiritually dead are not even slightly remarkable. The word 'even' is clearly used here, because it would have been surprising to many to learn that the gospel had 'even' been preached to people who were (literally) 'dead' at the time.

The fact is that 1 Peter 4:6 refers to the gospel being preached to the dead, so that they might be saved. The word 'dead' clearly means literally 'dead' for the reasons given above. This fact, together with the common language ('in the flesh', 'in the spirit') clearly links this verse to 1 Peter 3:19. Where, after all, is there any other scriptural reference to the gospel being preached to the dead apart from 1 Peter 3:19? And if people who are dead need to hear the gospel, does it not also necessarily follow that they must be in hell at the time?

The only honest conclusions one can draw from all of this evidence, is that it is possible to repent and to escape from hell and thereafter 'live in the spirit like God'. This also explains why people were baptised for the dead (1 Corinthians 15:29).

4.4.14. Jude

This single chapter epistle contains a number of statements about hell, some of which are likely to be advanced as evidence that the punishment of hell lasts for ever. The first of these is verse 6, which tells us that 'fallen angels' are held in 'everlasting chains'. We are then told about the punishment of wicked human beings. Their fate involves being consigned to 'eternal fire' (verse 7) and to a darkness that lasts 'for ever' (verse 13).

The first point to make about the 'chains' described in verse 6, is that they cannot be literal chains. Angels are spiritual beings (Hebrew 1:14), so the word 'chains' must symbolise the spiritual restraints that God places upon the fallen angels. The chains do not, therefore, possess an existence apart from the angels. Consequently, the chains must cease to exist as soon as those restraints are no longer in operation.

This is important, because verse 6 also tells us that the fallen angels are only held in these chains 'until' the Day of Judgement. If the 'chains' are symbolic and do not have an existence apart from the angels, then they must cease to exist on the Day of Judgement. The chains cannot therefore last literally for ever. Consequently, in this passage the Greek word ἀΐδιος must mean 'enduring' or 'long-standing', as opposed to 'everlasting'.

The final term to consider here is, 'for ever'. Here, the Greek phrase means literally 'unto the age'. Consequently, the phrase that is usually translated as, 'for ever and ever' means literally, 'unto the age of the ages'. The reason for this is that the Greek word for 'age' is αἰών, from which we get the word 'aeon', which means 'a long or indeterminate period of time'. The adjective derived from αἰών is αἰώνιος, and the translation of this as 'eternal' is discussed at 4.4.7. above.

It is clear from all of the linguistic and contextual evidence that none of these words necessarily means literally 'for ever'. As a result, none of the above verses prove that the punishments of hell are literally 'everlasting'.

4.5. SCRIPTURES ABOUT SALVATION

4.5.1. Ecclesiastes 12

The key words from this chapter are to be found in verses 5 to 7:

...man goes to his eternal home and the mourners go about in the street...and the dust shall return to the earth as it was, and the spirit shall return to God who gave it.

The Hebrew noun in the last clause can mean 'wind', 'breath' or 'spirit'. However, neither of the first two meanings makes any sense in this context. This verse must therefore be telling us that the spirits of men return to God when they die.

The New Bible Commentary acknowledges this, but argues that this tells us nothing 'about the final destiny of the spirit after it returns to God'[10]. This appears to suggest that the spirit of most men might be sent to hell after being returned to God.

However, these verses are concerned with the passage of man's spirit to its '*eternal* home', not its initial resting place. And we are told that a man's spirit returns to God. It follows from this that God must be man's 'eternal home'. This rules out the possibility of people being sent to hell for ever, unless one interprets the word 'eternal' here to mean a 'long or indeterminate period of time' (see 4.4.7. above), following which most people's spirits are sent to hell.

However, there is nothing in the Bible to support such a belief. Instead, it talks of people's spirits going to heaven or hell before the Judgement Day (Luke 16:23; 23:43; 1 Peter 3:19, 20). This cannot be reconciled with the idea that men's spirits go to be with God for a long period of time before most of them are sent to hell for ever.

This passage clearly indicates, therefore, that all men will be saved. God is the eternal home of the spirit of 'man' in general, not just for a small percentage of men. And all of our spirits will ultimately return to Him, as He is our 'eternal home'.

4.5.2. Matthew 19

Verses 16 to 26 of this chapter report how a rich man asked Jesus what he had to do to obtain eternal life. Jesus advised him that 'to be perfect' he needed to sell his possessions and give the proceeds to the poor. The young man said that he was a devout believer, but he went on his way downcast because he was also very rich.

Jesus then counselled His disciples about the obstacles that wealth presented to salvation, saying that it was easier for a camel to pass through the eye of a needle than for a rich man to enter the kingdom of heaven. Jesus's disciples were alarmed by this and asked Him, 'Who then can be saved?'

Jesus's reply is very revealing. Not only does He state that 'with men this is impossible'; He goes on to say that, 'with God *all things* are possible'. So, Jesus's disciples asked Him directly who could be saved, and He replied that with God all is possible. That is a clear statement that God is capable of saving all men.

This is important, because the Bible repeatedly states that God wants all to be saved (1 Timothy 2:4; 2 Peter 3:9). If God wants all men to be saved and it lies within His power to save them all, what would prevent this from happening? Jesus says in relation to salvation that 'with God all things are possible', and Ephesians 1:11

tells us that God 'accomplishes all things according to the counsel of His will'. How could both of these statements be true, if most of us were not saved?

In addition, why did Jesus make this statement in Matthew 19:26, if He believed that most people would be punished in hell for ever? How could the salvation of all men have even been 'possible' in Jesus's mind, if He *knew* that very few people would in fact be saved? The only answer to these questions is that Jesus clearly did not believe in a divine punishment that lasted literally for ever.

4.5.3. John 1

In this chapter, John the Baptist says of Jesus, 'Behold the Lamb of God, who takes away the sin of the world' (verse 29). John does not say how Jesus would take away sin. Elsewhere in the New Testament, however, we are told that it is Jesus's sacrificial death that 'takes away' our sins (Hebrews 10:11-14). And John re-emphasises the universality of this sacrifice in his first epistle when he says at 1 John 2:2:

> ...we have an advocate with the Father, Jesus Christ the righteous; and he is the atonement for our sins, and not only for ours but also for the sins of the whole world.

Sin did not end with Christ's death (1 John 1:8), so He did not 'take away' our sin in that sense. What John 1:29 must mean, therefore, is that Christ's death removed the effects of our sin by extending God's forgiveness to the whole of mankind. If the sins of the world are forgiven, then the world must ultimately be saved; punishment in hell for ever is completely incompatible with the concept of universal forgiveness.

It is clear, therefore, that Christ's death does not merely offer the possibility of forgiveness; it brings forgiveness. John 1:29 says Jesus 'takes away the sin of the world', not that He merely offers a possibility of it being taken away. How, in any event, could God say to us via John 2:29 that Christ's death offers the possibility of forgiveness to all, if God knows in advance that most of us will be condemned to hell for ever?

It is also clear from other scriptures that Christ's death does not merely bring about the possibility of redemption. For example, Hebrews 9:12 says that His death 'secures' eternal redemption, and Hebrews 10:14-18 tells us that Christ's sacrifice brings God's permanent forgiveness, perfecting us 'for all time'.

Because of these issues, orthodox commentators have tended to focus on the word 'world' in John 1:29, arguing that it does not mean literally everyone in the world for all time; instead, it means people from 'all corners of the world'. This reading, it will be argued, is justified by the fact that many other scriptures teach that most people will not be forgiven. Their sins will not be taken away, because they will be punished in hell for ever for those sins.

This interpretation significantly dilutes the meaning of the word, 'world' so that it means just 'a small fraction of the world'. However, the Greek word for 'world' here (κόσμος) is never used in this way in the Bible. It is principally used to mean one of two things: the planet or the whole of mankind[13]. In some places, particularly in the letters and gospel of John, it is also used to mean the world of unbelievers, hence the term 'worldly' (Titus 2:12)[13].

Despite this, some argue that 'world' is also used in another way in the New Testament, namely to refer to 'the world of believers'. It is argued that this is how it must be interpreted in various passages, such as John 1:29, 3:16-17, 6:33, 12:47, 1 Corinthians 4:9 and, 2 Corinthians 5:19.

However, there is nothing in these passages to require us to interpret the Greek word for 'world' to mean 'the world of believers'. It has only been construed in this way to avoid the obvious conclusion that everyone will ultimately be saved. Limiting the meaning of 'world' in this manner is only reasonable, if one can show that the Bible clearly teaches that not all people will be saved. As we have already seen, however, none of the scriptures we have examined require us to hold this belief.

4.5.4. John 12

In chapter 12:32, Jesus says, 'if I am lifted up from the earth, I will draw all men to myself.' The following verse then tells us what Jesus meant by this: it was a direct allusion to the manner of His death.

It can, of course, be argued that not all men who are drawn to Christ will be saved by Him. In what sense, however, could one say that 'all men will be drawn to Christ' if the vast majority go to hell for ever? There seem to be many people who never show the slightest interest in religion in this life, let alone feeling actually drawn to Christ in any way.

In addition, this verse does not say that everyone will just experience a sense of attraction to Christ. It tells us that Christ will actually draw 'all men' and that He will draw them 'to' Himself. All men cannot be said to have been drawn 'to' Christ, if most of them completely ignore His message and stay away from Him for the whole of eternity.

4.5.5. Romans 5

This chapter includes a comparison between the effect of Adam's sin with that of Christ's sacrificial death, which is summarised in verses 18 and 19 below:

So therefore, just as through one offence condemnation came to all men, so also through one righteous act justification of life comes to all men. For as through the disobedience of one man the many were made sinners, so also through the obedience of one righteous man the many will be made righteous.

The deliberate and powerful parallelism of these phrases clearly teaches that all men will be saved. Just as sin led to condemnation and death for all humanity, so Christ's sacrifice will lead to justification and life for the whole of mankind.

It might be argued that 'all men' does not literally mean 'all men' here, but refers to 'all believers'. Alternatively, it might be contended that Christ's sacrifice only leads to the possibility of life. Although the offer of life 'comes' to all men, it is not accepted by all, so not all are saved. To this, it might be added that verse 19 only says that 'many' will be made righteous; it does not say that 'all men' will be. It might also be pointed out that whilst there is clear parallelism here, there are also some obvious contrasts; hence, Paul's statement that 'the free gift is not like the effect of one man's sin' (verse 16), something which clearly indicates that the parallels can only be taken so far.

However, there are a number of serious flaws with these arguments. To begin with, Paul explains the contrasts in verse 16. In the case of Adam, one trespass led to *condemnation*; whereas the free gift occurred after *many trespasses* and brings *justification*. This says nothing, therefore, to justify interpreting 'all men' to mean anything other than literally 'all men'. And the second argument falls down when the two verses above are read together. From this it is clear that verse 19 follows on logically from the previous verse, as it starts with the word, 'for'. Verse 19 only tells us what follows from verse 18, therefore, and it does this by using different language to describe the message and implications of verse 18. Taken together, the two verses clearly indicate that 'all men' in verse 18 are synonymous with 'the many' in verse 19.

It is worth noting that verse 19 does not say that 'many will be made righteous'; it says 'the many will be made righteous'. Although the subtle nuances of the definite article in New Testament Greek are not universally agreed, one clear function is to refer back to a previous, indefinite noun. In this case, verse 19 refers back to the phrase 'all men' in verse 18. And we know that 'all men' means the whole of mankind here, as the Bible clearly teaches that all human beings are affected by Adam's sin.

It could be argued that 'all men' meant different things in the first and second parts of verse 18. However, this would obviously destroy the clearly intended parallels of the verse. It is also completely untenable to argue that an identical phrase has different meanings in the very same sentence, unless there is compelling evidence to justify this.

Here, there is no such evidence, as we have already shown that no scriptures teach that the punishment of hell is everlasting. As the interpretation of verse 19 hinges on the use of a particular phrase ('the many'), however, it is essential to carefully examine how this phrase is used throughout the New Testament.

The Greek word for 'many' is used as a noun about 80 times in the New Testament[14]. However, in only 10% or so of these cases is the phrase, 'the many' used. Where passages do contain this phrase, it appears as the subject and the object of the sentence in roughly equal proportions. The phrase, 'the many' can also be found in one of the gospels and two of the epistles.

This clearly indicates that the Greek word for 'many' is not always accompanied by the definite article. It also indicates that the phrase, 'the many' is not an individual stylistic issue, as it appears in different books that were written by different authors for different readers. We need to consider then in what circumstances the phrase, 'the many' is used. And to do this, we need to examine all of the passages in which this phrase appears.

The first example can be found in Mark 6:2, which says:

And when the sabbath came, He began to teach in the synagogue; and the many hearing were astonished...

Here, 'the many' clearly refers to the group of people who heard Jesus on this occasion. They were not just 'many' people generally; they were 'the many' people who were gathered in the synagogue at that time. So the word 'the' has clearly been used, because the passage had a specific group of 'many' people in mind.

The next passage is Mark 9:25, 26 which says:

And when Jesus saw a crowd running together, He rebuked the unclean spirit and said to it, 'Dumb and deaf spirit, I command you come out of him and never enter him again. And after crying out and much convulsion, it came out. And he was like a corpse, so that the many said that he had died.

As in Mark 6:2, 'the many' is used here as a pronominal phrase, to refer back to the indefinite group of people ('a crowd') in the previous verse, i.e. 'a crowd ran together' and 'the many (i.e. the crowd) said that [the man] had died'.

The definite article appears to have been used once again, therefore, because the verse is not talking about any vague or indefinite group of many people. Instead, it is referring to a specific collection of people, who were mentioned in an earlier sentence. Thus, the Greek follows the convention in many languages, that when something is introduced indefinitely, the definite article is always used to refer back to that particular object, e.g. 'he saw a bus arriving, and he got on the bus'.

The next example comes from Romans 5:12 to 16, which says:

Therefore as sin entered the world through one man and, through sin, death, so also death passed to all men inasmuch as all men sinned. For until the law sin was in the world, but sin is not counted when there is no law. But death reigned from Adam until Moses, even over those whose sinning was unlike that of Adam's transgression, who was a type of the one who was to come. But the free gift is not like the offence, for if the many died through the one offence, much more have abounded to the many the grace of God and the free gift...

Once again, the phrase 'the many' refers back to the large group of people introduced in the first part of this passage, namely 'all men'. So just as sin led to the death of 'all men', the free gift and God's grace also abounds to 'all men'.

Later on in this epistle Paul again uses the phrase 'the many' when he is talking about the body of Christ (Romans 12:3-5).

> ... I say to everyone among you not to think of himself more highly than he ought to think, but to think with sober judgement, each according to the measure of faith God has apportioned. For as we have many members in one body, but not all of the members have the same action, so we, the many, are one body in Christ, and each a member of one another.

As with the passages mentioned above, the phrase 'the many' here refers to a specific group of many people, who are clearly identified earlier in the passage. In this case, 'the many' comprises all of the members of the body of Christ.

The next two examples are both from 1 Corinthians 10, namely verses 17 and 33, which say:

> Because there is one bread, we, the many, are one body, as we all share the one bread.

> ...I also please all men in all things, not seeking my own advantage, but that of the many, in order that they may be saved.

As in the previous passages, the phrase, 'the many' clearly has a specific group of many people in mind. Here, these are 'all Christians' and 'all men' respectively. Once again, therefore, 'the many' is not used to simply denote 'many' in the sense of any indeterminate or large number of people; the noun preceded by the definite article refers to a definite group of many people.

Finally, in 2 Corinthians 2:17 Paul says:

> For we are not like the many who hawk the word of God, but as men of sincerity...

Here, the phrase, 'the many' also has a specific group of people in mind, namely the large number of people who in those times were peddling the word of God like salesmen. The use of the definite article, therefore, turns a general term ('many') into a phrase which identifies a specific group of people with whom the passage is directly concerned.

We can now turn back to Romans 5:18,19 and re-examine the passage in the light of this evidence:

So therefore, just as through one offence condemnation came to **all men[1]**, so also through one righteous act justification of life comes to **all men[2]**. For as through the disobedience of one man **the many[1]** were made sinners, so also through the obedience of one righteous man **the many[2]** will be made righteous.

As mentioned on page 295, the reasoning of both sentences is directly linked, as indicated by the word 'for' at the beginning of verse 19. In addition, the use of the phrase, 'the many' as opposed to 'many' in verse 19 supports the view that there are in fact only two groups of people in these verses: those who were affected by Adam's sin and those who will benefit from Christ's sacrifice.

The first group of 'the many' [1] is 'all men', as this is the corresponding phrase to which it is linked in the first sentence. We also know that the phrase, 'all men' in that sentence must mean literally every single human being on the planet, because of the Bible's clear teaching regarding the universality of sin.

For the same reasons, the second group that is described as 'the many' [2] must also refer back to the 'all men' in the previous verse. Unless we can show that this does not literally mean 'all men' as in the first clause, then the normal rules of exegesis require us to interpret this phrase in exactly the same way. We would otherwise have to conclude that 'all men' had two completely different meanings in the very same sentence, even though there was absolutely no evidence that this was the case.

It is also perhaps worth mentioning here that no textual variants of 'the many' in verse 19 are mentioned the *Novum Testamentum Graece*[15]. (This is a Greek New Testament with an extensive list of variant readings for each verse.) As far as we can establish, therefore, the phrase 'the many' would have appeared in the original text, and was not the result of a later scribal error. The only fair conclusion that we can draw from all of this, therefore, is that verse 19 is telling us in a very direct way that in the end 'all men will be made righteous'.

Elsewhere in the Bible we are told that 'the righteous' are God's sheep, and that they receive eternal life (Matthew 25:46) and will never perish (John 10:28). The reason for this is that nothing now or in the future can separate them from the love of God (Roman's 8:39). This must, then, be the joyful fate of 'all men', as all of us will eventually be 'made righteous'.

4.5.6. Ephesians 1

Verse 10 says that God plans 'in the fullness of time to unite all things in Christ, things in heaven and things on the earth'. Verse 11 then goes on to say that God 'accomplishes all things according to the counsel of His will'.

The word 'things' here clearly does not mean inanimate objects, as 'things' in heaven must be spiritual, not physical, entities. A similar use of the word 'things' appears in Colossians 1:19, 20, where it again clearly includes spiritual beings:

For in him all of the fullness [of God] was pleased to dwell, and through Him to reconcile all things to Himself, whether things on the earth or things in the heavens, making peace through the blood of the cross.

These verses in Ephesians chapter 1 tell us, therefore, that God's plans always come to fruition, and that one of these plans is that all beings in heaven and earth will be united under Christ. The souls of all men can only be united under Christ if all men are saved.

4.5.7. 1 Timothy 4

Verse 10 says: 'God is a saviour of all men, especially of believers'. The obvious question is: how can God be a saviour of all men, if most of them go to hell for ever? Those who believe that punishment in hell lasts for ever suggest the following answers:

(a) 'all men' only means 'all kinds of' men;
(b) God is only the *potential* saviour of all men;
(c) God 'saves' by sparing us from immediate punishment; and,
(d) the word 'especially' should be translated as 'namely'.

As regards (a), the Greek word does not always mean literally, 'all'. For example, when Paul refers to the Roman Christians as being filled with 'all knowledge' (Romans 15:14), he is clearly not saying that they have become omniscient. Nevertheless, the primary meaning of πας is 'all', and that is how it is usually interpreted[16]. This explains why there is a separate phrase for 'all kinds of' (πας γενος, e.g. Daniel 3:15) when this is the intended meaning.

Interpreting 'all' to mean 'all kinds of' would also still leave a problem for those who believe that most people will not be saved. The final phrase in the above quotation ('especially of believers') makes it absolutely clear that 'believers' are only a sub-set of 'all men'. Even if 'all men' did mean 'all kinds of men', therefore, they would still have to include some non-believers as well.

In addition, 'all kinds of men' would have to include non-believers, even if the phrase 'especially of believers' were removed from the second part of this verse. Non-believers are, after all, a 'kind' of men. In fact, the New Testament tells us that they are the most common kind of men to be found on the planet. So if 'all men' meant 'all kinds of men', it would have to include non-believers. God must therefore be the saviour of at least some non-believers.

As regards (b), we are told in the Bible that all scripture is 'God breathed' (2 Timothy 3:16, 17), and the 'scriptures' also include

Paul's letters (2 Peter 3:16). God does not just inspire men to write the scriptures, therefore; the words themselves emanate from Him. So, the scriptures are 'the very words of God' (Romans 3:2). And even where statements in the scriptures are not made by God directly, they are still described as being the utterances of God as they appear in the Bible (e.g., Matthew 19:5, c.f. Genesis 2:24).

The problem with (b), therefore, is this: 'how could God describe Himself as being the potential saviour of all men, if He knew in advance that He would not in fact save them all?' Reading 'saviour' to mean 'potential saviour' would also mean this verse was saying: 'God is the potential saviour...of *believers*'. However, the Bible teaches that God is the *actual* not the *potential* saviour of believers (Titus 3:5; see also John 10:28; Roman's 8:39).

The difficulty with (c) is that the word 'saviour' is not used in this way anywhere in the New Testament. We are told that Jesus's name means 'saviour', because He would 'save His people' (Matthew 1:21). That is what a saviour does. Furthermore, Luke 2:10 tells us that this 'great joy', this salvation, 'would be to all people', not just some of them.

If people went to hell for ever, however, they would only be temporarily *spared* from hell; they would not be *saved* from it. Furthermore, according to orthodoxy some would only be spared from hell for an extremely short period of time, as many teach that babies go to hell for ever when they die, because they have never heard the gospel and repented. It is hard to see how a baby that dies shortly after birth can be said to have been 'saved' by a God who creates it and then sends it to hell for ever a few minutes later.

This brings us to (d). This argues that the Greek word translated here as 'especially' actually means 'namely'. This was suggested by T.C. Skeat[17] and has been supported by others. However, the consensus amongst scholars is that the word means 'especially', as indicated by leading translations and Greek Lexicons.

The Greek word for 'especially' is μάλιστα, the superlative form of μάλα, which means 'very much'. It is hard to see how this word could come to mean, 'namely'. And in all the examples that Skeat provides, μάλιστα could still be read to mean 'especially'.

Even if μάλιστα was sometimes used to mean 'namely', it does not follow that this is how it is used in the New Testament. And even if it were, it would not follow that this is how it should be translated in 1 Timothy 4:10. There is also an obvious problem with reading μάλιστα to mean 'namely' here: it would equate 'all men' with 'believers'. According to orthodoxy all men will never become believers, as most will go to hell for ever. The only way that all men could be believers, would be if non-believers ceased to exist altogether, something which is clearly not taught in the Bible.

1 Timothy 4:10 is therefore telling us quite plainly that God is the saviour of all men. And God clearly cannot possess that role unless He actually saves all men. This conclusion is also strongly supported by other passages of scripture. For example, we are told many of the Samaritans recognised Jesus to be 'the Saviour *of the world*' (John 4:42). It might of course be argued that they were wrong to hold that belief. However, their testimony is also affirmed by the scriptures themselves, as 1 John 4:14 says:

And we have beheld and bear witness that the Father sent the Son, Saviour of the world.

Christ is the Saviour of the world, then, not just an elite part of it.

4.6. CONCLUSIONS

We have seen that the doctrine of everlasting punishment is not tenable, because it is illogical as well as being unjust and unscriptural. It is illogical, because the Bible teaches that God wants all men to be saved and that He is all powerful and knows everything, including the future. If non-believers went to hell for ever, this would mean that God had created them wanting them to be saved but knowing that they would go to hell for ever. If God knew this, He would not have created them in the first place. The Bible also tells us that God is against both sin and suffering. However, punishing sinners for ever would perpetuate both sin and suffering for all time. Furthermore, if everyone has freewill, we cannot logically rule out the possibility that all men might repent and be saved in the end.

Anyone who has endured extreme suffering knows how desperate it makes us feel. The idea of much worse suffering continuing for ever and ever, with absolutely no chance of escape, is the most barbaric of concepts. This is completely at variance with belief in a loving God, who the Bible tells us is infinitely more merciful and kind than we are (Matthew 7:9-11), and Who regards all of us as His children. Whatever our crimes are - and some people's are terrible - punishing them for ever and ever in this way is both cruel and disproportionate, as even the worst sins are nevertheless finite. If some people were truly beyond redemption, it is very hard, if not impossible, to see why God would not destroy them at some stage, rather than perpetuating their sin and suffering for all time.

Finally, the scriptures tell us that God will not be angry with us nor will he punish us for ever (Psalm 103:9), and that people can therefore escape from hell (1 Peter 3:19; 4:6). The Bible also directly teaches that everyone will be saved in the end. This is possible, because Jesus has taken away everyone's sins (John 1:29) and will eventually draw all men to Him (John 12:32), so that all of us will ultimately enjoy the gift of eternal life (Romans 5:18,19).

CHAPTER 5. MIRACLES AND REVELATION

5.1. INTRODUCTION

Miracles are acts of God that interfere with, and may completely reverse, the normal rules of the physical universe. The vast majority of people think there is absolutely no scientific evidence to support the existence of miracles, either now or in the past. Consequently, most people conclude that the references to miracles in the Bible were simply invented to lend credence to its teachings.

The Roman Catholic Church believes that miracles do still occur from time to time. They also believe that the bread and wine that are used in the Eucharist are miraculously transformed into the body and blood of Christ.

Amongst protestant denominations, however, there is quite a broad range of opinion on the subject of miracles. At one end of the spectrum, are those who believe that all of the miraculous gifts that the first Christians possessed are still held by true believers today. At the other end, are those who believe that all miracles ceased at the conclusion of the Apostolic Age, which culminated with the death of the last apostle. This is usually thought to have been John, the author of Revelation, the last book of the New Testament.

In this chapter, we will look at the grounds for these various points of view. We will also explore why miracles have not continued to the present day, or, if they have, why there appears to be little scientific evidence of their existence.

5.2. MIRACLES AND THE EARLY CHURCH

The Bible tells us that Jesus performed many miracles (John 12:37; Acts 2.22), including walking on water, calming a storm and raising the dead. The disciples also cast out demons and healed the sick (Mark 6:13; Luke 10:9), and before their apostolic ministry began, they were filled with the Holy Spirit on the Day of Pentecost. This gave them the miraculous power to speak in different languages, so they could communicate the gospel quickly to men of many different nationalities (Acts 2:1-21).

The Acts of the Apostles goes on to mention several instances of prophecy, healing and other miracles. These powers were also not limited to the apostles. Paul describes miraculous powers as 'gifts of the Holy Spirit' that were given to many Christians. They not only attested to the divine origin of the gospel message (Hebrew 2:4); they enabled the church to function as a unit, made up of different but complementary parts (1 Corinthians 12:4-31).

Several of the gifts of the Holy Spirit that Paul lists here are not necessarily miraculous in nature, namely wisdom, knowledge, faith and distinguishing between different spirits. It cannot be argued, therefore, that the unity of the church that was created by the gifts of the Holy Spirit would not be able to continue without those gifts that are miraculous in nature.

The miraculous gifts included the ability to speak in tongues (different languages) and the interpretation of tongues (1 Corinthians 12:10). One of the main benefits of these gifts was the ability to spread the gospel quickly and convincingly to people of different nationalities, as the apostles had on the Day of Pentecost.

The other gifts included healing, the working of miracles and prophecy. The gift of healing could presumably have included the skill and ability to heal by natural as well as supernatural means, as it is placed next to the gift of working miracles, which indicates that not all of the healing in question was miraculous in nature. This leaves the gift of prophecy.

Paul taught that some of the gifts of the Holy Spirit were more valuable than others, and he exhorted believers to 'earnestly seek *these* higher gifts' (1 Corinthians 12:31). The gift on which he placed greatest emphasis was prophecy, because of its power to encourage and inspire all who heard its message (1 Corinthians 14:4). Paul therefore urged everyone to desire the gift of prophecy (1 Corinthians 14:39).

5.3. THE GIFT OF PROPHECY

An integral part of the gift of prophecy is the ability to accurately foresee and predict the future. The importance of this aspect of prophecy is reflected in the fact that prophets were originally known as 'seers' (1 Samuel 9:9). This word literally means, 'one who sees'[1], a word that obviously refers to foresight as opposed to eyesight.

The central importance of prediction in prophecy is also demonstrated by the fact that the acid test of a true prophet was the accuracy of their predictions (Deuteronomy 18:21,22). Without the ability to predict the future, a person could not show that they were a true prophet. It is also clear that this ability had nothing to do with sound human judgement; men prophesied when they were carried along by the Holy Spirit (2 Peter 1:21).

It is of course true that not everything a prophet might say would consist entirely of predictions about the future. A large part of a prophet's message might involve applying that future knowledge to understanding the past or to showing people what they needed to do in the present. However, every utterance that is described as 'prophecy' in the Bible involves some element of prediction.

For example, Aaron is described as being Moses' 'prophet' (Exodus 7:1), and it is often suggested that this means a 'prophet' may simply be a spokesperson, 'forthtelling' rather than 'foretelling'. However, Aaron's role required him to convey predictions about the plagues that would arrive in the imminent future. Similarly, although the word 'prophecy' in Ezekiel 37:9 appears to simply be a divine command, the full wording of that prophecy includes a clear prediction about the future (verse 5).

The only case where a prophecy does not seem to include a prediction is found in the mocking words of those at Jesus's trial, who challenged Him to prophesy who had just hit Him (Matthew 26:68; Luke 22:64). Here, however, the word, 'prophesy' is clearly being used ironically by non-believers. This is clearly not a sound basis for arguing that not all prophetic acts include predictions.

The significance of this is that since the end of the Apostolic Age, whilst various predictions have been made by self-proclaimed prophets, none of them has come true. It does not follow from this, of course, that prophecy has ceased altogether. However, it is quite persuasive evidence that this is in fact the case.

Those who take a contrary view refer, in particular, to a speech by Peter in Acts chapter 2 on the Day of Pentecost, in which he explained their speaking in tongues by referring to Joel 2:28-32. According to most translations of Acts 2:17-21, Joel predicted that 'in the last days' God would pour out His Spirit on all people, causing them to prophesy and see visions. The passage concludes with a reference to the sun being darkened and the moon being turned to 'blood' before 'the great and glorious day of the Lord'. It is argued that 'the last days' here must therefore represent the final dispensation of the world, which began at Pentecost and will end with the Second Coming of Christ.

There are, however, serious problems with this interpretation. To begin with, the phrase 'the last days' does not appear in all versions of Acts 2:17. It also does not appear in the Hebrew or the Septuagint texts of Joel 2:28. The Hebrew text reads, אַחֲרֵי־כֵן, the literal meaning of which is 'after thus'[2], which is generally translated as 'afterwards'[3]. The corresponding phrase in the Septuagint of Joel 2:28 is μετα ταυτα. This literally means 'after these', and is usually translated as 'after these things'[4]. The latter is also the Greek phrase that appears in some versions of Act 2:17. So the original Hebrew of Joel 2:28 does not say 'in the last days' and neither do some of the Greek versions of Acts 2:17. It is clearly unsound therefore to base a doctrine entirely on this reading.

Secondly, even if 'in the last days' were the correct reading, it would not follow that prophecy and vision would continue *throughout* this period of time. We are also told that the sun would be darkened 'in' these last days. However, this does not mean that the sun would be darkened *throughout* this period.

If prophecy and vision did end, however, it raises three questions: when did this happen? why did it happen? and what implications does this have for the other gifts of the Holy Spirit? We will address each of these questions in the following pages.

5.4. THE END OF PROPHECY

5.4.1. Introduction

The next page provides an interlinear translation of one of the most significant of all Old Testament prophecies: Daniel's prophecy of the 'seventy sevens'. The interlinear text follows the right-to-left order of the Hebrew text, but the page after this provides a translation in traditional format. This is then followed by a detailed interpretation of the passage, which clarifies its meaning within the context of Daniel's other prophecies

All of the textual variants we know about are minor in nature, and none alter one clear message: all prophecy and vision came to an end within this period of 'seventy sevens'. As we will show, this coincided with the end of the Apostolic Age.

5.4.2. Daniel 9:21-27

בַּתְּחִלָּה	בֶחָזוֹן	רָאִיתִי	אֲשֶׁר	גַבְרִיאֵל	וְהָאִישׁ	בַּתְּפִלָּה	מְדַבֵּר	אֲנִי	וְעוֹד
at the beginning	in a vision	I saw	whom	Gabriel	the man then	in prayer	speaking	I	And still

וַיֹּאמֶר	עִמִּי	וַיְדַבֵּר	עָרֶב־מִנְחַת	כְּעֵת	אֵלַי	נֹגֵעַ	בִּיעָף	מֻעָף
and said	with me	and he spoke	evening offering	of time about	unto me	reaching	weariness	faint

וַאֲנִי	דָבָר	יָצָא	תַחֲנוּנֶיךָ	בִּתְחִלַּת	בִּינָה	לְהַשְׂכִּילְךָ	יָצָאתִי	עַתָּה	דָנִיֵּאל
and I	a word	went forth	your supplications	At beginning of	understanding	to teach you	have I come forth	now	Daniel

בַּמַּרְאֶה:	וְהָבֵן	בַּדָּבָר	וּבִין	אַתָּה	חֲמוּדוֹת	כִּי	לְהַגִּיד	בָאתִי
the vision	and understand	the message	so consider	you	precious	because	to explain	have come

וּלְחָתֵם	הַפֶּשַׁע	לְכַלֵּא	קָדְשֶׁךָ	וְעַל־עִיר	עַל־עַמְּךָ	נֶחְתַּךְ	שִׁבְעִים	שָׁבֻעִים
and to seal up	the transgression	to end	your holy	and upon city	upon your people	determined	seventy	sevens

וְלִמְשֹׁחַ	וְנָבִיא	חָזוֹן	וְלַחְתֹּם	עֹלָמִים	צֶדֶק	וּלְהָבִיא	עָוֹן	וּלְכַפֵּר	חַטָּאוֹת
and to anoint	and prophecy	vision	and to seal up	everlasting	righteousness	and to bring in	iniquity	to atone for	sins

יְרוּשָׁלִַם	וְלִבְנוֹת	לְהָשִׁיב	דָבָר	מִן־מֹצָא	וְתַשְׂכֵּל	וְתֵדַע	קֹדֶשׁ קָדָשִׁים:
Jerusalem	to rebuild	to restore	command	from going forth	and understand	So know	of holy holies

וְנִבְנְתָה	תָּשׁוּב	וּשְׁנַיִם	שִׁשִּׁים	וְשָׁבֻעִים	שִׁבְעָה	שָׁבֻעִים	נָגִיד	עַד־מָשִׁיחַ
and will be rebuilt	will return	and two	sixty	and sevens	seven	sevens	a prince	unto an anointed one

יִכָּרֵת	וּשְׁנַיִם	שִׁשִּׁים	הַשָּׁבֻעִים	וְאַחֲרֵי	הָעִתִּים:	וּבְצוֹק	וְחָרוּץ	רְחוֹב
will be cut off	and two	sixty	the sevens	and after	the times	distressing	but a moat	a city square

וְקִצּוֹ	הַבָּא	נָגִיד	עַם	יַשְׁחִית	וְהַקֹּדֶשׁ	וְהָעִיר	לוֹ	וְאֵין	מָשִׁיחַ
and its end	coming	the prince	of people	will destroy	and the sanctuary	and the city	anything	and not	an anointed one

לָרַבִּים	בְּרִית	וְהִגְבִּיר	שֹׁמֵמוֹת:	נֶחֱרֶצֶת	מִלְחָמָה	קֵץ	וְעַד	בַשֶּׁטֶף
to the multitudes	a covenant	and he will confirm	desolations	determined	fighting	end	until and	in the flood

שִׁקּוּצִים	כְּנַף	וְעַל	וּמִנְחָה	זֶבַח	יַשְׁבִּית	הַשָּׁבוּעַ	וַחֲצִי	אֶחָד	שָׁבוּעַ
abominations	of wing	and upon	and offering	sacrifice	will he end	the seven	and half of	one	seven

עַל־שֹׁמֵם	תִּתַּךְ	וְנֶחֱרָצָה	וְעַד־כָּלָה	מְשֹׁמֵם
upon causing desolation	shall pour out	and determined	even unto end	causing desolation

Translation

And I was still speaking in prayer when the man Gabriel, who I had seen in a vision at the start, faint with weariness, reached me about the time of the evening offering. And he taught me and spoke with me, and said:

'Daniel I came forth now to give you understanding. At the start of your prayers, a word went out and I have come to explain, because you are precious. So consider the message and understand the vision.

Seventy sevens are decreed for your people and for your holy city, to end the transgression and to seal up sins, and to atone for iniquity, and to bring in everlasting righteousness, and to seal up vision and prophecy, and to anoint the holy of holies.

Therefore, know and understand, from the going forth of a command to restore and rebuild Jerusalem unto an anointed one, a prince, there will be seven sevens and sixty two sevens. A city square and a moat will be rebuilt, but in distressing times.

And after the sixty two sevens an anointed one will be cut off and have nothing, and the people of the prince who will come will destroy the city and the sanctuary. And its end will be in a flood, and until the end there will be fighting; desolations are decreed.

And he will confirm a covenant with the multitudes one seven and half way through the seven he will end sacrifice and offering, on a wing of abominations causing desolation until the end; and what is determined shall be poured out on the one causing the desolation.'

5.4.3. Related Texts

(a) General

To understand this prophecy we have to look at its immediate and wider context. We will begin, therefore, with an outline of Daniel's contents, followed by a close examination of the key passages.

The book of Daniel is divided into 12 chapters. The first six cover events during Daniel's captivity, including his interpretation of the visions that kings Nebuchadnezzar and Belshazzar experienced (chapters 2, 4 and 5). The second six chapters cover various revelations Daniel received, namely:

Chapter 7: The Dream of the Four Beasts
Chapter 8: The Vision of the Ram and the Goat
Chapter 9: The Prophecy of the 'Seventy Sevens'
Chapter 10: The Vision of a Man
Chapter 11: The Kings of the South and the North
Chapter 12: The End Times

(b) Chapter 7: The Dream of the Four Beasts

In the first year of the Babylonian king, Belshazzar, Daniel has a vision in which he sees four beasts. These emerge from the sea in turn and resemble a lion, a bear, a leopard with four heads and a beast with iron teeth, bronze claws and ten horns. These horns are followed by another horn, which uproots three of those before it.

This last horn is boastful and wages war against the saints. God sits in judgement on the fourth beast, following which it is killed and thrown into a blazing fire. The other beasts remain for a period of time, but are stripped of their power. Daniel then sees one 'like a son of man' coming in the clouds, approaching God and being given power and glory and a kingdom that will never end.

Daniel is then given the meaning of his dream by one of the men in his vision. He is told that the four beasts are four kingdoms that will arise. Daniel is told that the fourth kingdom will be different from the others and will devour the earth, crushing and trampling it.

Daniel is also told that the ten horns are ten rulers of the fourth kingdom, who are followed by another ruler who humbles three rulers before him. The saints are handed over to this last ruler for 'a time, times and half a time'. The power of this ruler is ultimately taken away, however, and the saints are delivered into God's kingdom, which lasts for ever.

(c) Chapter 8: The Vision of the Ram and the Goat

This vision takes place in Belshazzar's third year. In it, Daniel sees a ram with two horns, one of which is longer than the other, but grows up after it. The ram charges west, north and south and does what it pleases, as none is able to stand up to it.

The ram becomes great, but is confronted by a goat from the west with a prominent horn between its eyes. The goat attacks the ram and shatters the ram's two horns. The ram is trampled underfoot and the goat reigns and becomes very powerful. However, at the height of its power its long horn is broken off and replaced by four prominent horns, pointing towards the four winds of heaven.

From one of the four horns grows another, which grows in power in the south and east and towards 'the Bountiful Land'. It then grows up to the heavens and throws down the stars, trampling them underfoot, even magnifying himself against 'the ruler of the host'. This horn then takes away the regular sacrifice and throws down the ruler of the host's sanctuary. As a result of a 'transgression causing desolation', a host and the regular sacrifice are given over to this horn, which prospers and throws truth down to the ground.

Daniel then hears one saint ask another about how long parts of the vision will last, namely those relating to the regular sacrifice and the desolating transgression that leads to both the sanctuary and the host being trampled underfoot. The answer that is given is that there will be 2,300 evenings and mornings before the sanctuary is 'vindicated'.

A man, Gabriel, then explains the meaning of the vision to Daniel. He says that the vision concerns 'the time of the end'. He explains that the two-horned ram represents the kings of Media and Persia, whilst the goat is the king of Greece, with the horn being its first king. The four horns that replace it are four kingdoms that emerge from Greece. After this, when the transgressors of those kingdoms have finished, a powerful king arises. He becomes very strong, but not by his own power. He deceives many and destroys mighty men and the holy people. He then takes his stand against 'the Ruler of rulers'. He is ultimately destroyed, but not by a human hand.

(d) Chapter 10: The Vision of a Man

This vision occurs in the third year of Cyrus, the king of Persia. In it, Daniel sees a man dressed in linen with a gold belt, whose face is like lightening. He tells Daniel that he has been helped by Michael, one of the first rulers, to resist the king of Persia. The man says that he comes now to explain what will happen to Daniel's people in the future, and he later adds that the arrival of a king of Greece is imminent.

(e) Chapter 11: The Kings of the South and the North

The man in the vision in chapter 10 tells Daniel that four more kings will appear in Persia. The fourth will stir up everyone against the kingdom of Greece. Following this, a mighty ruler will arise whose empire is divided between the four winds of heaven. His empire is then given over to others.

The king of the south becomes strong, but one of his rulers is even stronger. This ruler rules with great power, but he and the king become allies. The king's daughter goes to the king of the north to make an alliance, but it does not last. However, one of her offspring then rises up against the king of the north and carries off the booty to Egypt.

The king of the north then invades the king of the south's kingdom and eventually defeats him. The king of the south fights back successfully, only to be greeted by a further wave of fighting, including a rebellion from Daniel's people to fulfil a vision. This fight back is unsuccessful, however.

The king of the north then invades and defeats the king of the south, taking over 'the glorious land', which he has the power to destroy. He then makes an alliance with the king of the south. Attempts are made to destroy his kingdom via female infiltration, but this fails.

He then turns his attention to the coasts, but this is unsuccessful. He falls, but is not found. There is then a successor, who sends out a tax collector to maintain his kingdom. He is likewise defeated, but not in battle.

This successor is followed later by a despicable person, who obtains the kingdom by flattery. He sweeps away an army and a 'ruler of the covenant' and uses deceit to plunder and scatter all before him. He plans to defeat the king of the south, who raises a large army, but he fails as a result of internal conspiracies. The king of the north returns to his own country after seizing great wealth.

The king of the north's heart is still set against the holy covenant, however, and he invades from the south again. He is repelled in the coastlands by the ships of Kittim (Cyprus), but returns and sides with those who forsake the holy covenant. They profane the sanctuary and remove the regular sacrifice, erecting an 'abomination that causes desolation'. The wise stand up to him, but suffer from the sword, fire and exile. Many stumble, but only to be purged and refined for 'the time of the end'.

The king of the north now exalts himself above all others, even vaunting himself above every god, including 'the God of gods'. The only god he himself honours is an unknown god of battle. He then divides up the land 'for a price'.

At 'the end time', the king of the south pushes back. The king of the north responds with horses, chariots and ships and enters 'the glorious land'. Edom, Moab and Ammon escape, but Egypt, Lybia and Ethiopia are not spared. The king is troubled by news from the north and east, and places his tents between the seas in 'the glorious holy mountain'. When his end arrives, however, no-one comes to his aid.

Daniel is told that around this time Michael, a great ruler who protects Daniel's people, will stand up. There will then be a time of unprecedented trouble, but everyone whose name is written in 'the book' will be delivered. Many of those who 'sleep in the dust' will awake, some to eternal life and some to eternal punishment. The man then tells Daniel to shut up the words and seal the book until the time of the end.

Daniel then sees two other men, one of whom asks the man clothed in linen how long (literally 'until when') it will be to the end of these wonders. The man in linen replies that they will last for 'a time, times and half a time', a period which will culminate with the breaking of the power of the holy people.

Daniel does not understand this and enquires further. He is told that the words are sealed up until 'the time of the end' and only the wise will understand them. However, the man also tells him that from the time the daily sacrifice is taken away and the abomination that causes desolation takes place, there will be 1,290 days. Those who reach the 1,335 days are blessed, and Daniel is told that he will 'stand in his lot' at the end of those days.

(f) Chapter 9: The Prophecy of the 'Seventy Sevens'

Connections with Other Passages

This prophecy was delivered by Gabriel, which provides an immediate link to the vision in chapter 8, as Gabriel had only partially explained this (Daniel 8:13-26). The connection with the chapter 8 vision is reinforced by Daniel 9:23, as Gabriel exhorts Daniel to consider his message and understand 'the vision'.

The use of the definite article here signifies that Gabriel must be referring back to one of Daniel's previous visions. This must be the vision in chapter 8, as the meaning of the other vision was fully explained (Daniel 7:16). By contrast, Daniel clearly did not fully understand the vision in chapter 8 (Daniel 8:27). The latter must therefore have been 'the vision' to which Gabriel was referring in Daniel 9:23.

It follows from this that there must be some common ground between the vision in chapter 8 and the prophecies in Daniel 9. The only elements of the chapter 8 vision that were unexplained, however, were those relating to the four kingdoms that emerged from Greece (8:21,22). The ruler of one of those kingdoms dealt with a rebellion by the holy people by putting an end to the daily sacrifice, taking over the sanctuary and trampling it underfoot. This is the only common ground between this vision and the prophecy in Daniel chapter 9. Daniel 8:25 and 9:26,27 must therefore be describing the same events.

Daniel was also told that the vision in chapter 8 related to 'the time of the end' (literally an 'end time') and this same phrase is used in the second half of the vision in Daniel 11 to 12. This indicates that this part of the vision in Daniel 11 and 12 relates to the same events as the prophecy in Daniel 9.

This connection is reinforced by Daniel 11:31, which refers to 'the abomination that causes desolation'. As Daniel 9:27 is the only other place before this that refers to an abomination that causes desolation, Daniel 11:31 must be referring back to this event. This is confirmed by Matthew 24:15, which refers to 'the abomination that causes desolation spoken of by the prophet Daniel'. The use of the definite article means that Daniel must have only mentioned one 'abomination that causes desolation'. Daniel 9:27, 11:31 and 12:11 must therefore refer to the same event.

The connection between the visions in chapter 7 and 8 is confirmed by Daniel 8:1. This says that in the third year of Belshazzar Daniel saw a vision 'after' the one' he saw in 'the beginning'. i.e. in Belshazzar's first year. The Hebrew word for 'after' is clearly not being used here in a temporal sense, as this would make the second half of the sentence completely redundant. All scripture serves a didactic purpose (2 Timothy 3:16), and the final clause of Daniel 8:1 would be pointless if it was merely telling us that year three occurred 'after' year one!

Daniel 8:1 must therefore be using the word 'after' in the sense of 'in line with' or 'according to'. And there are many examples of this use of the word in the Old Testament. For example, 2 Chronicles 2:17 says that Solomon conducted a census 'after' ('in line with') the system employed by David. Similarly, Jeremiah 16:12 refers to people walking 'after' ('according to') the stubbornness of their hearts. Further examples appear in Deuteronomy 13:4; 1 Kings 11:6; 2 Kings 23:3; Job 31:7; Isaiah 65:2; Jeremiah 18:12; and, Hosea 5:11. Daniel 8:1 must therefore be telling us that the vision in Daniel 8 was 'after' the one in Daniel 7, i.e. it followed on from, was connected to, and was in the same vein as the dream of the previous chapter.

The connection between Daniel 7:24-26 and 9:27 is further supported by other links. To begin with, Daniel 7:25 says that the saints will be handed over to a ruler for 'a time, times and half a time', when he will seek to 'change their set times and laws'. The events in Daniel 12:7 also take place during 'a time, times and half a time' or three-and-a-half 'times'. As we have seen, Daniel 9:27 and 12:7 refer to the same events. The former also involves a 'three- and-a-half' time period, as the ruler ends the daily sacrifice in the middle of a 'seven', i.e. for three-and-a-half units of time.

The other links with the visions and the prophecy in chapter 9 mainly relate to the actions and character of the ruler. In both Daniel 7:8 and 8:9 the ruler is represented as a 'little horn'. In Daniel 7:25, the ruler speaks against 'the Most High', attacks the holy ones, tries to change their set times and laws, but is eventually destroyed by God. In Daniel 8:24 the ruler elevates himself against the 'Ruler of the Hosts', attacks the holy places and changes its 'set times' by cancelling the daily sacrifice. His power is also broken, but 'not by a human hand'. Similarly, Daniel 9:26 refers to a ruler who attacks the holy city and its sanctuary and changes its laws regarding daily sacrifice, before his just punishment is meted out to him.

The Timescale

All of the revelations in Daniel chapters 7 to 12 are therefore closely related to one another. The obvious next question is, 'when were these revelations fulfilled or when will they be fulfilled?' Daniel 9 tells us that they will occur within 'seventy sevens', a period that begins with a command to restore and re-build Jerusalem. What we need to know, therefore, is how long a 'seven' lasts, and the date of either the start or end of this period of 'seventy sevens'.

Many take the period 'seven' to mean 'seven years'. However, if Daniel 9:24 meant 'seven years', it could easily have said so, and 'three-and-a-half years' could have been used instead of the phrase, 'time, times and half a time'. The length of the period can, however, be determined from Daniel 12:11. This says that from the time the daily sacrifice is abolished and an abomination that causes desolation is set up, there will be 1,290 days. Verse 12 then adds, 'blessed is he who waits for and reaches 1,335 days'. The 1,290 days run from these events to the 'end time' when the power of the holy people is broken (Daniel 12:7). The 1,335 days must therefore run from those same events to the end of the last 'seven', as this is the point of complete safety when everything has been fulfilled. As the daily sacrifice occurred in the middle of the last 'seven' (Daniel 7:25, 9:27, 12:7), a 'seven' must last for 2,670 days (1,335 x 2), or 7.31 years (2,670 ÷ 365.2425). Hence, the period of 'seventy sevens' in Daniel 9:24 must equal almost 512 years.

Some believe this period began in the first year of Cyrus. However, Ezra 1:2-4 only refers to Cyrus's command to restore *the temple*, and Isaiah 44:28 only mentions his *prediction* about the re-building of Jerusalem ('you will be re-built'). Others suggest therefore that the period started in the 20th year of Artaxerxes I (444 BC?), when the king authorised the re-building of Jerusalem (Nehemiah 2:1-8).

However, the letters of authority that Nehemiah received did not *command* anyone to rebuild Jerusalem; they only gave *permission* to do so. There is also no reference to '*restoring*' Jerusalem, which would have required the Jews to return to their capital. The 'command' presumably therefore came from Nehemiah during the following twelve years, whilst he was governor of the area. Nehemiah mentions repeated opposition to the re-building work, but he may have delayed issuing a command, as he did not wish to 'lord it over the people' like his predecessors (Nehemiah 5:14,16).

These conclusions tie in with the analysis that follows, which dates the 'command to restore and rebuild Jerusalem' to 438 BC (508 years less 70*). This is based on Josephus's account and Matthew 24:1-34, which refers directly to 'the abomination that causes desolation spoken of by the prophet Daniel' (Matthew 24:15).

Matthew 24:1-34 needs to be read very carefully, however. Many assume this is solely a prediction about the end of the world. And some argue that Jesus thought His Second Coming was imminent, as He said that 'this generation' would not pass away until 'all these things' had taken place (verse 34). However, careful exegesis reveals that both of these interpretations are incorrect.

---

* Daily sacrifice ended on 14 July 70 AD according to Josephus. This occurred in 'the middle' of the last seven, and 69.5 sevens = 508 years.

The first point to note here is that Jesus began by predicting the complete destruction of the temple in Jerusalem (verse 2). In response to this prophecy, the disciples essentially asked Him *two* questions: (a) when would this be? and, (b) what would be the sign of His coming and the 'completion of the age'?

Jesus began by addressing the second question. In verses 4 to 14, therefore, He described how before the end there would be many false prophets, wars, famines and earthquakes in various places. These events would only be the beginning of the sufferings, however. Following this, many would fall away, and wickedness would increase. Despite this, the gospel would still have to be preached throughout the whole world; and only after this would the 'end of the age' take place. The nature of this description indicates that we are talking about a long period of time, which would extend well beyond the lifetimes of His disciples.

Jesus then answered the first question in verses 15 to 25. This passage begins with an explicit reference to 'the abomination causing desolation spoken of through the prophet Daniel'. Jesus then gives His disciples specific advice about what *they* should do during this period of time, counselling them to flee to the mountains and not to turn back to collect items of clothing. His final advice is not to believe anyone who announces Christ's return at this time. The reason He gives for this is that many more false christs and false prophets have yet to appear on the earth.

In verses 26-29 Jesus digresses briefly to contrast the signs of false christs at the time Daniel's prophecy is fulfilled with the unambiguous power and clarity of His own Second Coming. They are not to believe in these false christs, because His own Second Coming will be unmistakable – 'like lightening that shines from the east to the west'. It will also not only be preceded by carnage ('wherever the carcase is, there the eagles will be gathered'), but by great tumult in the heavens.

In verses 32 to 35 Jesus returns to the subject matter of the second question, namely when the destruction of the temple would occur. Jesus now makes it clear that this will happen within their lifetimes, as He says that His disciples (though not necessarily all) will witness these things (verse 33). He also adds that 'this generation will not pass away until all these things take place'.

The prophecy of Daniel provides us with a precise number of days, so it would have been possible to work out when the destruction of the temple would occur. Jesus compares this in verses 36 to 44 with 'the coming of the Son of man', which is entirely unexpected. Contrasting the time of His Second Coming with the prophecy of Daniel, He says, '<u>but</u> of that day and hour no one knows, nor the angels of heaven, nor the Son, but the Father only' (verse 36).

Despite this, some read Matthew 24 as a single sequence of events, with the Second Coming of Christ following shortly after the fulfilment of Daniel's prophecy. One of the main reasons for this is Jesus's statements in verses 33 and 34:

When you see all of these things, you know that the time is near, at the very gates. Truly, I say to you, this generation will not pass away until all these things take place

Some argue this indicates that the Daniel 9 prophecy relating to the last 'seven' will not be fulfilled until shortly before Christ's Second Coming. They therefore translate the word 'generation' in Matthew 24:34 to mean 'race', a reading that is only mentioned as a footnote in some versions of the Bible.

The first point is that this interpretation still restricts the meaning of '<u>all</u> these things', as it has to exclude those 'things' that relate to the Second Coming itself. Jesus clearly could not have been saying in verse 33, that when His disciples saw His Second Coming (verses 30,31) they would know that His Second Coming would be about to happen! The phrase 'all <u>these</u> things', therefore, clearly cannot refer to absolutely everything that Jesus had just talked about.

Secondly, the mainstream translations of the Bible do not regard 'race' as the natural meaning of the Greek word that is used here. In fact, one suspects that the word 'race' would not have even appeared as a footnote, had the word 'generation' not raised obvious questions about the timing of Christ's Second Coming.

A further issue with this reading of verses 33 and 34 is that it would mean Jesus simply did not answer the first question that was put to Him, namely, '<u>when</u> would the temple be destroyed?' We would have to assume that instead of providing any information about the timescale, He did not answer the question at all and simply said that the Jewish 'race' would still be existence at the time.

The only way to overcome these problems is by interpreting 'all these things' to refer back to the events described in Matthew 24:15 to 25. This reading is justified for the reasons given above, namely that verses 26 to 29 were a parenthetical digression from the main subject matter, namely the fall of Jerusalem. Jesus made this digression to contrast the signs of the false prophets with His own Second Coming, which He had already described at length in verses 4 to 14.

The possibility of this interpretation is not evident if the parallel passages in Mark 13:3-33 and Luke 21:5-33 are considered in isolation. However, this merely highlights the dangers of reading gospel passages in isolation. To gain a proper understanding of a gospel passage, one must look at the account in all of the gospels.

The interpretation of Matthew 24:33,34 that is proposed here is also supported by the fact that Jesus's words are directed at His own disciples. He tells them that <u>they</u> 'will see all these things' (verse 33). The phrase 'all these things' cannot include all of the events relating to Christ's Second Coming, as these were clearly not witnessed by the disciples. According to Matthew 25:31, when the Son comes in His glory (Matthew 24:30) He will judge 'all the nations'. This has clearly not yet taken place.

In particular, Jesus stated quite clearly that His disciples would see 'the abomination causing desolation spoken of by the prophet Daniel' (Matthew 24:15). It is also worth noting that in Luke's gospel, Jesus said that this desolation would occur shortly after Jerusalem had been surrounded by armies (Luke 21:20).

We know that Jerusalem was surrounded by armies in AD 70, when its temple was completely destroyed. The perpetrators were the people of 'a prince' of Rome, namely Titus, the son of the emperor Vespasian. According to Josephus, this war lasted for about 7 years[5]. In addition, during this period of time the high priest Ananias (an 'anointed one', Exodus 28:41) was murdered[6], and mid-way through that conflict Titus put an end to the daily sacrifice[7].

Interpretation of Daniel 7

The meaning of this vision is explained in verses 16 to 28. The four beasts represent four kingdoms, which mirror the four kingdoms in chapter 2. The first of the beasts in Daniel 7 is a lion with eagle's wings. This must be Babylon, because of what follows. In addition, it is the first kingdom chronologically in chapter 2, and the symbols that are used in Daniel 7 are associated with Babylon elsewhere in the scriptures (Jeremiah 4:7; 49:22; 50:17; Ezekiel 17:3).

The second is Media-Persia, as this kingdom was composed of two sides and one of them was more 'raised up' (bigger and more powerful) than the other. This also mirrors the imagery used to describe Media-Persia in Daniel 8:3,20, where the ram has two horns, one of which is 'raised up' higher than the other. In Daniel 7, the bear also has three ribs between its teeth, which ties in with Media-Persia's well-known conquests of Lydia, Egypt and Babylon.

The third beast is a leopard with four heads and four wings. As this succeeds Media-Persia, it must be Greece (Daniel 8:2). Daniel 11:3,4 also says that this kingdom is to be initially dominated by a great king before it is divided into four. This must be Alexander, as he was 'great' and his kingdom was broken up into four divisions.

The final kingdom is not mentioned by name in Daniel chapter 8. Unlike the other beasts, it has iron teeth and bronze claws. It also tramples everything underfoot, devouring all of the earth and waging war against the saints. Ultimately, it is defeated by God, just like the fourth kingdom in Daniel 2:44, which is also ultimately overcome by a divine kingdom that endures for ever. The only kingdom that 'devoured the whole earth' around this time was, of course, the Roman Empire.

We are also told that the fourth beast has ten horns, which represent ten of its rulers. After this, there is another ruler who wages war against the saints. He is described as 'a little horn', who uproots and humbles three rulers before him (Daniel 7:8, 24). This makes perfect sense as a description of Titus, who was the eleventh supreme ruler of Rome, excluding the triumvirates, none of whom were rulers in their own right. In addition, at the time that Titus 'waged war against the saints', he was only a prince; this ties in with the reference to the ruler being 'a little horn'.

We are also told in Daniel 7:8 and 24 that three rulers were 'uprooted' after the appearance of this 'little horn', who is said to have 'humbled' them. An explanation for this is that during the 12 months that Titus emerged on the scene, he and his father Vespasian made a bid for power and three emperors fell by the wayside in quick succession. This period is therefore known as the Year of the Four Emperors, and the three 'uprooted' rulers who were killed in that year were Galba, Otho and Vitellius. These three emperors were also humbled by Titus' achievements, which not only included his triumphant victory over the Jews, but the completion of the magnificent Coliseum of Rome.

If Daniel 7 refers to ancient kingdoms, therefore, then this fourth beast must be Rome. This was the only kingdom that 'devoured the whole earth' and came into conflict with the Kingdom of God. In addition, Jesus frequently referred to Himself as the Son of Man, which many have seen as a direct allusion to Daniel 7:13.

The destruction of the fourth beast (verse 11) does not, however, mean that Rome should have ceased to exist shortly after Titus's attack on Jerusalem. Verse 26 only says that it was the *power* of the beast's 'little horn' that was destroyed at this time. Titus' war with the Jews was therefore cut short for the sake of believers (Matthew 24:22), whose faith and whose kingdom triumphed over everything that Rome could throw at it (John 18:36-37).

Interpretation of Daniel 8

The vision in Daniel 8 supports this interpretation. Although the last kingdom is not named, we are told that its direct predecessors were Media-Persia and Greece. So the last kingdom must have been Rome. We are also told that the ruler who puts an end to sacrifice and destroys the sanctuary does not rule 'by his own power' (Daniel 8:24). This ties in with the fact that Titus was only a prince at this stage; he was therefore still acting 'by the power' of Vespasian.

We are also told that this 'ruler' did not perish by human hand (Daniel 8:25). And Suetonius tells us that Titus did not die in battle, but from an acute fever shortly after an inexplicable thunder clap from a cloudless sky, following which Titus:

...gazed up at the sky, and complained bitterly that life was being undeservedly taken from him – since he had done nothing at all which he had cause to regret, save for one thing only. What that was he did not reveal and it remains difficult to guess.[8]

Some do not agree that the visions in Daniel 7 and 8 relate to the same time, because Daniel 8:9 says that the 'little horn' comes 'from' the four divisions of the Greek empire. Many commentators therefore equate this ruler with Antiochus IV. This argument is inconclusive, however, as the Hebrew word for 'from' can also mean 'after' in a temporal sense. In addition, Daniel 8:23 indicates that the little horn does not need to be a Greek ruler, as he emerges in the 'latter part' of the Greek kingdom when its transgressors 'have finished', suggesting they had ceased to rule at this stage.

Moreover, Daniel is told that the vision in chapter 8 concerns 'the time of the end' (Daniel 8:17,19), which refers to the time when the power of the holy people would be broken (Daniel 12:7). This occurred with Titus's victory over the Jews and his destruction of Jerusalem and its temple. The 'little horn' in Daniel 7:8 and 8:9 must therefore refer to one and the same person.

Despite this, some have seen difficulties in reconciling the 2,300 days in Daniel 8:14 with the figures in Daniel 9:24-27 and 12:11,12. They have therefore argued that the visions in Daniel 8 and 9 must relate to completely different events.

However, there is no difficulty in reconciling these numbers. As we have seen, the 'sevens' in Daniel 9:24-27 were periods of 2,670 days. The last of these periods was marked by the arrival of 'the prince' (Daniel 9:25), and in this period he struck a pact with many (Daniel 9:27). It does not say that he would make this pact 'for one seven'; it simply says he would 'confirm a covenant with the many one seven'. This is analogous to saying that someone went to London 'one week'. The implicit preposition, therefore, is 'in', not 'for'. Hence, the prince confirmed a pact with many 'in' one seven not 'for' the whole duration of that 'seven'.

It also does not make sense to talk about 'confirming a pact' throughout a period of over seven years. Ratifying a pact is not a continuous process, but an act that occurs at a point in time. Josephus indicates that Titus arrived in early AD 67, where he was joined by Vespasian in Ptolemais. There he made a pact with a large body of men from Cesarea, Syria, and the forces of the kings Antiochus, Agrippa and Soaemus[9].

It is worth adding that 2,300 days is about 6.3 years, and according to Josephus the Jewish 'host' were 'trampled' from early 67 AD to May 73 AD, a period of about 6.3 years. We also know that the days of warfare in the last 'seven' did not run their full course, as they were cut short 'for the sake of the elect' (Matthew 24:22).

So within the last 'seven' there was a period of 2,300 days during which various events occurred. These included the trampling of the host, the end of daily sacrifice, the sin that caused desolation and the destruction of the sanctuary. Daniel 12:11,12, says that the days mentioned there run from the middle of the last 'seven', which could clearly overlap with the period of 2,300 days in Daniel 8:14. The 2,300 days in Daniel 8 do not therefore mean that this vision must relate to a different historical event.

A final reason that is advanced to support the view Daniel 8 and 9 refer to different events, is that the former says that the sanctuary would be 'vindicated' (Daniel 8:14), whereas Daniel 9 states that the temple would be 'destroyed'. However, the Hebrew word for 'vindicated' does not necessarily mean that it was 'restored'. It could simply mean that the sanctity of the temple was 'vindicated' by the destruction of those who had previously polluted it.

Interpretation of Daniel 11 and 12

This prophecy begins with the four-way division of the Greek kingdom, which we know occurred after the reign of Alexander the Great, 'the 'great king' (Daniel 11:3,4). It concludes by describing the actions of a ruler, whose forces are responsible for 'the abomination that causes desolation' (Daniel 11:31). Here, we know from Matthew 24:15 that this act occurred after the time of Jesus, but during the lifetimes of those to whom He was speaking.

As we have shown, the Roman 'king' whose people were responsible for these atrocities was Vespasian. His actions are described from Daniel 11:21 onwards, as he is a successor to the ruler in verse 20. The Hebrew does not require him to be the *immediate* successor of this ruler; he only has to be someone who at some stage 'stands in the place' that was previously occupied by that ruler. It is perfectly legitimate, therefore, to believe that the ruler in verse 21 comes from a succeeding kingdom, that is, he is a Roman rather than a Greek ruler.

It is interesting to note here that the ruler who is introduced in Daniel 11:21 is described as someone who does not at that stage possess the honour of a kingdom. In the case of Vespasian, this statement makes perfect sense, as he was only a governor at the time, not an emperor.

We have already seen how the details of Vespasian's attack on Jerusalem in AD 70 under the leadership of his son Titus provide a close fit to the description in Daniel 11:31-35. The question is, do the other details in Daniel 11:21 to 12:4 tie in with the evidence regarding Vespasian's life and his military career?

The lack of evidence to connect some statements in Daniel 11:21 et seq. with Vespasian, however, does not mean that such a connection does not exist. A number of historians have commented on the widespread propaganda that existed during Vespasian's reign. There is also good evidence that the key historians of the time were on Vespasian's payroll. So it would not be surprising if they did not record events that might reflect badly on their emperor.

For example, the Jewish historian who was renamed 'Josephus' was captured by Vespasian's forces and was later made a Roman citizen by him. Josephus therefore later referred to Vespasian as his saviour and patron[10], and described how he passed his work to Vespasian and Titus for approval beforehand[11].

As a result, there are clear signs of Roman influence in Josephus's writing. For example, he says that the seven branches of the altar lampstand represent the planets, whilst the twelve loaves on the altar table and the twelve stones on the high-priests vestments represent the twelve signs of the zodiac[12]. What Jew would have believed this? Leviticus 24:8 says that the bread was meant to be a lasting memorial 'from the sons of Israel'. Israel (previously Jacob) had twelve sons, who became the twelve tribes of Israel. So the loaves clearly represented the twelve tribes of Israel, as do the stones on the high priests garment, as stated in Exodus 28:9-12.

The significance of the lamp stand branches is not stated in Exodus 25:31-40. However, what Jew would have thought that they represented anything other than the creation week on which the whole Jewish calendar was based? The planets of the solar system are not mentioned in the Bible, and there are more than seven planets anyway!

The other main historian at the time was Tacitus. He was apparently born around 56 AD and began researching his *Histories* in 105 AD. Whilst Tacitus's accounts are at least one step removed from the eye-witness evidence, his comments about Vespasian and Titus are illuminating. He says of Vespasian that he launched Tacitus's career, which Titus then 'advanced' yet further[13]. He adds that he was writing during the reign of Trajan, when you were able to 'think what you like and say what you think'. The clear implication here is that this was not previously the case[13].

There is a clear risk, therefore, that the historical accounts of the period are slanted, perhaps even seriously inaccurate. It is also possible that certain events were left out altogether or perhaps not even commented upon, for fear of incurring the emperor's wrath

Despite these difficulties, the following suggest possible events to which the verses in Daniel chapter 11 and 12 might refer.

21 – he enters while at ease and seizes the kingdom by intrigues

Vespasian's rise to power clearly involved all of these elements according to the following details from Roman historians.

When Nero was succeeded by Galba, Vespasian sent Titus to pay tribute to him[14]. Just before Titus arrived, however, Galba was killed by an unknown group of assassins[15]. Otho replaced Galba, and Vespasian and a Syrian commander, Mucianus, swore allegiance to him. Several weeks later, however, Otho apparently committed suicide, shortly after burning all of his correspondence to avoid incriminating anyone. However, no-one witnessed these events[16].

Otho was replaced by Vitellius, and Vespasian agreed a pact against Vitellius. Vespasian also used a forged letter to persuade Otho's previous supporters to join him[17]. Vitellius eventually agreed surrender terms, but when he was about to sign this, Vespasian's troops attacked and killed him[18]. This all happened whilst Vespasian was in Egypt protecting the grain stores and consulting oracles. When Vespasian entered Rome, therefore, the fighting had died down and he was able to enter the capital 'at ease'.

22 - sweeps away opposing forces and the ruler of a covenant

Whilst Vespasian swept away the opposing forces of Vitellius, he dispatched his son Titus to defeat the people of the covenant, the Jews. Their religious ruler at the time was the high priest Ananias, who was 'swept away' during the conflict when he was murdered[6].

23 - practises deceit with those who join him

The comments on verse 21 provide ample evidence of deceit. In addition, Tacitus says Vespasian was not trusted[19], and Suetonius tells us that his greed and avarice caused him to swindle people[20].

24 - plunders, spoils and scatters and devises plots against the strongholds

This is perfectly in keeping with the account of the Jewish War. Vespasian's armies plundered and spoiled the temple in Jerusalem, scattering its riches in the process. The final stage of the war involved overcoming the remaining strongholds including the fortresses of Machaerus and, most notably, Masada, where Roman allied forces used engines based on those devised by Vespasian[21].

25 - stirs up forces against the king of the south

This verse and the following passage do not tell us which country or region the king of the south ruled. However, Edom, Moab, Ammon, Egypt, Ethiopia, Libya and Nubia are all mentioned by name (verses 41-43), which indicates that it was not one of these territories.

We are also told at various stages in this passage that the conflicts with the 'king of the south' are associated with the king of the north's enmity against the people of the covenant, i.e. the Jews (e.g. verses 28-30). This clearly indicates that there is at the very least a strong connection between 'the king of the south' and Israel.

The obvious candidates for the 'king of the south' are therefore the leaders of the Jewish uprising. A 'king' is, after all, any supreme ruler, and in the eyes of their people these leaders were their rulers at the time. The leader of the revolutionary forces during this period was Simon bar Giora, after whom coins were minted[22] and whom many people saw as their king[23].

25 - the king of south has a great army, but he does not stand due to plots against him

26 - his own army and those who eat his food will break him and many will be killed

Simon bar Giora had an army of 15,000[24]. However, the plotting and infighting between his followers and those of John of Gischala and Eleazar ben Simon led to their collective downfalls. In the siege of Jerusalem these parties turned on one another. Many lives and vital grain supplies were lost and many deserted to the Romans[25].

27 - both rulers speak falsely at one table; to no avail, as the end comes at the appointed time

This suggests the two leaders parleyed and tried to deceive one other. The king of the north then returned to his own land for reasons that are not explained. So is it possible that Vespasian met with Simon bar Giora in these circumstances?

According to Josephus, Vespasian rode to Jerusalem at the very time that Simon and his forces were encircling the city[26]. Vespasian then crushed all of the opposition in the neighbourhood of Jerusalem, but decided to return to Caesarea[27]. Here, he received news of further upheavals in Rome, which resulted in the accession of Vitellius. Vespasian's own men, however, declared *him* emperor, which prompted Vespasian to send Mucianus to Rome whilst he went to Egypt to secure the grain supplies. He therefore had to leave his son Titus to finish the war with the Jews[28].

Given the circumstances, it seems quite possible that Vespasian had a meeting with Simon bar Giora. They were both in the same place at the same time. They also shared a common purpose: to gain control of Jerusalem. Vespasian might have reasoned, therefore, that if he helped Simon to attack the city, this would assist his son Titus in ending the war more quickly. According to Josephus, Vespasian's strategy at this stage was to hold back and allow the warring Jewish factions to cancel each other out and thereby reduce the sizes of their armies[29].

It would also not be surprising if Josephus did not mention anything about such a meeting between Simon and Vespasian. To begin with, this might look like an act of weakness on Vespasian's part. In addition, whilst Josephus shows some grudging respect for Simon, he also describes him as a young hot-headed despot, who led a large group of bandits that plundered the countryside, killing many of his countrymen along the way[30]. He was clearly, therefore, not someone with whom he would want Vespasian to be associated.

28 - the king of the north returns to his land with great wealth

28 - his heart is still against holy covenant so he acts and returns to own land

Not long after the events of verse 27, Vespasian left for Rome with a vast amount of wealth[31]. Before he returned, he also 'acted' by giving Titus clear instructions to finish the war with the Jews. Vespasian thereby showed that he was still implacably determined to take the war to its bitter end. There was no urgent military or political need for him to do this. Nero had sent him to Israel, but he had been dead for a year. In addition, the Roman empire was in turmoil. So there was no burning need to crush the Jews so completely; there was much more important business to attend to at 'home'. The fact that he acted as he did clearly tells us that his heart was 'set' firmly against the holy covenant.

29 - he returns to come against the south, but it's different this time

30 - it's different because the ships of Kittim (Cyprus) come against him; he is grieved, retreats and is furious against the holy covenant

As we have seen, Vespasian 'came against' the south when he returned to Egypt to secure Rome's grain supplies. The above indicates that Vespasian was harried by ships from Cyprus, either on his journey to Egypt or from there to Rome. Once again, we are told that this made Vespasian furious with the holy covenant, indicating that the attack was carried out by or on behalf of Jews.

It is estimated that 3,000 Jews escaped to Cyprus during the war with Rome, joining an already sizeable Jewish presence there[32]. Josephus says that many of the Jews who were expelled from their towns formed a large pirate fleet, which raided along the route to Egypt, 'making it impossible to sail those seas'[33]. Given this, it is clear that quite a lot of vessels could have accumulated in Cyprus during the four years after the war had begun. This trend continued, as Cyprus witnessed a major Jewish rebellion against the Romans in AD 115, which is said to have claimed 240,000 Jewish lives[34].

Neither Josephus nor later Roman historians refer to Vespasian being attacked by ships from Cyprus. However, Josephus did not travel to Egypt, so only Vespasian and his Jewish attackers would have witnessed these events. If this did happen, then it would clearly have been humiliating for Vespasian. So it would not be surprising if he ensured the details were not recorded anywhere.

It certainly seems odd that we are told nothing about how Vespasian travelled to Egypt, whilst Titus's journey from there is described in great detail[35]. All we can say, is that Josephus clearly indicates that it was well-nigh impossible to travel to Egypt by sea without running the gauntlet of pirate attacks from displaced Jews. And the historical evidence indicates that a fair number of those ships could have come from, or been based in, Cyprus.

31 - an army from him profanes the holy temple

31 - they remove the daily sacrifice and place the abomination causing desolation

Josephus mentions the removal of the daily sacrifice[7]. He also details the 'abomination' of Roman standards being set up in the temple and sacrifices to Roman gods taking place there[36]. The 'king of the north' does not carry out these acts, however; 'an army from him' does this. And Josephus is keen to emphasise that it was the army that destroyed the temple, contrary to Titus's orders[37].

It is also worth noting here that Josephus sees these actions as the fulfilment of a prophecy that Jerusalem would be taken and the sanctuary burnt as an act of war at a time when the temple would be polluted[38]. The only known prophecies that make any reference to events of this kind are found in the book of Daniel.

32 - he ruins by flatteries those who do evil against the covenant

Those who did evil against the covenant here would be the Jewish zealot factions, who fought one another in Jerusalem and committed many atrocities against the sanctity of the temple[39].

The root of the Hebrew word translated here as 'flatteries' literally means 'smooth'. In this context, therefore, its meanings could range from suave, calm and slippery behaviour to direct blandishments, flatteries and fine promises[40].

We know from Josephus that Vespasian adopted a calm, softly-softly approach with the rebels that was designed to encourage the warring Jewish factions to destroy one another[29]. As indicated under verse 27 above, there is also good reason to believe that there would have been some contact between Vespasian and the rebels around this time, which may well have involved flatteries and deception.

36 - the king exalts himself above all gods and prospers

Like many Roman emperors, Vespasian was regarded as a god, and on his deathbed he apparently said, 'I must be turning into a god'[41]. Whilst this may have been a light-hearted comment, Vespasian clearly took these matters seriously. We are told that he approached 'the god of Carmel' and consulted the god Serapis in Egypt[42]. It is also claimed that Vespasian healed people, following which he apparently thought that there was no limit to his powers[43].

Vespasian's belief in the supernatural and his own importance in history are further exemplified by his treatment of Josephus. Here, we learn that Vespasian not only spared Josephus, but enriched and elevated him as a Roman citizen, solely because he prophesied that Vespasian would one day rule the world[44].

Moreover, Josephus, Tacitus and Suetonius all say that Vespasian was seen as the deliverer predicted by ancient Hebrew prophecies[45]. As Vespasian clearly took Josephus's views very seriously, he may well have identified himself with the 'son of man' in Daniel 7:14, 27, whose kingdom we are told would transcend all others and last for ever. If Vespasian equated himself with the Hebrew deliverer, he may well have seen himself as being above all of the other gods he had once believed in.

37/38 - he only honours the god of forces and a god his fathers did not know

The 'god of forces' was presumably Mars, the god of war. The other 'god' could in theory have been the Hebrew God or Serapis, both of whom would have been foreign gods as far as Vespasian's own people were concerned. We know that Vespasian consulted both gods and that he took Josephus's prophecies very seriously'[41].

However, these verses refer to 'a god', not 'the God'. We are also told that although Vespasian consulted the god of Carmel, he honoured Serapis and made him an imperial god, which paved the way for Serapis's introduction into Roman culture[46].

39 - he triumphs over the fortress of fortresses and divides the land for a price

According to Josephus the 'fortress of fortresses' (the strongest fortress) was Masada[47]. This was also the last major stronghold that Vespasian's forces had to overcome during the Jewish War.

Following the war, Josephus tells us that Vespasian appropriated Judea for himself. He then gave orders which permitted Bassus and the procurator Laberius Maximus to lease out the rest of the land, allowing 800 of Vespasian's soldiers to settle in Emmaus[48]. The leases would have required the payment of rent; hence the land was 'divided for a price'.

40 - at the end time the king of the south pushes; the king of the north pushes back with chariots, horses and many ships

The key to understanding this verse is not to see the events as following on from those up to verse 39, but rather as a résumé of the events so far described. This reading is in fact required by verse 41, which refers to the king of the north entering 'the glorious land'. However, according to the verse 39 he was already there, having defeated god's people, put an end to their daily sacrifice and divided up their land 'for a price'. The word 'and' at the beginning of this verse should therefore be translated as 'so'[49].

41 - Edom, Moab and the chief sons of Ammon escape

No historian refers to Vespasian or Titus attacking any of these territories. The war with Rome was of course against the Jews, not their near neighbours.

42 - he stretches his reach and Egypt does not escape

43 - he exercises control over Libya and Ethiopia (Nubia) and the riches of Egypt

We have already seen that both Vespasian and Titus marched on Egypt. They secured control over its wealth, in particular the natural riches it possessed in the form of its vital grain supplies. The fact that Egypt is mentioned separately by name also indicates that this is not 'the king of the south', as some have suggested.

44 - he seeks to destroy many when he gets troubling news from the north and east

Josephus does not mention Vespasian receiving troubling news whilst in Egypt. However, he must have received some bad reports, because shortly after he and Titus had arrived in Alexandria, Vespasian sent his son straight back to Jerusalem to destroy it[35]. Jerusalem is 'north and east' of Alexandria and Josephus tells us that thousands of people perished in the battles that followed.

45 - he plants his tents between the seas in a holy glorious mountain

Josephus says that Vespasian's forces under Titus were camped on the Mount of Olives[50], which is between the Dead Sea, the Mediterranean and the Sea of Galilee.

45 - yet he comes to his end and no-one can help him

Some interpret this to mean that the king of the north died at this time, whilst his army was encamped around Jerusalem. This is clearly not the case, as we are told that he prospered until the fury against Israel was completed (Daniel 11:36). Titus was also not killed in battle, as he died 'but not by human hand' (Daniel 8:25).

Daniel 11:45 does not tell us *when* the king of the north was to die, because this is not its purpose. Instead, as indicated by the word 'yet', this verse is contrasting the ruler's act of hubris in setting himself up in holy places with the helpless state to which he was later reduced, a condition from which no-one could help him. According to Suetonius, Vespasian died about 6 years after the war against the Jews, following an acute infection which led to severe dysentery[51]. He did not die by a human hand, therefore, and no-one was able to help him.

As regards Daniel 12, we are told in verses 1 to 4 that 'at that time' Michael would arise, a great ruler who would stand up for the sons of Daniel's people. There is then a time of unprecedented distress, following which some of Daniel's people are delivered, i.e. those whose name is 'written in the book'. Many of those sleeping in the dust awake, some to eternal life and some to eternal hostility. Daniel would be one of those who stood 'in his lot' at this time.

Michael is referred to on two other occasions in Daniel, where he is described as 'a ruler' (Daniel 10:13, 21). There are no known earthly rulers called Michael at this time, and on both occasions that he is mentioned in Daniel, he is described as aiding and supporting the angel who appears to Daniel. Moreover, in chapter 10:21 Daniel is told that Michael is 'your prince'. As Daniel's people had no earthly princes at this time, Michael must be a spiritual being. In addition, in the New Testament, the only Michael who protects God's people is an archangel (Jude 9, Revelation 12:7).

Our main concern in this passage, however, are the references to many people 'awaking from the dust'. The first point to make here is that this clearly says that 'many', rather than 'all', people would be raised from the dead. In view of this, some commentators do not see this as a reference to the general resurrection[52].

In addition, Matthew 24:21 says that the attack on Jerusalem (Luke see also 21:20) would involve a time of unprecedented distress that would never be equalled. Daniel 12:1 also says that the events at the time of these resurrections would involve unprecedented distress. So the events of Daniel 12:1 onwards could not have been either before or after the events described in Matthew 24:21, as the latter also involved unprecedented distress that would never be equalled again. Matthew 24:21 and Daniel 12:1 must therefore refer to the same period of time.

It is, of course, not unbiblical to believe that people are raised from the dead other than at the general resurrection. Matthew 27:52 refers to many saints coming back to life at the time of Jesus's death. If an event such as that described in Daniel 12:2 took place, however, one would expect there to be some reference to this in Jewish and Roman history, given that something extraordinary must have been witnessed by both the Jewish and Roman survivors.

This, however, is exactly what we find. Firstly, Josephus mentions the following event shortly before the destruction of the temple[53]:

A few days after the Feast, on the 21st of Artemisios [May-June], a supernatural apparition was seen, too amazing to be believed. What I have to relate would, I suppose, have been dismissed as an invention, had it not been vouched for by eyewitnesses and followed by disasters that bore out the signs. Before sunset there were seen in the sky, over the whole country, chariots and regiments in arms speeding through the clouds and encircling the towns. Again, at the Feast of Pentecost, when the priests had gone into the inner court of the Temple at night to perform the usual ceremonies, they declared that they were aware, first of a violent movement and a loud crash, then of a concerted cry: 'Let us go hence.'

Later, Tacitus provided the following account[54]:

Various portents had occurred at this time, but so sunk in superstition are the Jews and so opposed to all religious practices that they think it wicked to expiate them by sacrifices or vows. Embattled armies were seen to clash in the sky with flashing arms, and the Temple shone with sudden fire from heaven. The doors of the shrine suddenly opened, a superhuman voice was heard to proclaim that the gods were leaving, and at once there came a mighty movement of their departure.

The Bible also clearly teaches that there are two resurrections. The first involves believers who were persecuted by God's enemies; the second, general resurrection occurs much later (Revelation 20:5).

(g) Conclusions

The prophecies of Daniel 9:21-27 are linked with the revelations in Daniel chapters 7, 8, 11 and 12. All of these passages relate to an 'end time', which is defined as the time when the power of the Jewish people was broken (Daniel 12:7).

These events occurred within the lifetime of Jesus's followers, as He predicted that Daniel's prophecy would be fulfilled before that generation had passed away (Matthew 24:1,34). He said that not one stone of the temple would remain, and according to Josephus that is exactly what happened in AD 70[55].

We must now consider the important predictions within Daniel 9:21-27, as these relate directly to the questions being addressed in this chapter, namely, 'why do there appear to be no divine revelations and miracles in modern times?'

5.4.4. Interpretation

We now return therefore to the text of Daniel 9:21-27 on page 311, the key sections of which are reproduced below:

Seventy sevens are decreed for your people and for your holy city, to end the transgression and to seal up sins, and to atone for iniquity, and to bring in everlasting righteousness, and to seal up vision and prophecy, and to anoint the holy of holies.

Therefore, know and understand, from the going forth of a command to restore and rebuild Jerusalem unto an anointed one, a prince, there will be seven sevens and sixty two sevens. A city square and a moat will be rebuilt, but in distressing times.

And after the sixty two sevens an anointed one will be cut off and have nothing, and the people of the prince who will come will destroy the city and the sanctuary. And its end will be in a flood, and until the end there will be fighting; desolations are decreed.

And he will confirm a covenant with the multitudes one seven and half way through the seven he will end sacrifice and offering, on a wing of abominations causing desolation until the end; and what is determined shall be poured out on the one causing the desolation.'

We have established the length of the sevens, and when they began and ended (pages 319-324). We can now, therefore, consider the events that occurred within the last 'seven'. The first is that transgression will end; sins will be 'sealed up'. This clearly does not mean that sin would cease. It continued on earth and in the afterlife (Daniel 12:2). However, Christ's sacrifice put an end to the effects of sin (Romans 6:14; Hebrews 9:26), breaking down the dividing wall it created between God and man (Ephesians 2:14-17).

As sin and transgression mean essentially the same thing, the Hebrew verb translated here as 'to seal up' is used in the sense of 'to end', as the two verbs are used interchangeably, viz. '...to end the transgression and to seal up sins'. Consequently, in most versions of the Bible the above words are translated along the lines of, 'to finish transgression and to put an end to sin'.

The Hebrew verb 'to seal up' here clearly does not mean 'placing something on hold' with the possibility that it might start up again in the future. The effects of sin end for good. They end by being 'sealed up', just as a well ceases to be a well when it is sealed up.

In the next clause we read that this period would also see the 'sealing up' of 'prophecy and vision'. It would be untenable to argue that the same verb meant quite different things in the same sentence. This must be telling us, therefore, that prophecy and vision 'drew to a close' during this period of time.

Turning to the seventy sevens, these consist of seven 'sevens', sixty-two 'sevens' and the final 'seven'. The significance of the 'seven sevens' is not explained. However, the only event to which it could possibly relate is the re-building and restoration of Jerusalem.

After the sixty-two sevens that follow, an 'anointed one' arrives, who is also 'a prince'. The absence of the definite article before either noun means that this is not '<u>the</u> Christ', and not one New Testament verse connects this passage with Jesus. Gabriel also differentiates between 'your people' (the Jews) and 'the people of the prince'. If Jesus was 'the prince', they would be one and the same. However, it is 'the people of the prince' who destroy the city and its sanctuary, acts that were perpetrated by the Romans, not the Jews. So the prince in question must be Titus.

During the seventieth seven we are told of another 'anointed one'. The absence of the definite article means this cannot be referring back to the anointed prince in the previous verse. The juxtaposition here contrasts the fates of the two 'anointed ones': one is a prince, who is victorious; the other is cut off and has nothing. This contrast clearly indicates that the second person is a Jewish anointed one, not a Roman one. The only noteworthy Jewish 'anointed one' who was involved in this action was the high priest (Exodus 28:41), whose murder is singled out for specific comment by Josephus[6].

The prophecy relating to the creation of a pact or covenant with many has already been covered on page 327. This must relate to Titus's pact with the kings who joined forces with the Romans. And Josephus also tells us that mid-way through this last 'seven', Titus put an end to the daily sacrifice[7].

The very final clause of the passage on page 342 reminds us that the 'desolator' would not escape unscathed. The war was orchestrated, and in its later stages, commanded from afar by Vespasian. However, Vespasian died of an unpleasant and unidentified illness that attacked his bowels. This was the ignominious end that had been decreed for him. Like his son Titus, Vespasian did not die honourably in battle 'by human hand'.

If prophecy came to an end at this time, it would explain the prediction in Zechariah 13. This chapter begins by saying that a fountain would be opened in Jerusalem that would cleanse its inhabitants from sin and impurity. This is linked with Christ's sacrificial death, as John 19:37 says that Christ's death fulfilled the prophecy at Zechariah 12:10. Zechariah 13 then begins, 'in that day...', so we know that the events of Zechariah 13 took place not that long after Christ's death.

Zechariah 13:2,3 then says that God would remove all prophets from the land at that time, so that thereafter -

...when a man prophesies again, then his father and his mother who gave birth to him shall say to him, you shall not live for you speak lies in the name of Jehovah.

If prophecy ended at this time, it would also explain the severe warning in Revelation 22:18, which curses anyone who adds 'to the words of the prophecy of this book'. Why would it be wrong to add to those words if those additional prophecies came from God? And how could one speak and write down further prophecies without adding to the prophecies of Revelation? Would a further apocalyptic book called 'Revelations Two' not be adding to 'the words of the prophecy' of Revelation?

It is significant that no similar injunction or curse appears in any other book of the Bible. In addition, very few people who claim to prophesy today write them down and claim that they are further books of the Bible. It is as if God had revealed Himself to us as fully as He wished. And now we must live by faith and the scriptures, being deprived of the light of direct revelation that once was available to mankind. As Jesus said: (John 12:35):

You are going to have the light just a little while longer. Walk while you have the light, before darkness overtakes you.

This statement clearly predicted a future without the light of direct revelation. As a result, the last reference to prophetic acts is provided by Revelation chapter 11. This refers to a time when the temple would be given over to the gentiles and the city would be trampled for a period of forty-two months. This clearly relates to the prophecies of Daniel 9:24-27, as this is the only time when these events occurred. The forty-two months also tie in with the 'half a seven' and 'time, times and half a time' found in Daniel.

Revelation 11 tells us about two prophets who are killed in Jerusalem, but then raised to life, after which a voice is heard to say, 'come up hither', echoing the accounts of Josephus and Tacitus (page 340). Revelation 11 then mentions an earthquake that destroyed a tenth of the city, killing 7,000. This ties in with Josephus's reference to 'a violent movement and a large crash'[53]. As Josephus was outside the city, however, he would not have witnessed the damage or been aware of the casualties.

5.5. The End of Miracles

A miracle is an act of God that *directly* changes the material universe in some way, thereby interfering with the normal laws of nature. Miracles occur to show that a person or a message is approved by God (Acts 2:22), and this includes the miraculous gifts of the Holy Spirit (Hebrews 2:4).

If divine revelation has in fact come to an end, then there is no longer any need for miracles. Furthermore, Amos 3:7 says:

For the Lord Jehovah will do nothing unless He has revealed His secret counsel to His servants the prophets.

It is clear from its context that this is a general statement. God does not perform miracles without firstly revealing this to His prophets. As prophecy has ceased, there can be no miracles apart from those that have already been predicted. This explains why prophecy and miracles are so closely associated with one another (Psalm 74:9).

5.6. Conclusion

We do not see miracles today, as they were given to us for a time as signs to testify to the authenticity of God's true messengers. We now walk in the darkness, as Jesus told us we would (John 12:35). It is all the more important therefore that Christians carefully understand the scriptures (2 Timothy 2:15), and prove all things (1 Thessalonians 5:21) by not adding to His words (Proverbs 30:6) or going beyond what is written (1 Corinthians 4:6).

The scriptures are God's words and contain all we need for our learning and spiritual development (2 Timothy 3:16,17). They have therefore been preserved for all generations (Deuteronomy 29:29) in living languages. As Jesus said, 'Heaven and earth will pass away, but my words will never pass away' (Matthew 24:35).

CHAPTER 6. KNOWLEDGE AND FAITH

6.1. INTRODUCTION

Knowledge and faith are often represented as opposites. On the one hand, knowledge is associated with clarity and certainty. By contrast, faith is described as being 'blind'. Choices that are based on faith are therefore often seen as little more than acts of guesswork - 'leaps of faith'.

Knowledge is also closely associated with science and with things that can be verified by our senses: 'seeing', it is often said, 'is believing'. On the other hand, 'faith' is regarded as the realm of religion, which does not involve knowledge at all. Instead, faith is portrayed as something that calls for a blind trust in invisible things and concepts, the truth of which can never be verified.

These common perceptions, however, fall a long way short of reality. To begin with, science does not claim to provide knowledge, at least not in the sense of creating absolute certainty. Instead, the inductive method upon which science is based merely seeks to provide 'hypotheses' to help explain the evidence provided by our experiences. These hypotheses may become 'theories' and may even be regarded as 'laws' at some stage. However, there is nothing to prevent any of them from being revised or discarded altogether, even after they have been accepted as 'laws'.

Religions, however, often claim to provide knowledge in the sense of certainty. Furthermore, far from being blind, many religions see faith, not as hopeful guesswork or wishful thinking, but as a relationship of trust that stems from a certain knowledge of the truth. That claim often leads to the challenge, 'but how do you know?' This chapter seeks to address this question and some of the related issues that inevitably flow from it.

6.2. CERTAINTY

6.2.1. Scepticism

Behind the challenge of the question, 'but how do you know?' there may well lie a much more radical question: 'how can one be certain of anything?'

If we could not be sure of anything, this would clearly threaten the very basis of religion. As there is no empirical evidence to verify religious beliefs, if certainty by other means were impossible, it is hard to see how religion could be anything more than wishful thinking. As such, religion could not reasonably hope to command any strong claim to our attention, let alone persuade us to completely change our lives and follow its teachings.

The idea that we cannot be sure of anything is known as global scepticism. Simply stated, it argues that as one can always contemplate possible alternatives that cannot be disproven logically or otherwise excluded, all beliefs must be subject to perpetual doubt. And if legitimate doubt is inescapable, then certainty must be an unattainable goal.

This conclusion, however, is entirely self-defeating. If I cannot be certain of anything, then I must accept that I might be entirely mistaken in my belief that certainty is impossible. That conclusion might, for example, be the result of faulty reasoning or memory. Certainty might therefore be possible. In fact, others might be certain right now without my knowing it, and I might be certain at some stage in the near future myself.

It is also untenable to argue that certainty is impossible. If certainty did not exist, no-one would have ever experienced it. How then could we have a meaningful debate about its existence? Consider a man, for example, who had been born blind. He could not even begin to construct a meaningful definition of 'red', as this would not be something that he could extrapolate from his past experiences. One might be able to imagine a red giraffe by combining the concepts 'giraffe' and 'red', if one already knew about both of these things. If one had never seen anything at all, however, the word 'red' could have no meaning for that person whatsoever.

Such a person could, of course, construct a *grammatically* meaningful definition of 'red', by simply quoting details about wavelengths and other relevant factors. However, none of this would actually mean anything to someone who had absolutely no concept of sight at all. Such a person would be completely incapable of constructing an *experientially* meaningful definition of red; for them, any definition they created would simply be a collection of meaningless words.

Similarly, if no-one had ever experienced certainty, we might be able to create a *grammatically* meaningful definition by saying, for example, that 'certainty involved holding a belief about which one could not legitimately exclude all possible doubt'. The inclusion of the word 'legitimately' is essential here, as someone could of course exclude doubt quite erroneously. This could arise as a result of amnesia, a lack of imagination or simply because they were in a state of perpetual denial. Clearly, however, none of this would amount to certainty.

The problem with the above definition, however, is that the whole weight of this hangs on the word, 'legitimately'. In effect, this simply becomes a synonym for 'certainty', and as such it takes us no further forward in constructing an *experientially* meaningful definition of certainty. If we cannot be certain, the word 'legitimately' can have no meaning for us in this context; it is synonymous with 'certainty' about which we would know absolutely nothing.

It is important to note that we cannot interpret 'legitimately' to simply mean 'without making a mistake', and argue that we can fully understand the definition, as everyone knows about mistakes.

It is not enough to exclude doubt correctly; we must also *know* that we have done this. In short, we must be 'certain', and global sceptics insist that this is a state of mind that no-one has or ever will attain. If this is the case, however, then we would have absolutely no understanding of what certainty was. We would therefore be unable to talk about certainty meaningfully, let alone construct a watertight definition about what it entailed.

If we are uncertain, it would also not be rational to argue that certainty was impossible. This would be like the man who was born blind denying that red could ever exist, without possessing any concept of what red might be like if it did exist. If we *can* talk meaningfully about certainty, therefore, then we must be certain about some things. So what are we certain about and how exactly is certainty possible?

6.2.2. The Basis of Certainty

One fact about which all people are certain is their own consciousness. They may not know what is responsible for this, but everyone is sure when it is *they* and not someone else who is conscious. When they feel pain, they know that it is *they* who are in pain and not someone else. There is absolutely no doubt about the pain's existence or the fact that it is they who are involved in the suffering.

We can also see why we can be certain about things such as our own consciousness. We are sure about this, because we are in direct contact with the object of our knowledge. There are no logical steps of reasoning to separate our conclusions from their premises. And there are no physical gaps or mediums to separate us from the object of our knowledge. We are certain, because there is nothing to separate us from the thing that we are experiencing.

We only know about anything, however, by virtue of the changes that occur within our minds. When I see a chair, for example, everything I know about the chair is derived from the changes that occur within my own mind. How, then, could I be sure that the chair has a separate existence from myself, and is not simply an experience conjured up by my sub-consciousness?

We could argue that if we are certain about things that occur within us, then we must also know when experiences emanate from outside us. We should therefore be able to differentiate with certainty between internal and external experiences.

Being certain about one's consciousness, however, does not mean that one must also be certain about the content of our conscious experiences or their sources. Without further knowledge, the truth is that we would find it impossible to differentiate with certainty between vivid hallucinations created by our own minds and experiences produced by other persons or objects.

It might be argued, therefore, that we can only be sure about our own consciousness. We know that we are conscious, but we cannot be sure what is responsible for those conscious experiences. We also cannot be sure what we are or if there is anything or anyone else apart from us. All of our experiences could in theory stem entirely from changes within us, the product perhaps of our sub-conscious minds.

The idea that nothing and no-one else exists outside my own mind is known as *solipsism*. A less extreme version of this idea is *mental monism,* which argues that only minds exist. What both say is that we can only justifiably believe in the mind, as this is where all of our experiences take place. There is no need to believe that our experiences are caused by external entities, nor is there any basis for holding such a belief. There cannot be any evidence, therefore, to justify believing that there are any entities that have an existence outside our own minds.

If we can be certain about *one* thing, however, such as our own consciousness, then logically one cannot exclude the possibility that we could be certain about other things as well. If certainty is a reality – and it must be, for us to be able to talk about it meaningfully – then we must accept that certainty could arise in other circumstances as well. It would be self-defeating to argue otherwise, because to do so we would be concluding that we could be certain of at least two things: (a) that we are conscious, and (b) that we could not be certain of anything else. What, however, would give us certainty about (b) and why could we not be certain of other things if certainty about (b) were possible?

One way in which certainty about things outside ourselves might be possible, would be through a union with another mind. It might be possible for each person's identity to be preserved, whilst their knowledge was as directly accessible to another mind as if it were based upon their own direct experience. If this were possible, we could be certain of someone else's experiences in the same way as our own. We could be sure, not only that they were conscious, but that their certainty was as real as our own.

If a union between two minds were possible, it might also be possible for us to have the same kind of union with the mind of God. This would in turn enable us to be certain about the nature of all other persons and entities, because all of those things are entirely the product of God's mind. And as His knowledge is unlimited, He must possess complete and certain knowledge about all other persons and things.

To the extent that we could access that knowledge directly, we would be able to share in His certainty, as we would know things as they truly are, as opposed to how they might appear to be. The possibility of doubt and uncertainty would therefore be completely removed. Moreover, if God is infinite, omniscient and has always existed, there would be no possibility of any doubts based upon the possible existence of things outside God's knowledge.

6.2.3. Summary

The above is merely a brief outline of how certainty might be possible. It obviously does not attempt to cover wider aspects of these issues, which would clearly require a much lengthier chapter. However, it does at least provide the sceptic with a coherent account of how certainty might arise.

It also reminds us that science does not seek certainty or claim to have ever provided it. Instead, it only furnishes us with a number of working hypotheses, which appear to explain the available evidence, at least for the time being. The only logical position for science to adopt, therefore, is that all of its theories might be wrong, no matter how unlikely scientists might believe this to be.

This clearly blunts the edge of any epistemological challenge to religion. If atheists are not sure about anything, they must accept that they might be wrong about religion. By contrast, religion claims to deliver absolute certainty. And, as we have shown, it can clearly provide a coherent account of how that certainty might arise.

The remainder of this chapter looks at what the Bible says about these issues and the relationship between knowledge and faith.

6.3. THE BIBLE

6.3.1 General

The scriptures do not discuss knowledge or certainty in a philosophical way. What they do make clear, however, is that knowledge is an essential part of religion. Knowledge and faith are not therefore portrayed as opposites; instead they complement one another. Knowledge is the certainty that results from direct contact with the truth; faith is the attitude of complete trust that results from that knowledge.

6.3.2. Knowledge

Jesus said to His followers, 'you will know the truth, and the truth will set you free' (John 8:32). The importance of 'knowing', not just thinking, the truth is also emphasised by the apostle Paul (2 Timothy 2:25; 3:7), who says that God wants all men to possess a 'full knowledge of the truth' (1 Timothy 2:4).

In this life, the Bible says that all of us know about God's existence, as this is plainly evident from His creation (Romans 1:18-20). We also all retain a link with God, as He not only created our spirits (Numbers 27:16), but we also all 'live and move and have our being in Him' (Acts 17:28).

Believers 'know the truth' in a deeper way than others in this life, and will go on to possess a 'full knowledge of the truth' hereafter. For the present, however, Paul says that we all 'see through a mirror dimly' (literally, 'in a riddle') and only 'know in part' (1 Corinthians 13:12). It is only in the after-life that we will see 'face to face' and 'fully know as we have been fully known'. John echoes this, when he says:

Beloved, we are God's children now; but it is not yet clear what we shall be. But when it is made manifest, we shall be like Him, because we shall see Him as He is (1 John 3:2).

These verses emphasise that our knowledge in this life is incomplete and the experiences on which that knowledge is based are indirect; we only see via a reflection. In the after-life, however, our knowledge will be direct and will then 'mirror' the perfect knowledge that God has of us.

In His prayer in the Garden of Gethsemane, Jesus said that knowledge of God '<u>is</u> eternal life' (John 17:3). Believers already possess eternal life (1 John 5:13), therefore, as they have an intimate union with God, who 'abides' in them, as they 'abide' in Him (1 John 4:16,17). Ultimately, this union will be perfected and God and believers will become 'perfectly one' (John 17:23).

In this life, one of the main sources of knowledge about God is the Bible. We are told that all scripture is 'God breathed' (2 Timothy 3:16,17), which means that all of its words emanate directly from God (Romans 3:2). This explains why statements are described as being the very words of God, even when they are not directly spoken by Him in their original contexts (e.g., Matthew 19:5, c.f. Genesis 2:24).

As the words of the Bible are God's words, they are perfect communications. They do not contain irresolvable ambiguities; nor do they require speculative interpretations. To understand scripture, therefore, believers must not add to God's words (Proverbs 30:6) or go beyond what is written (1 Corinthians 4:6). That does not mean that they will not occasionally have to 'read the signs of the times' (Matthew 16:3) as well to apply their understanding of the Bible to the circumstances. Ultimately, however, certainty about the scriptures, like all knowledge, stems from the union with God's spirit that all true believers possess in this life (1 John 2:27).

The Bible therefore provides an account of knowledge that fully accords with the explanations outlined in 6.2 above. We have certainties in this life, but they are limited as much of our experience is indirect. The horizons of our knowledge are expanded by our union with God, but this knowledge is only perfected in the afterlife.

6.3.3. Faith

In the Bible the word 'faith' appears frequently in the New Testament, and the verb on which the Greek word for 'faith' is based is 'to believe'. These words broadly denote one of two things. (a) belief that something is true, and (b) trust in God.

The Bible attaches limited importance to the first kind of 'faith'. James 2:19 says, for example: 'You believe that God is one. Well done! Even the demons believe this *and* tremble!' Most passages of the New Testament are therefore concerned with 'faith' in the second sense of the word. And Hebrews chapter 11 describes numerous examples of unconditional trust in God, which are held up as being prime examples of the kind of 'faith' that justifies a man in the eyes of God.

Faith is not, therefore, a state of wishful thinking. It is a position of unconditional trust that provides solid evidence of the underlying truths to which it relates. As Hebrew 11:1 says, 'faith is the reality of things hoped for' and 'the proof of things not seen'.

In the Bible, therefore, faith is not seen as the opposite of knowledge; the two go hand-in-hand. Certain knowledge gives birth to the unconditional trust of faith. In 1 Timothy 4:3, therefore, Paul speaks of knowledge and faith in the same breath, referring to those who 'believe and know the truth'.

6.4. CONCLUSIONS

The challenge of scepticism is clearly not a difficult one to overcome. If I cannot be certain of anything, then I have to accept that I might be entirely mistaken in my belief that certainty is impossible. Moreover, if certainty were impossible, then no-one would have experienced it, so no-one would be able to have a meaningful discussion about it. If we accept that we can be certain about some things, however, then it should be possible to be certain about others, including religious beliefs.

Although empirical evidence is often regarded as the only source of true knowledge, at least in the popular perception, science regards its 'knowledge' as consisting of no more than a set of theories that could all be disproven, and about which therefore no absolute certainty can ever exist. By contrast, although faith is generally regarded as an act of wishful thinking, religion describes 'faith' as a state of trust that is grounded in certain knowledge.

We have also seen how it is possible for religion to provide a coherent account of how certainty might be possible. We are certain when we have direct, unobscured access to the object of our knowledge. This certainty therefore exists in relation to our own consciousness, but it is also capable of existing in relation to our union with other minds and ultimately with the mind of God.

It is no challenge for sceptics to argue that because *they* are not certain, no-one else can be either. In fact, to be consistent with their beliefs, sceptics must be open to the possibility that others might be certain about things, even if they are not. In short, it is clear that sceptics are logically obliged to admit that *they* might be wrong; believers are not.

CHAPTER 7. SUMMARY AND CONCLUSIONS

We have now thoroughly examined the principle objections to belief in God and to religion in general. We began by seeing that there must be a spiritual dimension to the universe, as materialism is clearly incapable of accounting for one fundamental in our lives – consciousness. The first chapter does a lot more than just defend belief in the soul, though; it completely vindicates it.

By contrast, the rest of the book is apologetic in nature, that is, it seeks to defend religious beliefs and argue that they are tenable, as opposed to trying to prove that any of them are true or are even more likely to be true than not.

In the second chapter, we looked in considerable depth at the challenges of the Theory of Evolution and science in general. It is worth making the point here that these are only challenges to those who believe in the biblical account of creation. They do not pose a threat to anyone who is religious, but who holds quite different beliefs about how life on earth developed. It should by now be clear, however, that the biblical account of creation can be defended, and defended very robustly.

The other challenges to religion have taken less time to answer. These are the issues relating to evil, suffering, doubt and the absence of miracles in our modern world. Even if those reading these passages remain entirely unpersuaded by the arguments, they cannot reasonably conclude that they do not at least provide logically tenable defences to belief in a loving God.

Once we accept that God might exist, we should be prepared to explore this possibility much further, in view of the huge implications it has for all of our lives. If this book achieves nothing else, it should at least cause the open-minded to reconsider any previously held beliefs on this subject.

APPENDICES

Appendix 1. Mammal Species

Biology of Mammals by Richard van Gelder (1971), page 7

Subdivision	Species	Notes
Montremata (platypus and echidnas)	6	
Marsupiala (marsupials)	242	
Insectivora (insectivores)	400	
Dermoptera (flying lemurs)	2	
Chiroptera (bats)	875	
Primates	166	
Edentata (toothless, e.g. sloths)	31	
Pholidota (pangolins)	8	
Lagomorpha (e.g. rabbits)	63	
Rodentia (rodents)	1,687	
Cetacea (aquatic)	84	Aquatic
Carnivora (carnivores)	284	Part aquatic
Tubulidentata (aardvark)	1	
Proboscidea (elephants)	2	
Hyracoidea (hyraxes)	11	
Sirenia (manatees and dugongs)	4	Aquatic
Perissodactyla (odd-toed hoofs)	16	
Artiodactyla (even-toed hoofs)	171	
Total	**4,053**	

<u>Less</u>	
Bats	-875
Cetacea	-84
Sirenia	-4
Seals*	-19
Sea lions*	-14
Walruses*	-2
Clean mammals (E)	-170
Unclean Mammals	**2,885**

* included in carnivora above and based on figures per Chapter 2. See Note 10 re sources.

Appendix 2. The Sumerian King List, Per Jacobsen and Vincente
[Chapter 2, Notes 64 and 69]

Year BC Reign Begins (Conventional Chronology)	Year BC Reign Begins (Dead Reckoning)	Ruler's Name	Reign Length	Notes & Variants > 50 years
		Pre-Deluge Era		
	-276,679	Alulim	28,800	
	-247,879	Alalgar	36,000	
	-211,879	Enmenluanna	43,200	
	-168,679	Enmengalanna	28,800	
	-139,879	Dumuzi	36,000	
	-103,879	Ensipazianna	28,800	
	-75,079	Enmenduranna	21,000	
	-54,079	Ubartutu	18,600	
			241,200	
		After the flood swept over, and the kingship had descended from heaven, the kingship was in Kish.		
		First Dynasty of Kish		
	-35,479	Gaur	1,200	
	-34,279	Nidaba	960	L_2 has 1200
	-33,319	Palakinatim	900	
	-32,419	Nangishlishma	3,480	years assumed to agree total
	-28,939	Bahina	3,480	years assumed to agree total
	-25,459	Buanum	840	
	-24,619	Kalibum	960	P_2 has 900
	-23,659	Qalumum	840	P_3 & Su_1 have 900
	-22,819	Zuqaqip	900	Su_1 has 600
	-21,919	Atab	600	
	-21,319	Mashda	840	Su_1 has 720
	-20,479	Arwium	720	
	-19,759	Etana	1,560	P_2 has 635
	-18,199	Balih	400	
	-17,799	Enmenunna	660	
	-17,139	Melamkishi	900	
	-16,239	Barsalnunna	1,200	
	-15,039	Samug	140	
	-14,899	Tizkar	305	
	-14,594	Ilku	900	
	-13,694	Iltasadum	1,200	
	-12,494	Enmenbaragesi	900	
	-11,594	Aka	625	
			24,510	

Year BC Reign Begins (Conventional Chronology)	Year BC Reign Begins (Dead Reckoning)	Ruler's Name	Reign Length	Notes & Variants > 50 years
		First Dynasty of Uruk		
	-10,969	Meskiaggasher	324	
	-10,645	Enmerkar	420	TL has 900
	-10,225	Lugalbanda	1,200	TL has 600
	-9,025	Dumuzid	100	
-2,600	-8,925	Gilgamesh	126	
	-8,799	Urnungal	30	
	-8,769	Utulkalamma	15	
	-8,754	Labashir	9	
	-8,745	Ennundaranna	8	
	-8,737	Meshe	36	
	-8,701	Melemanna	6	Su_2 has 900 years
	-8,695	Lugalkitun	36	Su_2 has 420 years
			2,310	Su_2 has 3,588 years
		First dynasty of Ur		
-2,500	-8,659	Mesannepada	80	time of Mesilim of Kish per Ch 2 N 71
	-8,579	Meskiagnunna	36	
	-8,543	Elulu	25	
	-8,518	Balulu	36	
			177	no mention of 1st dynasty of Lagash.
		Awan		
	-8,482	Three kings of Awan	356	
			356	
		Second Dynasty Kish		
	-8,126	Su... (?)	201	
	-7,925	Dadasig	1,249	years assumed to agree total
	-6,676	Magalgalla	360	
	-6,316	Kalbum	195	
	-6,121	See	360	
	-5,761	Gasubnunna	180	
	-5,581	Enbieshtar	290	
	-5,291	Lugalmu	360	
			3,195	L_1 has 3,792 years
		Hamazi		
	-4,931	Hatanish	360	TL has 6
			360	P_2 has 7 or 420 yrs

Year BC Reign Begins (Conventional Chronology)	Year BC Reign Begins (Dead Reckoning)	Ruler's Name	Reign Length	Notes & Variants > 50 years
		Second Dynasty of Uruk		
	-4,571	Enshakushanna	60	
	-4,511	Lugalure	120	name from Ni 9712b
	-4,391	Argandea	7	name from Ni 9712b
			187	
		Second Dynasty of Ur		
	-4,384	Lugalkinishedudu	146	years assumed to agree total
	-4,238	Lugalkisalsi	146	years estimated to agree total
	-4,092	….gi	145	years estimated to agree total
	-3,947	Kakug	145	years estimated to agree total
			582	P_2 reconstructed to give 116
		Adab		
	-3,802	Lugalannemundu	90	
			90	
		Mari		
	-3,712	Ansud	30	TL has 90 years
	-3,682	..zi	17	
	-3,665	…-lugal	30	
	-3,635	…-lugal	20	
	-3,615	…bimusmas	30	
	-3,585	…ni	9	
			136	
		Third Dynasty of Kish		
	-3,576	Kubaba	100	
			100	
		Akshak		
	-3,476	Unzi	30	
	-3,446	Undalulu	6	
	-3,440	Urur	6	
	-3,434	Puzurnirah	20	
	-3,414	Ishuil	24	
	-3,390	Shushin	7	
			93	

Year BC Reign Begins (Conventional Chronology)	Year BC Reign Begins (Dead Reckoning)	Ruler's Name	Reign Length	Notes & Variants > 50 years
		Fourth Dynasty of Kish		
	-3,383	Puzursin	25	
	-3,358	Urzababa	400	S has 6 years
	-2,958	Simudar	30	
	-2,928	Usiwatar	7	
	-2,921	Eshtarmuti	11	
	-2,910	Ishmeshamash	11	
	-2,899	Nannia	7	
			491	
		Third Dynasty of Uruk		
	-2,892	Lugalzagesi	25	
			25	
		Akkad		
-2350	-2,867	Sharrukin (Sargon)	56	
	-2,811	Rimush	9	
	-2,802	Manishtushu	15	
	-2,787	Naramsin	37	
	-2,750	Sharkalisharri	25	
	-2,725	Irgigi, Nanum, Imi, Elulu	3	
	-2,722	Dudu	21	
	-2,701	Shudurul	15	
			181	
		Fourth Dynasty of Uruk		
	-2,686	Urnigin	7	
	-2,679	Urgigir	6	
	-2,673	Kudda	0	
	-2,667	Puzurili	5	
	-2,662	Urutu	6	
			30	
		Gutium period		
		In the army of Gutium, at first no king was famous; they were their own kings and ruled for 3 years		
	-2,656	Imta	3	
	-2,653	Inkishush	6	
	-2,647	Sarlagab	6	
	-2,641	Shulme	6	

Year BC Reign Begins (Conventional Chronology)	Year BC Reign Begins (Dead Reckoning)	Ruler's Name	Reign Length	Notes & Variants > 50 years
	-2,635	Elulumesh	6	
	-2,629	Inimabakesh	5	
	-2,624	Igeshaush	6	
	-2,618	Iarlagab	15	
	-2,603	Ibate	3	
	-2,600	Iarla	3	
	-2,597	Kurum	1	
	-2,596	Habilkin	3	
	-2,593	Laerabum	2	
	-2,591	Irarum	2	
	-2,589	Ibranum	1	
	-2,588	Hablum	2	
	-2,586	Puzursin	7	
	-2,579	Iarlaganda	7	
	-2,572	Sium	7	
	-2,565	Tiriga - 40 days	0.11	
			91.11	text says 21 kings; there are 20
		Uruk		
-2170	-2,565	Utuhegal	427	IB has 26 years; TL & J have 7 years, 6 months, 15 days
			427	
		Third dynasty of Ur		
	-2,138	Urnammu	18	
	-2,120	Shulgi	46	
	-2,074	Bursin	9	
	-2,065	Shushin	9	
	-2,056	Ibbisin	24	
			106	text says 4 kings for 108 years
		Dynasty of Isin		
	-2,032	Ishbi-irra	33	
	-1,999	Shuilishu	20	
	-1,979	Idindagan	21	
	-1,958	Ishmedagan	20	
	-1,938	Lipiteshtar	11	
	-1,927	Urninurta	28	
	-1,899	Bursin	21	
	-1,878	Lipitenlil	5	
	-1,873	Irraimitti	8	

Year BC Reign Begins (Conventional Chronology)	Year BC Reign Begins (Dead Reckoning)	Ruler's Name	Reign Length	Notes & Variants > 50 years
		Dynasty of Isin		
	-1,865	Enlilbani	24	
	-1,841	Zambia	3	
	-1,838	Iterpisha	4	
	-1,834	Urdukuga	4	
-1,830	(see footnote) -1,830	Sinmagir	11	P_5 adds a later king, Damqilishu, who reigned for 23 years
			213	Text gives total as 13 (instead of 14 kings) reigning for 203 years,
		Summary		
		Rulers before Flood (8)	241,200	
		Rulers after Flood (134)	33,660	P_2 says 134 kings for 28,876 years; P4 has 139 kings for 32,243 years
		Total reign lengths	**274,860**	

Footnote

1st year of Hammarubi	1,792
To last year of Damqilishu*	4
Reign of Damqilishu	23
Reign of Sinmagir	11
	1,830

* Jacobsen places a 4 year gap between the end of his reign and the start of Hammurabi's reign

Appendix 3. C¹⁴ Dating: 1970 Results* & The Oxford History of Ancient Egypt

Dynasty	Monument	Conventional BC	C14, BC	Difference	Adjusted	Difference
1	Reed in mastaba 3357 of Aha (Menes?)	2,986	2,480	506	2,970	16
1	Wood in mastaba of 3504 of Wadji (Djet)	2,959	2,460	499	2,942	17
1	Wood in mastaba 3504 of Wadji (Djet)	2,959	2,390	569	2,844	115
1	Wood in mastaba 3504 of Wadji (Djet)	2,959	2,684	275	3,254	-295
1	Wood in mastaba 3504 of Wadji (Djet)	2,959	2,518	441	3,027	-68
1	Reed in mastaba 3035 of Den	2,945	2,560	385	3,082	-137
1	Wood in mastaba 3035 of Den	2,945	2,540	405	3,058	-113
1	Reed in mastaba 3503 of Merneith	2,931	2,710	221	3,278	-347
1	Reed in mastaba 3505 of Qa'a	2,890	2,450	440	2,928	-38
3	Reed in mastaba 3518 of Djoser	2,648	2,215	433	2,616	32
3	Flax rope in mastaba 3518 of Djoser	2,648	2,276	372	2,698	-50
4	Wood from pyramid of Sneferu	2,589	2,114	475	2,479	110
4	Wood from pyramid of Sneferu	2,589	2,029	560	2,364	225
4	Grass rope from funerary boat of Khufu	2,566	2,150	416	2,536	30
6	Wood from pyramid of Teti	2,323	1,940	383	2,228	95
6	Reed from mastaba of Teti	2,323	1,930	393	2,228	95
11	Wood from temple of Nebhepetra	2,004	1,650	354	1,845	159
11	Wood from chapel of Sankhara	1,992	1,830	162	2,088	-96
12	Reed from pyramid of Sesostris II (Senusret II)	1,870	1,740	130	1,962	-92
19	Reed from Ramesseum of Ramesses II	1,213	1,070	143	1,070	143
	Range			130 to 569		-347 to 225
				(439 years)		(572 years)

* I. Edwards, *Absolute Dating from Egyptian Records and Comparison with Carbon-14 Dating*

Appendix 4. C¹⁴ Dating: 1984 Results & The Oxford History of Ancient Egypt

Dynasty	Monument	Conventional BC	C14, BC	Difference
1	Charcoal in mastaba 3505 of Qa'a	2,890	3,163	-273
3	Charcoal from Step Pyramid of Djoser	2,648	3,203	-555
3	Wood from Step Pyramid of Djoser	2,648	2,901	-253
3	Wood from Step Pyramid of Djoser	2,648	2,857	-209
3	Wood from Step Pyramid of Djoser	2,648	2,816	-168
3	Charcoal from mortuary temple of Djoser	2,648	2,811	-163
3	Charcoal from mortuary temple of Djoser	2,648	2,465	183
3	Charcoal from pyramid at Saqqara of Sekhemkhet	2,640	3,263	-623
3	Straw from pyramid at Saqqara of Sekhemkhet	2,640	2,910	-270
3	Reed from pyramid at Saqqara of Sekhemkhet	2,640	1,307	1,333
4	Wood from pyramid of Sneferu at Meidum	2,589	3,570	-981
4	Wood from pyramid of Sneferu at Meidum	2,589	2,669	-80
4	Charcoal from pyramid of Khufu at Giza	2,566	3,809	-1,243
4	Wood from pyramid of Khufu at Giza	2,566	3,101	-535
4	Charcoal from pyramid of Khufu at Giza	2,566	3,090	-524
4	Charcoal from pyramid of Khufu at Giza	2,566	3,062	-496
4	Charcoal from pyramid of Khufu at Giza	2,566	3,020	-454
4	Charcoal from pyramid of Khufu at Giza	2,566	2,998	-432
4	Charcoal from pyramid of Khufu at Giza	2,566	2,988	-422
4	Charcoal from pyramid of Khufu at Giza	2,566	2,975	-409
4	Charcoal from pyramid of Khufu at Giza	2,566	2,971	-405
4	Reeds from pyramid of Khufu at Giza	2,566	2,950	-384
4	Charcoal from pyramid of Khufu at Giza	2,566	2,929	-363
4	Charcoal from pyramid of Khufu at Giza	2,566	2,909	-343
4	Charcoal from pyramid of Khufu at Giza	2,566	2,909	-343
4	Charcoal from pyramid of Khufu at Giza	2,566	2,869	-303
4	Charcoal from pyramid of Khufu at Giza	2,566	2,864	-298

Dynasty	Monument	Conventional BC	C14, BC	Difference
4	Mortar of limestone from pyramid of Khufu at Giza	2,566	2,853	-287
4	Charcoal from pyramid of Djedefra at Abu Roash	2,558	3,179	-621
4	Charcoal from pyramid of Djedefra at Abu Roash	2,558	3,046	-488
4	Charcoal from pyramid of Djedefra at Abu Roash	2,558	3,006	-448
4	Charcoal from pyramid of Djedefra at Abu Roash	2,558	2,974	-416
4	Charcoal from pyramid of Djedefra at Abu Roash	2,558	2,837	-279
4	Straw from pyramid of Djedefra at Abu Roash	2,558	2,699	-141
4	Straw from pyramid of Djedefra at Abu Roash	2,558	2,408	150
4	Charcoal from pyramid of Khafra at Giza	2,532	3,196	-664
4	Charcoal from pyramid of Khafra at Giza	2,532	3,188	-656
4	Charcoal/wood from pyramid of Khafra at Giza	2,532	3,147	-615
4	Charcoal from pyramid of Khafra at Giza	2,532	3,088	-556
4	Charcoal from pyramid of Khafra at Giza	2,532	2,841	-309
4	Charcoal from pyramid of Khafra at Giza	2,532	2,762	-230
4	Charcoal from pyramid of Khafra at Giza	2,532	2,723	-191
4	Charcoal from Sphinx Temple of Khafra	2,532	2,746	-214
4	Charcoal from Sphinx Temple of Khafra	2,532	2,085	447
4	Charcoal from pyramid of Menkaura at Giza	2,503	3,076	-573
4	Charcoal from pyramid of Menkaura at Giza	2,503	2,927	-424
4	Charcoal from pyramid of Menkaura at Giza	2,503	2,592	-89
4	Organic powder charcoal from pyramid of Menkaura at Giza	2,503	2,181	322
4	Organic powder charcoal from pyramid of Menkaura at Giza	2,503	2,136	367
4	Organic powder charcoal from pyramid of Menkaura at Giza	2,503	2,067	436
4	Charcoal from mastaba of Shepseskaf at Farroun/Saqqara	2,494	3,020	-526
4	Charcoal from mastaba of Shepseskaf at Farroun/Saqqara	2,494	2,983	-489
4	Charcoal from mastaba of Shepseskaf at Farroun/Saqqara	2,494	2,928	-434
4	Charcoal from mastaba of Shepseskaf at Farroun/Saqqara	2,494	2,873	-379
4	Charcoal from mastaba of Shepseskaf at Farroun/Saqqara	2,494	2,213	281

Dynasty	Monument	Conventional BC	C14, BC	Difference
4	Charcoal from mastaba of Shepseskaf at Farroun/Saqqara	2,494	2,197	297
4	Charcoal from mastaba of Shepseskaf at Farroun/Saqqara	2,494	1,622	872
5	Charcoal from pyramid of Userkaf at Saqqara	2,487	3,138	-651
5	Charcoal from pyramid of Userkaf at Saqqara	2,487	3,042	-555
5	Charcoal from pyramid of Userkaf at Saqqara	2,487	2,941	-454
6	Charcoal from pyramid of Userkaf at Saqqara	2,487	2,899	-412
5	Wood from pyramid of Userkaf at Saqqara	2,487	2,509	-22
5	Charcoal from mortuary temple at Abusir of Sahura	2,475	2,868	-393
5	Charcoal from mortuary temple at Abusir of Sahura	2,475	2,590	-115
5	Charcoal from mortuary temple at Abusir of Sahura	2,475	1,711	764
5	Charcoal from pyramid of Unas at Saqqara	2,345	2,899	-554
5	Charcoal from pyramid of Unas at Saqqara	2,345	2,669	-324
5	Charcoal from pyramid of Unas at Saqqara	2,345	2,589	-244
6	Charcoal from pyramid of Teti at Saqqara	2,323	3,217	-894
6	Wood under sarcophagus from pyramid of Teti at Saqqara	2,323	2,761	-438
6	Charcoal from mortuary chapel of Pepy II at Neit	2,184	3,126	-942
6	Charcoal from pyramid of Pepty II at Saqqara	2,184	2,419	-235
	Range			1,333 to -1,243
				(2,576 years)

Data from *Chronologies of the Near East (pp 585-606), Radiocarbon Chronology and the Historical Calendar in Egypt,* H. Haas et al.

Appendix 5. Old & Middle Kingdom C¹⁴ Dates* & The Oxford History of Ancient Egypt

Dynasty	Monument	Conventional BC	C14, BC (sigma 2)	Difference
1	Tomb 3357 Saqqara of Menes	2,986	2,770	-216
1	Tomb 3471 Saqqara of Djer's reign	2,973	2,996	23
1	Tomb 3504 Saqqara of Djet	2,959	2,967	8
1	Tomb 3035 Saqqara of Den	2,945	2,744	-201
1	Tomb 3505 Saqqara of Qa'a	2,890	3,214	324
3	Step Pyramid, Djoser	2,648	2,742	94
3	Temple complex of Djoser	2,648	2,666	18
3	Pyramid of Sekhemkhet	2,640	2,741	101
4	Tomb 17 of Sneferu at Meidum	2,589	2,391	-199
4	Bent Pyramid of Sneferu at Dashur	2,589	2,703	114
4	Sneferu's pyramid at Meidum	2,589	2,658	69
4	Khufu's pyramid at Giza	2,566	2,721	155
4	Djedefra's temple at Abu Roash	2,558	2,752	194
4	Djedefra's pyramid at Abu Roash	2,558	2,745	187
4	Pyramid of Khafre at Giza	2,532	2,741	209
4	Pyramid of Menkaure at Giza	2,503	2,663	160
4	Mortuary temple of Shepseskaf at Saqqara	2,494	2,748	254
5	Pyramid temple of Userkaf, Saqqara	2,487	3,011	524
5	Pyramid temple of Userkaf, Saqqara	2,487	2,288	-199
5	Pyramid of Userkaf, Saqqara	2,487	2,539	52
5	Queen of Userkaf's pyramid, Saqqara	2,487	2,380	-107
5	Temple and pyramid of Sahura at Abusir	2,475	2,328	-148
5	Temple of Unas at Saqqara	2,345	2,542	197
5	Pyramid of Unas at Saqqara	2,345	2,595	250
6	Pyramid of Teti at Saqqara	2,323	2,563	240
6	Pyramid of Pepi II at Saqqara	2,184	2,395	211
8	Pyramid of Quakare-Iby at south Saqqara	2,171	2,335	164
12	Pyramid of Senusret II at Illahum	1,870	1,912	42
12	Pyramid of Amenemhet III	1,786	1,756	-31
	Range			524 to -216
				(740 years)

*Near East Chronology: Archaeology and Environment: RADIOCARBON, Volume 43, pp 1297-1320: *Radiocarbon Dates of Old and Middle Kingdom Monuments in Egypt*, G. Bonani et al.

BIBLIOGRAPHICAL TABLE

CHAPTER 1

No.	Title	Published	Author/Editor	Page No./Ref.
1	Consciousness Explained	1993	D. Dennett	p 35
2	Reasons and Persons	1986	D. Parfit	p 276
3	A Brief History of Time	1995	S. Hawking	p 55
4	A Brief History of Time	1995	S. Hawking	pp 76,77
4	What does a Black Hole Look Like?	2014	C. Bailyn	p 158
5	A Brief History of Time	1995	S. Hawking	pp 76,77
6	The Self and Its Brain: An Argument for Interactionism	1984	K. Popper, J. Eccles	p 180
7	Hypnosis: Developments in Research & New Perspectives	2007	E. Fromm, R. Shor	p 299
8	Reasons and Persons	1986	D. Parfit	pp 245-247
9	Cognitive Science: The Science of Intelligent Systems	1994	G. Luger, P. Johnson, C. Stern, J. Newman	pp 120, 121
10	The Self and Its Brain: An Argument for Interactionism	1984	K. Popper, J. Eccles	p 362
11	Reasons and Persons	1986	D. Parfit	p 260
12	The Conscious Mind	1996	D. Chalmers	pp xi, xii
13	Quiddities: An Intermittently Philosophical Dictionary	1989	W. Quine	pp 132, 133
14	The Self and Its Brain: An Argument for Interactionism	1984	K. Popper, J. Eccles	p 440

BIBLIOGRAPHICAL TABLE

CHAPTER 2

No.	Title	Published	Author/Editor	Page No./Ref.
1	The New Bible Dictionary	1978	J. Douglas	pp 271, 272
2	Josephus, The Complete Works	1998	W. Whiston	pp 38, 39

BIBLIOGRAPHICAL TABLE			
CHAPTER 2			
No.	Title	Published	Author/Editor	Page No./Ref.
3	The New Bible Dictionary	1978	J. Douglas	pp 1338, 1339
4	Hebrew and English Lexicon of the Old Testament	1951	F. Brown	p 568
5	Biological Systematics	1998	A. Minelli	pp 108-113
6	A Textbook of Entomology	1967	H. Ross	pp 144, 145
6	The Insect's Structure and Function, 5th Edition	2012	R. Chapman	pp 351, 403-408
7	The Insect's Structure and Function, 5th Edition	2012	R. Chapman	p 351
8	The Cambridge Encyclopedia, 4th Edition	2000	D. Crystal	p 126
9	Horns, Tusks, and Flippers: The Evolution of Hoofed Mammals	2003	D. Prothero & R. Schoch	P 62
10	Biology of Mammals	1971	R. Van Gelder	p 7
10	The Cambridge Encyclopedia, 4th Edition	2000	D. Crystal	pp 981, 982 (seals, sea lions)
10	Dolphins, Wales and Porpoises: An Encyclopedia of Sea Mammals	1978	D. Coffey	p 157 (walruses)
11	The Cambridge Encyclopedia, 4th Edition	2000	D. Crystal	p 60
12	The Genesis Flood	1961	J. Whitcomb & H. Morris	p 65
13	The Genesis Flood	1961	J. Whitcomb & H. Morris	p 65
13	Hebrew and English Lexicon of the Old Testament	1951	F. Brown	pp 988a, 1041a
14	Collins Birds of Prey	2008	B. Gensbol & W. Thiede	p 7
14	Owls	1995	J. Sparks & T. Soper	p 7

BIBLIOGRAPHICAL TABLE
CHAPTER 2

No.	Title	Published	Author/Editor	Page No./Ref.
14	Seabirds	1976	D. Saunders	p 5
15	The Genesis Flood	1961	J. Whitcomb & H. Morris	pp 70-74
16	Noah's Ark: A Feasibility Study	1996	J. Woodmorappe	pp 129-133
17	Life in the Cold – Eleventh International Symposium	2000	G. Heldmaier & M. Klingenspor	pp 1, 2, 241
18	The New Bible Dictionary	1978	J. Douglas	pp 1321, 1322
19	The Cambridge Encyclopedia, 4th Edition	2000	D. Crystal	p 937
20	Amphibians of Europe	1984	D. Ballasina	p 25
21	The Biology of Reptiles	1982	I. Spellerberg	pp 37, 38
21	The Cambridge Encyclopedia, 4th Edition	2000	D. Crystal	pp 52, 239, 304, 656, 1016 - alligator, chelonia, crocodile, lizard, snake
22	The Life of Birds	1967	J. Welty	p 112
23	Introduction to Food Science & Technology	1973	G. Stewart & M. Amerine	p 6
24	Introduction to Food Science & Technology	1973	G. Stewart & M. Amerine	p 10
25	So Easy to Preserve	1984	S. Reynolds & P. Williams	p 275
26	Hebrew and English Lexicon of the Old Testament	1951	F. Brown	p 844
27	The New Bible Dictionary	1978	J. Douglas	p 82
28	Ships and Seamanship in The Ancient World	1995	L. Casson	p 188
29	Safety Investigation of Noah's Ark in a Seaway	1994	S. Hong, S. Na et. Al	Full text

BIBLIOGRAPHICAL TABLE
CHAPTER 2

No.	Title	Published	Author/Editor	Page No./Ref.
30	Chemical Oceanography (2nd Edition)	1975	J. Riley & G. Skirrow	Volume 1, pp 328 & 417
30	Environmental Chemistry	2013	P. O'Neill	p 173
31	The Wonders of Bible Chronology	1933	P. Mauro	p 14*
32	Noah's Ark: A Feasibility Study	1996	J. Woodmorappe	pp 11, 13, 20
33	The Life of Fishes	1976	N. Marshall	p 120
34	Noah's Ark: A Feasibility Study	1996	J. Woodmorappe	p 145
35	The Life of Fishes	1976	N. Marshall	p 123
36	The Origin of Species, Oxford World Classics	1998	C. Darwin	p 311
37	Biology of Mammals	1971	R. Van Gelder	p 78
38	The Cambridge Encyclopedia, 4th Edition	2000	D. Crystal	p 342
39	Dormancy and the Survival of Plants	1975	T. Villiers	p 37
40	Plant Reproductive Ecology: Patterns and Strategies	1990	J. & L. Doust	p 319
41	Plant Reproductive Ecology: Patterns and Strategies	1990	J. & L. Doust	p 295
42	Introduction to Algae: Structure and Reproduction	1984	H. Bold & M. Wynne	p 1
43	Introduction to Algae: Structure and Reproduction	1984	H. Bold & M. Wynne	pp 3, 10
44	Studies in Plant Survival: An Ecophysical Examination of Plant Distribution	1988	R. Crawford	p 114

* p14 less 40 years adjustment required per chapter 5 of this book

	BIBLIOGRAPHICAL TABLE			
CHAPTER 2				
No.	Title	Published	Author/Editor	Page No./Ref.
45	The Genesis Flood	1961	J. Whitcomb & H. Morris	pp 104-106
46	Analytical Biogeography	1988	A. Myers & P. Giller	pp 3,4
47	Biogeography	1979	E. Pielou	pp 192, 255
48	Biogeography	1979	E. Pielou	pp 29-31
48	The Cambridge Encyclopedia, 4th Edition	2000	D. Crystal	p 286
49	Biogeography	1979	E. Pielou	p 264
50	The Cambridge Encyclopedia, 4th Edition	2000	D. Crystal	pp 464, 548
51	Analytical Biogeography	1988	A. Myers & P. Giller	p 145
52	Geography of Life	1969	W. Neill	p 376
53	Biogeography	1979	E. Pielou	p 252
54	Biogeography	1979	E. Pielou	p 54
55	Geography of Life	1969	W. Neill	p 81
56	Biogeography	1979	E. Pielou	p 256
57	Geography of Life	1969	W. Neill	p 220
58	The Cambridge Encyclopedia, 4th Edition	2000	D. Crystal	p 866
59	The Genesis Flood	1961	J. Whitcomb & H. Morris	p 256
60	The Study of Man	1974	E. Clegg	p 196
61	Pears 2005/06 Cyclopedia	2005	C. Cook	L 117
62	The Cambridge Encyclopedia, 4th Edition	2000	D. Crystal	RR 1243
63	The Egyptians, An Introduction	2005	R. Morkot	p 71
64	The Tall Leilān Recension of the Sumerian King List	1995	C. Vincente	pp 236-238
65	The Sumerian King List	1939	T. Jacobsen	p 140

BIBLIOGRAPHICAL TABLE				
CHAPTER 2				
No.	Title	Published	Author/Editor	Page No./Ref.
66	The Sumerian King List	1939	T. Jacobsen	p 5
67	The New Bible Dictionary	1978	J. Douglas	p 501
68	The Sumerians	1971	S. Kramer	pp 163-164
68	The New Bible Dictionary	1978	J. Douglas	p 428
69	The Sumerian King List	1939	T. Jacobsen	pp 69-127
69	The Sumerians	1971	S. Kramer	pp 328-331
70	The Sumerian King List	1939	T. Jacobsen	pp 180-182
70	The Sumerians	1971	S. Kramer	pp 50-59
71	The Sumerians	1971	S. Kramer	p 32
72	A Test of Time	1995	D. Rohl	p 294
73	The Sumerians	1971	S. Kramer	pp 47-50
74	The Oxford History of Ancient Egypt	2000	I. Shaw	pp 12, 13
75	The New Bible Dictionary	1978	J. Douglas	p 1145
76	The Sumerian King List	1939	T. Jacobsen	p 108
77	The Sumerians	1971	S. Kramer	pp 205, 217
78	Royal Annals of Ancient Egypt: the Palermo Stone and its Associated Fragments	2003	T. Wilkinson	pp 23, 24
79	Berossus and Manetho, Native Traditions in Ancient Mesopotamia and Egypt	2001	G. Verbrugghe, J. Wickersham	pp 104, 185
80	Royal Annals of Ancient Egypt: the Palermo Stone and its Associated Fragments	2003	T. Wilkinson	p 76
81	The Oxford History of Ancient Egypt	2000	I. Shaw	p 12
82	Berossus and Manetho, Native Traditions in Ancient Mesopotamia and Egypt	2001	G. Verbrugghe, J. Wickersham	pp 186, 187

\multicolumn{5}{	l	}{BIBLIOGRAPHICAL TABLE}

BIBLIOGRAPHICAL TABLE				
CHAPTER 2				
No.	Title	Published	Author/Editor	Page No./Ref.
83	Manetho	1964	W. Waddell	pp 3-93
84	Berossus and Manetho, Native Traditions in Ancient Mesopotamia and Egypt	2001	G. Verbrugghe, J. Wickersham	p 103
85	Berossus and Manetho, Native Traditions in Ancient Mesopotamia and Egypt	2001	G. Verbrugghe, J. Wickersham	pp 111, 187-203
86	Ancient Egyptian Science: Volume II: Calendars, Clocks & Astronomy	2004	M. Clagett	pp 28, 29
87	Berossus and Manetho, Native Traditions in Ancient Mesopotamia and Egypt	2001	G. Verbrugghe, J. Wickersham	pp 156, 179
88	Journal of the Ancient Astronomy Forum: The Decline and Fall of Sothic Dating, El-Lahun Lunar Texts and Egyptian Astronomical Dates	2002	D. Lappin	Volume 9, pp 72, 73
89	Sothic Dating Examined, the Sothic Star Theory of the Egyptian Calendar	1995	D. Mackey	Chapter 10
89	Ancient Egyptian Science: Volume II: Calendars, Clocks & Astronomy	2004	M. Clagett	pp 333-335
90	Sothic Dating Examined, the Sothic Star Theory of the Egyptian Calendar	1995	D. Mackey	Chapter 10
91	Peoples of the Sea	1977	I. Velikovsky	p 219
92	The Oxford History of Ancient Egypt	2000	I. Shaw	p 11

BIBLIOGRAPHICAL TABLE			
CHAPTER 2			
No.	Title	Published	Author/Editor	Page No./Ref.
93	Tacitus The Annals	2008	J. Yardley	p 199 (Book 6, Part 28)
94	Herodotus The Histories	2003	A de Sélincourt, J. Marincola	p 124 (Book 2, Part 73)
95	A Dictionary of Ancient Roman Coins	1990	J. Jones	p 243
96	Quellen und Forschungen zur Zeitbestimmung der Ägyptischen Geschichte - Die Annalen und die Zeitlichen Festlegung des Alten Reiches der Ägyptischen Geschichte	1917	L. Borchardt	Volume 1, pp 55, 56
97	Ancient Egyptian Science: Volume II: Calendars, Clocks & Astronomy	2004	M. Clagett	p 327
98	Ancient Egyptian Science: Volume II: Calendars, Clocks & Astronomy	2004	M. Clagett	pp 331-333
99	The Oxford History of Ancient Egypt	2000	I. Shaw	p 481
100	Ancient Egyptian Science: Volume II: Calendars, Clocks & Astronomy	2004	M. Clagett	p 271
101	Ancient Egyptian Science: Volume II: Calendars, Clocks & Astronomy	2004	M. Clagett	p 260
102	Ancient Egyptian Science: Volume II: Calendars, Clocks & Astronomy	2004	M. Clagett	p 254
103	Ancient Egyptian Science: Volume II: Calendars, Clocks & Astronomy	2004	M. Clagett	pp 325, 326

	BIBLIOGRAPHICAL TABLE			
	CHAPTER 2			
No.	Title	Published	Author/Editor	Page No./Ref.
104	Sothic Dating Examined, the Sothic Star Theory of the Egyptian Calendar	1995	D. Mackey	Chapter 7
105	Ancient Egyptian Science: Volume II: Calendars, Clocks & Astronomy	2004	M. Clagett	p 406
106	The Oxford History of Ancient Egypt	2000	I. Shaw	p 481
107	A Test of Time	1995	D. Rohl	pp 154, 155
108	Sothic Dating Examined, the Sothic Star Theory of the Egyptian Calendar	1995	D. Mackey	Chapter 6
109	Ancient Egyptian Science: Volume II: Calendars, Clocks & Astronomy	2004	M. Clagett	p 196
110	Ancient Egyptian Science: Volume II: Calendars, Clocks & Astronomy	2004	M. Clagett	p 195
111	Ancient Egyptian Science: Volume II: Calendars, Clocks & Astronomy	2004	M. Clagett	pp 42, 43
112	A Test of Time	1995	D. Rohl	p 157
113	Theban Desert Road Survey in the Egyptian Western Desert (Vol 1). Gebel Tjauti Inscriptions 1-45 and Wadi el-Hol Rock	2002	J. Darnell	pp 49-52
114	Proceedings of the Colloquium, The Second Intermediate Period. Current Research, Future Prospects, British Museum: Egypt and the Levant: Egypt & Time	2004	M. Wiener	p 328

BIBLIOGRAPHICAL TABLE
CHAPTER 2

No.	Title	Published	Author/Editor	Page No./Ref.
115	A Test of Time	1995	D. Rohl	p 492
116	The Oxford History of Ancient Egypt	2000	I. Shaw	p 480
117	Ancient Egyptian Science: Volume II: Calendars, Clocks & Astronomy	2004	M. Clagett	pp 324, 357-366
118	A Test of Time	1995	D. Rohl	p 493
119	Journal of the Ancient Astronomy Forum (Vol. 9): The Decline and Fall of Sothic Dating, El-Lahun Lunar Texts and Egyptian Astronomical Dates	2002	D. Lappin	pp 78,79
120	Writings of Early Scholars in the Ancient Near East, Egypt, Rome, and Greece: Translating Ancient Scientific Texts	2010	A. Imhausen & T. Pommerening	p 140 (Alexandra von Lieven)
121	The History of Ancient Egypt	1992	N. Grimal	p 51
122	A Test of Time	1995	D. Rohl	p 17
123	A Test of Time	1995	D. Rohl	pp 157, 286
124	Journal of the Ancient Astronomy Forum (Vol. 9): The Decline and Fall of Sothic Dating, El-Lahun Lunar Texts and Egyptian Astronomical Dates	2002	D. Lappin	pp 82, 83
125	The Oxford History of Ancient Egypt	2000	I. Shaw	p 13
126	Science (Vol. 110): Age Determinations by Radiocarbon Content: Checks with Samples of Known Age	1949	J. Arnold, W. Libby	pp 678-680

	BIBLIOGRAPHICAL TABLE			
	CHAPTER 2			
No.	Title	Published	Author/Editor	Page No./Ref.
127	Philosophical Transactions of the Royal Society of London (Vol. 269) Absolute Dating from Egyptian Records and Comparison with Carbon-14 Dating	1970	I. Edwards	p 11
128	Chronologies of the Near East: Radiocarbon Chronology and the Historical Calendar in Egypt	1987	H. Haas et al	pp 585-606
129	Chronologies of the Near East: Radiocarbon Chronology and the Historical Calendar in Egypt	1987	H. Haas et al	p 585
130	Chronologies of the Near East: Radiocarbon Chronology and the Historical Calendar in Egypt	1987	H. Haas et al	p 586
131	Chronologies of the Near East: Radiocarbon Chronology and the Historical Calendar in Egypt	1987	H. Haas et al	p 592
132	Chronologies of the Near East: Radiocarbon Chronology and the Historical Calendar in Egypt	1987	H. Haas et al	p 588
133	Chronologies of the Near East: Radiocarbon Chronology and the Historical Calendar in Egypt	1987	H. Haas et al	p 589

	BIBLIOGRAPHICAL TABLE			
	CHAPTER 2			
No.	Title	Published	Author/Editor	Page No./Ref.
134	*Chronologies of the Near East:* Radiocarbon Chronology and the Historical Calendar in Egypt	1987	H. Haas et al	p 597
135	*Near East Chronology: Archaeology and Environment, Volume 43:* Radiocarbon Dates of Old and Middle Kingdom Monuments in Egypt	2001	G. Bonani et al	pp 1297-1320
136	*Near East Chronology: Archaeology and Environment, Volume 43:* Radiocarbon Dates of Old and Middle Kingdom Monuments in Egypt	2001	G. Bonani et al	p 1,299
137	The Mummy in Ancient Egypt: Equipping the Dead for Eternity	1998	S. Ikram & A. Dodson	pp 317-330
138	The Oxford History of Ancient Egypt	2000	I. Shaw	pp 479-482
139	Personal E-mail to author in 2008	N/A	J. Cockitt	All
140	Current Research in Egyptology 2006: The Radiocarbon Dating of Ancient Egyptian Mummies and their Associated Artefacts: Implications for Egyptology	2007	J. Cockitt & A. David	p 46
141	The Egyptians, An Introduction	2005	R. Morkot	p 86
142	Chronicle of the Pharaohs	2006	P. Clayton	p 28
143	Pears 2005/06 Cyclopedia	2005	C. Cook	F39

	BIBLIOGRAPHICAL TABLE			
CHAPTER 2				
No.	Title	Published	Author/Editor	Page No./Ref.
144	The Lost Dinosaurs of Egypt	2003	W. Nothdurft & J. Smith	pp 5, 19, 60
145	Pyramid Quest: Secrets of the Great Pyramid and the Dawn of Civilisation	2005	R. Schoch	pp 28, 29
146	The Chronology of Ancient Nations, Athar-ul-Bakiya of Albiruni	2010	C. Sachau	p 28
147	The Pyramids and Temples of Gizeh.	2004	W. Petrie	p 70
148	The Hall of Records, Hidden Secrets of the Pyramid and Sphinx	1980	J. Jochmans	p 39
148	Applied Palaeontology	2006	R. Jones	p 48
149	The Giza Power Plant	1998	C. Dunn	p 194
150	The Giza Power Plant	1998	C. Dunn	p 193
151	Pyramid Quest: Secrets of the Great Pyramid and the Dawn of Civilisation	2005	R. Schoch	p 73
152	Ancient Egypt, Myth & History	2005	Geddes & Grosset	p 38
153	Manetho	1964	W. Waddell	p 113
154	Current Research in Egyptology 2006: The Radiocarbon Dating of Ancient Egyptian Mummies and their Associated Artefacts: Implications for Egyptology	2007	J. Cockitt & A. David	p 45
155	China, a History	2009	J. Keay	p 28
156	The Cambridge History of Ancient China	1999	M. Loewe & E. Shaughnessy	pp 72, 73
157	The Cambridge History of Ancient China	1999	M. Loewe & E. Shaughnessy	p 2
158	The Cambridge History of Ancient China	1999	M. Loewe & E. Shaughnessy	pp 21-25

BIBLIOGRAPHICAL TABLE
CHAPTER 2

No.	Title	Published	Author/Editor	Page No./Ref.
159	Records of the Grand Historian of China	1961	Ssu'Ma Ch'ien; translated by B. Watson	Vol ii, p 487
160	Records of the Grand Historian of China	1961	Ssu'Ma Ch'ien; translated by B. Watson	Vol ii, p 492
161	The Cambridge History of Ancient China	1999	M. Loewe & E. Shaughnessy	pp 71, 72
162	The Cambridge History of Ancient China	1999	M. Loewe & E. Shaughnessy	p 68
163	The Wonders of Bible Chronology	1933	P. Mauro	pp 14, 85
164	The Genesis Flood	1961	J. Whitcomb & H. Morris	p 474 ff
164	How Old is the Earth	1991	A. Monty White	pp 23-30
165	How Old is the Earth	1991	A. Monty White	p 30
166	The Genesis Flood	1961	J. Whitcomb & H. Morris	pp 475, 476
167	The Genesis Flood	1961	J. Whitcomb & H. Morris	p 477
168	The Wonders of Bible Chronology	1933	P. Mauro	pp 20, 21, 28
169	The New Bible Dictionary	1978	J. Douglas	p 423
170	The Genesis Flood	1961	J. Whitcomb & H. Morris	pp 478, 479
171	The New Bible Dictionary	1978	J. Douglas	p 199
172	The Genesis Flood	1961	J. Whitcomb & H. Morris	pp 479, 480
173	The Genesis Flood	1961	J. Whitcomb & H. Morris	pp 481-483
174	The New Bible Commentary	1992	D. Guthrie, J. A. Motyer, A. Stibbs, D. Wiseman	p 122
175	A Brief History of Time	1995	S. Hawking	p 32

	BIBLIOGRAPHICAL TABLE			
CHAPTER 2				
No.	Title	Published	Author/Editor	Page No./Ref.
176	The Times, 3 April	1995	N. Hawkes, P. Stothard	p 14
177	NASA's Hubble Extends Stellar Tape Measure 10 Times Farther Into Space.	2014	J. Harrington	NASA News 10 April: p 1
178	Amateur Astronomy	1984	C. Ronan	p 197
179	Stars	1998	J. Kaler	p 92
180	Amateur Astronomy	1984	C. Ronan	pp 173, 174
181	Amateur Astronomy	1984	C. Ronan	pp 49-54
181	Getting the Measure of the Stars	1989	W. Cooper & E. Walker	pp 25, 34
182	Stars	1998	J. Kaler	p 96
183	Amateur Astronomy	1984	C. Ronan	p 184
184	Prisons of Light	1998	K. Ferguson	p 166
185	A Brief History of Time	1995	S. Hawking	p 121
186	Prisons of Light	1998	K. Ferguson	p 170
186	In Search of the Edge of Time	1993	J. Gribbin	pp 122, 123
187	A Brief History of Time	1995	S. Hawking	pp 115, 116
188	Stars	1998	J. Kaler	pp 78, 92, 93
189	Collins Pocket Guide. Stars and Planets	1993	I. Ridpath & W. Tirion	p 176
190	Realm of the Universe	1988	G. Abell	p 275
191	Variable Stars	1968	J. Glasby	p 74
191	Amateur Astronomy	1984	C. Ronan	p 67
191	Measuring the Universe: The Cosmological Distance Ladder	1999	S. Webb	p 183
192	Collins Pocket Guide: Stars and Planets	1993	I. Ridpath & W. Tirion	pp 136, 240
193	Collins Pocket Guide: Stars and Planets	1993	I. Ridpath & W. Tirion	p 108

BIBLIOGRAPHICAL TABLE
CHAPTER 2

No.	Title	Published	Author/Editor	Page No./Ref.
194	Understanding the Universe	2002	R. Prinja & R. Ignace	p 87
195	Collins Pocket Guide: Stars and Planets	1993	I. Ridpath & W. Tirion	p 246
195	Understanding Variable Stars	2007	J. Percy	pp 162, 163
196	Collins Pocket Guide: Stars and Planets	1993	I. Ridpath & W. Tirion	p 276
197	Gravity's Lens	1989	N. Cohen	p 23
198	Amateur Astronomy	1984	C. Ronan	pp 48, 49
198	Collins Pocket Guide: Stars and Planets	1993	I. Ridpath & W. Tirion	p 192
199	Realm of the Universe	1988	G. Abell	p 414
199	Collins Pocket Guide: Stars and Planets	1993	I. Ridpath & W. Tirion	p 223
200	Globular Cluster Systems (Cambridge Astrophysics)	2008	K. Ashman, S. Zepf	p 73
201	Amateur Astronomy	1984	C. Ronan	p 170
202	Amateur Astronomy	1984	C. Ronan	pp 178, 197, 208
203	Amateur Astronomy	1984	C. Ronan	p 178
203	Collins Pocket Guide: Stars and Planets	1993	I. Ridpath & W. Tirion	p 192
204	Realm of the Universe	1988	G. Abell	Appendix 17
205	Gravity's Lens	1989	N. Cohen	p 129
206	Gravity's Lens	1989	N. Cohen	pp 40, 65, 68
207	Realm of the Universe	1988	G. Abell	p 397
208	Amateur Astronomy	1984	C. Ronan	p 198
208	Astrostatistical Challenges for the New Astronomy	2013	J. Hilbe	p 63
209	Getting the Measure of the Stars	1989	W. Cooper & E. Walker	p 103
209	Realm of the Universe	1988	G. Abell	p 396

BIBLIOGRAPHICAL TABLE
CHAPTER 2

No.	Title	Published	Author/Editor	Page No./Ref.
210	Amateur Astronomy	1984	C. Ronan	p 198
211	Amateur Astronomy	1984	C. Ronan	p 198
212	Amateur Astronomy	1984	C. Ronan	p 197
213	Realm of the Universe	1988	G. Abell	p 435
214	Collins Pocket Guide: Stars and Planets	1993	I. Ridpath & W. Tirion	p 285
215	Gravity's Lens	1989	N. Cohen	p 122
215	The Cambridge Encyclopedia, 4th Edition	2000	D. Crystal	p 904
215	Realm of the Universe	1988	G. Abell	p 447
216	Realm of the Universe	1988	G. Abell	pp 7, 449
217	Quasars, Redshifts and Controversies	1988	H. Arp	pp 1-5
217	Gravity's Lens	1989	N. Cohen	p 173
218	Gravity's Lens	1989	N. Cohen	p 172
219	Hebrew and English Lexicon of the Old Testament	1951	F. Brown	p 21
220	Starlight, Time and the New Physics	2007	J. Hartnett	pp 115-118
221	Starlight, Time and the New Physics	2007	J. Hartnett	p 22
222	Realm of the Universe	1988	G. Abell	p 9
223	What about Origins?	1978	A. Monty White	p 64
223	Realm of the Universe	1988	G. Abell	p 412
224	The Sunday Times, 20 November	1994	A. Neil	p 8
225	Radiogenic Isotope Geology	1997	A. Dickin	p 13
226	Radon, A Householder's Guide	1997	Department of the Environment	p 7

BIBLIOGRAPHICAL TABLE
CHAPTER 2

No.	Title	Published	Author/Editor	Page No./Ref.
227	Geologic Time	1976	D. Eicher	p 138
227	Principles of Isotope Geology, 2nd Edition	1986	G. Faure	p VIII
228	Principles of Isotope Geology, 2nd Edition	1986	G. Faure	p 154
229	Principles of Isotope Geology, 2nd Edition	1986	G. Faure	p 123
230	Principles of Isotope Geology, 2nd Edition	1986	G. Faure	p 297
231	Radiogenic Isotope Geology	1997	A. Dickin	pp 51, 53
232	Principles of Isotope Geology, 2nd Edition	1986	G. Faure	p 72
233	Radiogenic Isotope Geology	1997	A. Dickin	p 34
234	Radiogenic Isotope Geology	1997	A. Dickin	pp 35, 36
235	Principles of Isotope Geology, 2nd Edition	1986	G. Faure	pp 145-147, 151, 327
236	Radiogenic Isotope Geology	1997	A. Dickin	pp 51, 89, 250
237	Principles of Isotope Geology, 2nd Edition	1986	G. Faure	p 74
238	Radiogenic Isotope Geology	1997	A. Dickin	p 78
239	Radiogenic Isotope Geology	1997	A. Dickin	p 74
240	Principles of Isotope Geology, 2nd Edition	1986	G. Faure	p 147
241	Principles of Isotope Geology, 2nd Edition	1986	G. Faure	p 329
242	Principles of Isotope Geology, 2nd Edition	1986	G. Faure	p 155
243	Radiogenic Isotope Geology	1997	A. Dickin	p 70

	BIBLIOGRAPHICAL TABLE			
	CHAPTER 2			
No.	Title	Published	Author/Editor	Page No./Ref.
244	Principles of Isotope Geology, 2nd Edition	1986	G. Faure	p 157
245	Principles of Isotope Geology, 2nd Edition	1986	G. Faure	p 158
246	Radiogenic Isotope Geology	1997	A. Dickin	p 69
247	Principles of Isotope Geology, 2nd Edition	1986	G. Faure	p 156
248	Principles of Isotope Geology, 2nd Edition	1986	G. Faure	p 159
249	Principles of Isotope Geology, 2nd Edition	1986	G. Faure	p 161
250	Principles of Isotope Geology, 2nd Edition	1986	G. Faure	p 257
251	Radiogenic Isotope Geology	1997	A. Dickin	p 83
252	Principles of Isotope Geology, 2nd Edition	1986	G. Faure	p 66
253	Radiogenic Isotope Geology	1997	A. Dickin	p 104
254	The Age of the Earth	1994	G. Dalrymple	p 80
255	The Age of the Earth	1994	G. Dalrymple	pp 80, 376
255	Radiogenic Isotope Geology	1997	A. Dickin	p 2
256	Principles of Isotope Geology, 2nd Edition	1986	G. Faure	p 469
257	Radiogenic Isotope Geology	1997	A. Dickin	p 441
258	Principles of Isotope Geology, 2nd Edition	1986	G. Faure	p 469
258	Radiogenic Isotope Geology	1997	A. Dickin	p 441
259	Radiogenic Isotope Geology	1997	A. Dickin	pp 400, 469
260	Radiogenic Isotope Geology	1997	A. Dickin	p 287
261	Principles of Isotope Geology, 2nd Edition	1986	G. Faure	p 101

BIBLIOGRAPHICAL TABLE				
CHAPTER 2				
No.	Title	Published	Author/Editor	Page No./Ref.
261	Radiogenic Isotope Geology	1997	A. Dickin	p 246
262	Radiogenic Isotope Geology	1997	A. Dickin	pp 287, 301
263	Radiogenic Isotope Geology	1997	A. Dickin	p 280
264	Radiogenic Isotope Geology	1997	A. Dickin	p 282
265	Radiogenic Isotope Geology	1997	A. Dickin	pp 398, 399
266	Radiogenic Isotope Geology	1997	A. Dickin	p 398
267	Radiogenic Isotope Geology	1997	A. Dickin	p 400
268	Principles of Isotope Geology, 2nd Edition	1986	G. Faure	p 120
268	Radiogenic Isotope Geology	1997	A. Dickin	p 107
269	Principles of Isotope Geology, 2nd Edition	1986	G. Faure	p 75
270	Geologic Time	1976	D. Eicher	pp 20, 21, 133
271	Radiogenic Isotope Geology	1997	A. Dickin	pp 154, 156, 209, 211, 238, 346, 408, 443, 456
272	Geologic Time	1976	D. Eicher	pp 65, 66
273	Principles of Isotope Geology, 2nd Edition	1986	G. Faure	p 288 re p 93 above
274	Radiogenic Isotope Geology	1997	A. Dickin	p 119
275	Principles of Isotope Geology, 2nd Edition	1986	G. Faure	p 304
276	Radiogenic Isotope Geology	1997	A. Dickin	p 105
277	Radiogenic Isotope Geology	1997	A. Dickin	p 121

| \multicolumn{5}{l}{BIBLIOGRAPHICAL TABLE} |
| \multicolumn{5}{l}{CHAPTER 2} |

No.	Title	Published	Author/Editor	Page No./Ref.
278	Radiogenic Isotope Geology	1997	A. Dickin	p 123
279	Principles of Isotope Geology, 2nd Edition	1986	G. Faure	p 301
280	Radiogenic Isotope Geology	1997	A. Dickin	pp 107, 111
281	Principles of Isotope Geology, 2nd Edition	1986	G. Faure	p 302
282	Radiogenic Isotope Geology	1997	A. Dickin	p 112
283	Radiogenic Isotope Geology	1997	A. Dickin	p 114
284	Radiogenic Isotope Geology	1997	A. Dickin	p 109
285	Radiogenic Isotope Geology	1997	A. Dickin	p 116
286	Radiogenic Isotope Geology	1997	A. Dickin	p 118
287	Radiogenic Isotope Geology	1997	A. Dickin	p 310
288	Principles of Isotope Geology, 2nd Edition	1986	G. Faure	pp 285, 286
289	Principles of Isotope Geology, 2nd Edition	1986	G. Faure	p 325
290	Principles of Isotope Geology, 2nd Edition	1986	C. Faure	p 328
291	Radiogenic Isotope Geology	1997	A. Dickin	p 129
292	Principles of Isotope Geology, 2nd Edition	1986	G. Faure	p 327
293	Radiogenic Isotope Geology	1997	A. Dickin	p 245
295	Principles of Isotope Geology, 2nd Edition	1986	G. Faure	p 93
296	Principles of Isotope Geology, 2nd Edition	1986	G. Faure	pp 96-98
297	Radiogenic Isotope Geology	1997	A. Dickin	p 257
298	Principles of Isotope Geology, 2nd Edition	1986	G. Faure	p 97
299	Principles of Isotope Geology, 2nd Edition	1986	G. Faure	p 100

	BIBLIOGRAPHICAL TABLE			
	CHAPTER 2			
No.	Title	Published	Author/Editor	Page No./Ref.
300	Radiogenic Isotope Geology	1997	A. Dickin	pp 261, 262
301	Radiogenic Isotope Geology	1997	A. Dickin	p 258
301	Principles of Isotope Geology, 2nd Edition	1986	G. Faure	p 98
302	Principles of Isotope Geology, 2nd Edition	1986	G. Faure	pp 104, 105
303	Principles of Isotope Geology, 2nd Edition	1986	G. Faure	p 103
304	Radiogenic Isotope Geology	1997	A. Dickin	p 274
305	Principles of Isotope Geology, 2nd Edition	1986	G. Faure	p 74
306	Principles of Isotope Geology, 2nd Edition	1986	G. Faure	pp 74, 101, 102
307	Principles of Isotope Geology, 2nd Edition	1986	G. Faure	p 100
308	Radiogenic Isotope Geology	1997	A. Dickin	pp 39, 40
309	Principles of Isotope Geology, 2nd Edition	1986	G. Faure	p 123
310	Radiogenic Isotope Geology	1997	A. Dickin	p 51
311	Principles of Isotope Geology, 2nd Edition	1986	G. Faure	p 163
313	Principles of Isotope Geology, 2nd Edition	1986	G. Faure	p 170
313	Radiogenic Isotope Geology	1997	A. Dickin	p 139
314	Radiogenic Isotope Geology	1997	A. Dickin	p 141
315	Principles of Isotope Geology, 2nd Edition	1986	G. Faure	p 170
316	Principles of Isotope Geology, 2nd Edition	1986	G. Faure	p 160

	BIBLIOGRAPHICAL TABLE			
	CHAPTER 2			
No.	Title	Published	Author/Editor	Page No./Ref.
317	Principles of Isotope Geology, 2nd Edition	1986	G. Faure	p 167
318	Principles of Isotope Geology, 2nd Edition	1986	G. Faure	p 162
319	Principles of Isotope Geology, 2nd Edition	1986	G. Faure	p 170
320	Principles of Isotope Geology, 2nd Edition	1986	G. Faure	p 191
321	Radiogenic Isotope Geology	1997	A. Dickin	p 57
322	Principles of Isotope Geology, 2nd Edition	1986	G. Faure	p 174
323	Radiogenic Isotope Geology	1997	A. Dickin	p 51
323	Principles of Isotope Geology, 2nd Edition	1986	G. Faure	p 183
324	Radiogenic Isotope Geology	1997	A. Dickin	p 53
325	Radiogenic Isotope Geology	1997	A. Dickin	p 56
326	Principles of Isotope Geology, 2nd Edition	1986	G. Faure	pp 388, 391, 444
327	Principles of Isotope Geology, 2nd Edition	1986	G. Faure	p 389
328	Principles of Isotope Geology, 2nd Edition	1986	G. Faure	p 390
330	Principles of Isotope Geology, 2nd Edition	1986	G. Faure	pp 391, 393
331	Principles of Isotope Geology, 2nd Edition	1986	G. Faure	p 392
332	Radiogenic Isotope Geology	1997	A. Dickin	p 366
333	Radiogenic Isotope Geology	1997	A. Dickin	p 368
334	Radiogenic Isotope Geology	1997	A. Dickin	p 367

BIBLIOGRAPHICAL TABLE
CHAPTER 2

No.	Title	Published	Author/Editor	Page No./Ref.
335	Geologic Time	1976	D. Eicher	pp 77-79
336	Principles of Isotope Geology, 2nd Edition	1986	G. Faure	p 396
337	Principles of Isotope Geology, 2nd Edition	1986	G. Faure	p 398
338	The Genesis Flood	1961	J. Whitcomb & H. Morris	p 256
338	Hydrology for Engineers	1982	R. Linsley, M. Kohler, J. Paulhus	p 15
339	Principles of Isotope Geology, 2nd Edition	1986	G. Faure	p 494
340	Hebrew and English Lexicon of the Old Testament	1951	F. Brown	p 1,007
341	Radiogenic Isotope Geology	1997	A. Dickin	pp 10, 413
342	Principles of Isotope Geology, 2nd Edition	1986	G. Faure	p 342
343	Principles of Isotope Geology, 2nd Edition	1986	G. Faure	p 345
344	Principles of Isotope Geology, 2nd Edition	1986	G. Faure	p 346
345	Principles of Isotope Geology, 2nd Edition	1986	G. Faure	p 348
346	Radiogenic Isotope Geology	1997	A. Dickin	p 422
348	Principles of Isotope Geology, 2nd Edition	1986	G. Faure	pp 354, 355
349	Principles of Isotope Geology, 2nd Edition	1986	G. Faure	pp 355, 356
350	Sedimentology and Stratigraphy, 2nd Edition	2009	G. Nichols	p 299

	BIBLIOGRAPHICAL TABLE			
	CHAPTER 2			
No.	Title	Published	Author/Editor	Page No./Ref.
351	Palaeomagnetism: Principles and Applications in Geology, Geophysics and Archaeology	1983	D.Tarling	p 200
352	A Geologic Time Scale	2004	F. Gradstein, J, Ogg, A. Smith	p 65
353	Palaeomagnetism: Principles and Applications in Geology, Geophysics and Archaeology	1983	D.Tarling	p 156
354	Palaeomagnetism: Principles and Applications in Geology, Geophysics and Archaeology	1983	D.Tarling	pp 149, 198
354	Essentials of Palaeomagnetism	2009	L. Tauxe, R. Butler, R. van der Voo, S. Banerjee	p 301
355	Essentials of Palaeomagnetism	2009	L. Tauxe, R. Butler, R. van der Voo, S. Banerjee	p 268
356	Essentials of Palaeomagnetism	2009	L. Tauxc, R. Butler, R. van der Voo, S. Banerjee	p 300
357	Essentials of Palaeomagnetism	2009	L. Tauxe, R. Butler, R. van der Voo, S. Banerjee	p 301
357	A Geologic Time Scale	2004	F. Gradstein, J, Ogg, A. Smith	p 65
358	Essentials of Palaeomagnetism	2009	L. Tauxe, R. Butler, R. van der Voo, S. Banerjee	p 304

BIBLIOGRAPHICAL TABLE				
CHAPTER 2				
No.	Title	Published	Author/Editor	Page No./Ref.
359	Climate Change: A Modern Synthesis	2013	G. Farmer & J. Cook	pp 300-306, 414, 415, 420, 421
360	Essentials of Palaeomagnetism	2009	L. Tauxe, R. Butler, R. van der Voo, S. Banerjee	p 307
361	Evolution: What the Fossils Say and Why it Matters	2007	D. Prothero	p 66
362	Sedimentary Geology, Volume 117, Issues 1-2: Syneresis Cracks: Subacqueous Shrinkage in Agrillaceous Sediments Caused by Earthquake-Induced Dewatering	1998	B. Pratt	pp 1-10
363	Evolution: What the Fossils Say and Why it Matters	2007	D. Prothero	p 67
364	Evolution: What the Fossils Say and Why it Matters	2007	D. Prothero	p 75
365	Geologic Time	1976	D. Eicher	p 79
366	Chemical Sediments and Geomorphology	1983	A. Goudie & K. Pye	p 333
367	Climatic Variations and forcing Mechanisms of the Last 2000 Years	1996	D. Jones, R. Bradley, J. Jouzel	p 454
368	Space and Time in Geomorphology	1982	C.Thorn	p 225
369	Moraines and Varves	1978	C. Schlühter	p 279
370	Moraines and Varves	1978	C. Schlühter	p 281
371	Moraines and Varves	1978	C. Schlühter	pp 281, 282
372	Space and Time in Geomorphology	1982	C.Thorn	p 226
373	Moraines and Varves	1978	C. Schlühter	p 290
374	Moraines and Varves	1978	C. Schlühter	p 298
375	Moraines and Varves	1978	C. Schlühter	p 297

BIBLIOGRAPHICAL TABLE				
CHAPTER 2				
No.	Title	Published	Author/Editor	Page No./Ref.
376	Evolution: What the Fossils Say and Why it Matters	2007	D. Prothero	p 62
377	Applied Palaeontology	2006	R. Wynn	p 5
378	Sedimentology and Stratigraphy, 2nd Edition	2009	G. Nichols	p 85
379	Sedimentology and Stratigraphy, 2nd Edition	2009	G. Nichols	p 309
380	Sedimentology and Stratigraphy, 2nd Edition	2009	G. Nichols	p 44
381	What about Origins?	1978	A. Monty White	pp 158, 159
382	Evolution: What the Fossils Say and Why it Matters	2007	D. Prothero	p 244
383	Evolution: What the Fossils Say and Why it Matters	2007	D. Prothero	p 282
384	The Greatest Show on Earth	2009	R. Dawkins	p 186
385	The Greatest Show on Earth	2009	R. Dawkins	p 416
386	Applied Palaeontology	2006	R. Jones	p 249
387	Applied Palaeontology	2006	R. Jones	p 250
388	Applied Palaeontology	2006	R. Jones	pp 191, 201, 205, 208, 251
389	The Greatest Show on Earth	2009	R. Dawkins	p 35
390	Evolution: What the Fossils Say and Why it Matters	2007	D. Prothero	p 238
391	The Greatest Show on Earth	2009	R. Dawkins	p 171
391	Evolution: What the Fossils Say and Why it Matters	2007	D. Prothero	p 327
392	Applied Palaeontology	2006	R. Jones	pp 251-259
393	Applied Palaeontology	2006	R. Jones	p 259

BIBLIOGRAPHICAL TABLE				
CHAPTER 2				
No.	Title	Published	Author/Editor	Page No./Ref.
393	Evolution: What the Fossils Say and Why it Matters	2007	D. Prothero	p 282
394	Applied Palaeontology,	2006	R. Jones	pp 251-253
395	Applied Palaeontology,	2006	R. Jones	pp 255-257
395	Arguments on Evolution	1989	A. Hoffman	pp 178, 204
396	Applied Palaeontology	2006	R. Jones	p 211
397	Applied Palaeontology	2006	R. W. Jones	p 273
398	Evolution: What the Fossils Say and Why it Matters	2007	D. Prothero	p 336
399	Evolution: What the Fossils Say and Why it Matters	2007	D. Prothero	p 342
400	Applied Palaeontology	2006	R. Jones	p 279
401	The Neanderthal in Us	2010	The Max Plank Institute for Evolutionary Anthropology	pp 1-3
402	Species Concepts and Phylogenetic Theory	2000	Q. Wheeler & R. Meier	p 5
403	Species Concepts and Phylogenetic Theory	2000	Q. Wheeler & R. Meier	pp 123, 126, 134
404	Species Concepts and Phylogenetic Theory	2000	Q. Wheeler & R. Meier	p 157
405	Sedimentology and Stratigraphy, 2nd Edition	2009	G. Nichols	p 312
406	Evolution: What the Fossils Say and Why it Matters	2007	D. Prothero	pp 101-103, 194,195
407	The Greatest Show on Earth	2009	R. Dawkins	p 410
408	Evolution: What the Fossils Say and Why it Matters	2007	D. Prothero	pp 3, 4
409	The Greatest Show on Earth	2009	R. Dawkins	p 334

BIBLIOGRAPHICAL TABLE
CHAPTER 2

No.	Title	Published	Author/Editor	Page No./Ref.
410	Evolution: What the Fossils Say and Why it Matters	2007	D. Prothero	p 6
411	Evolution: What the Fossils Say and Why it Matters	2007	D. Prothero	p 11
412	The Greatest Show on Earth	2009	R. Dawkins	p 163
413	Evolution: What the Fossils Say and Why it Matters	2007	D. Prothero	pp 105-107
414	The Greatest Show on Earth	2009	R. Dawkins	p 314
415	The Greatest Show on Earth	2009	R. Dawkins	p 320
416	The Greatest Show on Earth	2009	R. Dawkins	p 324
417	Evolution: What the Fossils Say and Why it Matters	2007	D. Prothero	pp 156-157
418	The Greatest Show on Earth	2009	R. Dawkins	p 297
419	Bat	2012	Wikipedia	N/A
419	Bats	2011	P. Richardson	p 17
420	Science, 25 November 2005:Vol. 310 no. 5752: 'Bats Have a Feel for Flight'	2005	Professor J. Zook	pp 1260-1261
420	Bats	2011	P. Richardson	p 17
421	Evolution: What the Fossils Say and Why it Matters	2007	D. Prothero	p 263
422	Bats	2011	P. Richardson	pp 5, 53, 79, 80
423	Bats	2011	P. Richardson	p 110
424	The Greatest Show on Earth	2009	R. Dawkins	pp 356-363
425	Anatomy of the Human Body	1918	H. Gray	p 912
425	Last's Anatomy, Regional and Applied	2011	C. Sinnatamby	pp 194,196, 208

BIBLIOGRAPHICAL TABLE			
CHAPTER 2			
No.	Title	Published	Author/Editor	Page No./Ref.
426	Atlas of Human Anatomy	2003	F. Netter	plates 120, 206, 223
427	Gray's Anatomy for Students	2009	R. Drake, A. Vogel, A. Mitchell	p 203
427	Atlas of Anatomy: Neck and Internal Organs	2006	M. Schuenke, E Schulte, L. Ross, U. Schumacher, E.Lamperti	pp 143, 144
428	Atlas of Human Anatomy	2003	F. Netter	plate 120
428	Morgan and Mikhail's Clinical Anesthesiology, 5th edition	2013	J. Butterworth, D. Mackey, J. Wasnick	p 310
429	Atlas of Anatomy: Neck and Internal Organs	2006	M. Schuenke, E Schulte, L. Ross, U. Schumacher, E.Lamperti	p 143
430	Walker's Pediatric Gastrointestinal Disease: Physiology, Diagnosis, Management, 5th Edition	2008	R. Kleinman, O. Goulet, G. Mieli-Vergani, I. Sanderson, P. Sherman, B. Schneider	p 50
431	Practical Gastroenterology: A Comprehensive Guide	2001	S. Bloom	p 16
432	Digestive Diseases in the Dog and Cat	1991	J. Simpson & R. Else	pp 39, 40
433	Physiology at a Glance	2005	J. Ward & R. Clarke	p 77
434	Autonomic Control of the Respiratory System	1997	P. Barnes	pp 9, 208
435	Autonomic Control of the Respiratory System	1997	P. Barnes	p 43

	BIBLIOGRAPHICAL TABLE			
	CHAPTER 2			
No.	Title	Published	Author/Editor	Page No./Ref.
436	Evidence for Recurrent Laryngeal Nerve Contribution in Motor Innervation of the Human Cricopharyngeal Muscle	1999	H. Brok, M. Copper, R. Ongerboer de Visser, A. Venker-van Haagen, P. Schouwenburg	Abstract
437	Access to Anaesthetics Primary FRCA: Physiology and Anatomy	2007	K. MacLennan	pp 203, 204
438	Principles of Airway Management	2003	B. Finucane & A. Santora	p 15
439	AMA, Archives of Surgery 1951;62(4): Multiple Divisions of the Recurrent Laryngeal Nerve, An Anatomic Study	1951	W. Armstrong & J. Hinton	p 539
440	The Greatest Show on Earth	2009	R. Dawkins	p 354
441	Cognitive Neuroscience	2010	M. Banich & R. Compton	p 16
442	Handbook of Optics, Third Edition Volume III: Vision and Vision Optics	2010	M. Bass, C. Decusatis, J. Enoch, V. et al	p 90
443	Cognitive Science: The Science of Intelligent Systems	1994	G. Luger, P. Johnson, C. Stern, J. Newman	p 167
444	Wheater's Functional Histology: A Text and Colour Atlas	2006	B. Young, J. Lowe, A. Stevens, J. Heath	p 408
445	Elements of Physiology; Being an Account of the Laws and Principles of the Animal Economy	2009	T. Aitkin	p 373
446	Ophthalmology	2007	B. James, C. Chew, A. Bron	p 171

	BIBLIOGRAPHICAL TABLE			
	CHAPTER 2			
No.	Title	Published	Author/Editor	Page No./Ref.
447	Retinal Glial Cells Enhance Human Vision Acuity, Physics Review Letters 104, 158102	2010	A. Labin & E. Ribak	pp 1-4
448	An Introduction to Clinical Perimetry	1938	H. Traquair	pp 7, 12
449	Evaluation and Management of Suspected Retinal Detachment, *American Family Physician* Apr 1;69(7)	2004	R. Gariano & C. Kim,	pp 1691-1699
450	Atlas of Human Anatomy	2003	F. Netter	plate 2
451	The Greatest Show on Earth	2009	R. Dawkins	pp 364, 365
452	Gray's Anatomy for Students	2009	R. Drake, A. Vogel, A. Mitchell	pp 284, 285
453	*Journal of Zoology*, (Volume 239) Reason for the Externalisation of the Testis of Mammals	1996	M. Chance	pp 691-695
454	Emergency Pediatric Radiology	2001	H. Carty	p 219
455	The Greatest Show on Earth	2009	R. Dawkins	p 370
456	Anatomy for Dental Students	1996	D. Johnson and W. Moore	p 118
456	Evolution of the Human Head	2011	D. Lieberman	p 136
457	Rhinosinusitis: A Guide for Diagnosis and Management	2008	E. Thaler & D. Kennedy	pp 146, 206
457	Anatomy for Dental Students	1996	D. Johnson & W. Moore	p 171
458	The Atlas of Birds: Diversity, Behavior and Conservation	2011	M. Unwin	p 15
459	The Greatest Show on Earth	2009	R. Dawkins	p 345

	BIBLIOGRAPHICAL TABLE			
	CHAPTER 2			
No.	Title	Published	Author/Editor	Page No./Ref.
460	Dinosaurs of the Air: The Evolution and Loss of Flight in Dinosaurs and Birds	2002	G. Paul	pp 144, 151
460	Systematic Biology, 59 (1): Tinamous and Moa Flock Together: Mitochondrial Genome Sequence Analysis Reveals Independent Losses of Flight among Ratites	2010	M. Phillips, G. Gibb, E. Crimp, D. Penny	pp 90-107
461	Dinosaurs of the Air: The Evolution and Loss of Flight in Dinosaurs and Birds	2002	G. Paul	pp 149, 151
462	Dinosaurs of the Air: The Evolution and Loss of Flight in Dinosaurs and Birds	2002	G. Paul	pp 153, 154
463	The Intelligence of Dogs	2006	S. Coren	p 23
463	Textbook of Veterinary Internal Medicine Expert Consult	2010	S. Ettinger	p 20
464	Molecular Biology and Evolution, 23(6):1144-1155. 2006L *Early Penguin Fossils, Plus Mitochondrial Genomes, Calibrate Avian Evolution*	2006	K. Slack, C. Jones, T. Ando, G. Harrison, R. Fordyce, U. Arnason, D. Penny	pp 1144, 1145
465	The Greatest Show on Earth	2009	R. Dawkins	p 351
466	The Greatest Show on Earth	2009	R. Dawkins	pp 379, 380
467	The Greatest Show on Earth	2009	R. Dawkins	p 384
468	The Greatest Show on Earth	2009	R. Dawkins	p 370
469	Pleasurable Kingdom: Animals and the Nature of Feeling Good	2007	Dr. J. Balcombe	p 52

BIBLIOGRAPHICAL TABLE
CHAPTER 2

No.	Title	Published	Author/Editor	Page No./Ref.
470	The Greatest Show on Earth	2009	R. Dawkins	p 340
471	The Complete Human Body	2010	A. Roberts	p 281
471	Principles of Dermatology, Fourth Edition	2013	J. Marks Jnr & J. Miller	p 8
472	Evolution: What the Fossils Say and Why it Matters	2007	D. Prothero	p 39
473	Reproduction in Mammals: Volume 3, Hormonal Control of Reproduction	1984	C. Austin & R. Short	p 226
474	Scientific American (6 September): Strange but True: Males Can Lactate	2007	N. Swaminathan	All
475	Evolution: What the Fossils Say and Why it Matters	2007	D. Prothero	pp 107, 108
476	Atlas of Human Anatomy	2010	F. Netter	plates 157, 163, 339-341
477	Gray's Anatomy for Students	2009	R. Drake, A. Vogel, A. Mitchell	p 434
478	Clinically Oriented Anatomy	2009	L. Moore, A. Dalley, A. Agur	p 566
479	THIEME Atlas of Anatomy: General Anatomy & Musculoskeletal System	2010	M. Schuenke, E. Schulte, U. Schumacher	p 136
480	Navigating the Adult Spine: Bridging Clinical Practice and Neuroradiology	2006	A. Fast, D. Goldsher	p 6
481	Functional Anatomy for Sport and Exercise	2008	C. Milner	p 86

BIBLIOGRAPHICAL TABLE
CHAPTER 2

No.	Title	Published	Author/Editor	Page No./Ref.
482	Low Back Syndromes: Integrated Clinical Management	2006	C. Morris	p 59
483	Anatomy at a Glance	2011	O. Faiz, S. Blackburn, D. Moffat	pp 66, 67
484	Clinical Neuroanatomy for Medical Students	2009	R. Snell	p 2
485	The Anaesthesia Science Viva Book	2008	B. Bricker	p 81
486	Take Back Your Back: Everything You Need to Effectively Reverse and Manage Back Pain	2010	B. Murinson	pp 155, 158
487	Evolution: What the Fossils Say and Why it Matters	2007	D. Prothero	p 39
488	Evolution: What the Fossils Say and Why it Matters	2007	D. Prothero	pp 107, 108
489	Ear, Nose, and Throat Diseases: With Head and Neck Surgery	2009	H. Behrbohm, O. Kaschke, T. Nawka, A. Swift	pp 237, 238
490	Why Evolution is True	2009	J. Coyne	pp 65, 66
491	Journal of Theoretical Biology, Volume 249	2007	R. Bollinger, A. Barbas, E. Bush, S. Lin, W. Parker,	pp 826-831
492	Bioinformatics: Tools and Applications	2009	D. Edwards, J. Stajich, D. Hansen	p 66
493	Pharmaceutical Biotechnology: Drug Discovery and Clinical Applications	2012	O. Kayser, H. Warzecha	p 133
494	Molecular Geometry of Body Pattern in Birds	2012	A. Lima-de-Faria	p 43

	BIBLIOGRAPHICAL TABLE			
	CHAPTER 2			
No.	Title	Published	Author/Editor	Page No./Ref.
495	Biological Computation	2011	E. Lamm and R. Unger	p 18
496	What Evolution Is	2002	E. Mayr	p 31
497	Evolution: What the Fossils Say and Why it Matters	2007	D. Prothero	pp 111-113
498	Marsupials	2006	P. Armati, C. Dickman, I. Hume	p 3
499	Marsupials	2006	P. Armati, C. Dickman, I. Hume	p 10
500	Marsupials	2006	P. Armati, C. Dickman, I. Hume	pp 5, 6
501	Marsupials	2006	P. Armati, C. Dickman, I. Hume	p 21
502	Marsupials	2006	P. Armati, C. Dickman, I. Hume	pp 13, 14
503	Marsupials	2006	P. Armati, C. Dickman, I. Hume	p 17
504	Applied Palaeontology	2006	R. Wynn Jones	p 5
504	The Natural History of Fossils	1980	C. Paul	p 15
505	Sedimentology and Stratigraphy, 2nd Edition	2009	G. Nichols	p 318
506	Evolution: What the Fossils Say and Why it Matters	2007	D. Prothero	p 52
507	Applied Palaeontology	2006	R. Wynn Jones	p 6
508	The Greatest Show on Earth	2009	R. Dawkins	p 97
509	Sedimentology and Stratigraphy, 2nd Edition	2009	G. Nichols	p 44

No.	Title	Published	Author/Editor	Page No./Ref.
	BIBLIOGRAPHICAL TABLE			
	CHAPTER 2			
510	Applied Palaeontology	2006	R. Wynn Jones	p 5
511	Sedimentology and Stratigraphy, 2nd Edition	2009	G. Nichols	pp 309, 310
512	Geologic Time	1976	D. Eicher	p 45
513	Geologic Time	1976	D. Eicher	p 13
513	The Natural History of Fossils	1980	C. Paul	p 181
514	Outlines of Historical Geology 4th edition	1941	C. Schuchert & C. Dunbar	p 53
515	Geologic Time	1976	D. Eicher	pp 54, 67
515	Sedimentology and Stratigraphy, 2nd Edition	2009	G. Nichols	p 322
516	Evolution: What the Fossils Say and Why it Matters	2007	D. Prothero	xxii and pp 60, 62
517	Evolution: What the Fossils Say and Why it Matters	2007	D. Prothero	p 75
518	Applied Palaeontology	2006	R. Wynn Jones	pp 284-291
519	Evolution: What the Fossils Say and Why it Matters	2007	D. Prothero	p 61
520	Evolution: What the Fossils Say and Why it Matters	2007	D. Prothero	p 228
520	The Greatest Show on Earth	2009	R. Dawkins	p 168
521	Evolution: What the Fossils Say and Why it Matters	2007	D. Prothero	p 263
522	The Greatest Show on Earth	2009	R. Dawkins	pp 168, 169
523	Evolution: What the Fossils Say and Why it Matters	2007	D. Prothero	pp 326, 327
523	The Greatest Show on Earth	2009	R. Dawkins	p 172

BIBLIOGRAPHICAL TABLE				
CHAPTER 2				
No.	Title	Published	Author/Editor	Page No./Ref.
524	Encyclopaedia Britannica Online, Homo Erectus	2012	C. Rightmire	p 3
525	Let's Review: Earth Science	2006	E. Denecke & W. Carr	p 492
526	The Biology of Disturbed Habitats	2011	L. Walker	pp 57- 59
527	Evolution: What the Fossils Say and Why it Matters	2007	D. Prothero	p 82
527	The Natural History of Fossils	1980	C. Paul	p 195
528	On the Origin of Species By Means of Natural Selection, 1st Edition (Introduction E. Mayr)	1966	C. Darwin	p 280
529	On the Origin of Species By Means of Natural Selection, 1st Edition (Introduction E. Mayr)	1966	C. Darwin	pp 172, 280
530	The Greatest Show on Earth	2009	R. Dawkins	p 147
530	Evolution: What the Fossils Say and Why it Matters	2007	D. Prothero	pp 79-82
530	Applied Palaeontology	2006	R. Wynn Jones	p 137
530	Geologic Time	1976	D. Eicher	p 99
531	Evolution: What the Fossils Say and Why it Matters	2007	D. Prothero	p 260
532	Evolution: What the Fossils Say and Why it Matters	2007	D. Prothero	pp 83, 84
533	Evolution: What the Fossils Say and Why it Matters	2007	D. Prothero	p 263

	BIBLIOGRAPHICAL TABLE			
	CHAPTER 2			
No.	Title	Published	Author/Editor	Page No./Ref.
534	Nature Magazine, Tetrapod Trackways from the Early Middle Devonian Period of Poland, (January; 463; 7277)	2010	G. Niedźwiedzki, P. Szrek, K. Narkiewicz, M. Narkiewicz, P Ahlberg	pp 43–48
535	Behavioral Evidence for the Evolution of Walking and Bounding before Terrestriality in Sarcopterygian Fishes	2011	H. King, N. Shubin, M. Coates, M. Hale	pp 1-6
536	Nature Magazine (Volume 413, 11 Oct.)	2001	D. Domning	pp 625 - 627
537	Applied Palaeontology	2006	R. Wynn Jones	p 275
538	The Rise of Homo Sapiens: The Evolution of Modern Thinking	2009	F. Coolidge & T. Wynn	p 129
539	The Rise of Homo Sapiens: The Evolution of Modern Thinking	2009	F. Coolidge & T. Wynn	p 27
540	American Journal of Physical Anthropology: Normal Neuroanatomical Variation in the Human Brain: An MRI Volumetric Study (Aug;118(4))	2002	J. Allen, H. Damasio & T. Grabowski	pp 341-358
541	Proceedings of the National Academy of Sciences of the USA, Genetic Evidence for Archaic Admixture in Africa (6 Sept. 10.1073)	2011	M. Hammer, A. Woerner, F. Mendez, J. Watkins, J. Wall	PNAS: 1109300108
542	Applied Palaeontology	2006	R. Wynn Jones	p 280
543	Baby Tale not Black and White (BBC News, 20 July)	2010	C. Murphy	All
544	Evolution: What the Fossils Say and Why it Matters	2007	D. Prothero	p 336

BIBLIOGRAPHICAL TABLE
CHAPTER 3

No.	Title	Published	Author/Editor	Page No./Ref.
1	Oxford Dictionary of English	2010	A. Stevenson	p 697
2	Oxford Dictionary of English	2010	A. Stevenson	p 636

BIBLIOGRAPHICAL TABLE
CHAPTER 4

No.	Title	Published	Author/Editor	Page No./Ref.
1	The New Bible Commentary	1970	D. Guthrie, J. Motyer, A. Stibbs, D. Wiseman	p 515
2	Hebrew and English Lexicon of the Old Testament	1951	F. Brown	p 936
3	Hebrew and English Lexicon of the Old Testament	1951	F. Brown	p 643
4	The New Bible Commentary	1970	D. Guthrie, J. Motyer, A. Stibbs, D. Wiseman	p 604
4	The New Bible Dictionary	1978	J. D. Douglas	p 575
5	Hebrew and English Lexicon of the Old Testament	1951	F. Brown	p 252
6	Hebrew and English Lexicon of the Old Testament	1951	F. Brown	p 823
7	The Analytical Greek Lexicon	1977	H. Moulton	p 62
8	The Analytical Greek Lexicon	1977	H. Moulton	p 11
8	Hebrew and English Lexicon of the Old Testament	1951	F. Brown	pp 761, 762
9	The Analytical Greek Lexicon	1977	H. Moulton	p 54

BIBLIOGRAPHICAL TABLE

CHAPTER 4

No.	Title	Published	Author/Editor	Page No./Ref.
10	The New Bible Commentary	1970	D. Guthrie, J. Motyer, A. Stibbs, D. Wiseman	p 1,244
11	The New Bible Commentary	1970	D. Guthrie, J. Motyer, A. Stibbs, D. Wiseman	p 1,245
12	The New Bible Commentary	1970	D. Guthrie, J. Motyer, A. Stibbs, D. Wiseman	p 577
13	The New Bible Dictionary	1978	J. Douglas	pp 1,339, 1,340
13	The Analytical Greek Lexicon	1977	H. Moulton	p 238
14	Strong's Exhaustive Concordance	1991	J. Strong	pp 885-887
15	*Novum Testamentum Graece*	1981	K. Aland, M. Black, C. Martini, B. Metzger, A. Wikgren	p 418
16	The Analytical Greek Lexicon	1977	H. Moulton	p 311
17	The Collected Biblical Writings of T. C. Skeat	2004	J. Elliott	p 263

BIBLIOGRAPHICAL TABLE

CHAPTER 5

No.	Title	Published	Author/Editor	Page No./Ref.
1	Hebrew and English Lexicon of the Old Testament	1951	F. Brown	p 909
2	Hebrew and English Lexicon of the Old Testament	1951	F. Brown	pp 29, 485
3	Hebrew and English Lexicon of the Old Testament	1951	F. Brown	p 30

BIBLIOGRAPHICAL TABLE
CHAPTER 5

No.	Title	Published	Author/Editor	Page No./Ref.
4	The Analytical Greek Lexicon	1977	H. Moulton	p 265
5	The Jewish War, Penguin Classics	1981	G. Williamson	pp 150, 153, 404, 405
6	The Jewish War, Penguin Classics	1981	G. Williamson	p 167
7	The Jewish War, Penguin Classics	1981	G. Williamson	p 344
8	Suetonius: The Twelve Caesars	2007	R. Graves & J. Rives	p 293
9	The Jewish War, Penguin Classics	1981	G. Williamson	p 194
10	Josephus, the Complete Works: The Life of Flavius Josephus 76	1998	W. Whiston	p 29
11	Josephus, the Complete Works: Against Apion 1:9	1998	W. Whiston	p 930
12	The Jewish War, Penguin Classics	1981	G. Williamson	p 304
12	Josephus, the Complete Works: The Antiquities of the Jews, 3.7	1998	W. Whiston	p 107
13	Tacitus: The Histories, Oxford World Classics	2008	W. Fyfe & D. Levene	p 3
14	Josephus, the Complete Works: The Wars of the Jews, 4. 9.2	1998	W. Whiston	p 825
15	Tacitus: The Histories, Oxford World Classics	2008	W. Fyfe & D. Levene	p 27
15	Suetonius: The Twelve Caesars	2007	R. Graves & J. Rives	p 253
16	Tacitus: The Histories, Oxford World Classics	2008	W. Fyfe & D. Levene	p 87
16	Suetonius: The Twelve Caesars	2007	R. Graves & J. Rives	p 261
17	Suetonius: The Twelve Caesars	2007	R. Graves & J. Rives	p 279
18	Tacitus: The Histories, Oxford World Classics	2008	W. Fyfe & D. Levene	pp 155, 156, 169

BIBLIOGRAPHICAL TABLE				
CHAPTER 5				
No.	Title	Published	Author/Editor	Page No./Ref.
19	Tacitus: The Histories, Oxford World Classics	2008	W. Fyfe & D. Levene	p 114
20	Suetonius: The Twelve Caesars	2007	R. Graves & J. Rives	p 286
21	The Jewish War, Penguin Classics	1981	G. Williamson	p 397
22	*Journal of Greco-Roman Christianity and Judaism (3): Messianic Hopes and Messianic Figures in Late Antiquity*	2006	C. Evans	p 30
23	The Jewish War, Penguin Classics	1981	G. Williamson	p 275
24	The Jewish War, Penguin Classics	1981	G. Williamson	p 307
25	The Jewish War, Penguin Classics	1981	G. Williamson	pp 286-289, 323
26	The Jewish War, Penguin Classics	1981	G. Williamson	p 278
27	The Jewish War, Penguin Classics	1981	G. Williamson	p 280
28	The Jewish War, Penguin Classics	1981	G. Williamson	pp 280-282
29	The Jewish War, Penguin Classics	1981	G. Williamson	p 264
30	The Jewish War, Penguin Classics	1981	G. Williamson	pp 188, 274, 275
31	The Jewish War, Penguin Classics	1981	G. Williamson	pp 384-386
32	Place of Refuge: A History of the Jews in Cyprus	2003	S. Panteli	p 32
33	The Jewish War, Penguin Classics	1981	G. Williamson	p 223
34	Dio's Rome, Volume 5, Echo Library	2007	Cassio Dio	p 100
35	The Jewish War, Penguin Classics	1981	G. Williamson	pp 286, 287
36	The Jewish War, Penguin Classics	1981	G. Williamson	pp 321, 344, 363

BIBLIOGRAPHICAL TABLE
CHAPTER 5

No.	Title	Published	Author/Editor	Page No./Ref.
37	The Jewish War, Penguin Classics	1981	G. Williamson	p 359
38	The Jewish War, Penguin Classics	1981	G. Williamson	p 265
39	The Jewish War, Penguin Classics	1981	G. Williamson	pp 245-250
40	Hebrew and English Lexicon of the Old Testament	1951	F. Brown	p 325
41	Suetonius: The Twelve Caesars	2007	R. Graves & J. Rives	p 287
42	Tacitus: The Histories, Oxford World Classics	2008	W. Fyfe & D. Levene	pp 102, 229
43	Tacitus: The Histories, Oxford World Classics	2008	W. Fyfe & D. Levene	p 228, 229
44	The Jewish War, Penguin Classics	1981	G. Williamson	pp 221, 222
45	The Jewish War, Penguin Classics	1981	G. Williamson	p 363
45	Tacitus: The Histories, Oxford World Classics	2008	W. Fyfe & D. Levene	p 241
45	Suetonius: The Twelve Caesars	2007	R. Graves & J. Rives	p 277
46	The Antichrist and the second Coming: a Preterist Examination, Volume I	2012	D. McKenzie	p 192
47	The Jewish War, Penguin Classics	1981	G. Williamson	p 58
48	The Jewish War, Penguin Classics	1981	G. Williamson	p 391
49	Hebrew and English Lexicon of the Old Testament	1951	F. Brown	p 251
50	The Jewish War, Penguin Classics	1981	G. Williamson	p 292
51	Suetonius: The Twelve Caesars	2007	R. Graves & J. Rives	p 287

BIBLIOGRAPHICAL TABLE
CHAPTER 5

No.	Title	Published	Author/Editor	Page No./Ref.
52	The New Bible Commentary	1992	D. Guthrie, J. A. Motyer, A. Stibbs, D. Wiseman	p 702
53	The Jewish War, Penguin Classics	1981	G. Williamson	p 361
54	Tacitus: The Histories, Oxford World Classics	2008	W. Fyfe & D. Levene	pp 240, 241
55	The Jewish War, Penguin Classics	1981	G. Williamson	p 374

GENERAL INDEX

Eccles, John	6, 10
Popper, Karl	10
Egypt	68-111
Einstein, Albert	129
Elephantine Stele	81, 87, 88
Enoch	120, 128
epilepsy	5, 7, 12
errorchrons	150, 162
Evolution, Theory of	1, 24, 26, 27, 41, 153, 175, 176, 188-201, 203, 205, 207, 208, 212, 213, 216, 217, 219, 221-224, 226-229, 231, 234-256, 358
faith	1, 7, 259, 263, 271, 285, 298, 306, 326, 344, 347, 353, 355, 356
fission tracks	171-173
flightless birds	221, 222, 224, 237
flood geology	179-182
food storage	43-47
free will	258-264
Gap Theory	26, 27
Gebel Tjauti Graffiti	81, 91, 92
Genesis genealogies	117-128
Gilgamesh	65
global scepticism	348-350
globular clusters	133, 134, 136,
Grand Canyon	181, 182
gravity	3, 5, 6, 220
H II regions	136, 137
Hammurabi	62, 64, 65
hibernation	38, 40, 41, 43, 44, 51, 54
Holy Spirit, sin against	279, 280
homo erectus	194, 245, 252, 253
homo habilis	245, 252
homo sapiens	190, 194, 231, 245, 252, 253

homologous structures	200-206
human body hair	228
human evolution	200, 245, 251-254
Hyades	132
Hyksos	79
hypnosis	7
Illahun Papyrus	81, 91, 92, 93
intermediate or transitional species	241, 244, 247-250
interstellar dust	131, 132, 133, 135, 136
isochrons	148, 150-152, 158, 159, 162, 165-167, 173
isotopes	153-156, 159-161, 166, 168, 175
Ivory Tablet of Djer	80, 81, 94
Jacobsen, Thorkild	63-67
Jehoiakim	122
Josephus	28, 74, 75, 324, 327, 329, 332-338, 340, 341, 343, 345
junk DNA	235, 236
Kepler, Johannes	138
Korean Research Institute of Ships and Engineering	50
light	24, 27, 128-146
magma	57, 149
main sequence fitting	132, 133
male lactation	229, 230
Manetho	68, 69, 74-77, 79, 104, 110, 111
mass extinctions	107, 187, 189, 190, 193, 200, 240, 241, 249
maxillary sinuses	219-221
Medina Habu Inscription	81, 86, 87
Mentuhotep III	104
meteorites	148, 151-153, 155, 162, 164-166
Meyer, Eduard	77, 90
Milankovitch Cycles	178, 179
Moses	28, 125, 126, 297, 307

mountain building	116, 180
Neanderthals	194, 252, 253
Noah	19, 25, 27-32, 34-38, 41, 43, 44, 46-48, 51, 54, 59, 62, 63, 67, 96, 110, 114, 116, 118, 120-125, 127, 129, 179-181, 184, 188, 237, 245, 286, 287
novae	134,135
Nurninsubur	62
oceanic islands	55, 56
open clusters	130
palaeomagnetism	175-179
palaeontology	154, 175, 177, 240-255
Palermo Stone	68, 71-74
parallax	129, 130
Parfit, Derek	5, 12, 13
Peleg	120, 127, 128
Pember, George	26
pezosiren portelli	244, 250, 251
phoenix	83, 84
Piltdown man	254
plate tectonics	55, 116, 166, 180, 237
Pleiades	132, 135
pleochroic haloes	173, 174
population, human	21, 29, 58, 60
potassium-argon dating	154, 163-165
pseudo-isochrons	151, 158, 162
quasars	139
radiometric dating	146-175, 177, 179, 182, 200, 241, 243
radon	147
recurrent laryngeal nerve	208-212
red shift	130
Relativity Theory	129, 143-145
Royal Annals of Egyptian Pharaohs	68, 71-73
RR Lyrae variables	133, 134, 136

rubidium-strontium dating	148, 152, 155, 157, 165-167
salinity	29, 50, 51, 52, 181, 183
salvation	15, 19, 260-262, 264, 267, 269-304
SC I Galaxies	137
scientific method	196-200, 347
seabirds	29, 57, 58
seeds	53, 54, 56, 206
siamese twins	8
sightless animals	223, 224
Sima Qian	112, 113
sin	20-22, 206, 220, 224-225, 257-259, 264, 268-271, 279, 280, 283, 285, 286, 292, 294-299, 304, 328, 342, 344
Sothic dating	77-94, 104
soul	1, 3-23, 259, 260, 261, 271, 300, 358
Sphinx	109, 110
Suetonius	326, 331, 336, 339
suffering	2, 16, 18, 20, 21, 53, 196, 200, 206, 220, 221, 225, 257-259, 264-268, 270, 271, 273, 277, 283, 287, 304, 321, 350, 358
Sumerian King List	61-68
supernovas	137, 138, 155, 156
syneresis cracks	181
Tacitus	83, 84, 329, 330, 335, 340, 344
Terah	120, 123, 125, 127
Theon	78, 81-83
thermoluminescence	173, 174
tiktaalik	244, 250, 251
Titus, Prince	324-327, 330, 331, 333-335, 337, 338, 343
tonsils	232, 233
Tower of Babel	22, 124, 127
trees	24, 33, 53, 56, 97, 169, 186, 224, 225
tunnelling	129
Turin Canon	68, 73, 74, 104, 111
uniformitarianism	176, 179, 185-187
uranium-lead dating	159-163

Urzababa	63, 67, 68
USS Dunderberg	50
Utu-hegal	61, 63
varves	169, 176, 180, 182-185
vas deferens	216, 217
vertebrate eye	212-216
Vespasian	324-339, 343
vestigial structures	196, 225-236
Wah mummy	104
Weld-Blundell Prism	61-63, 67
wiggle matching	98, 169
window of the Ark	46-48
Xia dynasty	112, 113
Ziusudra	62